D1600465

Sports and American Culture Series

BRUCE CLAYTON, EDITOR

HIGH-FLYING BIRDS

Jerry Mellecker

HIGH-FLYING FLYING BIRDS

The 1942 St. Louis Cardinals

Jerome M. Mileur

UNIVERSITY OF MISSOURI PRESS
Columbia and London

Copyright © 2009 by
The Curators of the University of Missouri
University of Missouri Press, Columbia, Missouri 65201
Printed and bound in the United States of America
All rights reserved
5 4 3 2 1   13 12 11 10 09

Library of Congress Cataloging-in-Publication Data

Mileur, Jerome M.
  High-flying birds : the 1942 St. Louis Cardinals / Jerome M. Mileur.
     p. cm.
  Includes bibliographical references and index.
  Summary: "Mileur provides a game-by-game account of the 1942
St. Louis Cardinals, world champions and the winningest team in
franchise history. He recounts the team's close pennant race against
the Brooklyn Dodgers and World Series victory over the New York
Yankees, while conveying the physical and mental demands on
the players within the context of wartime America"—Provided by
publisher.
  ISBN 978-0-8262-1834-6 (alk. paper)
  1. St. Louis Cardinals (Baseball team)—History. I. Title.
  GV875.S3M55 2009
  796.357'640977866—dc22
                                        2008046279

♾™ This paper meets the requirements of the
American National Standard for Permanence of Paper
for Printed Library Materials, Z39.48, 1984.

Designer and Typesetter: Kristie Lee
Printer and binder: Thomson-Shore, Inc.
Typefaces: Minion and Binner

~

To the memory
of my grandfather

AUGUST G. WILLI

who knew something
about baseball

~

CONTENTS

PREFACE

On March 2, 1942, Mort Cooper, ace pitcher for the St. Louis Cardinals, celebrated his twenty-ninth birthday at spring training in St. Petersburg, Florida, where he was getting into shape for the upcoming baseball season. On the same day, I celebrated my eighth birthday in Miss Shoemaker's second-grade class at the John A. Logan primary school in Murphysboro, Illinois. I had learned about baseball as a preschooler in the late 1930s and gone to a Labor Day doubleheader at Sportsman's Park in St. Louis in 1939. Mort Cooper started one of those games, something I learned from an old box score, not something I remembered. I was five at the time and have few memories of the game other than of the ballpark and the crowd. For years I thought we had left early before the second game ended. But from that old box score and the accompanying story, I learned that the second game had been called because of darkness with the score tied.

By 1942, I had learned how to read a box score, and I followed the season as it unfolded, rooting for the Cardinals and my favorite player, Mort Cooper. I went to two Cardinals games that year, both of which, as it happened, were pivotal in the season. The first was on Sunday, July 19, when the Redbirds swept a doubleheader from the Brooklyn Dodgers, with Mort Cooper winning the first game against Whitlow Wyatt and the second being determined on an inside-the-park home run by Enos Slaughter on which the Dodger center fielder knocked himself cuckoo crashing into the wall trying to catch the ball. My view of center field from the left-field grandstand was obstructed, but I remember all of the Dodgers running toward their fallen teammate while hundreds of fans poured out of the seats and onto the field, as was permitted then, creating a scene of great confusion. Other than that the Cardinals had won, I did not really know what had happened until the next morning's *St. Louis Globe-Democrat* carried a full account.

The other game I saw in 1942 was the second game of the World Series, the only World Series game I have ever attended. The Cardinals had lost the first game to the favored New York Yankees, though they mounted a spirited rally in the ninth that fell just short. They won the second game, then went on to take the next three as well to win the championship. A third-grader by then, I was called to the principal's office the day before the second game and told that my mother had called to say that I should get a haircut before coming home. My barber was "Shorty" Johnson, a rabid Cardinals fan, whose nickname came from his being a hunchback. Sitting in his chair, we listened to the Redbirds lose the first game. I had no idea at the time, of course, that the next day I would be sitting (or, more precisely, standing) in Sportsman's Park, watching the second game. Early the next morning, my grandfather and I boarded a train for St. Louis, arrived around eleven o'clock, and went to a bank where a business friend had the tickets. I was deposited in the lobby in the biggest chair I had ever seen, while my grandfather disappeared for what seemed like forever, but he returned finally with standing-room tickets and we set out for the game. We found a spot in the lower deck walkway behind home plate, and from there we cheered as the Cardinals took the lead, anguished when the Yankees fought back to tie the score, then exulted when the Redbirds prevailed in the end.

I was an only child and, on my mother's side of the family, an only grandchild. Her father, my grandfather, August Willi, loved baseball. A successful business-man and Democratic Party activist, he had played amateur ball while working in St. Louis in the late 1890s for a team called the "Shamrocks." As the name sug-gests, it was an Irish club, and he, a Swiss German, was a "ringer" who, according to others in the family, was a very good hitter. A photograph of the team shows his decidedly un-Irish face in the center of some classic Gallic mugs. As his only male heir, I had no choice but to be a baseball fan, and I was more than willing to oblige. It was he who taught me about the game, how it was played, why certain things were done, who the good players were, and how to read a box score. He tried also to teach me how to play the game. I learned how to bunt from him, but he died when I was ten, and, without my private coach, whatever talent I might have had for the game never reached a level of any consequence.

I became a college professor, teaching and writing about American politics. But along the way, in the early 1980s, two friends and I bought a minor-league team in the Double A Eastern League. At the time, it played in Holyoke, Mas-sachusetts, near where I was employed at the University of Massachusetts. It moved from there to Nashua, New Hampshire, and a few years later to Har-risburg, Pennsylvania, where it remains, though I have not been its owner since the 1994 season. Owning a minor-league team is different from owning a major-league team in that you have no voice in decisions about players or managers. Nevertheless, it afforded regular contact with major-league officials, principally those involved with player development, and also provided a window upon the game I had never expected to have. When I retired from teaching in 2004, I told friends that since it is said one reverts to childhood in old age, I was going to do so frankly and write something about the 1942 St. Louis Cardinals and their season. The genesis of this book therefore lies in the desire to relive one year of my childhood.

~

A book, like baseball, takes a team. I have benefited from the support of many people, none more so than Timothy Wiles, Claudette Burke, and Freddy Berowski at the National Baseball Hall of Fame in Cooperstown, who helped me through their rich holdings. My thanks go to them and also to Deborah Cribbs at the St. Louis Mercantile Library and Carol Warren and Keith Zimmerman at the St. Louis Public Library for help with basic research. The W. E. B. Du Bois Library at my home institution, the University of Massachusetts Amherst, held or acquired materials essential to my work, and my gratitude extends to friends there for help that over the years goes well beyond the pages of this book. Pat Kelly and John Horne at the Baseball Hall of Fame were most helpful in my obtaining rights to photographs, as was Karen Schnurr at Allied PhotoColor in St. Louis. Lonce Sandy-Bailey provided technical assistance in preparing the manuscript for submission, without which it would never have left my home.

A special thanks goes to two longtime friends. Glen Gordon, my onetime chair, dean, and provost at the University of Massachusetts Amherst, grew up in Brooklyn and shared firsthand accounts of games at Ebbets Field, its crowds, and the intensity of the Cardinals-Dodgers rivalry as seen from the other side. Bob Robertson, a fraternity brother who signed with the Cardinals as a pitcher in the late 1940s, shared experiences and stories about being with coaches and instructors at the Redbirds' minor-league training site in Albany, Georgia, and also gave me a general idea of what it was like to be in the St. Louis system with all the many prospects they always had.

Finally, I am grateful to my spring training buddies who gather every March in Florida to assess Redbird chances for the upcoming season: Roland Banscher, Jay and Jeff Demerath, Terry Jones, Lois Pierce, Ron Story, and George Sulzner. Some read major portions of the manuscript; others offered advice and assistance in research; all were forgiving of my sometimes endless jabbering about the 1942 Cardinals and their season. They all know their baseball. Several played the game a lot better than I ever did, and all gave generously of their support and encouragement. Last, but surely not least, my thanks go to Beverly Jarrett, John Brenner, and the staff at the University of Missouri Press. Thanks also to Mary McClintock and Claudia Vander Heuval for help in preparing the final manuscript. In the end, however, an author, like the manager of a team, is responsible for any errors in the final product.

HIGH-FLYING BIRDS

INTRODUCTION

There had never been a championship team like the 1942 St. Louis Cardinals. It was almost entirely home-grown. Led by the innovative baseball executive Branch Rickey, the Cardinals had pioneered in developing the farm system, in which a major-league team builds a network of minor-league teams and grows its own talent. From the 1920s to the 1940s, this system produced a steady stream of players. Some became stars, others made important contributions to the club's success, and still others were sold to competing major-league teams to help finance the minor-league operation. At one time, St. Louis either owned or had working agreements with thirty minor-league teams. In 1942, the number was twenty-two, but even this was more than twice the number of any other major-league club. Before 1942, every Redbird championship team had key contributors who came from other organizations—Grover Cleveland Alexander, Billy Southworth, Frankie Frisch, Leo Durocher, and others. But in 1942, all eight of the everyday starters and all but one of the starting pitchers were home-grown. Only Harry Gumbert, a sometime starting pitcher, and outfielder Coaker Triplett, who replaced Stan Musial in games against some lefthanders, did not come from the team's farm system.

In this, the Cardinals contrasted sharply with their principal National League rival in 1942, the "Bums" of Brooklyn. Only two of the Dodgers' regulars—infielder Pee Wee Reese and outfielder Pete Reiser—had made their major-league debuts with Brooklyn, and both of them had come from minor-league organizations of other teams. Only two pitchers on the Brooklyn roster had begun their major-league careers with the Dodgers. On the other hand, in the American League, the New York Yankees, destined to be the Cardinals' World Series opponents, were built much as the Redbirds were. With ten minor-league teams, the vaunted Bronx Bombers had the second-largest farm system after the Cardinals. In the 1942 World Series the only Yankee regulars drawn from other teams were first baseman Buddy Hassett, who had come up originally with the Dodgers, and right fielder Roy Cullenbine, who first saw the light of major-league day with the

Detroit Tigers. Of the starting pitchers, staff ace "Red" Ruffing had come up with the Boston Red Sox, but all the others were products of the Yankees' farm system. Noting all the home-grown talent on the Birds and Bombers, Whitney Martin of the Associated Press dubbed the 1942 World Series a "county fair" series in which both teams showed off the "prize pumpkins" grown on their farms. "Probably never before has a series been so dominated by home grown talent," he wrote, adding that it "would seem to prove the farm system of building major league clubs has it all over the assembly system six ways from Sunday."[1]

The 1942 Cardinals were also distinctive for their youth. They were celebrated by many veteran sportswriters as the youngest team in both age and experience ever to win the National League pennant and the youngest ever to win a World Series as well. Most writers qualified this by saying "probably"; none tried to document the claim. There seems little doubt, though, that the Cardinals of 1942 were the youngest in average age and years of major-league experience since World War I to win the pennant and World Series. Before 1915, however, it is less clear. A case can be made that the 1914 Boston Braves had a younger starting team than the Cardinals, though their reserves were older. Moreover, the Braves had only one rookie in their starting lineup—outfielder Larry Gilbert—and he played in only about half of their games, whereas the Cardinals started two rookies—Stan Musial and George Kurowski—and had two others on the bench who received significant playing time during the season.[2] Two other Cardinal rookies played prominent roles on the pitching staff: Johnny Beazley, who won twenty-one games, and Murry Dickson, who appeared in thirty-six games, most of them in relief.

There were only two Redbirds with five or more years of big-league service: Terry Moore with seven and Jimmy Brown with five. It was much the same with the pitchers. After Gumbert, the "old-timers" were Mort Cooper and Max La-nier with four years each in the big leagues, while the rest of the staff included four pitchers with two or fewer years of experience. St. Louis typically fielded young teams because Rickey believed in selling or trading veteran players to give younger ones a chance. This was the case in 1942 when star first baseman Johnny Mize was sent to the New York Giants before the start of the season and two veterans—pitcher Lon Warneke and catcher Gus Mancuso—were sold to the Chicago Cubs and New York Giants respectively early in season. None of Rickey's St. Louis clubs, however, had been as young and inexperienced as the 1942 Cardinals.

Toward the end of the season, nothing drew more comment than the remarkable stretch run of the Cardinals, which ranks among the greatest in baseball history and may indeed have been the most impressive ever. From August 14 to the end of the season they won forty-three games and lost only eight, a winning percentage of .843. There had been great stretch drives before, like the twenty-one consecutive wins of the Chicago Cubs in September 1935 to overtake the Cardinals for the National League crown, but none had covered a period of time as long as fifty-one games. The Cardinals' achievement in coming from ten games behind Brooklyn in early August was most often compared with that of the so-called Miracle Braves in 1914, who went from last place in mid-July to winning the National League pennant. But the Braves' streak was not as long, nor was their winning percentage as high as that of the Cardinals.

The race for the 1942 National League pennant was itself unusual. There had been many close, hotly contested pennant races in previous seasons, especially in the National League. Many of these were dogfights lasting until the final day of the season, with two or more teams battling back and forth, winning, then losing, then winning again until only one was left standing in the end. Many teams had come from well behind in the standings to capture a pennant, but in most of these cases the team leading the race faltered badly or collapsed altogether. From the second week of August, when the Redbirds began their run, until the end of the 1942 season, the Dodgers played at a .725 pace against teams other than the Cardinals—good enough to win the pennant in a normal year. The Cards were somewhat better against teams in the league other than Brooklyn, winning at an .844 pace, but the real difference between the two teams was that St. Louis beat Brooklyn five of the final six times they played in late August and early September. The Cardinals drew even with the Dodgers in their final game in Flatbush, then moved ahead the next day when Brooklyn lost a doubleheader while the Redbirds split one. After that, the two teams fought to the finish. In the final week of the season, neither lost a game. St. Louis took the pennant on the final day, winning both ends of a doubleheader to finish the season with 106 wins to Brooklyn's 104. St. Louis reporter Martin J. Haley of the *Globe-Democrat* called it "the most amazing performance in all major league baseball history," a claim that should not be dismissed as mere hometown puffery.[3]

～

Major-league baseball in 1942 was different in many ways, large and small, from today's game. There was less specialization, less emphasis on power hitting, at least in the National League, and of course all the players were white. Teams typically had only two coaches in addition to a manager. There was no hitting coach, no pitching coach, and no bullpen coach. Veteran players—catcher Gus Mancuso and pitcher Lon Warneke—worked with young pitchers in spring training, as did minor-league managers and coaches. It was also common for the big-league manager to serve as third-base coach, as Billy Southworth did. Players left their gloves on the field after innings, a practice that continued until 1954. The gloves presented potential hazards to the defense, but there is no evidence that they had any effect on any game during the Cardinals' 1942 season. The gloves themselves were unlike today's, being two pieces of leather stitched together with some padding but without a preformed pocket or netlike webbing, which meant that when left on the field they would lie flat and close to the ground. Gloves were not the only obstacles on the playing fields. News photographers were permitted on the field with their heavy Graflex cameras to capture action shots for their papers. Only three umpires were normally assigned to a game, which meant that base umpires had to change positions in the course of play depending on where runners were on base.

One difference did have an effect on the National League race in 1942. There were no warning tracks in the outfield, and the outfield walls, many of them made from concrete as in St. Louis, had no padding. Brooklyn center fielder Pete Reiser, generally considered the team's best player, crashed into the wall in a July game with the Cardinals, suffered a concussion, and was never the same player after that. At the time he was injured, he was leading the league in hitting with a .349 average, but he ended the season with an average more than one hundred points below that. Cardinal fans will remember what a similar collision with an outfield wall in 2006 did to Jim Edmonds. Unlike Edmonds, Reiser kept trying to play, but through August and September he was forced from games repeatedly by headaches and dizziness.

The game was also played differently in 1942, especially game strategy in the National League. From the 1920s on, the American League became more and more the home of the new power game. All of its best teams featured home-run hitters: Babe Ruth and Lou Gehrig with the Yankees, Jimmie Foxx and Al Simmons with Philadelphia, Hank Greenberg with Detroit. The same was true in 1942 when three Yankees—Charlie Keller, Joe DiMaggio, and Joe Gordon—combined to hit sixty-seven home runs, seven more than the entire Cardinal team, whose top slugger, Enos Slaughter, had thirteen. The National League still played the older game of "scientific" baseball that featured pitching, defense, speed, situational contact hitting—such as the bunt and the hit-and-run—and aggressive baserunning to force mistakes by opponents. The 1942 Cardinals were the very model of this style of baseball.

Pitching was also different. Pitching staffs were smaller because a "quality" start meant going nine innings, or longer if a game went into extra innings. New York Yankee starters completed 88 of the team's 154 games in 1942, while Cardinal starters finished 66 of the games they began. The Redbirds carried nine pitchers for most of the season, but only eight saw much action, and all eight served as both starters and relievers. Even ace Mort Cooper, who won twenty-two games and was named the National League's Most Valuable Player, made three appearances in relief. Some pitchers worked more out of the bullpen than others, but the concept of a "closer" did not exist. The emphasis on complete games also affected game strategy. In late innings of a low-scoring and close game, it was common for the starting pitcher to hit for himself even with the tying or winning run in scoring position. Indeed, sportswriters often remarked on how unusual it was to employ a pinch hitter for a starter who was pitching well, even if the game had gone far into extra innings.

The scale and economics of baseball were very different from today for owners and players alike. Player salaries, while much better than those of ordinary working Americans, rarely exceeded four figures, and the Cardinals "enjoyed" the reputation of being perhaps the cheapest team in either league. The highest-paid Redbird in 1942 was pitcher Lon Warneke with a salary variously estimated at $12,500 and $15,000. He was sold to the Chicago Cubs at midseason in a deal that enabled St. Louis to recover most of what had been paid to him. As a rookie, Stan Musial's contract was reportedly for $4,800, but that was substantially more than the $3,000 paid to the team's other rookie regular, George Kurowski. By winning the World Series, each player received a $6,800 share in revenues; for Kurowski that meant he earned more than twice as much for playing five World Series games as he had earned during the entire 154–game regular season. Other than Warneke, only pitcher Mort Cooper and outfielders Terry Moore and Enos Slaughter had contracts for more than $6,800 a year. And there were few sources of income for players other than their contracts. Occasionally they made additional money through advertising opportunities or public appearances or a glove or bat contract. Moreover, players had to provide much of their own equipment: teams gave them a home and a road uniform (shirt and pants), a cap, and stirrup stockings, and they provided bats and balls, but players had to purchase their underwear, sanitary socks, gloves, and spikes.

Financially, baseball was a split-level house. New York, Boston, and Chicago were home to the "rich" clubs. Teams in all the other cities had to struggle to balance the books, and some ran in the red year after year. Ticket sales were the largest source of revenue for owners, and teams were heavily dependent on game-day walk-up sales, especially for weekday games.[4] Advertising on outfield fences and scoreboards, as well as concession and souvenir sales, added modestly to the till, but there was no television and in 1942 the Cardinals sold radio rights for thirty thousand dollars. New York teams often drew a million or more fans in a season, but the Cardinals usually had to balance their books on an attendance of just over half that number. The Redbirds did have a revenue stream from the sale of players from their farm system, but much of this revenue went back into the team's large minor-league system itself. With night baseball still a novelty, most weekday games started around 3 p.m. so that businessmen could put in almost a full day of work, attend a game (usually played in two hours), and be home for dinner. Sunday doubleheaders, two games for the price of one, were scheduled almost every week and were big draws because workers, families, and out-of-town fans were able to attend. In its more intimate atmosphere and proximity to the players, a game at Sportsman's Park in 1942 was more like one in a minor-league park today than one at Busch Stadium.

Finally, professional baseball dominated the sports scene in America in 1942. Professional football and basketball were insignificant rivals; college football and basketball commonly received more space on sports pages than did their professional counterparts. Boxing and horse racing were the other two major professional sports, and there was extensive coverage of local high school and amateur leagues, but nothing could match the popularity of baseball: it was without question the national pastime. News coverage of baseball was intense but very different from today. Because there was no television, fans looked to newspapers for game reports and photographs of the action, as they had for decades. St. Louis had three major dailies in 1942: the morning *Globe-Democrat,* which carried full reports and box scores of the previous day's game; the early afternoon *Post-Dispatch,* which often carried partial reports of games in progress as well as brief accounts of games played the day before; and a late-afternoon paper, the *Star-Times,* which reported more fully than the *Post-Dispatch* on games played at home or in a western city and gave accounts of completed games in the East. All of the papers depended heavily on wire services or hired special reporters for important games away from home. The *Sporting News,* published weekly in St. Louis, covered only baseball, with reports on all major-league teams, box scores with brief accounts of all big-league games played the previous week, reports on all the minor leagues, and general stories about the business of baseball. During 1942, it included a weekly page on military service teams and players in uniform, as well as a special series on baseball during World War I.

CHAPTER 1
War Comes to Baseball

The U.S. House of Representatives was packed. Members from both branches of Congress were gathered for a joint session, joined on the floor of the House by cabinet officers and justices of the Supreme Court and ringed by congressional staff standing around the side and back walls. The public gallery was filled with military personnel, officials from the War and State Departments, and advisers from the White House, as well as members of the public. The press gallery was crowded; security was tight. The mood was somber. There was none of the casual camaraderie, the easy joviality, the good-natured bantering common in gatherings of politicians. It was instead an unusually quiet and solemn assemblage. At 12:30 in the afternoon on December 8, 1941, a grim President Franklin Roosevelt made his way slowly to the rostrum, assisted by his son James, and stood before microphones that would carry his words beyond the House chamber to millions of Americans in their homes and workplaces across the nation. He leaned heavily on the podium, in front of a large American flag that hung behind Speaker of the House Sam Rayburn and Vice President Henry Wallace, who were seated just above and directly behind him.

"Yesterday, December 7, 1941—a date which will live in infamy," the president began. The familiar shake of his great head punctuated his next words: "the United States of America was suddenly and deliberately attacked by the naval and air forces of the empire of Japan." For the next three minutes, Roosevelt spoke in only general terms about the attack on Pearl Harbor, for the full extent of the damage—the loss of men, ships, and aircraft—would not be known for a week. He concluded by asking the Congress to declare that "since the unprovoked and dastardly attack" by the Japanese, "a state of war has existed between the United States and the Japanese empire." By 12:40 the speech was over, the joint session of Congress had adjourned, and Roosevelt was on his way back to the White House.

He had left his office to the cheers of a great throng that had gathered on Pennsylvania Avenue; he returned to a largely silent crowd.

Events moved rapidly on Capitol Hill after Roosevelt's speech: at 1 p.m. the Senate unanimously adopted the resolution declaring war on Japan, and ten minutes later the House did the same by a vote of 385–1.[1] At 4 p.m. the resolution was delivered to the White House by Garrett Whiteside, clerk of the Senate Committee on Enrolled Bills, who as a House clerk in 1917 had typed the declaration for World War I.[2] Ten minutes later, surrounded by the leaders of Congress, President Roosevelt signed the document, and a nation whose people had not wanted war was at war nonetheless. Two days later, Germany and Italy declared war on the United States. Roosevelt, calling for a "rapid and united effort" for victory "over the forces of savagery and barbarism," asked for and received a declaration of war against them in return, this time without a dissenting voice in the Congress.[3] The nation suddenly faced a war on two fronts: one in the Pacific, the other in Europe.

The week before Pearl Harbor, professional baseball's minor leagues held their fortieth annual meeting at the George Washington Hotel in Jacksonville, Florida. Executives from major- and minor-league clubs came together in a festive environment of good cheer, back-slapping, and storytelling for a meeting at which the principal order of business, as always, involved the governance of the minor leagues and their relationship with the major leagues. The majors asked the minors to standardize the baseball used in all of their leagues to make it easier for big-league talent scouts to evaluate the players. In addition, the majors wanted to simplify the process by which players were moved from one level to another and to give big-league clubs more protection over players they owned. William G. Branham, president of the National Association of Professional Baseball Leagues, governing body for the minors, brought good news about the 1941 season: all forty-one leagues had completed their schedules and more than fifteen million fans had attended minor-league games, an increase of three million over 1940.[4] Branham also reported that the military draft established in 1941 had taken 277 players from minor-league rosters, but he did not see this as a problem and predicted a rosy future for minor-league baseball.

The St. Louis Cardinals sent a delegation of thirty-six people to the meetings that included representatives from all their farm clubs except Sacramento, as well as team president Sam Breadon and vice-president Branch Rickey. The Cardinals had no urgent business at the meetings. Breadon told reporters that there were no trades "in the fire," a sentiment Rickey echoed, saying that they would be "good listeners." The Cardinals did make a modest deal, selling pitcher Hank Gornicki to the Pittsburgh Pirates. In 1941, Gornicki had won twenty-two games for the Double A farm club in Rochester, New York, but he did not figure in Redbird plans for the 1942 season. They also had some "housekeeping" to do as a result of Burt Shotton resigning as manager of their Double A Columbus, Ohio, club to take a coaching job with the Cleveland Indians. Eddie Dyer was tapped to move up from Class A to Double A, while Clay Hopper took the reins of the Class A club at Houston.[5] Dyer would one day manage the Cardinals, while the paths of Shotton and Hopper would cross again later in the 1940s when both would be in the Brooklyn organization.[6]

When the minor-league meetings ended on December 5, everyone headed home, the big-league officials to prepare for the annual major-league meetings scheduled to convene the following week on December 8 in Chicago. Many team officials, managers, sportswriters, and some players began to arrive in the Windy City on Sunday, December 7, where they were greeted by the news of Pearl Harbor. As the Congress in Washington was listening to President Roosevelt's war message, baseball executives were meeting in a subdued atmosphere of their own, sharply different from that at the minor-league meetings just days before. Unlike minor-league chief Branham, National League president Ford Frick had delivered an ominous warning to baseball at the minor-league meetings, saying that the game faced "critical difficulties" that would present "as stern a test as at any time in its one hundred year history." Frick was referring to the military draft and shortages of materials like Australian wool and horsehide needed for baseballs, but with the nation suddenly at war, his remarks now took on a larger meaning. Team officials were faced with not only the question of how to improve their teams for the 1942 season but also the far larger question of whether there would even be a 1942 baseball season. Many remembered that the 1918 season had been cut short by World War I, ending on Labor Day with the World Series played in early September, and they wondered if the same or worse was to be their fate again.[7]

Since the German invasion of Poland in September 1939, the American press had reported almost daily on the war in Europe, following the advance of Nazi troops across the continent: Denmark, Norway, then Holland, Belgium, and finally France. The British escape from Dunkirk and the massive, almost nightly German air assaults on London and other cities in England had been front-page news in 1940, often with large headlines and dramatic photographs. Radio too brought regular reports from newsmen in beleaguered Britain. In the summer of 1941, the major war news shifted to the bloody German assault on the Soviet Union.[8] While isolationist sentiment remained strong at home, the Roosevelt administration had nonetheless taken a stand in the war with its Lend-Lease program to aid Britain and the Soviet Union in their resistance to the Axis forces. The nation's first peacetime draft had brought the war home to the major leagues as several players had been called into service in 1941, most notably Detroit Tigers slugger Hank Greenberg and Philadelphia Phillies pitcher Hugh Mulcahy.

The news about fighting in Asia had not been as prominent in the press, and except for those living on the West Coast with its sizable Japanese population, the Asian war seemed less significant to most Americans. Japan had overrun Manchuria, held China in a death grip, and harbored territorial designs on all of oil-rich Southeast Asia. U.S. negotiations with Japan were ongoing in Washington, and while most Americans, according to opinion polls, thought war with Japan was inevitable, few thought it was imminent.[9] The relationship between the Asian conflict and the war in Europe was unclear to most Americans, and because most of them traced their ancestry to the nations of Europe, more attention was given to the fighting there. Still, some in the St. Louis contingent to the winter baseball meetings might have read a column by Bertram Benedict in the Sunday, December 7, 1941, edition of the *St. Louis Post-Dispatch* that warned, "Never before have the American people been so close to war as in the present crisis with Japan."

The suddenness, the improbability, and the apparent devastation of the Japanese attack on Pearl Harbor had stunned baseball's executives, but they went ahead with their meetings and with plans for the 1942 season, all the while acknowledging that it might never be played. "Back in the first war," Washington Senators owner Clark Griffith recalled, "we were advised to continue, to keep life as nearly normal as possible. We were prepared to close our gates then, but were advised against such procedure." He added, "We will carry on now and be guided by the sentiment and needs of the nation." National League owners adopted a resolution directing Ford Frick to offer President Roosevelt "their complete cooperation and assistance in this time of national crisis," pledging that "individually and collectively we are yours to command."[10]

The American League echoed the dedication of the so-called Senior (older) Circuit, but its more immediate business was a proposal from St. Louis Browns president Donald Barnes to move his team to Los Angeles for the 1942 season. St. Louis had fielded two major-league teams since 1902, when the Browns replaced Milwaukee in the infant American League. At the time, St. Louis was the fourth-largest city in the nation, prosperous, growing, a center of railroading that was known especially for its shoe industry and its breweries.[11] The city had a rich history, having played a central role in the opening of the West, and its rapidly expanding and ethnically diverse population had grown to almost six hundred thousand by 1900. Settled originally by the French, St. Louis had become a predominantly German-American city, albeit with a growing Irish immigrant population. The 1904 World's Fair brought the city international attention and acclaim, and in many ways marked the pinnacle of its achievement. After World War I, St. Louis went into a long period of slow decline, accelerated in the 1920s by Prohibition, which hurt its breweries, and a decade later by the Great Depression, which had a devastating impact.[12] By 1942, St. Louis could no longer support two major-league teams. The Browns had remained in operation through the 1930s only with substantial financial support from other American League teams. The team's owner had concluded that the only solution was to move the franchise elsewhere.[13]

Calling Los Angeles a "logical and desirable city" for a major-league team, Browns vice-president William DeWitt had spent months persuading other owners to support the move and had won tentative approval for it. He had worked out a schedule for the league that showed how travel to the West Coast could be arranged. But as DeWitt lamented, "December 7, 1941, screwed up the whole thing."[14] The league rejected his proposal, believing—correctly—that since the federal government would have to commandeer space on trains to move troops and materiel, travel would be difficult enough to schedule even within the compact geography of major-league baseball in the early 1940s, in which St. Louis was the westernmost city.[15] The Browns would have to wait another twelve years before leaving St. Louis for Baltimore before the 1954 season. Los Angeles would not be home to a major-league club until 1958 when the Brooklyn Dodgers moved west.

Night baseball continued to be controversial. Night games were relatively new to the major leagues, which limited teams to no more than seven per season. Teams in financial difficulty, like the Browns and the Washington Senators, wanted to play more "arc light" games because they drew larger crowds than those played during daytime hours.[16] The American League voted to increase the number of night games, but the National League voted against it. The game's long-serving and autocratic commissioner, Kenesaw Mountain Landis, broke the tie by siding with the National League. With patriotism running high, the leagues agreed to make a $25,000 gift to the military and also to donate all receipts after expenses from the major-league All-Star Game to an equipment fund for use by the Army and Navy.

~

Traditionally, the major-league meetings had been a marketplace for trading players as teams prepared for the upcoming season. But the advent of war created new uncertainties that made trade talks problematic. "It's tough to know what to do," William DeWitt of the Browns lamented, noting that a team might have two men for a position, trade one of them, then have the military take the other. Yet, trades were made. The Cardinals sold catcher Don Padgett to Brooklyn, prompting *Post-Dispatch* columnist J. Roy Stockton to note that the Dodgers "did considerable shopping at the St. Louis Cardinal store before winning the 1941 pennant."[17] Three Brooklyn regulars—outfielders Joe Medwick and Pete Reiser and catcher Mickey Owen—had all been obtained from St. Louis, as had starting pitcher Curt Davis and manager Leo Durocher. The Cardinals made bigger news on the last day of the meetings. For weeks there had been speculation that the club would deal star first baseman Johnny Mize, and late in the proceedings, after many had already left Chicago, the Redbirds sent Mize to the New York Giants for pitcher Bill Lohrman, catcher Kenneth O'Dea, and $50,000.[18]

Signed by the Cardinals in 1930, Mize had arrived in St. Louis in 1936 and quickly became one of the league's best hitters for both average and power. In six seasons with the Cardinals, "Big Jawn," as he was known affectionately, had compiled a .330 batting average, leading the National League in 1939 with a .349 mark. He also averaged more than twenty-six home runs a year, setting the club's single-season record with forty-three round-trippers in 1940. Mize had injured his shoulder late in the 1941 season, and his recovery had been slow. Moreover, he had annoyed manager Billy Southworth by not being in uniform and on the bench with his teammates for games in the final weeks of the season as the club battled for the pennant, preferring instead to wear street clothes and sit in the grandstand or press box. More important to Branch Rickey, however, was that Mize's batting average had dropped to .317 and he hit only seventeen home runs. Mize was only twenty-nine, but he had a history of injury, and his decline in performance led Rickey to suspect that he might have peaked as a player. In addition, Rickey had a high regard for first-base prospect Ray Sanders, who seemed ready for the big time. In 1941, playing for the Cardinals' Double A team at Columbus, Ohio, Sanders had hit .308 and driven in 120 runs. He was also fleet afoot and an excellent defensive player, whereas Mize was a slow runner and average at best defensively.

The Cardinals had a long history of dealing veteran players for cash and replacing them with prospects from the team's highly productive minor-league system. This practice helped the club, never awash in money, to balance its books, as the deals at once reduced payroll and added revenue. In 1937 the Cardinals sold pitcher Dizzy Dean to the Chicago Cubs for $185,000. The garrulous hurler had teamed with his brother Paul to win a combined forty-nine games for the colorful 1934 champions known as the Gas House Gang. Two years later, the Dodgers sent players and cash in excess of $100,000 to the Cards for Joe Medwick and Curt Davis, and after the 1939 season Brooklyn acquired Mickey Owen for $60,000. Early in the 1941 season, Rickey peddled starting pitcher "Fiddler" Bill McGee to the Giants for an undisclosed amount of cash. And there were many players of less prominence, like Padgett, who were sold for lesser amounts of money. If Cardinals fans were troubled by the Mize trade, he was not. Learning about it while hunting, Big Jawn declined to criticize the trade: "All I'm thinking about now is ducks. We killed 34 yesterday," he said, "and we're going back there today."[19]

The day after the Mize trade, the Brooklyn Dodgers made a major trade of their own, sending four players to the Pittsburgh Pirates for All-Star shortstop

Arky Vaughan. The widely respected Roy Stockton of the *St. Louis Post-Dispatch* called it the most important trade of the winter meetings. The Dodgers already had a great young shortstop and future Hall of Famer, Harold "Pee Wee" Reese, which meant that Vaughan would play third base, an upgrade over the incumbent Harry "Cookie" Lavagetto, who had been lost to military service.[20] It also meant that Brooklyn's rookie sensation of 1941, Pete Reiser, who had led the National League in hitting, could shift from infield to full-time duty in center field, improving the Dodgers' defense there.

As baseball's winter meetings ended, the war was the dominant fact of life for the game's leaders, as it would be throughout the 1942 season and beyond. Connie Mack, the venerable owner and manager of the Philadelphia Athletics, issued stern advice to his players, saying that when their contracts arrived they should "sign up and shut up." "None of us knows what the season holds in store, and there'll have to be a limit to our financial commitments," Mack said. "It doesn't seem right that the club owner should have to take all the risk . . . the player has been pretty well taken care of, year in and year out, whereas there've been plenty of clubs in distress even in prosperous baseball years."[21] Mack was not alone among owners in his concern about the costs of operating in 1942. The St. Louis Browns released all four of their scouts. "We are confronting a situation that nobody knows or can know much about," Browns president Donald Barnes later explained. "We released the scouts as an economy measure," he said, adding, "we're not the only club cutting down. Detroit has released four or five scouts. . . . There may be no minor leagues in a few months . . . there won't be much of anything for scouts to do." Barnes concluded plaintively, "We can't know what's going to happen in the majors."[22]

After the meetings, the Cardinals sparked a firestorm of criticism in St. Louis by announcing a second $100,000 dividend for the year. Each time, much of the dividend went to team president Sam Breadon, bringing his income from the club to more than $100,000 for the year. Branch Rickey also shared in the profits, adding around $30,000 to his base salary of $50,000 for the year. Sportswriters were quick to wonder whether the sale of Mize had been to improve the team or the bank accounts of Breadon and Rickey. Rickey had often talked of "addition by subtraction" as a way to strengthen a team, but it was unclear to many in the press how subtracting Mize while the Dodgers were adding Vaughan computed to a positive outcome for St. Louis. Some of the Cardinals' players very likely had their doubts as well. Johnny Mize may not have been speaking only for himself when he complained to *Brooklyn Eagle* columnist Harold Parrott in an April interview that the Redbirds could have won the 1941 pennant if they had brought outfielder Stan Musial and pitcher Howard Pollet to the big-league club sooner in the season. "The St. Louis Club is run backwards," Mize said. "I mean the Cardinals themselves are run for the benefit of the minor league clubs in the chain system." Mize predicted that the Cards "probably won't win" in 1942, because something always happened to them. He added, "Is it any wonder I'm happy to be a Giant and out of St. Louis at last?" Parrott noted that "revealing the player merry-go-round on the Cardinals tickled Mize."[23]

~

During the week of the winter baseball meetings, the war news, as President Roosevelt acknowledged in a radio address, had been "all bad." The Japanese attack on Pearl Harbor was accompanied by simultaneous assaults on targets across the China Sea and in the Pacific from the Philippines in the north to Malaya, the oil-rich Dutch East Indies, and New Guinea in the south. The speed and range of the Japanese assaults was stunning.[24] Most Americans reacted to Pearl Harbor with anger and wanted revenge, though many residing on the East Coast and especially on the West Coast were also fearful that the war would come to the American mainland. Reports circulated that Japanese planes had been sighted over several cities along the Pacific coast, and local officials, many with military assistance, reacted immediately. In San Francisco there were blackouts almost every night in the week following Pearl Harbor and an air-raid alert that lasted for an hour and thirty-four minutes. In Los Angeles, soldiers and agents from the Federal Bureau of Investigation rounded up many Japanese residents to be incarcerated in a makeshift facility. Antiaircraft batteries were set up at key communication sites and power stations all along the coast. The Rose Bowl game was moved from Pasadena, California, to Durham, North Carolina. Military officials in California called the situation "dangerous" and said there was "every reason to believe there will be an attack."[25]

The public response on the East Coast was much the same. There were air-raid warnings in Boston and New York, and schoolchildren were sent home. In Jacksonville, Florida, the military base was blacked out, with the post commander warning that it was "not a test blackout." "This is serious so far as we are concerned," he added ominously.[26] Radio stations went off the air at night, and reports of German submarine activity picked up all along the Atlantic seaboard.

It was a week before the grim details of the attack on Pearl Harbor were fully known. Eighteen ships had been sunk or badly damaged, eight battleships among them, in addition to which three hundred aircraft were damaged, most of them destroyed. The toll in human lives totaled 2,403, while another 1,178 were wounded. The heaviest loss of life came on the battleship *Arizona*, which blew up when hit by bombs, sank within minutes, and carried 1,103 sailors to a watery grave. The nation was numb as it got the news and saw newspaper and newsreel photographs of the damage. The military commanders on Oahu, both Army and Navy, were made scapegoats for the losses, relieved of their commands within days of the attack, and retired from the service. By mid-December, Congress had approved a draft for men twenty to forty-five years of age, but also required all men ages eighteen to sixty-five to register.[27]

Before Pearl Harbor, the Roosevelt administration had been talking with Japanese officials about their respective interests in Asia, but the primary focus of the American government had been on the war in Europe. A strong isolationist lobby at home had prevented both serious preparations for war and direct military assistance to any of the combatant nations, though there had been an increase in the production of military weapons and equipment and the Lend-Lease program gave indirect support to Britain and the Soviet Union. British Prime Minister Winston Churchill had met with President Roosevelt at Newfoundland in August 1941, where they reached agreement on the "Atlantic Charter," declaring in general terms the war aims of the two nations. Churchill came away confident that Europe was of first importance to Roosevelt. But the attack on Pearl Harbor and the U.S. declaration of war on Japan led him to worry that Asia might take priority over Europe in the war plans of the Americans.

Within two days of the Japanese attack, Churchill wired Roosevelt seeking another meeting and offering to come to Washington. He left England on December 12 by ship and arrived in Washington ten days later. As thousands of young men were rushing to enlist in the military, overwhelming local boards and military officials, and as baseball's leadership was preoccupied with whether there would be a 1942 season, Roosevelt, Churchill, and their advisers and military staffs began meetings at the White House to plan a joint war effort. In a little more than two weeks, as David Bercuson and Holger Herwig write, they drafted "the war plan that both nations would follow in the first year or so of the war" and "established a system of joint theater command and put in place a mechanism—the Combined Chiefs of Staff—that would pull the levers to make that system go."[28] Moreover, they agreed on a joint statement of their war aims and called for an all-out war production program to defeat the Axis powers. The United States, however, had no plan for mobilizing war production, managing the economy, or securing the nation at home—or, for that matter, preparing its people for war.

Differences remained between Britain and the United States, but to Churchill's relief, Roosevelt agreed that victory in Europe should be the first objective. On Christmas Eve, after a fierce battle for Manila, General Douglas MacArthur, who had not been told of Roosevelt's decision to pursue victory in Europe first, withdrew to the island of Corregidor, conceding Manila to the Japanese. The day after Christmas, Churchill addressed a joint session of Congress, flashed his famous V for Victory sign, and left the podium to a standing ovation that closed the deal on the grand alliance. The war was on. The question remained whether the 1942 baseball season would be on as well.

CHAPTER 2

Winter of Uncertainty, Spring of Hope

As the new year arrived, the overriding question for major-league baseball was whether there would be a season. Beginning with the National League resolution putting its teams at the disposal of President Franklin Roosevelt, baseball mounted a public relations campaign that associated those in the game with all Americans dedicated to doing their patriotic duty whatever the costs. In its first issue after Pearl Harbor, the *Sporting News* set the tone in an editorial entitled, "Uncle Sam, We Are at Your Command!" Known as the "bible of baseball" for its authoritative and comprehensive coverage of the game, the Sporting News was also widely seen as a semiofficial house organ for the sport. While the editorial noted that the major leagues were ready to cancel the season if so ordered, its real purpose was to make the case for playing the 1942 season. The editorial emphasized the importance of baseball to American life, asserting that the game was "born in America, propagated in America and recognized as the National Game"; that it epitomized the American values of hard work, fair play, and respect for rules; and that "all those engaged in the sport are Americans first, last and always." Playing the season, the editorial concluded, would provide continuity for the nation, sustain hope at home, and offer a diversion from the grim work at hand for the troops abroad.[1]

In early January, Clark Griffith of the Washington Senators and other owners urged baseball commissioner Kenesaw Mountain Landis to ask Roosevelt for clarification of baseball's role in wartime. A conservative southern Republican, Landis had been outspoken in his disdain for Roosevelt, so much so that, in the opinion of *Washington Post* columnist Shirley Povich, the commissioner "was not welcome at the White House."[2] Griffith, on the other hand, was on friendly terms with the president and knew him to be a baseball fan who often attended Senators games at Griffith Stadium. The Washington owner also had an influential ally in Robert Hannegan, chairman of the St. Louis Democratic city committee and political adviser to then-Senator Harry Truman. Well connected with baseball in St. Louis, Hannegan was a close friend of Browns president Donald Barnes and had been a high school classmate of Browns vice-president William DeWitt.[3] Landis sent a handwritten letter to Roosevelt seeking his direction; Hannegan and Griffith met with the president soon thereafter. Griffith, who wanted to play more night games in Washington, took the opportunity to suggest that it might be good for the country if the major leagues were to schedule more night games.

Roosevelt responded promptly to erase all uncertainty about the season. In what came to be called his "green-light" letter, he wrote to Landis: "I honestly feel that it would be best for the country to keep baseball going. There will be fewer people unemployed and everybody will work longer hours and harder than ever before. And that means that they ought to have a chance for recreation and for taking their minds off their work even more than before." Roosevelt added, "I hope that night games can be extended because it gives an opportunity to the day shift to see a game occasionally."[4]

Baseball thus had its season, but with it came another question: whether to increase the allotted number of night games. Many owners had reservations about night baseball. Yankees president Edward Barrow thought it a fad, "a wart on the nose of the game."[5] Landis had doubts as well, fearing games at night would have an adverse impact on players, especially on their eyesight, and would give license to those with loose morals. The major leagues had banned the use of artificial lights for games until 1935, when the first night game was played in Cincinnati, one of seven scheduled that year by Larry MacPhail, then general manager of the Cincinnati club.[6] In 1942, five big-league stadiums—those of the New York Yankees, Boston Red Sox, Detroit Tigers, Boston Braves, and Chicago Cubs—were still without lights. While officials in the game fretted, sportswriters embraced the green-light letter and night baseball. Shirley Povich said it gave a "tremendous boost" to night baseball, while Dan Daniel of the *New York Herald Tribune* called it "the most important approval the game has got in all its history." Griffith, who had engineered the whole thing, called the president's letter a "command."[7] In the end, the National League went along grudgingly with the American League, and the number of night games for each team was increased to fourteen.[8] The Washington Senators were the exception; they were authorized to play twenty-one games under the lights because the nation's capital was a city of "day-shift" workers.[9]

~

January brought good news to the Cardinals' organization. The *Sporting News* named the team's skipper, Billy Southworth, its Major League Manager of the Year for 1941. For Southworth, it meant redemption. "Billy the Kid," as he was known in his playing days, had been a member of the 1926 Cardinals team that edged the Cincinnati Reds by two games in a hotly contested race to win the club's first National League pennant of the twentieth century, then went on to best Babe Ruth and the New York Yankees four games to three in the World Series to be champions of baseball. Small in stature, standing just over 5'8" and weighing 170 pounds, Southworth had been acquired in a trade with the New York Giants in June 1926 and did much to solidify the Cardinals' outfield defense. He also stabilized the batting order, adding speed and hitting .317 in ninety-nine games. His greatest moment came in a September contest against his former team. The Giants, managed by John McGraw, had taken a three-run lead in the first inning, only to have Southworth stroke a home run to cap a five-run second inning that put the Cards ahead to stay. It was a crucial late-season win.[10]

Southworth was named manager of the Cardinals in 1929, but his style, modeled after that of McGraw and other tough guys for whom he had played, grated on the players and produced a near mutiny. Many of the players were Southworth's former teammates, and they thought the "Kid" had become the "Martinet." In midseason Southworth was demoted to Rochester, where he had managed the team to the International League pennant the year before. He enjoyed a great run of success at Rochester, eventually winning pennants in four consecutive years from 1928 through 1931. He left the St. Louis organization in 1933 to become a coach with the New York Giants, but his tenure there was brief. During spring training, in an angry exchange with Bill Terry, he took a swing at the Giants' manager and was promptly fired. One St. Louis sportswriter explained that Southworth was a "victim of the grape."

Southworth was out of baseball for several years, but returned to the Cardinals' organization in 1936 to manage teams in the low minors. By 1939 he had worked his way back to Rochester, and in 1940, with the Cardinals off to a poor start, Sam Breadon fired Ray Blades as manager and brought Southworth back to St. Louis. The decision was made without consulting Branch Rickey and was the first public break between the two, a break that would become final after the 1942 season when Rickey left St. Louis for Brooklyn.[11] Southworth made the most of his second chance. Taking over a club in seventh place, he led the Cardinals to a 69–40 record for the rest of the season and a third-place finish. His managerial style had clearly changed. "A slap on the back and a word of encouragement are worth more than anything else," he said after learning of his selection by the *Sporting News*. "I talk to my players man-to-man—the way I should want to be talked to myself." He added, "I try to make the clubhouse a friendly place. I want the players to come early each day and create comradeship."[12] Still a disciplinarian, Southworth had learned how to enforce his rules with kid gloves.

In naming Southworth its Manager of the Year, the *Sporting News* noted the large number of injuries the Cardinals had experienced in 1941 that put every regular except shortstop Marty Marion on the bench for various lengths of time. In all, the regulars lost more than 283 playing days. Enos Slaughter and Walker Cooper were the major casualties, being out of action for two months each with broken collar and shoulder bones. In addition to the everyday players, pitcher Mort Cooper had elbow surgery in June that sidelined him until the middle of September.

The 1941 pennant race itself was one of the hardest and most closely fought two-team battles in National League history. It was like the trench warfare of World War I in which a team would advance one day, then fall back the next. The Cardinals were in first place for seventy-three days; the Dodgers held the top spot for seventy-eight; the two were tied seven times; and they were almost always within two games of each other. From early June to around Labor Day, the lead changed hands twenty-one times. The two teams played each other twenty-three times during the season, with each winning eleven times and the remaining game ending in a tie. "Never," Roger Craemer concludes, "were two big league teams more evenly matched."[13] The season came down to a three-game September series in St. Louis, with the Dodgers holding a one-game lead and the Cardinals, due to all the injuries, fielding a makeshift lineup. The teams split the first two games. In the third, Cooper, back from arm surgery, held the Dodgers to three hits and one run, but Whitlow Wyatt was better, shutting out the Redbirds 1–0 to build a two-game lead that Brooklyn held to the end of the season.

The Cardinals also learned in January that Rogers Hornsby, the greatest Cardinal of them all to that time, had been elected to the Baseball Hall of Fame. The Hall was still a new institution, having opened its doors in 1939 with the induction of thirteen of the game's immortals. Hornsby was the first *modern* player (one from the twentieth century) to be elected since 1939. The "Rajah," as he was known, joined two others in the Hall who had played briefly for the Cardinals: Cy Young, who won 45 of his 511 career victories in a St. Louis uniform, and Grover Cleveland "Old Pete" Alexander, who pitched the Redbirds to their first World Series triumph in 1926, a team for which Hornsby had been the manager.

Generally acclaimed the greatest righthanded hitter of all time, Hornsby posted batting statistics rarely seen before his time or since. He was National League batting champion seven times, including six times in a row. His .424 average for the 1924 season remains the highest for any player since 1900, while his career average of .358 tops all National Leaguers and is second only to Ty Cobb in major-league history. Hornsby twice won the Triple Crown, leading his league in batting average, home runs, and runs batted in. The only other player to win two Triple Crowns is American Leaguer Ted Williams of the Boston Red

Sox. Hornsby is the only player ever to hit .400 with twenty or more home runs in three different seasons, and he set the Cardinals' single-season home-run mark with forty-two in 1922, a record that stood until broken by Johnny Mize with forty-three in 1940 (Mize's record stood until Mark McGwire hit seventy home runs in 1998). But perhaps Hornsby's most remarkable feat is that over five seasons from 1921 to 1925 he *averaged* better than .400 in hitting.

Hornsby had worn out his welcome with the Cardinals' owners during his pennant-winning year in 1926 and was dealt to the New York Giants in the off-season.[14] Loved by the fans, his trade set off an angry firestorm of protest among the Cardinal faithful, but Hornsby went on to antagonize just about everyone else with whom he came into contact in baseball. He quickly fell into disfavor with the Giants, who dealt him to the Boston Braves after one year. He played one year in Boston, leading the league in hitting, but at season's end he was traded to the Chicago Cubs, where he stayed for four years before returning to St. Louis as manager of the Browns. Hornsby was a difficult man—a loner who did not smoke or drink alcohol, who did not hang out or socialize with his teammates, and who avoided both reading and movies to protect his eyesight. He could be and often was, Jim Hunstein writes, "uncivil, mean, insulting, and belligerent," but Hunstein adds, "he was fair about it. He treated everyone the same."[15] J. Roy Stockton of the *St. Louis Post-Dispatch*, who followed Hornsby's career up close, thought him the "squarest, bluntest, cussingest," most "stubborn" and "bull-headed" of men, but one "without guile or subterfuge." People might not like Hornsby, Stockton allowed, but they trusted him.[16] Hornsby was a great player who deserved to be among the first dozen chosen for the Hall of Fame, but his abrasive character combined with the view of some that he was not a team player turned enough of the Hall's electors against him to prevent his entry with the first group of the game's all-time greats in 1939.

~

The winter months in baseball are spent preparing for the coming season, making repairs to the ballpark and playing field, planning promotional and marketing campaigns, and getting ready for spring training. The latter would take the Cardinals once again to St. Petersburg, Florida. They announced a schedule of twenty-two exhibition games in the Grapefruit League, including nine against the defending World Champions, the New York Yankees, that the *Sporting News* speculated might be "a preview of the 1942 World Series."[17] For the first time, all of the Redbirds' games were to be against big-league clubs—"facing the real thing throughout the training period," an optimistic Sam Breadon commented, adding that, at manager Southworth's request, training would start a week earlier than usual to give pitchers and catchers more time to get ready and also to give the manager and his coaches more time to evaluate a number of highly prized rookies who would be in camp. The plan also called for the team to stay in Florida longer than usual, not leaving until the week before the start of the major-league season. On the way north they would travel with the Detroit Tigers, playing exhibition games in North Carolina and Tennessee before arriving in St. Louis for the annual two-game city series with the Browns. Roy Stockton of the *Post-Dispatch* applauded the plan as "the most intelligently arranged in Cardinal history."[18]

Of the Cardinals' prospects, none was more anxiously awaited or faced higher expectations than Stanley Frank Musial, whose rise to the big leagues late in the 1941 season was the stuff of storybooks. Signed as a pitcher, he injured his arm playing the outfield and had struggled to recover. In a 1941 spring game against the major-league club, he was hit hard and sent back to the Cardinals' minor-league training site at Albany, Georgia, where the decision was made to move him permanently to the outfield. None of the minor-league managers wanted an outfielder who could not throw, but Ollie Vanek finally agreed reluctantly to take him for the Class C Western Association club in Springfield, Missouri. Musial, whose arm grew stronger as the season progressed, promptly went on a tear at the plate, hitting .379 with ninety-four runs driven in and twenty-six home runs in eighty-seven games. Promoted midseason to the Double A Rochester club, he continued to hit, compiling a .326 average in fifty-four games and starring in the International League playoffs.[19] Brought to St. Louis in September for the final two weeks of the major-league season, Musial impressed by hitting .426 in twelve games, prompting the Chicago Cubs manager to ask, "Can he be *that* good?" and leading Billy Southworth to marvel: "In all my experience I don't think I've seen a better-looking young ball player come up."[20]

As the Cardinals were putting the final touches to their spring training plans, a controversy arose with the New York Giants. Bill Terry, the team's manager, declared that Johnny Mize, dealt to the Giants at the winter meetings in December, was a "partial cripple" as a result of injuries sustained in 1941. Terry threatened to return Mize to St. Louis and get his fifty thousand dollars back if Mize was not ready to play by spring training. Branch Rickey assured the Giants, "We wouldn't insist on any club keeping a player we sold if he was not fit to make himself worth the purchase price."[21] Mize struggled initially in spring training, but returned to form in time for the start of the season. He would hit .305 for the New Yorkers in 1942 and continue to be a top slugger for years thereafter.

⁓

The war was ever present in the minds of baseball officials and sportswriters during the months after Pearl Harbor. It meant higher costs for all the clubs. Railroad passenger rates had increased by 5 percent in November 1941 and were to go up another 10 percent by the time of spring training. The cost of travel for the Cardinals in the 1941 season had been around $25,000; it was expected to be closer to be $30,000 in 1942. Hotel costs were also rising, sometimes by as much as 25 percent. For traveling secretaries of major-league clubs, about the only cost that remained constant was the $3.50 per day meal allowance players received while away from home.[22]

The effects of the war were greater for the minor leagues. William Branham, who had been upbeat at the minor-league meetings before Pearl Harbor, now anguished about the impact of the war on his leagues. Almost six hundred minor-leaguers were in the armed forces by late February as spring training began, most of them younger players from lower-level leagues. The New York Yankees, with fifty of their minor-league players in service, had already scaled back their player development operation from twelve minor-league teams in 1941 to ten clubs in 1942. A few leagues had canceled their seasons; others would play with six teams rather than the usual eight. Branham was worried as well about wartime shortages of tires and gasoline. Most minor-league teams were in towns without public transportation so that fans had to drive to the parks, and almost all minor-league teams traveled to road games by bus.[23]

Dodger president Larry MacPhail, who had been an Army captain in World War I, took the initiative on how major-league clubs might contribute to the war effort. Speaking in early February at the ninth annual New York baseball writers dinner, he laid out a four-point program designed to raise money and provide entertainment for the nation's servicemen and women. MacPhail suggested that in addition to proceeds from the July All-Star game the majors should play a second game between the winner of this game and an All-Star service team, with proceeds from it going to aid military relief. He called on everyone in baseball, including the players, to accept part of their salaries in war bonds and urged teams to use open dates on their schedules to play exhibition games against service teams at Army and Navy camps. In addition, he recommended that teams set aside a portion of every admission to buy a bomber for the Air Force to be named the "Kenesaw Mountain Landis." Finally, MacPhail announced that the Dodgers would donate the receipts from a specially designated home game to a servicemen's welfare agency.[24]

In their February meeting, baseball owners accepted most of MacPhail's proposals and agreed also to follow his example of scheduling a home game with all gate receipts going to a military relief agency. Like other teams, Sam Breadon said the Cardinals would distribute a special military ticket that would admit servicemen and women in uniform free of charge. The only MacPhail suggestion that bombed was that major-league baseball purchase a bomber.[25] Through this war program, baseball was assured, Richard Goldstein writes, that in 1942 "hardly a day would go by without a reminder that the 'national pastime' was a national resource, making itself useful to the war effort beyond serving as a morale boost-er through its mere presence."[26]

～

Cardinal players and officials began to arrive in St. Petersburg in the third week of February. Infielder Jimmy Brown was the early bird, checking in five days before training was to start on February 23. Accompanied by his wife and their golf clubs, he lamented that rain prevented their getting to the golf course right away. Brown had come to Florida earlier in the month to work as an instruc-tor at the Joe Stripps baseball school at Orlando after having spent most of his winter hunting and fishing. He settled comfortably into one of the plush chairs in the spacious lobby of the Bainbridge Hotel and was immediately set upon by reporters. The Bainbridge had been the Florida spring training home of the Cardinals since 1938. It was a familiar and comfortable lodging whose owner, Bain Hayward, and his wife knew everyone in the Redbird traveling party except the first-year players, and treated all as if they were family. In addition, longtime Bainbridge chef Bill Richards knew the tastes and appetites of the players and always found premium cuts of beef because he knew the players loved steaks.

Brown told reporters, "Our first job is to beat the Dodgers, they're the champs." He praised the Cardinals' young pitchers, especially Howard Pollet, who had come to the majors late in the 1941 season to win five games in the closing weeks. He had praise as well for the "old heads," pitcher Lon Warneke and catcher Gus Mancuso, who had worked hard with all the pitchers. "They molded our young pitchers into seasoned performers," Brown said, "working with them daily and showing them the ropes. Gus and Lonnie babied them along all season and . . . well, just take a look at their records." As for the war, Brown thought the draft likely to be the great leveler as the Cardinals had already lost two outstanding pitching prospects to the military, John Grodzicki and Freddy Martin, both of whom would pitch for St. Louis after the war.[27]

Brown was not alone at the Bainbridge for long, as players and team officials began arriving daily. Pitcher Mort Cooper checked in after having spent the winter in Florida, near Deland, where he went fishing for thirteen straight days with Johnny Mize. It provided the big righthander with the first fish story of the spring as he claimed to have caught eight large bass in one afternoon. The team's traveling secretary, Leo Ward, the organization's best-dressed man, led the "official" party, which included trainer Harrison J. Weaver, equipment man-ager Maurice "Butch" Yatkeman, and veteran coaches Clyde "Buzzy" Wares and Miguel "Mike" Gonzalez. Gonzalez, a loquacious Cuban who was often quoted in ways that highlighted his accent, came with his wife and eighteen-month-old son and told everyone that "little Mike" would sign a Cardinals contract as soon as Branch Rickey put $25,000 in the bank for him. "Not before," Señor Gonzalez said. "No, sir . . . I say to [little Mike] you wanna pitch batting practice? He say, no, I professional ball player. No pay, no pitch . . . Smart dummy, just like papa," Gonzalez joked, using one of favorite expressions.[28]

Billy Southworth joined the growing Cardinal family and, reflecting on base-ball in wartime, told the press that players owed the country "more enthusiasm, more spirit, more color" as their part in maintaining public morale. "Since the president has asked baseball to carry on during the war it is up to us to give fans something to take away from the games with them," the Redbirds' skipper de-clared. "The players must realize that the reason they are not in service is because they had dependents and that they owe it to their country and dependents to give their utmost."[29] As for the upcoming season, Southworth told Roy Stockton of the *Post-Dispatch* that the team had a "hazard" to overcome: "Too many persons have told us too many times that we had too much hard luck last year and that we would win in a breeze this year. That's bad." Rather than his players getting the idea that the team is "pretty good," he continued, "we must get the other slant, that we're not much good and that we'll have to struggle hard to get any-where."[30]

Branch Rickey materialized in St. Petersburg the same weekend as Southworth, telling reporters that "the initial morale of the club is that of a pennant winner." He praised the pitching staff as the best since he had joined the Cardinals in 1918 and predicted that it would be the greatest "surprise" about the team. "Quality and quantity considered," Rickey intoned, "the pitching staff is better than in the days of Jesse Haines" and the Cardinal championship teams in the late 1920s and early 1930s. He thought the staff deep in starting pitching with righthanders Mort Cooper and Lon Warneke and southpaws Ernie White, Howard Pollet, and Max Lanier, and deeper yet in the bullpen with veterans Harry Gumbert, How-ard Krist, Bill Lohrman, and Clyde Shoun and rookies Murry Dickson and Max Surkont. "This club is set for a championship race," he declared. "It's a pennant club."[31] His remarks seemed to give manager Southworth all the more reason to fear the "hazard" of overconfidence. Reflecting on wartime baseball, Rickey voiced a somewhat different concern: whether, in light of war needs, adequate medical personnel and supplies would be available for the players.

Billy Southworth believed in a meticulously organized, rigorous, no-nonsense spring training in which players would work hard, but he also wanted them to enjoy themselves and bond together as a team. In the first week, the Cardi-nals concentrated on physical conditioning—stretching, running, throwing—in which pitchers especially could work through the aches and pains that came after a winter of inactivity. There would also be hitting and fielding practice, and pepper games. Southworth was a great believer in pepper games as training for reflexes and quickness, calling them the foundation of spring training that alone could prepare a team for the season.[32] The schedule called for four separate workouts each day. The team was divided into two groups, the first of which practiced from 10 to 11:30 in the morning, then returned in the afternoon from 1:30 to 3:15; the other group went from 11 to 12:30 and again from 3 to 4:15. After the first week, as conditioning exercises continued and before exhibition games began, the players would be divided into two teams for intrasquad games to give newcomers plenty of time to show what they could do. Morning workouts would continue even after exhibition games began.

Southworth believed that spring training was mainly for the pitchers, all of whom would throw off the mound to live hitters every day. "Every pitcher will serve 'em up in batting practice for five minutes and not a minute longer," the manager said, "after which he'll report to the clubhouse, get a rubdown, put on dry clothes and come back for his turn at the plate."[33] Southworth was careful in the use of his pitchers, keeping records throughout the season of innings pitched by each so that none would be overworked.[34] The pitchers would also spend a lot of time on fielding practice, which meant seemingly endless drills of covering first base on bunted or slowly hit balls, on finishing a delivery to the plate in a position to make a fielding play, and on backing up third base and home plate on base hits to the outfield. "It is mighty valuable insurance to have a good fielding man in the box," Southworth pointed out, "just like having a fifth infielder."[35] He also wanted his pitchers to practice their hitting, and especially their bunting. All of the players appeared to be in decent shape, none was overweight, but the manager wanted them in peak condition for the long season ahead to guard as best he could against a recurrence of the many injuries that had cut them down the year before.

Southworth also believed in vitamins. He brought twelve thousand B-1 vitamin pills to spring training and put all the players on a daily regime of three tablets at breakfast. Players had various names for the B-1 pills, calling them the "morale vitamin," the "wham vitamin," and the "oompah vitamin."[36] The Cardinals also experimented with arch supports in their baseball shoes. Street shoes, Southworth pointed out, have arch supports for walking comfort, but not so baseball shoes. The club's trainer, "Doc" Weaver, had invented a latex arch support for the players but had trouble getting the aluminum and rubber to make them. He finally found what he needed from stock discarded by a manufacturer and made arch supports for all the players. Jimmy Brown enthused about them: "I mean, they're the `nuts.'" He was confident that they would "sure go good on those hard diamonds this summer." Weaver was known for his inventions. Several years before, he had come up with a device inserted into the nose that filtered air to help players who suffered from hay fever. Players called it a "schnozzle plug."[37]

Redbird players continued to check into the Bainbridge Hotel, but one late arrival drew the most press attention. It was "Old Pete." Named for Grover Cleveland Alexander, Old Pete was the team's pitching machine—a "rubber-armed, steel shanked hurler of baseballs," as the *St. Petersburg Times* described it. Cardinal scout Joe Mathes was towing Old Pete to camp, but rather than putting the machine on a flatbed truck, he mounted it on two tires with no springs. Before getting to the training site, Old Pete broke in two, "near what he probably calls his universal joint," Mathes reported. The pitching machine was one of Branch Rickey's innovations in training methods, and like a good parent, he was anxious about the condition of his offspring. The machine had been used for the first time in 1941 and had received a mixed welcome: some players spent hours using it, while others would have nothing to do with it. Old Pete was expected to provide even better practice in 1942 as improvements enabled the machine to pitch high, low, inside, or outside at many different speeds, including one faster than any human could hurl a baseball. But Old Pete, unlike its namesake, could not break off a curveball, although he did throw a "wiggle" that was something like the hop on a fastball. The machine not only gave hitters more practice but also gave pitchers more relief, saving wear and tear on their arms. Bryon Moser, who had built the machine, was called upon to put Old Pete together again, which he did, and by the end of the first week of practice, Old Pete was in St. Pete and ready for action.[38]

~

The war had become a fact of life for baseball in the spring of 1942. *Star-Times* columnist Sid Keener reported that in previous years, after workouts and games were finished for the day, the talk among players had always been about baseball. But now players gathered in the hotel lounge most nights to listen to news about the war on radio broadcasts or to read about it in the newspapers. They would "digest" reports "about bombings, sinking of vessels, air raids, sabotage, espionage and draft calls to service." As spring training was just getting under way, President Roosevelt, in another of his Fireside Chats, spoke to the nation about the war, and every member of the Redbirds listened to what he had to say. After Roosevelt's talk, Keener wrote, "there was no conversation among the Cardinals about 'knocking off Brooklyn's Dodgers.'" "This is 1942," he added. "It's World War II," and for all the similarities with spring trainings past, "there were striking differences" as well.[39]

Since December, news about the war had not been good. Japanese troops swept across a broad expanse of Southeast Asia and the Pacific, occupying the Philippines, Wake Island, Guam, Hong Kong, Malaya, Singapore, and Thailand, and pressing forward with invasions of Burma, oil-rich Sumatra, Java, Borneo, and New Guinea. On the day of his talk, Roosevelt had ordered General Douglas MacArthur to abandon Corregidor, leaving behind General Jonathan Wainwright and several thousand American troops dug in on the Bataan Peninsula across from Manila, where they would fight a heroic but losing battle in the following weeks. Meanwhile, Germany was on the offensive again in North Africa, where General Erwin Rommel's tank corps was moving relentlessly toward Egypt with the goal of controlling the Suez Canal and the great oil fields of the Middle East beyond. In Russia, Nazi forces that had driven to the thresholds of Moscow and Leningrad in 1941 were preparing to renew their offensive. Only days before his talk, Roosevelt had ordered Japanese Americans to evacuate California, Alaska, and western parts of Washington, Oregon, and Arizona. Eventually, they would be forcibly removed by the military and taken to War Relocation Centers for the duration of the conflict.[40]

Sixty-one million Americans, the largest radio audience to that time, tuned in to hear the president explain what the war was about, what we were doing, what was required, and to be assured that the Allies would prevail in the end. Roosevelt had chosen February 23 for the talk because it was the day after the birthday of George Washington, then a national holiday, and he used the moment to draw a parallel between the nation's revolutionary struggle for independence from tyrannical rule little more than a century and a half earlier and its present fight to preserve the freedom won by the courageous American colonists. As in his first inaugural, delivered ten years earlier in the depths of the Great Depression, he urged the nation once more to find comfort in the knowledge it had nothing to fear but fear itself, though he did not reprise that familiar phrase. There were, however, real reasons for fear. Since early January, German submarines had been destroying large numbers of unarmed freighters, tankers, and other cargo ships all along the eastern seaboard from Boston, New York, and Newark south through the Caribbean to the mouth of the Mississippi River. And on the day of the president's talk, a large Japanese submarine surfaced near Santa Barbara, California, and shelled an oil refinery for twenty minutes.

Reminders of the war were everywhere. Tourism was down in Florida by an estimated 25 percent, which meant there were fewer fans in the stands for spring games and also at the dog tracks. Shortages of rubber and wool caused the price of baseballs to go up to seventeen dollars a dozen, a two-dollar increase over the year before. The Pittsburgh Pirates announced that the team would have "girl ushers" at Forbes Field because the war had taken 215 of the 300 boys on their list of ushers. Jack Doyle, the oddsmaker in New York City, lamented that it was hard to set odds on the season without knowing how the war would affect the various teams. But for all its presence, the war did not disrupt the lives of players in Florida all that much, and not at all when they were on the playing field. Marty Marion later recalled having heard the news about Pearl Harbor while sitting in his car in the driveway of his farm in South Carolina. "When I heard it on the car radio," he said, "I thought, 'Uh-oh, everything is going to break loose.'" But when spring training arrived, he continued, "nothing had changed. We went back to St. Petersburg as usual. I didn't have any idea that 1942 would be any different than any other year." "Players just think about having to play a game every day," Marion explained.[41]

One thing different in 1942 had nothing to do with the war, but rather with the appearance of the first woman sportswriter to cover the baseball camps. She was Jeanne Hoffman of the *Philadelphia Evening Bulletin*, twenty-three years old, who veteran reporter Burton Benjamin called a "girl baseball scribe" and described as "tall, blond, pretty . . . quite pretty."[42] A California native, she took a newspaper job rather than attend Stanford University, and at age seventeen was the first "girl" to cover the Pacific Coast League. A cartoonist as well as a reporter, she moved to Philadelphia in 1940 and took up residence in the YMCA to learn firsthand about male psychology. In the Cardinals' camp, she was pictured interviewing Walker Cooper and Lon Warneke, saying she was there as a "straight-away" sportswriter to report on the game. There would be no "women's angle," though she did intend to write about a ballplayer's life away from the stadium. Asked if she thought the war would lead to more women sportswriters, Hoffman replied, "No," explaining that "most women sports writers are terribly dull."[43] Anything but dull herself, she persuaded Phillies manager Hans Lobert to let her throw batting practice, with his stipulation that "the boys keep their minds on their work."[44]

~

As the Cardinals began their training, only the wet and blustery weather through the first week of practice disrupted an otherwise tranquil start. Some lifelong residents called it the worst weather they could remember at that time of year. On the first day, the Redbirds were greeted by a damp and chilly wind that blew off Tampa Bay and across Waterfront Stadium, which was only a short distance from the water. The few fans who turned out to watch looked like snowbirds as they sat bundled in heavy overcoats. Southworth acknowledged that the weather was far from ideal for player conditioning, but he nonetheless wanted his charges to work up a good sweat and begin to get the stiffness and soreness out of their bodies for the harder work to come. As the second week began, cold and wind continued to assault the players, though they were able to play an intrasquad game between rain showers one day. Finally, at midweek, a hot, bright "typical" Florida day dawned and the players ran through their best workout of the spring. The rest of the week remained sunny and warm as exhibition games began. Baseball, however, took a back seat to golf in the local sports pages during the first week of March, as the St. Petersburg Open was played at Lakewood Country Club. Its $11,000 in prize money had drawn all the big names in the game: Byron Nelson, Ben Hogan, and the eventual winner, Sammy Snead.

Sam Breadon arrived in St. Petersburg on the first of March and took up residence in his usual corner room on the fourth floor of the Bainbridge. He was accompanied by his "teammate" George Vierheller, director of the St. Louis Zoo. The next day, Breadon, who was in his sixties, put on a Cardinal uniform and with Vierheller went through morning workouts with the team. Vierheller had become director of the zoo shortly before Breadon had become president of the Cardinals in 1920, and both had led their organizations to national prominence—even international in the case of the zoo. These workouts were an annual rite of spring for Breadon, who had started them in the 1920s when the team trained in Bradenton, Florida, and who had worn out several companions. But Roy Stockton noted that "Vierheller stays with him, through good bounces and bad, kinks in the back and charley horses."[45] The daily workouts continued until Breadon and Vierheller returned to St. Louis at the end of the month.

One of the big stories each spring was always about players holding out for more money and refusing to sign contracts until they got what they wanted. War or no war, it was no different in 1942.[46] The Cardinals always had one of the lower payrolls in the National League, and with all their rookies it was probably the league's lowest in 1942. Breadon and Rickey had reputations as cheapskates—tight-fisted, hard bargainers when it came to player salaries. Lon Warneke was the highest-paid Redbird with a salary generally estimated at between $12,000 and $15,000; Terry Moore was the only other Cardinal thought to be paid as much as $10,000, while Enos Slaughter and Mort Cooper were two or three thousand away from five figures. Rookies were paid much less. But while low in comparison with other major-league clubs, these salaries were above the average annual income of ordinary Americans, which was about $2,000.[47] In 1942, second baseman Frank "Creepy" Crespi was the only Cardinal holdout, and he agreed to a contract soon after training began. The club did have a second quite unusual holdout in Eddie Lake, an infielder who was asking for a $150 *cut* in pay and assignment to a minor-league club. Branch Rickey allowed that he had "never known a case like it."[48]

If spring training had gotten off to a tranquil start for the Cardinals, the same could not be said for their St. Pete neighbors, the New York Yankees, or their National League rivals, the Brooklyn Dodgers. The problem for the Yankees was the large number of players holding out for higher salaries. The team had so many holdouts that an intrasquad game in the first week of spring training had to be canceled because too few players were in camp to make up two teams. Moreover, the New York holdouts were the team's brightest stars: pitcher Charles "Red" Ruffing, catcher Bill Dickey, second baseman Joe Gordon, left fielder Charlie Keller, and most of all center fielder Joe DiMaggio. The DiMaggio holdout was something of a family affair as brothers Dominic with the Boston Red Sox and Vince with the Pittsburgh Pirates had also declined the contracts they were offered. All of the Yankee holdouts signed contracts over the first weekend in March except DiMaggio. It was the middle of the second week before New York president Ed Barrow reached agreement with the "Yankee Clipper" on a salary the press estimated to be $42,000. "We reviewed the situation pleasantly," Joe reported. "I am satisfied with the terms we agreed upon."[49]

Holdouts were the least of the problems for the Dodgers. Their spring training, which began a week after that of the Cardinals, opened in acrimony and descended into turmoil, with team president Larry MacPhail at the center of it all. The club had arranged to spend the first week of training in Havana, Cuba, but at the last minute was told by the War Department that it could not go there by ship because of all the German U-boat activity in the area. Flying, however, meant that everyone was restricted to thirty-five pounds of luggage, which annoyed the players, who could not take their golf clubs, and manager Leo Durocher, who could not take the five trunks of clothing he always brought to Florida. Compounding matters, the team's equipment had been taken to Cuba by boat before the ban, and no one was entirely sure how, or even if, it could be returned. In addition, several players objected to the trip, among them pitcher Kirby Higbe, who complained that he could not get anything to eat in Havana. He finally showed up late and was fined $500.

While in Havana, MacPhail hired private detectives to follow each of the players, coding the players by the numbers on their uniforms. Many of the Dodgers frequented a popular nightspot that doubled as a house of ill repute, and did not return to the team hotel until four or five o'clock in the morning. "You never saw anything like this place," Higbe recalled years later. "The most beautiful girls in Havana . . . music, soft lights, drinks, and about fifteen rooms."[50] The detectives reported everything to MacPhail, and when the team returned to the United States their reports were discovered by customs officials, who thought the coded messages were suspicious and refused the team reentry until persuaded that they really were the Brooklyn Dodgers. By the next day Leo Durocher had read the reports, and according to Higbe that was when "the real thunder and lightning came," as the manager slapped fines on a number of players and suspended pitcher Johnny Allen indefinitely. Another heated exchange soon followed, after which Durocher tossed the reports away and ended Allen's suspension after one day.[51]

If Cuba was not enough, several Dodger players came to camp with personal grievances against MacPhail, and he with them. First baseman Dolph Camilli, who in 1941 led the National League in home runs and runs batted in, was in disfavor with his boss; rumor had it that he had thrown a punch at MacPhail during the previous season. MacPhail had tried to trade Camilli in the off-season, but failed. Camilli also missed part of spring training when he came down with toxic poisoning, and, with second baseman Billy Herman, who had back problems, he was sent to Johns Hopkins Hospital for treatment. Fred "Dixie" Walker was also an unhappy camper. A fan favorite, Walker had hit .311 for the Dodgers in 1941 and had batted under .300 only once in the previous six years, yet he was told by MacPhail that he would have to fight to keep his right-field job. Even matrimony produced acrimony, as Pete Reiser left the team for a day without permission to get married and was fined $200. A day later, Pee Wee Reese also got married, apparently with club approval, as he was not fined for saying, "I do." Through it all MacPhail kept threatening to trade his major holdout, ace pitcher Whitlow Wyatt, and was very public about other Dodgers he might send along with him, frequently mentioning the name of outfielder Joe Medwick.

∼

The Cardinals opened their Grapefruit League schedule with three games against their springtime cross-town neighbors, the New York Yankees. Though still not at full strength with only two regulars from their World Series club in the lineup, the Bronx Bombers nonetheless prevailed in the March 6 opener by a score of 8–7 in ten innings. Rookie Johnny Beazley threw three hitless innings to start for the Cards, but the New Yorkers scored five times in the fourth inning against Ernie White and picked up additional runs in the sixth and seventh. The Redbirds fought back to tie in the seventh, only to lose in the tenth on a throwing error by rookie second baseman Buddy Blattner. Stan Musial, looking like the player he was reputed to be, got three hits, including a double and an inside-the-park home run. The Yankees won again the next day 3–2 before the Cardinals finally got their first spring win 4–2 in a Sunday afternoon contest.

The Cards lost again the next day 7–5 to the Cleveland Indians, but then got hot and won eight straight games, including two over the Yankees. They knocked off the Cincinnati Reds twice, Detroit once, and Cleveland once before meeting the Yankees in another weekend set of two games. Mort Cooper, Harry Gumbert, and Howard Krist combined to shut out the New Yorkers 4–0 on seven hits in the first of these games as the St. Louis defense sparkled. The Cards won again the next day 5–3 behind solid pitching from rookies George "Red" Munger and Murry Dickson and veteran Clyde Shoun. After the Yankees, the Cardinals took two more from Cleveland, with Max Lanier and Johnny Beazley combining on a four-hit shutout. During the eight-game winning streak, Redbird pitchers gave up only thirteen runs, and the rookie hurlers performed especially well. The defensive play continued to impress, as the infield turned four double plays in one game against the Indians, and the offense was solid, producing on average more than five runs a game, though it had shown little power.

The Cardinals lost three of their next four games, including a 4–2 decision to Brooklyn, which was the only time the two teams met in Florida. Kirby Higbe quieted the Redbirds' bats, while the Dodgers played long ball with St. Louis pitching, Augie Galan and Pee Wee Reese homering off Clyde Shoun and Harry Gumbert. But the game was lost on an error by Gumbert, who failed to touch the bag on a close play at first, allowing what proved to be the winning run to move into scoring position. The Cards' skid continued with a 4–3 loss to the Yankees, as Joe DiMaggio hit his first home run of the spring high over the left-field bleachers and into Tampa Bay on one bounce. Musial, who had begun to struggle at the plate after a fast start, made the defensive play of the day, running at full speed, diving, catching the ball, and doing a somersault. The Cardinals ended their losing ways the next day with a 6–3 win over the Yanks that included a display of the daring baserunning and slashing style that would become the team's trademark.

The Cardinals won again the next day against the Cincinnati Reds, then got a break in the spring schedule with an open date, following which they again shut out Cleveland 1–0, with Mort Cooper and Clyde Shoun holding the Indians to four hits. The Washington Senators moved in to take a 2–1 decision from the Redbirds, after which the Birds got an unscheduled day off as rain washed out their second meeting with the Dodgers. Under clear skies, the Cardinals went back to work for their final weekend series with the Yankees. It was Knot Hole Gang Day for the Saturday encounter, and Waterfront Park was overflowing with boys and girls admitted free of charge. Before the game, players from both teams gathered at home plate for a moment of silence in memory of the Yankee great Lou Gehrig, who had passed away the previous year. With a strong outing from Mort Cooper, the Redbirds topped the Yankees 8–1, aided by sloppy and lethargic play by the New Yorkers. The Cards also took the Sunday contest 3–2, thereby winning the spring series from the World Champions six games to three.

With the days of spring training dwindling to a precious few, Dallas Graham of the Associated Press lamented the absence of "rube rookies" in any of the big-league camps. "Years ago," he reminisced, "the awkward, gangling newcomers [came] out of the hills of No'th Ca'lina or old Kaintuck wearing their first store-bought and ill fitting suit and had to comb the hayseed out of their unkempt hair. You could send them for the key to the city or a lefthanded monkey wrench and know that they would be gone all afternoon." They "mistered everybody," Graham continued, "and seemed astonished at the happenings out in the wide open world and such contraptions as the radio and telephone . . ." There's not much fun in spring training anymore, he sighed. The kids are all "sophisticated" and "regimented," and baseball has become a "college man's game." It is "big business now," he groused.[52] *Star-Times* columnist Sid Keener saw the "juvenile big leaguers" on the 1942 Cardinals in much the same light. They were "an excellent take-off on 'Kollege Kids,' or a page from Esquire," "fashion-plates" in their dress and "very Hollywoodish" in their appearance. It was quite a change from the Gas House Gang of 1934, Keener wrote, with Pepper Martin's "unshaven face, polo shirts, scuffed shoes, corn cob pipes, [and] baggy trousers."[53]

The Cardinals wrapped up their Florida exhibition season the first week of April, winning four of the six games played before breaking camp on Monday, April 6. Most major-league clubs, including the Yankees and Dodgers, had left Florida by the end of March to "barnstorm" north, playing a week of games in towns across the South and along the eastern seaboard against their farm clubs, military teams, and an occasional major-league team. There were risks in these games, played on subpar fields against opponents trying to impress the major-leaguers, as the Brooklyn Dodgers learned when in one game center fielder Pete Reiser crashed into an outfield fence in a futile attempt to catch a long drive. He was not hurt seriously, but was stunned and left the game. The Cardinals headed north in company with the Detroit Tigers, with whom they would play games in Durham and Winston-Salem, North Carolina, and Johnson City, Tennessee, before reaching St. Louis. The Cards won the first two of these games, but bad weather forced cancellation of the third.

∼

The Cardinals finished their exhibition schedule with a record of 20–9, the third best among teams training in Florida. The best record belonged to the other St. Louis team; the Browns had gone 11–2 against major-league teams. Departing Florida, a bullish Sam Breadon called the 1942 Cardinals "the best young ball-club we've ever assembled." "I am not conceding this National League pennant to the Brooklyn Dodgers," he huffed, "regardless of preseason statements by Larry MacPhail and Leo Durocher." The Dodgers had power, Breadon conceded, but "we have pitchers, excellent youngsters, a splendid team spirit, and Billy South-worth for our manager."[54] Southworth shared the owner's optimism, saying the Florida stay had been "easily our most successful training season." "Training is fun for my boys," Southworth added. "I have to stop them sometimes. Never have to urge them on."[55]

The team also received high marks from outsiders. Saying he "looked with great admiration at the Cardinals," *Chicago Sun* sportswriter James Hearns thought them "the most interesting team in the majors whether they're playing a game or working out" because "they actually like this game." "There's something about those Cardinals," Hearns smiled, "the running, laughing, sweating, playing Cardinals. In the South," he concluded, "there's no other camp like the Red-birds."[56] Gayle Talbot of the Associated Press agreed: "The Cardinals have shown more zip and fire than any club in training in Florida," he wrote. "They are the fastest team in baseball today and old timers say they might be the fastest ever." Dale Stafford of the *Detroit Free Press* echoed Hearns and Talbot. After watching the Cardinals defeat the Detroit Tigers in seven of eight spring training games, he thought them the best. The 1941 Cardinals, he opined, had been "the best team in the National League, if not all of baseball, but they couldn't maintain their good health." It would come down, he predicted, to the Dodgers' hitting against "fine pitching and superb defensive play by the Cardinals." Adding an exclamation point, Paul Scheffels of United Press commented, "It's hard to pick a flaw in the makeup of the Cardinals this year."[57]

Not everyone, of course, thought the Cardinals would win. Yankee coach Art Fletcher conceded that St. Louis had strong pitching and good speed, but "Brooklyn has power [and] some how we kinda string along with power."[58] Judson Bailey of the Associated Press seemed to agree. "The Dodgers," he wrote, "are a well-balanced collection of veterans, old and time tested" with the "know how" to win, whereas he saw the Cardinals as "mainly young and fast" with pitchers "as good, or better than those of any other big league club" but who lack "the experience and power of the Dodgers."[59] Veteran sportswriter Grantland Rice questioned whether the Dodgers were not getting a "trifle gray around the edges," but was assured by MacPhail that Brooklyn had "youth and experience perfectly mixed."[60] Like Bailey, most pundits saw the race as between a time-tested old stallion and a frisky young colt. Brooklyn manager Leo Durocher was among those who did not believe the colt was a good bet. He was confident that his club was better. His effusive claims about the superior strength of the Dodgers prompted Roy Stockton of the *Post-Dispatch* to suggest, "Perhaps the Cardinals won't bother to play out the season. It's hardly worth while, the way Leo talks."[61]

St. Louis writers, for the most part, were cautious. Stockton believed that should the Cardinals beat the Dodgers, "it will be a triumph of courage, harmony, youth and speed over seemingly superior forces," while John Wray, the senior *Post-Dispatch* sportswriter, saw the Cardinals as "a nice level ball club which can rise to greatness if it gets plenty of hitting and the breaks the team failed to get last year."[62] The exception was *Star-Times* columnist Sid Keener, who was ecstatic about the Cardinals' spring training. It had been marked, he enthused, by "thorough cooperation by every player," by a "splendid team spirit," and by the absence of any "temperamental athlete" in camp. "Billy Southworth," Keener's paean continued, "is a mastermind as the coach at third base. He realizes the lack of fence-busting power" and sends everyone "a-running at every opportunity. Getting that extra base will win close games," he prophesied. In addition, the pitching staff, a mix of "juvenile phenoms" and veterans, "may be the best in the league," while the team's "sparkling defense" promises to snuff out opposition rallies with "double plays on the infield and brilliant catches in the outfield." "Southworth's new material," Keener concluded, "is the most promising this press box occupant scouted at the spring training camp in many years."[63]

As he moved north, Southworth knew that there were still unresolved questions about his club. He did not have a set starting lineup, as left field and first base remained unsettled. Stan Musial had not lived up to expectations, hitting only .199 in Florida, and some began to wonder if his hitting the previous September had been a flash in the pan.[64] None of the regulars was hitting: Enos Slaughter, Walker Cooper, and Terry Moore were mired in the .220s; Jimmy Brown and Frank Crespi were only slightly better; Johnny Hopp and Marty Marion were worse. Only second-year outfielder Harry Walker had a good spring at the plate. Ray Sanders, tapped as Johnny Mize's successor at first base, had proved to be a good contact hitter, spraying line drives for singles and doubles, but he had shown none of Mize's power. Southworth may have had some quiet concerns about his pitching as well. The rookies had drawn rave notices in Florida, but veteran Lon Warneke was not ready to start the season and Mort Cooper's legs were not in top shape. In addition, Howard Pollet was nursing a tender arm.

CHAPTER 3
Baby Birds Leave the Nest

As opening day approached, National League president Ford Frick once again proclaimed baseball's intimate connection with America. "Baseball's outlook for 1942 exactly coincides with the outlook of the nation," he declared, "no better, no worse, no different. Our game is so much a part of our national life that as long as the United States exists, there will be baseball."[1] Few, if any, Americans doubted that the United States would be around for a long time, and most no doubt felt the same about baseball. Still, the war had not been going well since President Roosevelt's February fireside chat. The gravity of the situation was not apparent to all Americans because news coverage of the war was generally upbeat as setbacks were not reported in full. This annoyed many on the front lines, among them Lieutenant Robert Kelly, one of the sailors who helped evacuate General Douglas MacArthur from Corregidor. Newspapers "had us winning the war," he complained to a reporter. Those on the front lines "could see these victories. There were plenty of them," Kelly continued, and "they were all Japanese." "The resulting deception was not inadvertent," John Morton Blum observes. "While the Japanese early in 1942 were overpowering the small, ill-equipped American garrisons on Pacific islands, the armed services invented heroic situations presumably to encourage the American people." War correspondents were usually far removed from the actual combat, and their reports were rewritten by others even farther removed from the fighting who, Robert Sherrod noted, "gave the impression that any American could lick twenty Japs."[2]

The sweep of the Japanese across the Pacific following Pearl Harbor had not abated. By mid-February, they had driven American and Filipino forces out of Manila and also captured the "unconquerable" stronghold of Singapore, where eighty-five thousand British troops surrendered in "the worst defeat in the history of British arms."[3] In late February, Japan inflicted the worst naval defeat on the Allies since Pearl Harbor, wiping out more than a dozen U.S., British, Dutch, and Australian warships in the Battle of the Java Sea, and then occupied Java. In early March, the Japanese invaded New Guinea, just off the northern coast of Australia, and shortly after MacArthur arrived in the Land Down Under on March 12, having abandoned Corregidor, Japan bombed the city of Darwin on Australia's north coast.

Meanwhile, in North Africa, German and Italian armies under General Erwin Rommel had captured the British stronghold in Libya and pushed English and Commonwealth forces back into Egypt. With spring coming, the Nazi war machine was gearing up to renew its offensive in the Soviet Union, and despite $1 billion in U.S. Lend-Lease aid—tanks, warplanes, guns, clothing—Russian prospects were dire. Closer to home, German submarines continued to terrorize shipping along the Atlantic seaboard and throughout the Caribbean. Since Pearl Harbor, the Federal Bureau of Investigation had been busy rounding up Germans and Italians suspected of enemy activity, most of them in the big cities of the North and along the coastal South. Meanwhile, Americans on the West Coast continued to fear an invasion from Japan and felt little relief when Japanese American residents were removed to special compounds away from the area.[4]

As major-league teams headed home from Florida to open the season, the war news grew even worse. On the first of April, after almost two months of relative inactivity, the Japanese launched an all-out assault on the thirty-six thousand American and Filipino troops still on Bataan north of Manila. Exhausted, many of them ill, and with food and ammunition in short supply, they resisted as best they could for a week before giving up. It was the first time in U.S. history that an entire American army had surrendered.[5] As the Japanese were taking Bataan, they also pressed forward with their invasion of Burma, advancing toward southern China. They moved as well against India, bombing Ceylon, a strategically important piece of land off the southern tip of India. Days later they bombed two ports in India itself.

The few Allied successes were heralded with bold headlines and excited front-page stories disproportionate to the relative importance of the news. Still, there were encouraging signs. Through March and into April, Britain repeatedly sent its high-flying bombers on missions against industrial sites in Germany and France, targeting those in the Ruhr Valley in particular, but also damaging German submarine maintenance facilities at the French port of St. Nazaire. In early April, the British launched a massive air assault—three hundred bombers—on factories producing war goods near both Paris and Cologne.

There were some successes in the Pacific as well. A U.S. and Australian air attack destroyed a large part of the force Japan was mobilizing for an invasion of Australia. In addition, thousands of American combat troops had been arriving in Australia for more than a month, giving the Allies an advantage in manpower and greater hope that Australia could be defended. U.S. and British submarines began to enjoy occasional successes. In March, American subs invaded Japanese territorial waters to sink three ships, while British subs in the Mediterranean destroyed a large Italian shipment of war materiel headed for North Africa. At the end of March, the U.S. Navy announced that it had sunk twenty-five German submarines off the Atlantic coast. Declaring the U-boats "our worst menace," a Navy spokesman added that Germany was beginning to pay "a terrible price in both submarines and men." [6]

Following cancellation of their final exhibition game, the Cardinals boarded a train for St. Louis and arrived at Union Station on Friday, April 10, too late in the afternoon for any practice before meeting their American League counterparts, the Browns, in the annual city series. Since the mid-1920s, the fortunes of the Browns and Cardinals had moved in opposite directions. In 1926, as the Redbirds won their first National League title and first World Series, the Browns, who had the better teams in the first half of the decade, dropped to seventh place in the eight-team American League. In the fifteen years from 1927 through 1941, the Cardinals won four more pennants, two World Series, and finished second or third in the National League six times. The Browns, on the other hand, finished in the top half of the American League just twice over this period, the last time in 1929, and were last or next to last seven times. But after a strong showing in Florida, hope sprang anew that the team's fortunes were about to improve.[7]

Saturday dawned overcast and chilly with a biting wind snapping at the almost five thousand well-bundled fans assembled to watch baseball on a day more suitable for football. The Browns were the home team, so the Cardinals were dressed in their road gray uniforms and occupied the first-base visitors' dugout. The Redbirds sent Ernie White to the hill against Bob Muncrief, who had won thirteen games for the Browns as a rookie in 1941. The Cards drew first blood with a run in the second and followed it with two more in the third on a bases-loaded single by Stan Musial. The Birds went on to a 7–2 win as White and Harry Gumbert held the Browns to four hits. There was no change in the weather for Sunday's game, but there was a change in the outcome as the Browns prevailed. A smaller crowd of around three thousand turned out to watch Max Lanier struggle through three innings, giving up four runs on only three hits but six walks. The Browns added a run off Lon Warneke in the fifth. Trailing 5–2, the Cardinals came back, scoring twice in the seventh on a pinch-hit double by Musial, but could get no closer and lost 5–4.

After the game, the Browns boarded a train for Chicago, where they would open their season against the White Sox, while the Cardinals stayed home for their Tuesday opener against the Chicago Cubs. The Baseball Writers Association announced that its members, to no one's surprise, had picked the Yankees to take the American League pennant. "Anybody picking a club to beat the Yanks," Shirley Povich of the *Washington Post* opined, "is a case for the violent ward."[8] In the National League, a surprisingly large majority of the writers picked the Cardinals to finish ahead of the Dodgers: forty-six of the seventy-two ballots were for St. Louis, twenty-three for Brooklyn, while Cincinnati was the choice of four writers, including J. G. Taylor Spink, publisher of the *Sporting News*.[9] The Reds had an impressive staff of veteran starting pitchers—Paul Derringer, Bucky Walters, Elmer Riddle, and Johnny Vander Meer—and would get an exceptional year from a fifth veteran, Ray Starr. But Cincinnati lacked depth on the mound, and after trading catcher Ernie Lombardi over the winter, the Reds also had an uncertain offense that they had tried to patch with youngsters and some retreads from the American League. The poll of baseball writers notwithstanding, most observers thought the National League race in 1942 would be a replay of 1941, with St. Louis and Brooklyn battling it out from day one for the title. New York oddsmaker Jack Doyle saw it that way and made the Redbirds an ever-so-slight favorite over the Dodgers.

The St. Louis and Brooklyn teams were similar in many ways. Both played the hard, aggressive National League game, where pitching, defense, speed, and "scientific" baseball were prized more highly than raw power. The Dodgers, encouraged by their "old-school" manager, Leo Durocher, were something of a throwback to the earlier John McGraw era in their aggressive play (more pitches thrown at opposing hitters, more runners sliding hard into bases with spikes flying). The Cardinals were more of a finesse team, using speed to surprise opponents and pressure them into misplaying balls and making other mistakes. For all their similarities, however, the two teams were quite different in how they had been constructed and in age and experience. The Cardinals were built through their farm system, whereas the Dodgers had been assembled through trades and purchases. All but one of the Cardinal position players, those on the bench as well as the starters, were products of the St. Louis minor-league system. The exception was Coaker Triplett, who arrived in the majors with the Chicago Cubs in 1938 and was acquired by the Cardinals in 1941. All of the pitchers also came from their farm system, save for Harry Gumbert, who spent six years with the New York Giants before being dealt to St. Louis in 1941, and the little-used Lloyd "Whitey" Moore, who was acquired from Cincinnati during the 1942 season and appeared in only nine games.[10]

In contrast, all of the Dodgers' position players and most of their pitchers, including all of the starters, had come from outside the Brooklyn organization. No fewer than eight came from St. Louis, including three of their everyday players—left fielder Joe Medwick, center fielder Pete Reiser, and catcher Mickey

Owen—plus reserve infielder Lew Riggs, backup outfielders Johnny Rizzo and Stanley "Frenchy" Bordagaray, and starting pitchers Curt Davis and Max Macon, the latter brought up in midseason. Others in the Brooklyn organization also had ties to the Cardinals: Durocher was the shortstop on the Gas House Gang, the 1934 Cardinals world championship club; team president Larry MacPhail got his first job in baseball with the Columbus farm club of St. Louis; and Branch Rickey, Jr., son of the St. Louis general manager, was the farm director, the youngest one for any major-league team. Only two of the players were "home grown," pitchers Ed Head and Les Webber, both of whom worked primarily in relief, though Head was an occasional starter. Several of the Dodgers' regulars had been plucked from other minor-league systems on the advice of Brooklyn's "bird dogs" in the field. Shortstop Harold "Pee Wee" Reese was acquired from Louisville, a farm club of the Boston Red Sox; outfielder Fred "Dixie" Walker, dubbed the "Peeple's Churce" by his legions of loving fans in Brooklyn, came from the Detroit Tigers after years of bouncing around their farm system; and ace righthander Whitlow Wyatt, in his thirties, was purchased from the minor-league Milwaukee Brewers after nine unimpressive years with three different American League clubs.[11]

"Most major league managers want experienced players," Roy Stockton of the *Post-Dispatch* observed. "They don't want to have to double as psychologists, to lead rookies out of mazes of worries. But Billy Southworth rather prefers the youngsters."[12] The Dodgers were a veteran team whose players were older and had far more major-league experience than those of the Cardinals. In an era when thirty-five was thought old for a ballplayer, the Dodgers had fourteen players thirty or older, three of them thirty-five or more. The Cardinals had four, and one of them, Lon Warneke, would be traded to the Cubs in July.[13] Indeed, two Dodger regulars—second baseman Billy Herman and third baseman Arky Vaughan—together had played more games in the major leagues than the entire St. Louis starting lineup. The oldest Cardinal was infielder Jimmy Brown, who at thirty-two had been with St. Louis for five years. The most experienced Redbird was center fielder Terry Moore, who at twenty-nine had been in the majors for seven years. Five of the Dodgers' regulars had seven years or more of major-league experience, while five of the St. Louis regulars had two or fewer years of major-league playing time, two of them rookies with about three weeks of experience between them. Only two Dodgers had two years or fewer in the big time—Pee Wee Reese with two years and Pete Reiser with one—and they had no rookie regulars. Overall, the average major-league experience of Brooklyn's everyday players was six and a half years; for St. Louis it was two and a half. The gap in experience between the two teams' pitching staffs was even larger. The top four Dodger starters averaged eight and a half years in the majors; the Cardinal starters less than two. One Brooklyn starter, Larry French, had almost as many years in the big leagues as the top four St. Louis starters. The Dodgers had two pitchers with no more than one year in the majors; the Redbirds had five. It was clearly a contest between the Baby Birds of St. Louis and dem Ol' Bums of Brooklyn.

The two teams also played in stadiums that were different both in their design and in the character of the fans that filled them. Sportsman's Park, located in north St. Louis and owned by the Browns, opened in 1902 as the first all-concrete stadium in the major leagues and had been home to both the Browns and Cardinals since the early 1920s. Originally, the stadium had a single deck, but expansions in 1909 and 1926 added a second deck that reached from the right-field foul pole to the left-field foul pole, with open bleachers in left and center fields, a covered pavilion in right, and a seating capacity of 34,500 (standing room added another two thousand to attendance). Lights were installed in 1940 largely on the initiative of Cardinals owner Sam Breadon.[14]

None of the major-league fields in 1942 was symmetrical, and some, like the elongated Polo Grounds, were of curious design for baseball. In Sportsman's Park, it was 353 feet down the foul line from home plate to the left-field wall, about the average for National League parks, and 310 feet down the right-field line, a distance shorter than in most other ballparks, but the pavilion in right field was covered with a screen that ran from the foul pole to deep right–center field and whose height lengthened the distance for home runs.[15] The distance to straightaway center field was 425 feet, greater than in any other National League park except New York's Polo Grounds and Philadelphia's Shibe Park. The so-called power alleys in left and right center were also deeper than in most other stadiums. The outfield walls of solid concrete stood almost twelve feet high, while the pavilion screen raised the right-field height to thirty-three feet. It was a friendly park for pitchers, as balls could be hit great distances and still be in play, but they would be caught only if a team had fleet-footed outfielders. The best Cardinal teams had consistently featured strong pitching with fast, far-ranging outfielders. The 1942 outfield of Stan Musial, Terry Moore, and Enos Slaughter fit that mold, and indeed remains the best all-around trio in team history.

The Dodgers' home, Ebbets Field, opened in 1913, and in contrast to Sportsman's Park it had almost as many quirks in its design as it had quirky fans in the grandstand. Ebbets Field was built on the site of the Pigtown garbage dump in the Flatbush area, and like all stadiums in its time had undergone numerous renovations. In 1942 it had a double-deck grandstand that extended from the right-field foul pole around to the left-field foul pole and across to center field. There was a small covered section of box seats in center field, but no seating in right field. The entrance to the stadium featured a rotunda, an eighty-foot circle in Italian marble with ticket booths stretching almost halfway around. From its twenty-seven-foot ceiling hung a chandelier with twelve baseball-bat arms holding twelve lights shaped like baseballs, and the tile floor was designed with slightly raised stitches to simulate those on a baseball.

The playing field was smaller than at Sportsman's Park. The distance down the line from home to the left-field fence was three feet longer than the left-field line in St. Louis, but center field was twenty-five feet shorter and the power alleys were also shorter by twenty-five to fifty feet, except for a point in right center that was 415 feet from home plate. The distance down the line in right field was 247 feet, the shortest of any National League park except the Polo Grounds, but a wall rose in right running from the foul pole to the center-field seats that reached the height of thirty-eight feet, which like the pavilion screen in St. Louis compensated for the short distance to the wall. The wall itself was concave in design, with a scoreboard that jutted five feet into the playing field at a forty-five-degree angle, and the wall had something like 289 different angles from which balls could bounce in myriad directions. There was also a large gate in right center, and it too could change the direction of balls in play. The shorter distances, in addition to the double deck in left and the high wall in right which blocked winds, made Ebbets Field more friendly to hitters than most fields, and the 1942 Dodgers were clearly designed with that in mind.

St. Louis fans were also different from those in Brooklyn, and indeed from those in other two-team cities. Unlike in Chicago, where class differences created two sets of fans, upper-class northsiders for the Cubs and working-class southsiders for the White Sox, in St. Louis the fans were comfortable rooting for both the Cardinals and the Browns. Unlike in Brooklyn, where baseball united the city's diverse ethnic populations against outsiders, especially those across the East River, baseball in St. Louis was a game in which players, friend and foe alike, were applauded for good performances. The city's two major-league clubs were a matter of civic pride, but they had no larger social significance. St. Louis fans were as loyal to their teams as those in other cities were to theirs, were excited when their team won and suffered quietly when it lost, but for them life went on relatively undisturbed regardless of the outcome of the baseball season. By 1942, a generation of Redbird fans had known nothing but competitive teams, and they took winning as a normal condition of life, but a losing season, for all its disappointment, was taken more or less in stride. Losing never evoked a strident, "Wait 'til next year," the mantra in Brooklyn, but rather a confidence that the team would get it right next year and be a winner once more. For the most part, their patience was rewarded on the field by the Cardinals, though the same could not be said for the dwindling number of Browns fans.

Dodger loyalists, who had endured more than a decade of laughable, lovable losers from the mid-1920s until the late 1930s, had a more fatalistic view of baseball. The Bums had in fact been bums whose play was often comical. But working-class Brooklynites identified with the Dodgers as underdogs like themselves, and they were devoted to the team. They expected the Dodgers to lose and went to games to enjoy themselves in what were at times outlandish ways, but as the team began to win their behavior did not change, remaining as passionate and zany as ever, marking them as different from fans anywhere else in baseball.

St. Louis had Mary Ott, whose horse-laugh and screeching cries of support for her favorite players could be heard throughout Sportsman's Park.[16] But this was nothing compared with Brooklyn, where Hilda Chester, a former bloomer girl, sat in center field wielding a large cowbell to encourage the Dodgers; where Jack Pierce, a businessman always dressed in suit and tie, sat behind the visitors' dugout popping balloons through games; where Eddie Bataan wore his explorer's hat and blew a tin whistle whose shrill note pierced all parts of the park; where "Shorty" Laurice and his Dodgers Sym-phony serenaded fans between innings, playing more or less the same tune; and where organist Gladys Gooding once welcomed the umpires to the field with a rendition of "Three Blind Mice."[17] When a Dodger hit a home run, someone in the radio booth would slide a carton of Old Gold cigarettes down the screen behind home plate and everyone would go, "Woooooooooah," voices rising. A home run came to be called an "Old Goldie." Dodger fans had little patience with anyone rooting for the other side, but they directed most of their venom at opposing players and especially at umpires. Tra-ditionally, the New York Giants were the team most hated by Brooklyn fans, but in the 1940s, as the Dodgers fought the Cardinals year after year for the pennant, it was more and more St. Louis that was the target of their special ire.

The managers and executives of the two clubs were also different. Billy South-worth of the Cardinals was soft-spoken and reflective, steady and upbeat in anything said about his team and players. His brief tenure in 1929 had taught him to treat players evenhandedly and with respect; he never reprimanded a player in front of another and regularly gave credit for success to them, reserving blame for himself.[18] He prided himself on being organized and efficient in his work and enjoyed the respect, even affection, of his team as well as that of others around the league, including umpires.

None of this could be said of Dodger manager Leo Durocher, described by one critic as "an accomplished linguist in the artful use of profanity." Durocher could be charming off the field, but on it he was one of the most disliked figures in the game, whose personality transferred to his team to make it the most hated in the league as well. Durocher, Peter Golenbock writes, was "a gambler and street hustler who combined ferocity with guile to outwit, outmaneuver, and outrage the opposition," noting that "even Babe Ruth, who liked almost everyone, hated Durocher." "Only Cobb," Arthur Mann adds, "was more hated by fellow players." Many of Durocher's own players disliked him but also loved playing for him. His aggressive no-holds-barred, anything-to-win, nice-guys-finish-last approach appealed especially to the veterans and made the Dodgers as much feared as hated. Playing against the Cardinals, his former team, regularly brought out the worst in Durocher. He often reacted "uncontrollably" and "irrationally" when facing them, Gerald Eskenazi recalls, especially if the Dodgers were losing.[19]

The St. Louis front-office team of Sam Breadon and Branch Rickey had worked well together for twenty-five years, but by 1942 it was clear that the bloom was off the rose in their relationship. Though it was not generally known at the time, Breadon had informed Rickey a year earlier that his contract would not be renewed after the 1942 season. Each of them brought dignity to the game and was widely respected within baseball. But each was also stubborn, tight-fisted, and rather remote in his day-to-day relations with players. Marty Marion remembered Breadon and Rickey as "very tough" bosses. "You knew they owned the ballclub but that was it. They didn't even talk to you; the only time you ever saw them to talk to was at contract time."[20] Beyond these similarities, the two were an odd couple, different in temperament, interests, and character.

Rickey was raised in rural southern Ohio and was a devout Methodist, a "tee-totaler" and "hymn singer" to his critics. He did not attend Sunday games, and he objected to beer advertising in the park but was overruled by Breadon.[21] A graduate of Ohio Wesleyan and the University of Michigan law school, Rickey taught briefly at Allegheny College and was, Murray Polnar writes, an "intellectual in an anti-intellectual profession, a reader among men for whom books were suspect."[22] An astute judge of player talent and one of the greatest innovators in the game's history, Rickey had played for a couple of years in the majors as a catcher, then worked for the St. Louis Browns before joining the Cardinals in 1917. The farm system was his creation in the early 1920s; with it he could "grow" his own talent. Rickey concluded that this was the only way to make St. Louis successful in a small-market, two-team city where financial resources were insufficient to compete successfully with the rich teams in New York and Chicago for more-established players. Derided at the time as "chain-store baseball" and hated by baseball commissioner Kenesaw Mountain Landis, the farm system was the key to the Cardinals winning their first championship in 1926 and to sustaining them thereafter as one of the league's top teams.[23]

Rickey developed new methods for training as well: a sliding pit where players could get instruction and more practice, four strings strung together in a rectangle to outline the strike zone so pitchers could learn better control by hitting the strings, and "Old Pete," the pitching machine, so hitters could get more practice without overworking the arms of the team's pitchers. Rickey was energetic, always on the go, and always talking as he went. He was a compelling public speaker, much in demand by service clubs. He loved the limelight and had strong, well-informed views on a wide range of public issues. An active Republican and popular fund-raiser, he was courted by some Republican leaders in Missouri to be their party's candidate for various offices, including governor and senator. Indifferent about his dress, he enjoyed cigars as much as props as for their smoke and cultivated an image of great rectitude. His grandson, Branch III, recalls his being "Victorian in manner, rumpled Churchillian in appearance."[24] Others thought of him as "the Brain" and the "Mahatma."

Unlike Rickey, Breadon grew up in the big city, in New York's Greenwich Village, and migrated to St. Louis around 1900 to make his fortune in the new and growing automobile business. Though he lived in St. Louis for almost half a century, he never entirely lost his New York accent, as when he spoke of the "Cawd'nals." A Democrat, though not so public in his politics as Rickey, his was a rags-to-riches story as he worked his way up from auto mechanic to owner of a dealership. He first bought stock in the Cardinals as a favor to a friend. Quiet and reserved in manner, he was at the same time a friendly man, gracious in conversation, a good mixer, who enjoyed drinks with his close friends and associates and frequently joined his rich baritone voice with theirs in barbershop harmonies. Breadon and Rickey were not social friends. For most of their time together, Rickey ran the team while Breadon took care of business and the hiring and firing of managers. "Between them, Breadon and Rickey made one of the greatest front office teams in baseball history," Robert Burnes of the *St. Louis Globe-Democrat* observed. "Rickey was the dreamer, Breadon was the sound businessman."[25]

As a businessman, Breadon had a reputation for being cold-blooded, confident in the soundness of his own judgment, almost impossible to dissuade when he settled upon a course of action, but also highly principled and completely honest. If tight-fisted with players (critics called him "cheap"), Breadon was often generous with former players, coming to the aid of Rogers Hornsby, Grover Cleveland Alexander, Mort Cooper, and others after their playing days were behind them and they were down on their luck. Little of this was known at the time as Breadon, who did not like the spotlight and was no headline seeker, feared that mention of it would make him appear to be a publicity hound. At the time he sold the team after the 1947 season, only three men in the history of the National League had been owners for as long, or longer, than Breadon. League president Ford Frick took the occasion to laud Breadon, saying that "no man had contributed more to the National League and few men to baseball than Sam."[26] He never sought or received the accolades that were showered upon Rickey, nor did he suffer the criticism that often came Rickey's way. Breadon seemed happiest when watching games from his box next to the Cardinals' dugout, where he could be, as Roy Stockton of the *Post-Dispatch* wrote, "a fan above everything else."[27]

The Dodgers' team president was much different. There was no one in baseball quite like Larry MacPhail, described by William Klingaman as "a clownish, bellicose, red-haired and red-faced wild man . . . an unpredictable self-destructive genius."[28] In background, temperament, and behavior, MacPhail was almost the opposite of both Rickey and Breadon. He grew up a rich kid in Grand Rapids, Michigan, who had advantages that neither of the Cardinals' executives had enjoyed. He got his start in baseball through Rickey, who knew him from the University of Michigan and hired him to run the Cardinals' Double A Columbus ball club.[29] MacPhail's marketing genius was soon apparent, but he was also soon fired by Breadon, who did not share his spend-money-to-make-money philosophy.

On Rickey's recommendation, MacPhail was hired as general manager by Cincinnati, where he built the Reds teams that won pennants in 1939 and 1940, though he was not around to enjoy them. A loudmouth and a heavy drinker, MacPhail had difficulty controlling his temper after a few drinks and was fired in Cincinnati after taking a drunken punch at owner Powell Crosley. He was then hired by Brooklyn almost out of desperation; the team was deeply in debt, near bankruptcy, and needed someone with his talent for promotion. MacPhail was given a largely free hand and the assurance that ample funds would be available. The first thing he did was to repair and repaint Ebbets Field at considerable expense to the ball club. He next acquired a $100,000 bank loan with which to purchase first baseman Dolph Camilli from the Philadelphia Phillies. MacPhail went on to become, in Peter Golenbock's words, "the embodiment of Brooklyn," fiery, profane, given to outbursts, hot-headed, ornery, and impetuous. He was stubborn and wanted things done his way, traits he did share with Rickey and Breadon, and he never hesitated to criticize his players to the press, a trait not shared by the St. Louis pair. With Durocher, MacPhail reinforced the image of the Dodgers as "a hard-drinking, scrappy, rough-hewn, brawling bunch," an image earned both on the field and in the front office.[30]

～

On opening day, all teams scheduled ceremonies filled with bands and dignitaries, but it was always the ceremony in the nation's capital, where the president came to toss out the first ball, that sustained baseball's primacy in American sports. Nothing validated baseball's claim to be the national pastime more effectively than the president's symbolic first pitch. The *Sporting News* carried the message clearly in its opening-week issue with a drawing of President Roosevelt, arm raised, baseball in hand, posed before the American flag, surrounded by cartoon figures representing all sixteen major-league teams. The headline read, LET'S GO, ALL YOU AMERICAN PLAYERS AND FANS![31] In the week before the season started, Washington owner Clark Griffith and American League president Will Harridge made their annual trek to the White House to be photographed presenting Roosevelt with a season pass and an invitation to opening day. Now in his third term, Roosevelt had made more "starts" on opening day than any of his predecessors, but this year was special because it had been his "green-light" letter saying "play ball" that had given the government's sanction to the season. Roosevelt promised to be at the game, but as opening day arrived his assistant Stephen Early notified Griffith that the burden of war work made it impossible for the president to attend. Instead, Roosevelt went to the White House bullpen to tap Vice President Henry Wallace as his replacement. With managers Bucky Harris of the Senators and Joe McCarthy of the Yankees by his side and Griffith, Harridge, and a host of dignitaries in the background, Wallace delivered the pitch that got the season off to its official start.[32]

In St. Louis, the cold weather of the weekend city series was gone, replaced by a sunny, almost balmy day with temperatures in the mid-seventies by game time. But residents of St. Louis, a city settled originally by the French, were also greeted this day by alarming war news from France, where World War I hero Henri Philippe Pétain had stepped down as head of the French government in favor of Pierre Laval, the nation's leading exponent of collaboration with Germany. Laval was now the "civil supervisor" for all of France, heading a new government whose policies were sure to be much more sympathetic to the Nazis. The British immediately took an "exceedingly grave view" of this change, thought it a "tactical defeat" for the Allies, and believed that intervention by Germany had forced the change.[33] The United States recalled its ambassador, Admiral William D. Leahy, to await developments and also announced that it would not maintain normal relations with the new Vichy government (so named for the city in which it was headquartered). Sumner Welles, acting secretary of state, made it clear that the United States would continue to support Free French forces wherever they were effective. Within days, Laval issued a pledge of friendship with the Nazi regime, telling the French people that their choice was between rapprochement with Germany or "seeing our civilization disappear."[34]

As baseball's leaders anticipated, opening day provided a welcome distraction from news of a world at war. Almost twenty thousand fans turned out for the start of the 1942 season in St. Louis, 20 percent of them guests of the Cardinals. Sportsman's Park, entering its forty-first year, had received a facelift over the winter and looked elegant. All of the seats had been repaired or replaced, the grandstand given a fresh coat of paint, and the advertisements on the outfield fences, dugout roofs, and scoreboard freshened for the new season. Groundskeeper Bill Stocksick had installed a lush new infield of fresh sod—grass that he knew would never withstand the rigors of constant play by two teams. By midseason, the continuous use of the field and the scorching-hot St. Louis summers would turn the playing surface almost as hard as the stadium's concrete walls. By July and August, everyone, visitors and home teams alike, would be complaining that it was the worst infield in the majors. With the war in mind, Ed Browning had designed the 1942 Cardinals scorecard in red, white, and blue with the Statue of Liberty on the cover. For fans not at the game, the broadcast team of Dizzy

Dean and Johnny O'Hara was ready to report the action over radio station KWK with Falstaff beer as their sponsor, as were their competitors France Laux and Bob Lyle, who did the play-by-play on KXOK for Hyde Park beer.[35]

The pregame ceremonies were a grand display of patriotism. With red, white, and blue bunting gracing the facade of the grandstand, seven bands marched onto the field, including military bands from Scott Air Force Base, the Missouri National Guard, and the Washington University Reserve Officers Training Corps. Marching groups from the Ferry Street Naval Armory and the state National Guard were also among the more than one thousand people who took the field to welcome the season with a tribute to the nation's soldiers, sailors, and marines, another thousand of whom were sitting in the grandstand in uniform as guests of the Cardinals. Shortly before the scheduled 2:30 start of the game, a large contingent of servicemen paraded to the center-field flagpole, where Old Glory was raised toward the heavens as the assembled bands played the national anthem. When the last band disappeared, William D. Becker, in his second year as mayor of St. Louis, was joined by numerous dignitaries to throw out the ceremonial first ball.

Unfortunately for the Cardinals, the game did not go as well as the pregame ceremonies. The Cubs jumped on Mort Cooper for two runs in the first inning as third baseman Stan Hack led off with a single to center. The next two Chicago hitters went down easily, but right fielder Bill Nicholson lined a single to center that Terry Moore fielded quickly to hold Hack at second. It made little difference, however, as Cooper unleashed a wild pitch to the Cubs' diminutive left fielder Dominic Dallessandro, advancing both runners. Dallessandro was then given an intentional walk to load the bases, but the strategy backfired when lefty-swinging first baseman Phil Cavaretta looped an outside pitch to left for a single and two runs. The Birds came back to take the lead with three runs in the fourth inning, a rally that featured the first argument of the new season. With Enos Slaughter on first, Ray Sanders hit an easy grounder to Chicago second baseman Lou Stringer, who bumped Slaughter in tagging him out, then threw too late to first to get the speedy Sanders. Cubs manager Jimmie Wilson leaped from the dugout to claim that Slaughter had interfered with Stringer, and when his protest became too vehement (or perhaps too personal), first-base umpire Al Barlick threw him out of the game. The inning continued with Jimmy Brown hitting a towering fly ball to left center that fell in for a double, scoring Sanders from first, and catcher Ken O'Dea followed with a home run onto the pavilion roof in right to give St. Louis a one-run lead. It was a short-lived, though, as the Cubs sent Cooper to the showers with three runs in the sixth. The Redbirds had several scoring opportunities over the final innings but failed to capitalize on most of them, losing the game 5–4.

St. Louis got a measure of revenge the next day behind the four-hit pitching of "Handsome" Harry Gumbert, as the veteran righthander was often described by St. Louis writers. Gumbert was shaky at the start as Chicago scored single runs in the second and fourth innings, but thereafter he settled down to retire the last sixteen Cubs hitters in order. The Cardinals tied the score in the fourth on a Terry Moore triple, a walk, and two singles, and won the game with two runs in the seventh. The Birds collected eight hits against two Chicago pitchers, including doubles by Musial and Brown as well as Moore's triple. The big hits, however, came from shortstop Marty Marion, whose single in the third helped to tie the game and whose single in the sixth won it. The final game of the series was a slugfest won by the Cardinals 11–6. Most of the scoring came early. The Cubs pummeled St. Louis starter Ernie White for six hits and five runs. Bill Nicholson delivered the knockout blow in the third with a leadoff single. The Redbirds returned the favor, touching Chicago starter Dick Errickson for two runs in both the first and second, then ending his day in the third as they knotted the score at 5–5. Bill Lohrman took over for White in the third inning and went the rest of the way, yielding eight hits but only one run to get credit for the win as the Cards scored four times in the fourth and added single runs in the seventh and eighth. St. Louis rookies led the attack: Stan Musial had three hits, including a home run, while Ray Sanders collected two singles. The series was a good start to the season for both Musial, with six hits in fourteen tries, and Sanders, with four hits in twelve attempts.

The Dodgers opened their season in the Polo Grounds against their ancient rivals, the New York Giants, and took two of the three games. It did not take long for the old rivalry to heat up. The fireworks began in the second game when outfielder Johnny Rizzo and third baseman Arky Vaughan protested umpiring decisions on close plays that went against them. After the game, Leo Durocher exploded in the clubhouse about the umpiring, prompting a bit of satire from *Brooklyn Eagle* writer Tommy Holmes: "The Dodgers, you see, never admit they lost one—they're always bilked, bamboozled, or out lucked. S'great stuff!"[36] Meanwhile, the Giants were upset by the beanballs they believed Brooklyn hurlers had thrown at them, responsibility for which they laid at the feet of the Dodgers' manager. It was, in short, a typical Dodgers-Giants series to launch the season.

As the Cardinals moved to Pittsburgh for the Pirates' home opener, the Dodgers returned home for theirs against the Philadelphia Phillies. It was an "opening day tradition at Ebbets," *Eagle* correspondent Harold Parrott noted, that "the program always seems to be unannounced [and] unplanned." He recalled that when Ebbets Field opened in 1913 a corps of dignitaries marched solemnly to the center-field flagpole only to discover that no one had remembered to bring the flag. On another occasion, the game began before it was realized that borough president Raymond Ingersoll had not thrown out the ceremonial first pitch. The game stopped, the pitch was thrown, and the game resumed.[37]

In 1942, all seemed to go well. Players from both teams lined the first- and third-base lines as a color guard with a soldier, sailor, and marine marched to center field, flag in hand, while the Brooklyn Edison American Legion band and the Fort Hamilton band formed in front of home plate to play the national anthem as the Stars and Stripes were sent skyward. Borough president John Cashmore dutifully tossed the first pitch and the game began. But when the Dodgers came to bat in the bottom of the first, a rotund fan in the upper deck pulled a cornet from under his topcoat and got the biggest laugh of the afternoon when he played "Here Comes the Bride" as newlywed Pee Wee Reese stepped to the plate. Reese tipped his cap to the musician, who followed with a jazzed-up version for Pete Reiser when he took his first turn at bat. Also at the game was Dodger fan Robert Anderson, who had not missed a home opener in ten years, but whose attendance in 1942 was placed in jeopardy when he was notified by his draft board to report for induction into the military on April 7. To preserve his streak, Anderson filed as a conscientious objector, figuring that any investigation would take at least a couple of weeks. The Dodgers went on to beat the Phillies 7–1, but opening day in Brooklyn was only incidentally about the game.

～

When the Cardinals arrived in Pittsburgh on April 17, they and the nation got an emotional lift from easily the best news yet about the war. Early that morning, a squadron of B-25 bombers under the command of Colonel James "Jimmy" Doolittle rose from the deck of a carrier in the Pacific and headed for Japan. A onetime professional boxer who had been a fighter pilot in World War I, Doolittle had earned a doctoral degree in aeronautics from the Massachusetts Institute of Technology after the war. He had achieved a number of "firsts" in aviation, including being the first to fly "blind," using only instruments from takeoff to landing. He was also famous as a racer and held several transcontinental air records. Now, he was racing toward Japan to bomb Tokyo. Like the Japanese in their attack on Pearl Harbor, Doolittle used Tokyo radio stations to guide his five-and-a-half-hour flight. Just past noon on April 18 his squadron dropped their loads on Tokyo, the port cities of Yokohama and Kobe, and the city of Nagaya, hitting oil refineries, electrical plants, steel mills, railroad centers, port facilities, and airplane factories.[38] The military significance of the attack was negligible—little damage was done to Japan's war-making capacity—but as David Kennedy observes, the raid packed "a momentous psychological wallop."[39] It made Japan appear vulnerable and reinforced the determination of Japanese leaders to eliminate the United States and Britain as military powers in the Pacific. To Americans, the raid was retaliation for the sneak attack on

Pearl Harbor, except that Doolittle had hit Japan's capital city, whereas Japan had struck only a distant outpost of the United States.

Doolittle had once lived in St. Louis, which gave the news stories a local connection. But later in April, St. Louisans had an even closer connection to the war as they welcomed the return of their first real hometown hero, Lieutenant Commander Edward H. O'Hare, who had single-handedly shot down five Japanese fighter planes and damaged a sixth to protect an aircraft carrier from the enemy. Just days before in a White House ceremony, Roosevelt had presented him with the Congressional Medal of Honor. In a noontime parade through downtown St. Louis, the handsome O'Hare and his wife rode in an open car, waving happily to the crowd estimated at sixty thousand as confetti and shredded paper streamed down.[40]

In Pittsburgh, the Cardinals once again fell behind early when the Pirates tallied three times in the third inning on a triple by third baseman Bob Elliott and a single by left fielder Ed Stewart. Lon Warneke started for St. Louis and was the victim of the Pirates' attack, but pitched through seven innings before giving way to Max Lanier. The Cards scored one run in the seventh and made a bid to tie the game in the ninth. With one out, Slaughter doubled. Sanders looped a fly ball over the infield that fell in for a two-base hit, but Slaughter held at second, fearing the ball might be caught, and could advance no farther than third base. Brown followed with a long sacrifice fly to score Slaughter, but O'Dea flew out to end the game in a 3–2 loss. The Pirates won again the next day behind lefthander Ken Heintzelman, who scattered five hits in throwing a shutout. Pittsburgh again got on the board early with three runs off Redbird starter Ernie White, who struggled through six innings and took the loss. St. Louis won the final game of the series, barely escaping the Pirates' rally in the ninth. Rookie righthander Johnny Beazley pitched brilliantly for eight innings, mixing a good fastball with a great curve to strike out seven. But after Beazley walked the first two batters in the ninth, Billy Southworth went to his bullpen for Gumbert. Errors by Brown and Sanders and a wild pitch followed, but Gumbert retired the Pirates after two runs had scored, securing a 3–2 win for the Redbirds. Slaughter was the offensive star for the Cards with a double to drive in their first run and an infield hit that he stretched into a double, enabling him to score what proved to be the winning run on Jimmy Brown's single. It was the kind of aggressive and opportunistic baserunning that would characterize the 1942 Redbirds.

After an open date, the Cardinals returned to Sportsman's Park, where their bats came alive in a two-game sweep of the Cincinnati Reds to give them five wins in their first eight games. Mort Cooper went the distance in the series opener for his first win of the season, striking out seven and walking one. The St.

Louisans pounded out twelve hits, including Musial's second home run, on their way to an 8–0 win. The next day, Gumbert hurled a complete game, giving up seven hits but only a ninth-inning run that came on a scratch double by second baseman Chuck Aleno and a Texas League single by catcher Ray Lamanno. The Cards meanwhile collected eleven hits and six runs to defeat Elmer Riddle, who had posted the league's best winning percentage in 1941 with a record of 19–4.

After the brief home stand, the Cardinals returned to the road for three games in Chicago, where their bats again fell silent as they lost the first two and saw the third rained out. In the first contest, the stocky lefthander Max Lanier held the Cubs to seven hits, but one was a home run by Lou "the Mad Russian" Novikoff, who led off the sixth by driving a letter-high fastball into the left-field seats. It was enough for a 2–1 Cubs win. The Cards threatened repeatedly throughout the game, getting seven hits against Big Bill Lee, who also gave up five walks, but they failed to hit when it counted except for Brown's double in the third that plated their only run. Howard Pollet made his first start of the season in the second game of the series, but was wild and failed to get through a first inning in which he gave up two hits, two walks, and threw a wild pitch, enabling the Cubs to score three times. Murry Dickson finished the inning, making his initial appearance of the season. He pitched well, yielding only one run in four and a third innings. Chicago's rookie southpaw Johnny Schmitz held the Redbirds in check for seven innings until an error by first baseman Babe Dahlgren put a runner on base who came home on a Walker Cooper home run. The Cards got another run in the ninth but lost 4–3. It was their fourth one-run loss in the first ten games.

After the third Chicago game was rained out, the Birds returned home for a Sunday doubleheader with Pittsburgh. In the first game, lefty Ken Heintzelman once again shut out the Cardinals. Lon Warneke, the venerable "Arkansas Hummingbird," started for the Cards and gave up a run in the seventh, which was all the support that Heintzelman required. The lefthanded-hitting Stan Musial, who after a good start at the plate had fallen into a slump, was replaced for the first time with a righthanded hitter, Coaker Triplett, a practice Southworth would continue throughout the season. In the nightcap, the Cards broke on top with three runs in the second inning, two of them on Sanders's first home run of the young campaign. The Pirates answered with four runs of their own in the fifth, ending the day early for St. Louis starter Mort Cooper. The Cardinals tied the game in the seventh on Moore's sacrifice fly, then spotless relief pitching from Lohrman, Howard Krist, and Ernie White held Pittsburgh scoreless from the sixth through the eleventh. But the Redbirds could not fathom Pirate lefthander Aldon Wilkie, who took over for starter Eldon "Rip" Sewell in the fifth and held them to one run over the final eight innings. The game was called after the eleventh because of darkness and ended in a tie. Cards owner Sam Breadon had pushed the start of the doubleheader back to 2:00 from the usual starting time of 1:30 to let fans have Sunday dinner with their families before heading to Sportsman's Park, but the later start meant fewer hours of daylight for the twin bill.

After an open date, the Cardinals finished April at home with three games against the New York Giants. Musial remained on the bench for the first two, in which lefties Cliff Melton and Carl Hubbell started for the Giants. The Cards took the first game against the New Yorkers in ten innings, 5–4, with the winning run driven in by Johnny Hopp, who started at first base for the ailing Ray Sanders. The game went back and forth as Harry Gumbert was hit hard through the first six innings and left with one out in the seventh. Lanier replaced him and sparkled in relief, shutting out the Giants over the final three and two-thirds innings to get the win. The second game also went ten innings, but this time New York won 4–3. Going into the ninth, the Giants had built a three-run lead for their great lefthander, "King Carl" Hubbell, who had held the Cardinals scoreless. But in the ninth, the Redbirds rallied to tie the score. Terry Moore and Walker Cooper doubled for one run, and Brown followed with a single to drive in another. Ace Adams replaced Hubbell and promptly gave up a game-tying double to pinch hitter Estel Crabtree.[41] The Giants wasted no time in coming back to score a run against Bill Lohrman in the tenth, and Adams held St. Louis scoreless in their half of the inning for a 4–3 New York win. Howard Pollet then faced the Giants in the rubber game of the series. Pitching as he had in 1941, he took a shutout into the ninth inning. Meanwhile, the Redbirds' hitters broke out of a team slump, getting eleven hits and seven runs against Hal Schumacher and Tom Sunkel, three of the runs scoring on a double by Pollet. In the ninth, Pollet tired and the Giants rallied, bunching three of their four hits for three runs, but the lefty worked through it to win 7–3.

St. Louis finished April with a .500 record, seven wins and seven losses, not the start for which they had hoped. Brooklyn, meanwhile, ended the month with fourteen wins and only three losses for an .824 winning percentage. After two wins and a loss in each of their first two series, the Dodgers had won ten of eleven for the rest of the month. As May approached, they stood atop the National League, four games ahead of the second-place Pirates, five ahead of the Cubs, and five and a half ahead of the Cardinals, who were in fourth place. Tommy Holmes of the *Brooklyn Eagle* marveled that "probably no team ever got off to as fine a start as Brooklyn's Dodgers did this season."[42] Boston Braves manager Casey Stengel was more reserved in his view of the Brooklyn start, pointing out that they had been beating up on some of the league's weaker teams. Stengel thought the Dodgers, a predominantly lefthanded-hitting team, might find the going more difficult against stronger clubs with good southpaw pitching.

Numbers told the story about the Cardinals, who simply were not hitting. In their opening series with the Cubs, they averaged .284 as a team, and had done better at .315 in their two games soon after with the Reds. The Cards scored thirty-three runs in those five contests, but in their other ten games they hit only .231 and crossed the plate just twenty-eight times. Compared with Brooklyn, St. Louis had scored an average of four runs a game while giving up 3.2, whereas the Dodgers had averaged seven runs a game and held opponents to 2.7 runs. Almost all of the Redbird games had been tightly contested, with seven games— five of them losses—decided by one run. Only two of the Dodgers' games had been settled by one run, of which Brooklyn had won one.

After a slow spring in Florida, Musial got off to a fast start when the season began, with six hits in the opening series with the Cubs, but then fell into a slump and managed only six more hits the rest of the month and a batting average of just .158 after the initial series. He was not alone in starting slowly. Terry Moore and Ray Sanders were hitting around .260, while Marty Marion had a meager .128 average and his double-play partner Frank Crespi was little better at just over .200. Only Enos Slaughter, Jimmy Brown, and the catching tandem of Ken O'Dea and Walker Cooper were hitting over .300, and Brown, the leadoff hitter, had driven in 30 percent of the team's runs during the month. Billy Southworth, however, said he was "not worrying about the hitting," assuring fans, "We went through the same thing in the South."[43]

Cardinal fans may have wondered how poor hitting in March was reason for optimism about poor hitting in April as they tried to share Southworth's faith in the team. The series against the Giants at the end of April marked the first appearance of Johnny Mize in St. Louis since his trade the previous winter. Mize delivered five singles in fifteen at bats and drove in a couple of runs against his former team. With their team slumping, many St. Louis fans must have wondered, "What if?" What if Big Jawn still wore a jersey with that brace of birds on a bat across the chest, instead of one with the words "New York"?

CHAPTER 4

The Not So Merry May

By the spring of 1942, the effects of war could be seen and felt everywhere in the country. Men in uniform were a common sight, especially in the nation's large cities and near the more than one hundred new military bases and camps, which sprang up mostly in the South. Commercial buildings were converted to military use, among them the spring training hotels of the Cardinals and Yankees in St. Petersburg. Newspapers were filled with photographs of local soldiers and sailors, and of airplanes, tanks, and warships, as well as with maps of combat areas. Movie Tone and Pathe News newsreels shown before feature films in movie theaters brought scenes of actual combat to audiences across the country. More and more men were employed in war industries, many in the dozens of new shipyards built in cities along the Atlantic coast and Gulf of Mexico that had never before known one. Increasing numbers of women joined men on the production lines. Children collected tinfoil to be recycled and used in the war effort, began their school days with the Pledge of Allegiance, sang patriotic songs, and regularly brought money to class to buy savings bond stamps. Workers faced gasoline rationing and a rubber shortage; housewives had to manage the food stamps required to purchase rationed meats and produce; families planted Victory Gardens, collected scrap metal, and on Sundays joined their neighbors at church in prayers for those in the military.

Major-league baseball may have provided a distraction from the war, but it did not provide an escape. The Cardinals and Browns, like other major-league clubs, asked fans to return foul balls hit into the grandstands; the balls were sent to Army and Navy camps for use by servicemen. St. Louis fans complied and made a point of lustily booing anyone, including a soldier in uniform, who hesitated to throw a ball back on the field for deposit in a large, clearly visible barrel that sat beside the home team's dugout. Several hundred men in uniform could be seen at every game, and the National Anthem, previously played only on special ceremonial occasions like opening day and July 4, was now heard before every game.[1]

There were fewer fans at games. Attendance was down almost 10 percent in the first month of the season, as the war was having an adverse effect on entertainment businesses in general.[2] In East Coast stadiums, areas were designated as bomb shelters with signage throughout the park directing fans where to go for greatest safety. Stevens Brothers concessionaires set up canteens in the three New York ballparks at which uniformed military persons could purchase a hot dog, soda, or bag of peanuts for a nickel rather than the dime charged ordinary fans. Regular announcements were made by baseball executives about baseball's contributions to the war effort. In addition, the *Sporting News* published weekly reports on major- and minor-league players in service and launched a weekly feature on baseball during World War I.

The greatest concern to all teams was that the draft would claim key players for military service during the season.[3] St. Louis fans grew nervous in late April when Enos Slaughter left the team briefly to meet with his local draft board in North Carolina. Slaughter had been classified 3A, a deferment status for married men, but his status was called into question when he divorced his wife, claiming she had been unfaithful to him. After meeting with Slaughter, the board postponed any action, leaving Slaughter's long-term availability to the Redbirds in doubt. Some suggested that the early-season struggles of the Cardinals were attributable to their having so many young players distracted by concerns about the draft. But in fact many of the kids on the club, including Stan Musial, were married, had families, and were classified 3A, while others, like Marty Marion, George Kurowski, and Ray Sanders, had suffered childhood injuries that led to their being ruled physically unfit for military service and classified 4F. One of the questions raised regularly in the press by critics of wartime baseball was how a professional athlete, able to withstand the rigors of a physically demanding sport, could be physically unfit for the military, and many players classified 4F underwent repeated examinations to confirm their injuries were sufficient for a draft exemption.

∼

The Cardinals began May at home with a two-game series against a hot Boston Braves club riding a five-game winning streak. The first game was a slugfest in which the two teams had eleven extra-base hits, five of them home runs. The Braves broke on top with two runs in the first inning, but the Cards came back with two in the second followed by single runs in the third and fourth to take a 4–2 lead. The Bostonians erased that lead and took one of their own with five runs in the sixth off Lon Warneke. St. Louis came back again with one in the bottom of the sixth, but failed to add any more in the seventh or eighth. Trailing by two in the ninth, the Redbirds put a runner on base with two outs and Stan Musial at the plate. The rookie already had a double and home run for the afternoon. This time he connected with a fastball from Braves' pitcher Dick Errickson, just acquired from the Cubs, lifting it high onto the pavilion roof to tie the score at 7–7. Johnny Beazley worked a scoreless tenth against Boston, and Johnny Sain appeared on his way to doing the same to the Cardinals in the bottom half of the inning, getting two quick outs, but then he threw a fastball to a fastball hitter, Ken O'Dea, who planted it on top of the pavilion. It was the fourth round-tripper of the game for the Cards and sent the tiny Friday afternoon crowd of just over a thousand home happy.

The big sports story the next day was a horse race, not baseball, for it was Derby Day at Churchill Downs in Louisville, Kentucky. The race was won by the favorite, Shut Out, ridden by jockey Wayne Wright, who emerged at the top of the stretch and pulled away to capture the roses by more than two lengths. Indicative of the times, the playing of the National Anthem drew more applause than did "My Old Kentucky Home." As Shut Out was winning the Derby, the Braves' lefty Lou Tost was tossing his own shutout against the Cardinals. There was no miracle finish for the Redbirds this day, only rain that led to the game being called at the end of six innings with Boston leading 1–0. Mort Cooper started for the Birds and went all six, but he was not sharp, giving up six hits and twice escaping innings with the bases loaded. The Braves' run came on a Sibby Sisti home run that just made it into special field seats in left field. The game was plagued by rain showers, with the diamond requiring continuous repair until a heavy downpour in the seventh stopped play altogether. After thirty minutes, the umpires declared the field unplayable. Southworth insisted that another attempt be made to repair the field, but Sam Breadon told the umpires that the team did not have enough fresh dirt and other materials on hand to repair the damage, and the game was lost.

The Brooklyn Dodgers moved into St. Louis on May 3 for a three-game series that began with a Sunday doubleheader. The aggressive play of the Dodgers, which many thought more than just aggressive, had already engulfed them in controversy. St. Louis radio announcer Dizzy Dean told *Brooklyn Eagle* columnist Harold Parrott, "The other clubs are laying for them Bums this year. That's all I hear in the dugouts—how they are going to take the Dodgers down a few notches." "They got it coming," the Giants' Harry Danning had told Parrott earlier. "They pop off too much." But not to worry, he added, because "they'll be fighting among themselves before another month."[4] Before they left St. Louis, the Dodgers were fighting again, but with umpires and not one another.

Brooklyn arrived on the west bank of the Mississippi River after having suffered their first back-to-back losses of the season to the Pittsburgh Pirates. Their aces, Whitlow Wyatt and Kirby Higbe, were ready for St. Louis, where 23,871 greeted them at Sportsman's Park, the largest crowd of the young season for the Cardinals. Almost all wanted to see the Redbirds take two, and they would not be disappointed. Wyatt did not survive the opening frame of the first game, as the Cards tagged him for three hits to go with two walks and two Dodger errors to score five times, the big hit being a grand slam by O'Dea, continuing his heroics from the Boston series. Manager Leo Durocher also failed to survive the first inning, being tossed after, as one reporter saw it, "a long, tiresome, useless flow of words and accompanying gesticulations" that followed a four-pitch walk to Terry Moore. Durocher had come to home plate ostensibly to speak with his catcher Billy Sullivan, but was sent back to the dugout when umpire Ziggy Sears judged this to violate a new league rule that prohibited managers from leaving the bench to contest ball and strike calls. Durocher retreated to the dugout but continued to protest. Umpire Tom Dunn walked over to the Brooklyn bench from first base, words followed, and Durocher was banished. This provoked an even more spirited debate as tempers flared. Dodger coach "Fat Freddy" Fitzsimmons became embroiled in the argument, his face reddening in anger, and he was tossed from the game as well. Enraged, Fitzsimmons tried to punch Sears but was physically restrained by other umpires and some Brooklyn players. Dunn went into the Dodgers' dugout to try to quiet matters, and after a twenty-seven-minute delay the game was resumed.[5]

In the second inning, the Cardinals batted around for the second time, adding three more runs to take a commanding 8–0 lead. Brooklyn got two of those back in the third, only to have the Redbirds answer with two more runs of their own. Trailing 10–2, the Dodgers were not about to go meekly. In the fourth, they bombarded Harry Gumbert, scoring five times, three coming on a home run by St. Louis native Pete Reiser. Their attack continued in the fifth with three runs against Johnny Beazley to knot the score at 10–10. Ernie White came on to pitch for the Cards, working through several jams to hold the Dodgers scoreless in the final four innings. At the same time, the Cardinals touched Johnny Allen, Brooklyn's fourth pitcher of the day, for four runs in the seventh, with O'Dea's bases-clearing double being the big hit in the 14–10 win. Before the game-winning rally, however, Billy Southworth was ejected for violating the same rule that sent Durocher to the locker room.

The first game took three hours and six minutes to play, a very long time in an era before television commercials when any game lasting much over two hours was thought to be long. The second game did not start until after 5 p.m. Neither Higbe nor Max Lanier was sharp at the outset. Brooklyn scored first, taking a one-run lead in the second, but the Cards came back with four in the fourth, highlighted by a bases-loaded triple by Jimmy Brown that chased Pete Reiser to the deepest part of center field, where he still could not catch up with the long drive. Larry French relieved Higbe, and after a few pitches ran afoul of the law as home plate umpire Dunn went to the mound, accused French of pitching without having his foot in contact with the pitching rubber, and swept the slab clean. The Dodger lefty promptly kicked some dirt back onto the rubber, which drew a warning from Dunn. This angered Brooklyn first sacker Dolph Camilli, who had joined the others on the mound. He kicked yet more dirt to cover the rubber entirely, which drew another warning from Dunn. Camilli reacted angrily, had to be restrained by teammates, and was thrown out of the game by Dunn.

When play resumed, Dunn was subjected to a blistering barrage of verbal abuse from players in the Dodgers' dugout, to which he responded by throwing two more players out of the game. After the war of words, Brooklyn could manage only one more tally off Lanier and lost 4–2 in a game that was called because of darkness after the visitors batted in the sixth. Stan Musial had a big day in the doubleheader, with four hits in five tries, including two doubles and two runs batted in, and also a dazzling back-handed catch high against the left-field wall to rob Reiser of an extra-base hit. Monday was an open date, which gave the Dodgers time to reflect upon their now four-game losing streak, during which the Cardinals had gained three games on them.[6] It also gave Roy Stockton time to weigh in on league rules and the behavior of the Dodgers. "If [National League president] Frick really wants to make the Brooklyns change their tactics, he might try a few suspensions." "Players and managers do not worry about fines," Stockton opined, but "suspensions would be real punishment, a blow to the team's pennant chances."[7] Frick handed out fines to Durocher and several of the Dodgers with the warning that anyone who continued to violate the "anti-squawk" rule, for which both Durocher and Southworth had been banished, could be suspended. "Fans come to the parks to see ball games," he said with disgust, "not to sit in on stupid time killing arguments at the plate." In an appeal to patriotism he added, "In these war days, it is unjust to the spectators to ring in unnecessary delays."[8]

The third game was a classic pitcher's duel between two southpaws, veteran thirty-four-year-old Larry French for Brooklyn and twenty-one-year-old rookie Howard Pollet for the home club. Through six innings, they posted goose eggs on the scoreboard. In the seventh, the Dodgers pushed across a run when, with Pee Wee Reese on first, French stroked a single to center. Moore charged the ball, tried for a shoestring catch, but missed. Slaughter, backing up the play, had trouble corralling the ball, enabling Reese to scamper around the bases from first to score. The Cards tied the contest in the eighth on a bunt for a hit, a bunt for a sacrifice, and an error by second baseman Billy Herman. The game went to extra innings tied at one with the starters still on the mound. In the tenth, Joe Medwick saved the day for the visitors with a leaping catch against the left-field wall. In the eleventh, Pollet got the first two Dodgers. Medwick then bounced a grounder to third for what should have been the third out, but Jimmy Brown booted it for an error. Owen followed with a single, moving Medwick to second, and French drove Medwick home with a single into right center. The Dodgers added a second run in the frame to claim a 3–1 win. It was a masterful performance by French, who mixed off-speed pitches, curveballs, and knuckleballs to limit the Redbirds to just four hits in eleven innings and end Brooklyn's four-game skid.

The Cardinals wrapped up their home stand with a two-game set against Philadelphia. It was chilly for the first game, but while the day was cold, the Redbirds were not. They broke out their bats in a manly display of power for a slim Ladies Day crowd of fewer than one thousand, pounding three Phillies hurlers for eleven runs on fourteen hits, six for extra bases. Both Terry Moore and Enos Slaughter belted home runs, while Jimmy Brown had a triple. Moore also smacked a double and drove in three runs. But most encouraging to Southworth was that the offensive explosion involved the whole team as all of the starters except Marion joined the hit parade. Even pitcher Mort Cooper hit safely. On the mound, Cooper went the distance for his second win, giving up six hits and three walks but only two runs. The Redbird defense sparkled behind him, turning two double plays in the 11–2 win. The weather for the second game was more foul than for the first, as cold and blustery winds blew through St. Louis and forced cancellation of the May 7 contest. The only action was in the front office, where the Cards sold pitchers Bill Lohrman to the New York Giants and Clyde Shoun to the Cincinnati Reds. The decision had been made to go with the younger hurlers, so neither of the veterans figured into the team's plans. Dealing them brought several thousand dollars to the team coffers.

~

On May 8, the Cardinals departed on their first extended road trip, which would take them to all of the eastern cities. Meanwhile, in Brooklyn, the Dodgers were hosting the New York Giants in the first military relief game of the season, from which all proceeds would go to benefit the military. Brooklyn president Larry MacPhail turned responsibility for the game over to the Navy Relief Society so his club could avoid paying taxes on revenue that went to charity. Scheduled as a twilight game, there were 42,822 tickets sold for it, breaking the Ebbets Field record of 41,109 set in 1934. Everyone who entered the stadium had to buy a ticket, including all of the players, umpires, front office personnel, vendors, ushers, policemen, public officials (including New York mayor Fiorella LaGuardia), and even the Legionnaires and musicians who entertained the crowd in elaborate pregame ceremonies. The game raised almost sixty thousand dollars for Navy relief, to which the team's concessionaire added another thousand from the sale of scorecards. The event's success gave great satisfaction to MacPhail, whose idea it had been that all teams play such games.

Trailing the Dodgers by two games, the Cardinals began their road trip in Cincinnati, banging out nine hits in a 5–2 win. Brown drove in the first two Redbird runs in the fifth against Reds' starter Elmer Riddle. Slaughter and Sanders followed with solo homers in the sixth for two more runs. Lon Warneke went the distance for his first win of the year, surviving a poor start in which Cincinnati bunched five of its eight hits in the first two innings, but the Reds could score only once, their run coming on a bases-empty home run by first baseman Frank McCormick in the second. Cincinnati added a run in the sixth on a circuit blow by rookie catcher Ray Lamanno, and the Cards did likewise in the ninth off Clyde Shoun, who had been their teammate only hours before.

But just as suddenly as the Cardinals had begun to hit the way management had expected, they quit. The Birds lost the second game 5–2 to the Reds' Johnny Vander Meer, another lefthander, who struck out seven. It was the fifth time St. Louis had lost to a southpaw in the first three weeks of the season. Hoping to reverse this pattern, Southworth added righthanded hitters to the starting lineup against Vander Meer, replacing Musial and Slaughter with George Kurowski and Coaker Triplett, neither of whom got a hit. The next day was a study in utter futility as Cincinnati pitching blanked the Redbirds in both ends of a Sunday doubleheader. Ray Starr beat Mort Cooper 1–0 in the first game, with St. Louis hitters failing in clutch situations time after time, hitting into three double plays. In the second game, Bucky Walters struck out ten and scattered four hits in cruising to a 3–0 whitewash of the Cards. Johnny Beazley started for St. Louis, gave up only five hits, and matched Walters through six innings of shutout ball. But in the seventh, Frank McCormick looped a double to center field on which Moore got a late break, Lonny Frey and Ival Goodman walked, and pitcher Walters singled home two for all the runs he needed. The Monday open date was welcomed by the Cardinals, who were suddenly on a three-game losing streak as they moved to Philadelphia.

The City of Brotherly Love proved no more hospitable than Cincinnati, as the last-place Phillies sent the Cards to their fourth straight loss. Frank Hoerst, another lefty, held St. Louis to two runs on six hits. The Phils scored a single run in the first off starter Max Lanier, but the Redbirds took the lead in the second on a two-run double by Marty Marion. The Phillies reclaimed the lead in the third, bunching four singles for two runs, ending Lanier's day. The bullpen held the Phils scoreless after the third, but to no avail as the Cards also failed to score and lost 3–2. St. Louis finally ended its losing ways the next day with a 9–1 win behind Lon Warneke. The veteran dazzled Philly hitters with a deceptive slider, striking out five and holding them to four hits after Danny Litwhiler's two-out home run in the first inning. All of the snoozing bats of the Cardinals awoke simultaneously as every regular had at least one hit in a fifteen-hit assault on a quartet of Philly pitchers. The top of the batting order did most of the damage: Brown collected three hits, including two doubles; Musial had two singles and a triple that drove in a run; Moore added a single and a double; and Slaughter rapped three singles to plate three runners. Rain denied St. Louis a third try at Philadelphia pitching, and the team moved on to Boston, where the Redbirds split a two-game series with the Braves.

The hot bats that left Philadelphia were chilled in the New England "spring," a season largely unknown to the region. Birds starter Harry Gumbert was no mystery to Boston batsmen, but backed by strong defensive play he put down repeated threats through seven scoreless innings. Al Javery did much the same to the Cards until the sixth, when singles by Slaughter and O'Dea gave St. Louis a 2–0 lead. Gumbert's luck expired in the eighth as the Beantowners tied the score on two singles, a double, and a sacrifice fly. Then the Braves won the game in the ninth against Beazley without getting a hit. Tommy Holmes walked to lead off, went to second on Paul Waner's sacrifice, and advanced to third on an error by the Redbirds' pitcher. Beazley gave the next Brave a free pass to first to load the bases, after which catcher Clyde Kluttz, who had driven in the tying run, launched a long fly to left that brought home the game winner. With the 3–2 win, Casey Stengel's surprising Bostonians were alone in second place behind the Dodgers while the Cardinals dropped below .500, six and a half games behind Brooklyn.

The Cardinals got back to .500 the next day behind Mort Cooper. In a ragged tilt on a windy day, St. Louis fielders made four errors, while Boston pitchers walked eleven Redbirds. The sloppy play caused Cooper to lose his temper and his control in the third as the Braves scored three times to tie the game. But his brother Walker, the Cardinals' catcher, knew what to do and kept yelling, "Don't get red out there!" which always made Mort chuckle and usually got him back on track. With his brother's help, Mort Cooper held Boston to only one run thereafter in the 7–4 St. Louis win. It was no doubt pleasing to Southworth that his club had finally beaten a lefthander, Lou Tost, whom the Birds dispatched in the second inning on their way to an eleven-hit game. The win gave the Cards a record of four wins and six losses for the trip, disappointing in itself, but more so because the Dodgers had gotten hot again, winning six of the seven games they played over the same period. The Cardinals' pitching had been the best of any team in the majors, but their "powder puff attack," as *Star-Times* columnist Sid Keener described it, had produced only 117 runs and a team batting average of just .255 while the Dodgers had scored 177 runs and hit .273. As the Birds boarded the train to New York to wrap up their first eastern sojourn against the Giants and Dodgers, they were in sixth place, six and a half games behind Brooklyn and only half a game ahead of the seventh-place Cincinnati Reds. "If it's always darkest just before the dawn," Stockton of the *Post-Dispatch* wrote wistfully, "the sun should come up quickly for the Cardinals."[9]

~

Like the Cardinals, the American war effort was struggling as April turned
to May. News reports told a story of one "strategic" retreat after another by the
Allies. In the first week of May, British forces abandoned the city of Mandalay in
central Burma, where U.S. General Joseph Stilwell acknowledged that the Allies
had taken "a hell f a beating," adding, "We got run out of Burma and it is embar-
rassing as hell."[10] In the same week, the Japanese pressed north through central
Burma to invade the southern Chinese province of Yunnan, where despite fierce
resistance they advanced farther and farther into China. In early May, Japanese
bombardment of the island of Corregidor at the entrance to Manila Bay became
relentless, with day-and-night attacks from both the air and land-based artillery. It wore down the resistance of General Jonathan Wainwright and his fifteen
thousand American and Filipino troops, who had held out for almost a month
after the fall of Bataan but were finally forced to surrender on May 6. Shortly
thereafter all resistance in the Philippines ended, and the entire territory fell
under Japanese control.[11]

In the second week of May, the front pages of St. Louis newspapers blazed
with reports of the "greatest battle of the war" underway in the Coral Sea between
New Guinea and Australia.[12] It began when Japan launched a large invasion force
headed for Port Moresby on the southern underside of New Guinea. Control of
Port Moresby would complete a solid southeastern perimeter for Japan's newly
won Pacific territories and also provide a base from which to threaten Australia. The United States had cracked the Japanese naval code well enough to
know about the operation in advance and moved to counter it. The engagement
itself stretched across hundreds of miles of ocean and was conducted entirely by
carrier-based aircraft, the first time in naval history that a sea battle had been
fought without the opposing ships being in sight of one another.[13] Losses were
heavy on both sides. Newspapers carried detailed accounts of Japanese losses but
not the full extent of U.S. losses. While Japan claimed significant U.S. losses, the
War Department acknowledged only that three American planes had been shot
down.[14] A full accounting of U.S. losses was not made public for several months,
which for the moment left the happy but erroneous impression of a far more
decisive American victory. David Kennedy concludes that the battle of the Coral
Sea "represented an allied victory," but left the Allies with a military capacity for
little more than harassment while "Japan still held all the high cards and all the
power of initiative."[15]

On May 11, the War Department finally confirmed that three weeks earlier U.S.
planes had indeed bombed Tokyo and other cities in Japan, but provided little
additional information about the assault. A week after that, Colonel James Doolittle was introduced in Washington in a White House ceremony as the leader

of the American attack force and given the Congressional Medal of Honor by President Franklin Roosevelt. Seventy-nine others in the seven-bomber squadron were given the Distinguished Flying Cross, including Lieutenant Charles Lee McClure of University City, a St. Louis suburb. The War Department was silent with respect to losses of men or planes and also as to the location from which the planes had taken flight, which remained a mystery to the Japanese. President Roosevelt finally told reporters jokingly that the planes had come from Shangri-la, which was reported in the German press as serious news.

As the Japanese drove farther into China and Germany launched its summer offensive in the Soviet Union, there was little genuinely good news about the war. But Americans were not fully aware of this. Winston Groom notes that "victories were often touted when the results were murky and defeats were turned into victories in the press or kept out of it entirely by censorship."[16] Instead, the public ceremonies for Doolittle and the positive, albeit incomplete, news about the battle of the Coral Sea gave Americans a renewed sense of optimism about the eventual outcome of the war. On May 20, reflecting this winning spirit, the weather bird cartoon that accompanied daily forecasts on the front page of the *St. Louis Post-Dispatch* carried the caption: "O'Hare. Doolittle. Come on, Southworth."

$\sim$

Arriving in New York on May 17 to face Mel Ott's Giants, the Cardinals found Brooklyn sportswriters already suggesting that, given the Dodgers' fast start and superb play, the National League pennant race might already be over. The Cards were also greeted by news that New York's police commissioner, Lewis Valentine, had banned night baseball in the city as part of regulations designed to "dim out" the coast to protect shipping from attacks by German submarines.[17] At the Polo Grounds, the Redbirds found two lefthanders waiting to face them in a Sunday twin bill. In the first game, Carl Hubbell limited the Cards to eight hits and one run, a home run by Ray Sanders, for a 7–1 Giants win. In the nightcap, Cliff Melton limited the Birds to two runs for six innings. But just as it began to appear that the Brooklyn writers might be correct about the pennant race, the erratic St. Louis offense came to life to score two runs in the seventh and four more in the eighth for an 8–6 win and a split of the doubleheader, keeping their record at .500 for the season.

On Monday, the Redbirds pounded three Giants pitchers for fifteen hits as they scored early and often on their way to a lopsided 16–4 victory. St. Louis starter Lon Warneke was shaky from the start. Despite a comfortable four-run lead after two innings, he could not get through the third. Lanier replaced him to go the last six and two-thirds innings for the win. Lefty Dave Koslo started for the Giants and was driven from the game in the second inning, the second southpaw in two days beaten by the Birds. Walker Cooper and Jimmy Brown led the attack, the Cards' catcher driving in four runs on two doubles while the third sacker knocked home four with a single and a double. New York started a fourth lefthander, "Prince Hal" Schumacher, heir apparent to "King Carl" Hubbell, against the Cardinals in the final game. But the Birds got to him quickly for three runs in the second, two more in the sixth, and then finished his day with another pair in the seventh for their third win in the four-game set. Howard Pollet, who had missed recent turns in the pitching rotation with elbow discomfort when throwing a curve, started and gave up only three hits and an unearned run through six innings before tiring in the seventh. He picked up the 8–4 win with help from Johnny Beazley.

From the Polo Grounds, St. Louis moved across the East River to Ebbets Field for a two-game encounter with the red-hot Dodgers, who were riding an eight-game winning streak. They had taken ten of eleven on their current home stand and opened a seven-and-a-half-game lead on the Cardinals. Mort Cooper started the first game and wasted no time in putting an end to Brooklyn's winning ways. In his best performance of the season, the righthander had near perfect control, mixing fastballs with curves and other off-speed pitches to whitewash the Dodgers 1–0 on a two-hitter in which no Dodger runner got past first base. It was the first time the Dodgers had been shut out in 1942. Brooklyn's Whitlow Wyatt pitched well, holding the Redbirds to four hits, but one was a long triple off the center-field wall by Walker Cooper, who then scored the game's only run on Frank Crespi's fly to Dixie Walker, who was playing center field while Pete Reiser was laid up with a bad back.

The second game with the Dodgers was canceled due to bad weather, and the Cardinals headed for home. By taking five of their final six games, the Redbirds salvaged a 7–6 record from their first eastern swing, but still returned to St. Louis trailing first-place Brooklyn by six and a half games. Of their six losses, three were by one run and two were shutouts. The Cardinals' pitchers had done their job; the hitters had not. The team batting average for the trip was just .236, and 40 percent of the hits had come in three of the thirteen games. In the other ten games the Cardinals had hit barely .200. There was, moreover, a power outage: three-fourths of their hits had been singles and almost all the rest doubles. The Cardinals were getting runners on base (they drew an average of more than four walks a game), but they could not get the hit needed to drive runners home. Three players—Enos Slaughter, Walker Cooper, and Jimmy Brown—accounted for half the runs scored by the team, and only Slaughter and Cooper had hit over .300 on the road. Stan Musial had an especially disappointing trip. Save for one game in which he got three hits, the rookie outfielder batted only .179. Southworth juggled his lineup at times, trying especially to get more righthanded hitters to the plate against lefthanded pitchers, and for several games he benched Marty Marion, who was buried in an extended slump, in favor of rookie Buddy

Blattner at shortstop. Nothing worked. Johnny Mize and the deal that sent him to the Giants began to loom large in press commentaries about the team's offensive woes.

The Cardinals were no doubt happy to get home, if only for a short two-day, three-game weekend series against Cincinnati. It would not, however, be a happy stay. The series began well enough as the Redbirds took the first game 6–3. Ernie White started but left in the second inning with none out and St. Louis trailing 3–0. The Cards came back to tie the game with three runs in the sixth off Reds' starter Bucky Walters and went ahead in the seventh on Musial's three-run home run, his fifth home run of the season. With the victory, St. Louis cut the Dodgers' lead to five games and also moved into sole possession of second place. It was, however, a different story the next day as Cincinnati swept both ends of a Sunday twin bill. In the first game, Johnny Vander Meer locked up with Mort Cooper in a tight pitcher's duel. The Cardinals took the lead with a run in the second, and Cooper held the Reds scoreless until the sixth, when Cincinnati tallied twice to go ahead. Cooper left for a pinch hitter in the seventh as the Cards scored a run to tie the game. Beazley entered in relief and threw a scoreless eighth, but then gave up the winning run in the ninth when the Redbirds' defense collapsed behind him. In the nightcap, Ray Starr tossed a masterful three-hit shutout in which all but six putouts were on ground balls to Cincinnati infielders. It was the second time in the month that the Reds had taken both ends of a doubleheader from the Cardinals, who dropped back to six and a half games off Brooklyn's league-leading pace.

As St. Louis was preparing to leave for a seven-day, eight-game swing around the National League's three western cities, it was reported that Southworth had fined a player $200, a substantial sum in 1942. The manager refused to comment, saying it was "a matter between the club and the player" and that, "if it was ever mentioned publicly, it would be because [the player] told somebody about it." Defending the amount of the fine, Southworth asked reporters, "Do you think it does any good to fine a big leaguer $50? That's chicken feed." "I make the rules to be observed," Southworth added firmly. "The boys know that now."[18] This was the only such incident reported during the season. The young Cardinals, unlike some of their predecessors in St. Louis, were a respectful and responsible group, comfortable with the serious but sociable clubhouse Southworth wanted.

As the team left for Chicago, its bench was strengthened by the return of the versatile Johnny Hopp, who had been laid up with a broken thumb. Hopp could play all three outfield positions as well as first base, was a solid hitter, and was also the fastest runner on the team, possibly the fastest in the entire league.[19] In the first game in Chicago, Ernie White took the mound and went the distance while the Redbirds collected thirteen hits in a 10–2 win. Southworth had juggled his lineup once more, putting George Kurowski at third base, moving Jimmy Brown to second, benching Frank Crespi, and inserting Walker Cooper into the third slot in the batting order ahead of Slaughter. Cooper responded with two hits, including a double, and knocked home two runs. Kurowski, hitting in the seventh spot, also collected two hits, one a double, while Moore stroked three hits, Musial two including a double, and Slaughter two with a home run.

The Cardinals also took the second game of the series in a duel of lefthanders. The Cubs' Vern Olsen matched the Cards' Max Lanier through seven scoreless innings, but in the eighth a home run by Terry Moore put St. Louis on the board. Chicago came back an inning later to tie the score in the bottom of the ninth. Olsen, who had been injured in spring training and was making his first start for the Cubs, ran out of gas in the tenth as the Redbirds pushed across two runs for a 3–1 lead. The Cubs threatened in their half of the inning, but failed to score when Stan Musial made a leaping catch of a long drive off the bat of shortstop Len Merullo to secure the victory. The insertion of Kurowski at third and the switch of Brown to second would become permanent after these games, and would prove to be the critical lineup change in the St. Louis season. Of more immediate concern to Southworth, however, was that after the first game a large lump, "big as a chestnut," developed under White's pitching arm, preventing him from raising it to the throwing position. He would not pitch again for four weeks and not win again until July.

The Cards moved on to Pittsburgh for single games on May 27 and 28, winning both. The first game saw Hopp replace the injured Ray Sanders at first base and the rookie Murry Dickson make his first big-league start.[20] The game was a see-saw affair in which Pirate miscues contributed to most of the Cardinals' runs. St. Louis scored first, in the top of the second, only to have the Pirates tie the game in the bottom half of the frame. The Birds moved ahead with single runs in the third and fifth, the first scoring on an error by shortstop Alf Anderson and the second on a dropped throw by catcher Babe Phelps. The Pirates came back with two in the sixth to knot the score once more. With the game still tied, Musial led off the eighth with a triple. The Bucs' starter, Rip Sewell, retired the next two Cardinals, and it looked as if Musial might be stranded at third, but Marty Marion reached the blooper-ball specialist for a clean single to center to score Musial. When Pirate center fielder Vince DiMaggio, rushing to field the ball quickly, let it skip past him to the wall, Marion was able to circle the bases to score as well in what would be a 5–3 Redbird victory. Johnny Beazley picked up the win in relief of Dickson, who acquitted himself well as a starter, allowing Pittsburgh only four hits in just over six innings.

There was excitement in the grandstands before the start of the second contest. A spectator, Glenn Titus, chief chemist of the Pittsburgh Coke and Iron Company, suffered a cerebral hemorrhage and died just minutes before the night game was to begin. There was a brief delay, after which Cardinals nemesis Ken

Heintzelman took the mound for the Pirates. The lefty, who had shut the Birds out twice in April, once again baffled them, limiting the St. Louisans to two runs on six hits for nine innings. But this time he was matched against Mort Cooper, who gave up only one run through eight innings. In the ninth, however, Cooper tired and turned the pitching chores over to Beazley with one out, the game tied, the bases loaded, and the dangerous Elbie Fletcher coming to the plate. The rookie righthander was equal to the challenge, getting Fletcher to hit into a double play, and the game went to extra innings. In the eleventh, with the clock at the witching hour, Kurowski and Marion led off with bunt singles and Frank Crespi, hitting for Beazley, singled home the go-ahead run. Harry Gumbert came in to hold the Buccos scoreless in the bottom of the eleventh for a 3–2 win. A game that began with a death ended in a fight as an angry fan jumped out of the stands to assault umpire Tom Dunn. Police broke up the struggle, but Dunn declined to press charges, pointing out that his partner Ziggy Sears had made the disputed call and the attack on him was simply a case of mistaken identity.

Southworth continued to tinker with his batting order, moving Slaughter into the number three spot and Cooper into the fourth as the "cleanup" hitter. It seemed as if his prayers were finally being answered as the top of the batting order had been on a hitting tear since leaving St. Louis. Moore, batting second, had ten hits in twenty tries, Slaughter seven in sixteen at-bats, and Cooper nine in eighteen. But Southworth also knew that more than tinkering might be needed in the near future because Slaughter had received notice from his draft board that he had been reclassified as 1A. Yet with the team playing well, the manager declared, perhaps with fingers crossed, that "the race has just begun" for the Redbirds.[21] The "beginning" ended quickly, however, when the Cardinals reached Cincinnati for a Memorial Day doubleheader in which the Reds' pitchers continued to be a puzzle to Redbird batters.

Facing Johnny Vander Meer, who had beaten them earlier in the month, the bats of Moore, Slaughter, and Cooper went cold on what was otherwise a steaming-hot day along the banks of the Ohio River. All three were hitless against the Cincinnati lefty, who gained his second win of the season over St. Louis and his eleventh against them in fourteen career decisions. The Reds scored all of their runs in the third inning, aided by a rare misplay of a fly ball by center fielder Terry Moore, and won the game 3–2. The Cardinals came back to take the nightcap and avoid a third doubleheader loss to the Reds. They struck early, scoring five times in the second inning and adding three more in the third on their way to a 10–5 win. Slaughter led the attack with a home run and four runs driven in. Lon Warneke, again the beneficiary of the scoring outburst, pitched into the sixth for his third win of the season. It was a tough day for Cincinnati outfielders. Mike Marshall broke his ankle sliding into second base in the opener, and Harry Craft and Gerald Walker collided in the second game while chasing a long fly. A deep cut in his chin forced Craft from the game. Walker continued playing, but later had to be helped from the field when he became groggy while standing in the batter's box. Pitcher Bucky Walters, a former third baseman, finished the game in center field for the Reds.

The Cardinals returned to Chicago for a Sunday doubleheader on May 31 and were greeted by more than thirty-four thousand fans, the largest Cubs crowd in almost a year. The Redbirds took the first game behind the shutout pitching of Howard Pollet, who scattered ten hits while striking out five. George Kurowski, now playing every day at third, saved the shutout when he stabbed a line drive and turned it into a double play. He also stole home in the sixth for the Cards' second run after Johnny Hopp, starting his fifth straight game at first base, had driven Slaughter home with the first run. In the eighth, however, the Redbirds' aggressiveness on the base paths cost them the services of Stan Musial, who sprained his ankle sliding into home while trying to score from first base on a double by Kurowski and had to be helped from the field. The injury made him unavailable for about a week. The second game did not get past the first inning. After Stan Hack led off for the Cubs with a walk, a sudden downpour stopped play. Half an hour later, it appeared to Chicago officials that the game could be resumed, but it turned out that the umpires had already called the game and left the stadium before waiting the required thirty minutes. An irate Jim Gallagher, the Cubs' general manager, protested to league president Ford Frick, demanding that he make a public statement explaining the actions of the umpires.

The Cardinals thus ended their week-long swing around the westernmost National League cities, winning six of seven games to bring their season mark to 25–18. They had again moved into second place but were still six games behind the Dodgers, who finished May on the road, winning five of seven. The rest of the National League teams were strung out behind the front-runners: Boston third, eight games back; New York and Cincinnati each nine and a half games out of first; Chicago eleven; Pittsburgh and Philadelphia farther behind. The season had passed Memorial Day, the traditional "quarter pole" in baseball's pennant races, and the Dodgers and Cardinals would soon be the only horses still in the race. Cubs manager Jimmy Wilson was not optimistic about St. Louis's chances, not because they were so far behind Brooklyn, but because the running Redbirds expended "too much energy, entirely too much. No team can keep charging around a park the way they do and stay in one piece."[22] While the National League race would go to the wire, the American League pennant race had seven teams chasing the New York Yankees, who at 33–11 were a commanding eight games ahead of second-place Detroit. Despite a ten-day swoon near the end of June, the Bronx Bombers would never be seriously challenged on their way to a second straight pennant.

~

No player on the 1942 Cardinals was more admired by his teammates than Terry Moore. "When you read interviews with various 1942 Cardinals," Rob Neyer and Eddie Epstein write, "two things keep popping up: their ability, willingness, or intention to take the extra base whenever possible, and the leadership of center fielder Terry Moore." "Terry was our leader and captain," Stan Musial recalled years later. "We all looked up to him [and] often went to him with our problems, on or off the field." George Kurowski agreed: "He was the father of the ballclub. If we had any troubles or anything, we would go to Terry. He's the one that kept us in good spirits." Enos Slaughter called him the team's "inspirational leader," while Harry Walker credits Moore with making the 1942 Cardinals a "close team."[23] The players also saw Moore as their spokesman. Using him as a buffer against inquisitive newsmen, the young Cardinals would regularly tell them, "See the Captain."

A ballplayer's ballplayer, Moore worked hard, played hard, and expected no less from others. His teammates remember him as a good-natured enforcer, not a "rah-rah" guy but someone who would remind rookie and veteran alike how they should play the game. "If we made a mistake," Kurowski recalled, "Terry Moore would pinch the back of our neck and tell us what we did wrong. And he had bear claws for hands, so you felt it."[24] He would "chew out anybody he didn't think was giving a hundred percent," Musial remembered. Max Lanier agreed, saying that Moore would "get on you if you did something wrong," but added that he "always praised you when you did something good, too."[25] Moore also discouraged fraternizing with players on other teams. "When we'd play the Brooklyn Dodgers," Harry Walker remembered, "Terry would never let me go to the other dugout and talk to my brother Dixie." The respect Moore enjoyed from his teammates extended to other teams as well. "No player in the league perhaps is more genuinely admired and respected by rival players," Dick Farrington of the *Sporting News* observed, adding that it was said "the Cardinals are built around speed, hustle, and Moore."[26]

A southerner by birth, Moore grew up in St. Louis, where he attended Roosevelt and Humboldt high schools. His parents separated while he was in school, forcing him to take various jobs from the time he was fifteen to help support his mother.[27] One was working as a pressman for the Bemis Bag Company, printing advertising on paper bags. Moore also joined the company's St. Louis Muny League team as an outfielder and occasional pitcher. In 1932, at the age of twenty-one, he was playing for a team in a semi-pro league in Collinsville, Illinois, whose manager, Bill Walsh, was a scout for the Cardinals. On Walsh's recommendation, Branch Rickey signed Moore and sent him to the Cards' Double A team at Columbus, Ohio, late in the season, where he played in three games and went hitless in seven times at bat. In 1933, Moore returned to Bemis because the pay was better than that offered by the Cardinals, but in 1934 Rickey persuaded him to try baseball again. After a year divided between Elmira in the Class A Eastern League and Double A Columbus, he joined the Cardinals in 1935 as a twenty-three-year-old rookie playing for the defending champions, the Gas House Gang.[28] In his first year, Moore won the everyday center-field job from the veteran Ernie Orsatti, played brilliantly in the field, and hit .287 in 119 games until his season was ended early by an injury.

A line-drive hitter who sprayed the ball to all fields, Moore had a .284 batting average for his seven years with the Cardinals from 1935 through 1941 and hit .288 in 1942. He had a good eye at the plate, with more career walks than strikeouts (in 1942, he drew fifty-six walks and struck out only twenty-six times). Like all the Cardinals, he had good speed and was a daring base runner. But Moore was best known for his defense. He was widely regarded by friend and foe alike as the best outfielder in the National League. Indeed, the veteran New York sportswriter Arthur Daley ranked Moore with Joe DiMaggio and Tris Speaker as the best center fielders ever to play the game.[29] His teammates raved about his play. Slaughter called him "the greatest defensive center fielder I ever saw," while Dizzy Dean told reporters that he did not care who started when he pitched so long as Moore was in center field. Marty Marion thought him as good as any center fielder of his time: "I'm taking nothing away from Joe DiMaggio [but] he was no better than Terry . . . Willie Mays had more flair, but believe me, in center field, Terry was everything Willie was."[30] Opponents agreed. Brooklyn manager Leo Durocher said no one was better than Moore. "If it's hit in the air," the Dodgers' skipper said, "he'll get it."[31] Brooklyn ace Whitlow Wyatt echoed his boss, calling Moore "the best center fielder I ever seen."

Center field in St. Louis was one of the most expansive fields in the National League. Moore always played shallow ("right behind second base," the Dodgers' Kirby Higbe recalled), but with great instincts and speed he got good jumps on fly balls and could range widely to all reaches of center field at Sportsman's Park. Moore had very large hands, but wore a small glove with about three-inch fingers. On more than one occasion, he made catches bare-handed—and indeed practiced fielding grounders and fly balls with his bare hands. In addition to its size, center field in St. Louis had a difficult playing surface. With two teams using the field and the blistering summer sun baking it, the outfield surface was unusually hard and often uneven, with patchy grass that caused balls to skip or bounce erratically, making agility and ambidexterity great assets. Moore played the outfield like an infielder and made a point of taking infield practice at every opportunity. "Nobody charged balls from the outfield like Moore," an admiring Enos Slaughter recalled. In addition, Moore had a powerful and accurate arm. "I always thought more about fielding than hitting," Moore recalled. "I didn't take as much pride in hitting as I should have. It seemed I could win more ball games with good fielding."[32]

An All-Star from 1939 through 1942, Moore teamed with Slaughter and Stan Musial to compose, for one season at least, the best outfield in St. Louis history, perhaps the best the National League had ever known, and one of the best in the history of the game. All three outfielders had great speed, great instincts, played their positions aggressively, and except for Musial had exceptionally strong throwing arms. Moreover, they were all good hitters. Two of them—Musial and Slaughter—are now members of baseball's Hall of Fame.

All of the Cardinals' players wanted to win the pennant in 1942, but none more than Moore. He had never played on a pennant winner, although his Redbird teams had come close on three occasions. They had finished second in 1935 when the Chicago Cubs won twenty-one straight games at the end of the season to pass them and capture the flag, second in 1939 when their last-ditch drive to catch Cincinnati fell short, and second yet again in 1941 when injuries to key players led to their narrow defeat by Brooklyn. One of those injuries was to Moore, who was hit in the head with a pitch in late August and was still feeling dizzy from it when the 1942 season began. "About the middle of the year," he recalled, "it just stopped and by the end of '42 I felt wonderful."[33] By the end of the 1942 season, everyone associated with the Cardinals felt wonderful, but no one in St. Louis was yet feeling wonderful as May rolled into June.

CHAPTER 5
The Swoon in June

As May ended, many St. Louisans were most unsettled not by baseball or faraway battles, but by beer—or more precisely, the rationing of beer. The War Production Board announced that the production of bottled beer would be cut by 30 to 40 percent to conserve on materials used in the manufacture of bottle caps. August Busch of Anheuser-Busch quickly assured city residents that beer would continue to flow, but that more of it would now come from the tap than from a bottle. To the city's large German population, for whom going to the corner bar to get a bucket of beer on draught was a familiar trip, the Busch plan was a happy resolution of the matter. Other brewers calmed public fears by promising to increase the volume of beer sold per cap by bottling more of it in quart containers. Meanwhile, local newspapers continued to offer advice on how to deal with wartime shortages. Women were counseled that they would get more mileage from a pair of silk hose if they were careful in laundering them and if they turned stockings inside-out and rolled them on instead of sticking their feet directly into them. They were also advised to carry "stocking glue" to seal any snags before they became runs. As St. Louis women were trying to prevent runs, the St. Louis Cardinals were trying to score some.

~

The Cards had an open date on Monday, June 1, but instead of returning directly to St. Louis from Chicago, they stopped in Rantoul, Illinois, for a game with a military team at the Chanute Field training base for the Army Air Corps. Part of baseball's program to support the war effort called for teams to entertain those in service by using open dates to play exhibition games at military bases. It was an opportunity for the troops to get autographs, have photographs taken, and otherwise fraternize with big-league players. More than four thousand spectators crowded into the small ballpark on the base to watch the Redbirds defeat the service team 10–3. The Cards had one big inning in which they sent eleven men to the plate and scored six times. The big hit was a home run by Ray Hayworth, a veteran catcher who got into only one regular-season game for the Birds in 1942. The little-used Whitey Moore pitched for the major-leaguers and went the distance, giving up eleven hits and being aided greatly by a defense that turned three double plays.

The Cardinals returned to Sportsman's Park the next day to start a series with Boston, while the Dodgers had begun June in Pittsburgh with a 17–3 blasting of the Pirates. After the game, the commandant of the forces from Flatbush announced his "war aims" for the club's western swing: "We plan to reduce these cities one-by-one. We will attempt to raze only war industry targets in Pittsburgh, Chicago, and Cincinnati, but St. Louis will feel the full brunt."[1] The Boston–St. Louis game featured neither the fireworks nor the bombastic oratory of the Dodgers-Pirates engagement. Each team scored a run in the first inning, after which the starting pitchers, Mort Cooper for the Cardinals and Jim Tobin for the Braves, took command to hold the other side scoreless. In the bottom of the sixth, the Redbirds finally broke through, scoring twice after loading the bases without a hit. Slaughter was hit by a pitch leading off. After an out, Harry Walker (playing for Musial, who was still sidelined with an ankle injury) drew a walk. Both runners moved up a base when Hopp bounced out. Braves manager Casey Stengel decided to walk Kurowski intentionally to face the light-hitting Marty Marion. Tobin's knuckleball had frustrated Cards hitters all day, but with the bases loaded, Tobin, perhaps fearful of a wild pitch, threw a fastball that Marion lined into left center for the inning's only hit and its two runs.

The Cardinals added another run in the seventh, while Cooper continued to blank the Braves. But he faded in the ninth with a 4–1 lead, and the Braves rallied to score two runs on a Sibby Sisti triple. With only one out and the tying run on third, Billy Southworth summoned Johnny Beazley, who quickly retired the next two hitters on a fly to short right and a grounder to Marion, saving the 4–3 win for Cooper. It was the thirteenth relief appearance for the rookie righthander, whose cockiness and fastball reminded some of Dizzy Dean. He was a favorite of Branch Rickey, who believed Beazley had a chance to be "one of the great pitchers in the league" in part because of his talents but also because "he is smart and courageous."[2]

The Cards' military relief game was scheduled for June 3 at 5:30 p.m., and as was the practice elsewhere, everyone entering the park—players, umpires, club officials, radio and press, and park workers, as well as fans—paid admission. The Redbirds had put on an exhibition for troops on Monday; now soldiers from Ft. Leonard Wood put on one for them. There was a display of large artillery pieces, jeeps, field telephones, machine guns, and "other instruments of modern war" under the grandstand that fans could inspect as they entered the park. Once in their seats, they watched as eight hundred soldiers went through maneuvers, demonstrating rifle and gas mask training, the use of 30- and 50-caliber machine guns and 60- and 81-millimeter mortars, and concluding with a bayonet charge. Colonel George Ramsey represented the troops at the flag-raising ceremony. The game drew 14,449 spectators. While more tickets than that were sold, Sam Breadon was disappointed in the turnout, saying the front office had put a lot of effort into promoting the event and "expected much better." After expenses, the game raised $13,838.73, more than the $9,948.28 raised by the Browns in their military relief game, but not close to the amount raised by the Dodgers.

The game began in sweltering ninety-degree heat, but if the weather was hot, the Cardinals were not. Lefty Lou Tost, who had shut the Birds out earlier in the year, put an end to their five-game win streak. Murry Dickson started for the home team but could get only one out before departing in the first inning. Boston scored three times in the first, then added another run in the top of the fifth. Tost threw four scoreless innings before the Redbirds scored two runs in their half of the fifth. In the sixth, the Birds loaded the bases with no one out, ending the day for Tost. Johnny Sain took over, and the big righthander promptly slammed the door on the Redbirds, getting out of the inning with no runs scored when the previous day's hero, Marty Marion, hit into a double play. Sain pitched in and out of trouble over the final three innings, but held St. Louis scoreless. The game ended dramatically when, with the bases loaded, Enos Slaughter scorched a line drive that was caught by first baseman Max West and turned into yet another double play. The three-game series did end on a happy note for the Cardinals, as they downed the Braves 6–2 in the finale with Lon Warneke going the distance. The Redbirds scored five times in the second inning against Boston's rookie southpaw William Donovan. Extra-base hits by Walker Cooper and George Kurowski, combined with two Boston errors, did the damage, after which the outcome was never in doubt.

The eastern invasion continued with the arrival of the New York Giants, who had one of their many lefthanders, Dave Koslo, ready to open the four-game series. Once again lefthanded pitching befuddled the Redbirds. They managed only four hits against the little southpaw in a 3–1 loss, their only run coming on a third-inning triple by Jimmy Brown after a walk to Marty Marion. It tied the game at the time, but in the sixth Johnny Mize untied it with a home run off Max Lanier. The Giants added an insurance run in the ninth, but Mize's home run provided the winning margin and sent the fans home grumbling about the off-season trade that sent Big Jawn to New York. Musial was missing from the lineup for the fourth straight game. His replacements, Harry Walker and Coaker Triplett, had gone only three for fourteen in his absence, and Southworth was anxious to have his freshman left fielder back in the lineup.

Heavy rains fell on St. Louis, postponing Saturday's game, and the field on Sunday showed the effects. The outfield was soaked with puddles everywhere, but the scheduled doubleheader was played nonetheless. The Cardinals took the first game 4–1 as their young lefty Howard Pollet bested the Giants' great but aging postsider Carl Hubbell. King Carl threw four no-hit innings, but left after the fifth when the Redbirds got to him for three runs with Pollet's double driving home the first. Hubbell was off to the worst start of his career, his left arm so twisted from throwing screwballs that he could no longer deliver the pitch with its once-devastating effectiveness, leaving him to rely more on curves and canniness. In the second game, Mort Cooper went the distance, shutting out the New Yorkers 2–0 on four hits. Stan Musial made his return to the St. Louis lineup, playing in both games and collecting a single in the second. But the big hit in the nightcap was Johnny Hopp's first home run of the season, which gave Cooper all the runs he needed.

With Monday an open date, the Cardinals could look back on their best two weeks of the season, having gone 6–1 on the road to end May and 4–2 at home to start June. Still, they had gained no ground on the Dodgers. Hopp was now playing first base and Kurowski third on an everyday basis while Brown had replaced Crespi at second. It give the Cardinals' lineup a better mix of left- and righthanded hitters. They nonetheless continued to struggle at the plate, posting a woeful .217 team batting average for the six games in June. The team average would have been worse had not the lower end of the order, the sixth through eighth hitters, averaged over .300 during the home stand. Pitching was carrying the club as it awaited a critical three-game series with the Dodgers set to begin the next day. This was a "must" series for the Cards, Roy Stockton of the *Post-Dispatch* wrote.[3] Vernon Tietjen of the *Star-Times* agreed, seeing it in near apocalyptic terms: the Cardinals were "peeking over the brink of pennant oblivion" where two Dodger wins would "presage the next closest thing to the end of the race."[4]

If St. Louis sportswriters saw the three-game series as crucial to Redbird chances, their counterparts from Brooklyn were no less concerned about what it meant for their team. "The Dodgers are feeling pretty cocky these days with their big lead and their recent five out of six on this Western trip," Tommy Holmes of the *Brooklyn Eagle* wrote. But the Dodgers, he continued, "have been completely unsuccessful in impressing the Cardinals with their championship majesty as they have the rest of the league," having lost three of their four meetings to St. Louis. Billy Southworth had his Dodger killer, lefthander Max Lanier, rested and ready for the first game, with Cards ace Mort Cooper set to follow in the second. No one admired Cooper more than Brooklyn manager Leo Durocher, who told reporters, "There's a real pitcher, a real professional . . . my type of pitcher, too, a guy who really pours it in for nine innings."[5]

Then the rain came. On Tuesday, heavy thunderstorms rolled across the Midwest, drenching St. Louis and forcing postponement of the scheduled night game that was to open the series. On Wednesday, the storm system hung on, soaking an already drenched field and forcing cancellation of the second game scheduled for that afternoon. Thunderstorms with bursts of heavy showers continued through Thursday, wiping out the entire series. The Thursday game had been moved from afternoon to evening in the hope that the rain might pass by then. The Cardinals' schedule called for a Friday night game; had the Thursday game been played, it would have been the first time that night games were played back-to-back in the major leagues. It was a challenge for reporters to explain why the games were canceled because wartime restrictions forbade reporting weather conditions. Cards announcer Dizzy Dean solved the problem by telling listeners to stick their heads out a window and they would know why games were not being played, while one Dodger scribe told readers, "let's just say it wasn't snowing."[6]

The cancellation of the entire Brooklyn series posed major problems in rescheduling the games. There would now be back-to-back doubleheaders in July and a Monday night game added on August 26 for which the Dodgers would have to leave New York after a day game with the Giants to reach St. Louis for a night contest the next day. The washout of the series also delivered "a soporific wallop to the Cardinals' box office," Roy Stockton of the *Post-Dispatch* pointed out. The games had been widely promoted, fans were excited, and the series was expected to draw forty-five to fifty thousand fans. "It would have been the season's most profitable series to date for the Redbirds," Stockton continued, adding that "little can be salvaged from the loss."[7] To the cash-strapped Cardinals' front office, this was a huge setback. To the players, it meant an opportunity lost to play the Dodgers when the Redbirds were playing their best baseball of the season.

In addition to Breadon's financial frustrations, there were reports from New York that the Cardinals, being so far behind the Dodgers, were preparing to sell Mort Cooper to the Giants. Clearly irritated by the rumor, Breadon responded by pointing out that "the Cardinals have beaten Brooklyn three out of four so far," and asked rhetorically, "So why should we give up?" He declared flatly, "We have no intention of selling Cooper's contract to anyone."[8] The Redbirds owner was no doubt annoyed by the reminder of fan displeasure over deals of other stars and by having to defend the team's practice of selling veteran players while not spending to acquire any. He reminded reporters that he and Branch Rickey had given St. Louis a contending team almost every year for the past fifteen seasons, during which time the Cardinals had finished in first place or in the first division more often than any other National League team. Baseball was a hard sell with two major-league teams in the city, Breadon maintained, pointing to the previous season when the Cards, "with a club as attractive as any club in either league," had an attendance of just 640,000 whereas Brooklyn, with a smaller park, had drawn almost twice as many. But the fact that the club had declared two five-dol-lars-per-share dividends after the 1941 season, one of them on the heels of the Mize sale, provoked Stockton of the *Post-Dispatch* to write: "A city that can do for the Cardinals what the area has done since Sam Breadon decided it was a good investment deserves a little more attention to the needs of the seat holders, with a little less worry over the melons of the major stockholders."9

~

On June 1, St. Louisans awoke to headlines reporting a massive night attack by Britain's Royal Air Force on the German city of Cologne, a manufacturing center in the heavily industrial Ruhr Valley. The *St. Louis Post-Dispatch* called it the "most devastating air blow in history," as one thousand planes, coming in waves only seconds apart for ninety minutes, dropped hundreds of tons of incendiary and high-explosive bombs on Germany's fifth-largest city, leaving it engulfed in flames. In a radio address announcing the bombing, Prime Minister Winston Churchill told the British people that this was "a herald of what Germany will receive, city by city, from now on."10 Indeed, the very next night, another one thousand British bombers struck the city of Essen, also in the Ruhr Valley, but this second air attack was not nearly so destructive as the Cologne attack because the bombing was ill planned, so much so that the huge Krupp munitions works went largely untouched. Smaller assaults were made on other industrial cities in the Ruhr Valley over the next several days and weeks, as well as on targets along the coast of France. At the end of the month, another one-thousand-bomber attack was launched against Bremen with mixed results.11

Air warfare was still in its infancy at the start of World War II, still controversial, and these raids were largely experimental, testing aircraft, navigation, bombs, strategy, and tactics. The British wanted to undermine morale, especially among industrial workers, by destroying all German cities of one hundred thousand or more inhabitants. Not everyone agreed with this strategy, and the results varied greatly.12 The United States did not participate in these attacks. The buildup of its Eighth Army Air Force in Britain was moving forward rapidly, but its planes would not be used against European targets until mid-August, and even then only on a limited basis. It would be March 1943 before the combined U.S. and British air forces began their relentless pounding of German cities to gain the air superiority necessary for a land invasion of the continent. Nevertheless, these massive assaults in June 1942 boosted morale in Britain, much as Doolitttle's bombing of Tokyo had done for Americans. American optimism about the war was no doubt boosted as well by the dramatic reports of the British raids that appeared in the U.S. press repeatedly throughout the month.

As the British were bombing German cities, Japanese planes attacked a U.S. naval station at Dutch Harbor, Alaska. Four bombers and fifteen fighter planes inflicted minimal damage, but the attack raised new fears among West Coast residents of a Japanese invasion. The attack on Dutch Harbor proved to be a diversion to draw attention away from Midway Island, which was the real Japanese target. But tensions were heightened even in the Midwest heartland of America. As the Cardinals were preparing for their military benefit game on June 3, the Elmwood Ordinance Plant, forty miles south of Chicago, blew up. The plant was a shell-loading facility, and the explosion occurred on the loading line. The blast, which left fifty-seven dead or missing, was unnerving to thousands of people who lived within the one-hundred-mile radius of the plant in which the blast was felt. FBI investigators rushed to the scene but found no evidence of sabotage.[13]

British bombing of German cities had to share headlines in early June with reports of an attack by Japanese carrier planes on Midway Island in the central Pacific. The huge naval engagement gripped the attention of the nation for several days until on June 7 the announcement came that the Japanese had broken off the battle and were withdrawing their forces. It was a great and unequivocal victory for the United States. Japan had committed much of its navy to the intended invasion of Midway, including four of the carriers used at Pearl Harbor, a force that was "the largest assemblage of seapower ever to sail under the Japanese flag, the biggest yet seen in the Pacific and the most powerful in all history."[14] The Japanese hoped once again that the element of surprise would be on their side, but this time U.S. intelligence had broken the Japanese naval code and knew of the attack in advance. The United States marshaled its forces and lay in wait for the Japanese. In the ensuing battle, good fortune as well as surprise was on its side when, after a series of ineffectual assaults, American dive bombers discovered the enemy flotilla while the Japanese were reloading their planes. In five minutes three of the Japanese carriers were sunk, and a few hours later U.S. planes found and sank the fourth. Japanese losses were massive. Among the U.S. losses was the carrier Yorktown, which was itself part of the surprise because the Japanese thought it had been sunk in the battle of the Coral Sea.[15]

The defeat of the Japanese at Midway, David Kennedy concludes, "had done nothing less than turn the tide of the Pacific war" and "put the Imperial Japanese Navy at a disadvantage from which it never recovered."[16] The success delighted the usually gruff Admiral Ernest King, chief of American naval operations, who noted that it was the first decisive Japanese naval defeat since 1592. He may not have been so delighted to read the *New York Times* report of the battle, which gave credit to the Army Air Force, not to the Navy.[17] The news from Midway lifted American spirits more than anything in the six months since Pearl Harbor. It blocked Japanese expansion to the east, but undaunted, Japan renewed efforts to capture Port Moresby to the south, this time by land, and also targeted the

Solomon Islands in a continuing effort to strengthen its defensive perimeter. The Japanese also continued to advance in China as well, but after threatening to invade India, which caused the British to commit massive reinforcements of men and weapons to its defense, they chose instead to secure what they already held.

In Europe, there was a lull in the fighting on the Russian front in May, but there was no lull in North Africa. Instead, there was a massive buildup of troops and equipment as both sides prepared for a battle, one observer noted, "on a scale that had never been seen in the desert before." In the first week of June, German and Italian units commanded by Erwin Rommel launched their offensive; by the second week, they had split the British defenses and were pressing forward, inflicting heavy casualties. On June 20, Rommel's Afrika Korps captured the strategic fortress of Tobruk and with it a vast store of arms, equipment, and fuel. Australian journalist Alan Moorehead, embedded with the Allied forces, called it "the blackest night they had faced in more than two years of fighting."[18] The British retreat continued into Egypt, and by month's end there was panic in the cities of Alexandria and Cairo over their prospective capture by Axis forces.

$\sim$

The Cardinals put whatever disappointment they felt about the Dodgers series behind them as they prepared to finish their home stand against the lowly Philadelphia Phillies, who were already well on their way to losing 109 games in 1942. Three days of rain following an open date had completely disrupted Southworth's pitching plans, such as they were. The Redbirds did not have a set rotation, in part because Ernie White and Howard Pollet had struggled with arm ailments on and off all season. Only Mort Cooper started on a regular basis every fifth day; otherwise, Southworth juggled Warneke, Lanier, Gumbert, and occasionally Beazley, Dickson, and even Krist with Pollet and White when the latter were able to pitch.[19] The manager opted for Cooper to open the Philadelphia series, and big Mort responded with a five-hit, one-run complete game that the Redbirds won 2–1. Tommy Hughes held the Cards to only six hits, but one of them was a first-inning triple by Slaughter to drive home Terry Moore, after which Slaughter scored the second run on an infield out. The Phillies' only run came in the fourth when, with a man on first, Danny Litwhiler drove a ball into left center on which Musial, attempting to make the catch, slipped on the wet turf and got just enough of his glove on the ball to deflect it past Moore, who was backing up the play. By the time the ball was retrieved, the runner had scored. In the fourth the game was held up for forty minutes as rain paid another visit to the already waterlogged field at Sportsman's Park, but play resumed with Cooper returning to the mound to shut down the Phils without allowing a runner past first.

It was Cooper's seventh win of the year. The righthander was seen by some as a "surgical gift" to the team after his arm operation the previous year to remove bone chips from his right elbow that made throwing his fastball and especial-ly his curve very painful. He chewed aspirin on the mound to dull the pain, a practice he continued even after the surgery. The Cardinals' team doctor, Robert Hyland, performed the operation, and Cooper returned to action in September. Surgery on pitchers' arms was not commonplace in the early 1940s.[20] Hyland was generally reluctant to reach for the scalpel, believing that most pitchers' problems were in their heads rather than their arms. In his view, the "chief reason" for arm problems was that pitchers got "too much attention"—they were "coddled," spent too much time on the trainer's table, and got too much rest. He also thought that pitchers fooled around with too many "trick" pitches, some of which, like Carl Hubbell's screwball, put great strain on the arm. He also knew that advances in medical science had recognized several different afflictions, once grouped simply as a "sore arm," for which there were specific causes and treatments other than surgery.[21]

The rain, which had delayed completion of Friday's game, refused to go away, continuing into Saturday and forcing postponement of the game that day. The Cardinals must have felt something like Joe Btfsplk in the popular comic strip *Li'l Abner* who was continuously under a rain cloud, but at last clear weather returned on Sunday, enabling the Cards to wrap up their home stand by sweep-ing the Phillies in a doubleheader. Lon Warneke notched his fifth win in the first game with a six-hit, route-going performance, while Stan Musial led the eleven-hit Cardinals' attack with two singles and a double, driving in two of the nine Redbird runs. The only Philly run came on a fourth-inning home run by former Cardinal Ernie Koy. Walker, Slaughter, and Brown each had a stolen base for St. Louis, which was unusual for the fleet-footed Cards. For all their speed, the Cardinals did not attempt to steal that often, preferring instead to use their quickness on the base paths to put pressure on the defense by going from first to third or from second to home on balls hit to shallow parts of the outfield or that were not fielded cleanly by infielders. Billy Southworth, who doubled as third-base coach as was then the custom, also liked to use the bunt as a tactical weapon, not merely to sacrifice runners into scoring position but also for base hits and squeeze plays.[22] The quickness and speed of the team was an asset on defense as well, especially in the outfield where Musial, Moore, Slaughter, and Harry Walker regularly delighted fans with sensational catches after long runs.

The Phils drew first blood in the second game of the Sunday twin bill when Danny Litwhiler singled home two runs in the first. The Redbirds, however, came back to score five times in their half of the inning, with the big hit a home run by first baseman Johnny Hopp. Gumbert started for the Cardinals, and after the first inning had Philly hitters beating the ball into the dirt all afternoon. St. Louis infielders had seventeen assists. After the sixth, Handsome Harry weak-ened, giving up single runs in the seventh and eighth. He turned mound duties over to Howard Krist in the ninth, who was unable to hold the lead as the Phils tied the contest. In the bottom of the ninth, with the help of an error by first baseman Nick Etten, the Cardinals loaded the bases. With one out, Slaughter smacked a sharp grounder to Etten, who fielded it cleanly and won the race to first but forgot that it was only the second out of the inning. Realizing his mistake, Etten threw frantically to the plate but too late as Marion dashed across with the winning run. It was a day that Etten, one of his team's best hitters, would want to forget. In the eighth with one on, one out, and the Phillies two runs behind, he inexplicably bunted and was thrown out easily.

Following their three-game sweep of the Phillies, the Cardinals left on their second swing through the East, beginning with two games against the Giants, followed by five in Brooklyn with the Dodgers. Pollet took the mound to face Carl Hubbell in the series opener against the Giants. It was a back-and-forth contest: the Cards went ahead with one run in the third; the Giants tied it with one in the fourth. Both teams scored in the sixth, the Giants' run coming on a solo home run by Johnny Mize. A weary Pollet left in the sixth with one out as Johnny Beazley took over to shut down any further scoring. Beazley's free-wheeling fastball had already marked him as one of the league's genuine power pitchers, and he had emerged as Southworth's favorite late-inning reliever. Hubbell continued to pitch well into the tenth, when Enos Slaughter, who had tripled earlier, lifted a home run into the short right-field stands at the Polo Grounds to put the Redbirds ahead by one. Beazley then closed out the Giants in the bottom half of the inning for a 4–3 win. Marty Marion, whose bat was warming up with the approach of summer, came through twice in the clutch, once with a double and again with a long sacrifice fly, knocking in a pair of runs, while George Kurowski had his fifth consecutive two-hit game.

St. Louis continued its winning ways the next day behind Mort Cooper, who won his eighth straight game, striking out eight and blanking Mel Ott's crew on five hits. Kurowski provided the only runs Cooper would need with his first major-league home run. The Redbirds were now riding the crest of a seven-game winning streak in which their starting pitchers had turned in five complete games, three of them shutouts. The team was also hitting better, led by the bottom of the batting order, the seventh- and eighth-place hitters, Kurowski at .375 in the seven games and Marty Marion even better at .411. As they headed for Ebbets Field, the Birds had pulled to within four and a half games of the front-running Dodgers, and they hoped now to spring their own Midway (midseason) surprise on dem Bums of Brooklyn. This required beating a team that boasted four of the league's top six hitters. Pete Reiser, who had won the batting title as a rookie in 1941, was again leading the league with a .363 mark, followed by Joe Medwick at .330 and looking every bit as good as he had in the late 1930s with the Cardinals. Mickey Owen at .310 and Dixie Walker at .308 were fifth and sixth among the league's top hitters. The Cardinals, meanwhile, had no .300 hitters.

～

After a doubleheader loss to the Cincinnati Reds on May 24, Billy Southworth had shaken up his starting infield, installing George Kurowski at third and moving Jimmy Brown to second. A few games later, Johnny Hopp took over at first. The team almost magically began to play better ball. From their May 25 win against the Cubs through their June 16–17 sweep of the Giants, the Cardinals had won fifteen and lost only three and were beginning to look like the team that Rickey and Southworth had envisioned in spring training. The moves sent Frank Crespi and Ray Sanders to the bench. A skilled shortstop and second baseman, Crespi was an ideal utility infielder who proved his value in that role when Brown was out for several games with an injury. The highly touted Sanders, projected as Mize's replacement at first base, had struggled at the plate and shown little power. A fastball hitter, Sanders's batting average dwindled against all the breaking-ball lefties and soft-throwing righties the team had faced.

A strong infield defense was critical to a team whose pitchers relied on a lot of ground-ball outs, and the Redbird infield in 1942 was a good one. At shortstop, Marty Marion was the cornerstone. "All he has to do is throw his glove on the diamond," Braves manager Casey Stengel said, "and Breadon's got an infield." Marion had sure hands, expansive range, good leaping ability, and a strong, accurate arm. He made everything about fielding look easy. "I've looked at a lot of shortstops in my day," the venerable Connie Mack opined, "but that fellow is the best I've seen." Baseball writers agreed in a 1950 survey, ranking Marion second only to Honus Wagner, with whom he was most often compared, as the best shortstop in the first half of the twentieth century. As for his contemporaries in both leagues, New York sportswriter Red Smith concluded, "none of them could make the plays that Marion could make at shortstop."[23] Marion's defensive prowess earned him many nicknames: Burt Shotton dubbed him "Slats" after a comic-strip character who, like Marion, was tall and skinny; Frankie Frisch labeled him "the octopus" because he was all arms and legs and sucked up so many ground balls; Bill Dickey said he was a "flying ghost" who materialized from nowhere to make a play; others called him the "vacuum cleaner" and the "grounds keeper," but the nickname Marion liked best was "Mr. Shortstop."[24] His defensive play was all the more remarkable in that the Sportsman's Park infield was considered the worst in the National League. It was "hard as a rock," Marion remembered. "The ball came at you like a rocket, and you never knew which way it was going to bounce."[25]

Born in South Carolina, Marion was a descendant of Francis Marion, the "Swamp Fox" of Revolutionary War fame. He attended Georgia Tech for one year before signing with the Cardinals in 1936 and broke into the majors in 1940 as the Redbirds' everyday shortstop, hitting .278 in 125 games. A "gap hitter," Marion stroked line drives between the outfielders often enough in 1942 to lead the major leagues with thirty-eight doubles. Marion made himself into a good situational hitter. An accomplished bunter with excellent speed, he became a reliable hit-and-run man who could shoot the ball to the right side of the diamond behind a base runner going from first to second. He was also a tough out in the clutch. "I would bear down when a hit meant something," Marion recalled, acknowledging that he did not do this at other times. He was popular with his teammates, especially the pitchers. Mort Cooper credited Marion with more saves than anyone else on the team because he "turns sure hits into double plays." He was also popular with the press, prompting Marion to remark, "You've got to be a really no-good guy for the press to dislike you."[26]

That Marion was a major-leaguer at all was something of a medical miracle. One of his legs was shorter than the other due to a childhood accident in which he jumped off a high embankment, landed wrong, and broke his right leg so severely that part of the bone was exposed. Doctors set the leg, but a few weeks later realized it was an inch and a half shorter than the left one. Surgeons operated to correct the problem and, as Marion recalls, his leg was "wired together," sewn up with "forty-eight stitches in the thing."[27] He was on crutches for almost a year but recovered to play high school baseball even though one leg remained a bit shorter than the other. Marion's condition resulted in a 4F classification that kept him out of the armed services in World War II, but it did not affect his ability to play baseball, though eventually it led to back problems that shortened his career.[28]

The real medical miracle on the ball club, however, was third baseman George Kurowski. He had grown up in Reading, Pennsylvania, the opposite end of the Keystone State from Donora, the hometown of his teammate, fellow rookie, and fellow Pole Stan Musial. As a child Kurowski suffered a serious injury to his right arm. The arm was treated improperly, leading to a severe case of osteomyelitis. To save the arm, surgeons removed three inches of bone, leaving a gap in the bone that remained. Cardinal physician Robert Hyland, whose surgery saved the career of Mort Cooper, was amazed that Kurowski could throw a baseball or swing a bat with authority, much less play baseball at the major-league level. "I have seen the arms of many ball players in my day," Hyland said, but "nothing to compare with this." The Redbirds' doctor called Kurowski a gift to medical science as well as to the Cardinals, adding that he regularly carried X-rays of Kurowski's arm to show other physicians, who were always amazed that its owner was a major-league ballplayer.[29]

The removal of bone made Kurowski's right arm shorter than his left, and he carried it, Marty Marion said, like the hind leg of a dog. Signed by the Redbirds in 1937, Kurowski made it to the big leagues for five games at the end of the 1941 season, then won a full-time job in 1942. His role leaving spring training was to be a reserve infielder who could play second as well as third base. At 5'11" and 190 pounds, Kurowski had a stocky build with heavy thighs and legs, but he had good quickness, was sure-handed, and, playing next to Marion at shortstop, strengthened the left side of the Cards' infield defense. "Kurowski is all over the left side of the infield on defense," New York sportswriter Frank Graham observed, adding that he "throws hard, slides on his face [and] takes a terrific swing at the ball."[30] He was an aggressive hitter who often said he got three strikes and intended to use them all. In the batter's box, Kurowski, called "Whitey" because of his light blond hair, stood almost on top of the plate, hanging over it slightly, and thus presented an inviting target for any pitcher. But Musial noted that getting knocked down only made Kurowski a better hitter: "He really would wake up when aroused."[31] He swung a 33-ounce, 34½-inch bat that he gripped at the knob, saying this gave him better control. "I was pretty much a pull hitter early in my career," Kurowski said. "The injury to my arm made me turn my right wrist over. Much of the time I couldn't buy a base hit to right field."[32] He "bought" a lot of them in the other direction, including some of the most memorable of the 1942 season.

At thirty-two, second baseman Jimmy Brown was more than two years older than any other position player on the 1942 Cardinals. Only Terry Moore had been with the Cardinals longer than the diminutive 5'8½" 165-pound infielder. A native of North Carolina, Brown came from a large farming family with five brothers and three sisters, and he continued to farm in the off-season on thirty acres near Jamestown, North Carolina, where he grew tobacco, corn, and peanuts. Brown had attended what is now North Carolina State University, where he was discovered by Frank Rickey, brother of the Cards' general manager, who signed him to a St. Louis contract in 1933. In his five years with the Redbirds, the blue-eyed Brown had played every infield position except first base, having been the team's regular second baseman in 1937, its regular shortstop in 1939, and its regular third baseman in 1941, dividing time between these positions in his other two years. In shifting him from third to second, Southworth was simply moving him from one familiar position to another. Brown did not possess Frank Crespi's defensive skills at second base, especially in making the pivot on double plays, but he was very fast, covered a lot of ground, and had a strong arm.

A switch-hitter, Brown brought a lifetime .292 batting average into the 1942 season. He was the leadoff hitter for the team despite the fact that he rarely drew a walk and consequently had a low on-base percentage. At the same time, he was a good clutch hitter, finishing third on the 1942 team in runs batted in with seventy-one, one fewer than Stan Musial, who finished second behind Slaughter's ninety-eight. He was popular with the other players, who regarded him as a great teammate. Max Lanier said that Brown was the player who "did most to inspire his team."[33] An aggressive base runner, fearless in the way he played, Brown was admired by Pittsburgh manager and old Gas Houser Frankie Frisch, who called him "a great fellow to have on your ball club . . . the kind of fellow who loves to win, will break his neck trying and has no use for anybody who doesn't feel the same way he does." There is no evidence that Brown ever broke his neck, but he did have a plate in his skull that came from a baseball accident. Brown struggled at the plate in 1942, posting the lowest batting average of his career at .256, but Branch Rickey paid him the ultimate tribute after the season, saying, "The Cardinals could not have won without Brown. He contributes his share to the team and then so very much more."[34]

First baseman Johnny Hopp came from an athletic German immigrant family. He had been a football and track star at Hastings College, while his brother Harry was a halfback at the University of Nebraska and played professionally with the Detroit Lions. Hopp was a Southworth favorite. Both were from Nebraska, but it was Hopp's versatility and hell-for-leather style of play that his manager most admired, perhaps because it reminded him of himself. Hopp was also popular with his teammates, who called him "Cotney" because of his cotton-colored hair, but sportswriters preferred the nickname "Hippity" for reasons of alliteration as well as Hopp's rabbit-like quickness. Early in the season, he played behind smooth-fielding rookie Ray Sanders at first base. Handsome, easygoing, and a bit of a comic, Sanders was well-liked by his teammates, who called him "Gabe" for his resemblance to movie star Clark Gable. But when Sanders did not hit as expected, Hopp took over.

More than adequate defensively at first, though lacking Sanders's grace, Hopp was a throwback to the Gas House Gang in his rough-and-ready approach to the game, challenging defenders, flying around the bases, and belly-sliding into them. He came to the major leagues full-time in 1940 and his versatility had been a godsend in 1941, when almost every Cardinal starter was injured and out of action for extended periods. Hopp, who was lefthanded, alternated between first base and all outfield positions and hit over .300 in 134 games. A speedster, the fleetest of the fleet Cardinals, Hopp's daring style of play was evident in the 1941 season when he scored from first on a single in one game and from second on an infield out in another. He struggled in the first half of 1942, playing irregularly, due in part to injuries, but from July on he was an everyday player and had an increasingly larger role in the team's success.

Frank Crespi had been the regular second baseman for the 1941 Cardinals, when he paired with Marty Marion to be the premier keystone combination in the league. No one made the pivot on the double play better than Crespi. A St. Louis native, he had dark eyes and a glowering countenance that hid a mirthful spirit. But Crespi brought a combative and fiery spirit to the game and was an ideal utility infielder. He had large hands that seemed to envelop anything close to him, and he always fielded balls low and very close to the ground where only creepy, crawly things were to be found, which led to the nickname "Creepy." [35] His large hands also enabled him to use a thick-handled bat unlike any other employed by a Redbird, with a larger surface that was better for hitting singles than home runs.

~

It was a happy and confident flock of Redbirds that left Gotham for Flatbush to battle the Dodgers in a five-game weekend series. The Cardinals were riding a hot streak and had moved closer to the league leaders. They hoped to make the race much closer before they left the unfriendly confines of Ebbets Field. They knew the challenge before them. The Dodgers had become the scourge of the National League. They were a good, smart, veteran team that knew all the tricks and played hard. Many in the National League said "too hard": they were said to be a dirty team. More and more opponents came to hate the Dodgers for their overly aggressive and often dangerous style of play: pitchers regularly threw high and tight near a batter's head to "loosen 'em up" and back them off the plate; runners regularly went high and hard into bases with spikes glistening to intimidate defenders. "If I had a ball club as good as Durocher's," Braves manager Stengel said, "I wouldn't throw at a ball club as bad as mine."[36] The Dodgers were also hated for their cockiness, their swagger, their arguing over every umpire's decision that went against them, and their loud, crude, relentless, and threatening bench jockeying. While the Dodgers wanted to beat everyone, there was no team they wanted to beat more than the St. Louis Cardinals.

The series opener was set to begin at 7 p.m. in daylight and end under the lights in what Larry MacPhail called a "twight" game, neither a twilight nor a night game.[37] It started on a warm family note with a pregame ceremony in which Dodger first baseman Dolph Camilli was named the outstanding father in sports for 1942. The father of five, Camilli was presented with a gold medal by Jean Cagney of Brooklyn, sister of film star Jimmy Cagney. When the game began, lefty Larry French, who had beaten the Cards earlier in the season, took the mound for the Dodgers, opposed by St. Louis southpaw Max Lanier, who owned one of the Redbird wins over Brooklyn. St. Louis struck quickly, scoring in the second inning on a double by Walker Cooper and a triple by Coaker Triplett, but the Cards' left fielder was stranded at third when neither Kurowski nor Hopp could bring him home. The Cardinals added another run in the third on successive singles by Lanier, Terry Moore, and Enos Slaughter. But the Dodgers came right back to score in their half of the third on singles by Mickey Owen, Pee Wee Reese, and Arky Vaughan.

In the bottom of the sixth, the contest turned into a "brawl" game when Joe Medwick, who led off with a walk, tried to advance to second on a short passed ball but was gunned down by Walker Cooper. Medwick was easily out yet slid hard into Marty Marion with spikes ominously high. Marion knocked his legs down with his glove, and the two exchanged unpleasantries that were followed quickly by punches. Second baseman Frank Crespi jumped into the fracas, tackling Medwick, taking him to the ground, where Crespi, joined by Johnny Hopp, began to pummel the Dodgers' left fielder. Father of the Year Camilli, who was at the plate when the free-for-all began, raced to second base and dove on top of Crespi. Dixie Walker, in the on-deck circle as the next hitter, followed Camilli, joining the fray by charging headlong into Kurowski, who came away with a black eye. Players from both benches poured onto the field and punches began to be thrown indiscriminantly but with little effect. The umpires moved quickly to separate the combatants, most of whom were by now simply shuffling around the scene throwing nothing more harmful than menacing looks at one another. Calm was restored and the field finally cleared after about twenty minutes. Medwick and Crespi were ejected and later fined twenty-five dollars each by the league. Dixie Walker had to be helped to the dugout, having injured his left ankle. His hand was also "tenderly caressing his jaw," which had been the recipient of a well-directed fist.[38]

Joe Medwick was among those Dodgers who wanted most to beat the Cardinals. He had come up through Branch Rickey's farm system, joining the Redbirds for twenty-six games at the end of the 1932 season and then starring for them over the next seven years. A powerful righthanded hitter in the tradition of Rogers Hornsby, he also shared many of the Rajah's personality traits, including a preoccupation with his own performance. Popular with the fans, Medwick was less popular with his teammates. Don Gutteridge, who joined the Cardinals in 1936, thought Medwick had a "sour disposition," was a "bit of an egotist," and "not a very likable guy."[39] But he could hit. He led the league in doubles and runs batted in for three consecutive years from 1936 through 1938 and led in hitting and home runs as well in 1937, winning the Triple Crown, a feat no National Leaguer has accomplished since. The press had several (printable) nicknames for Medwick: "Muscles," which he rather liked, for his physique; "Ducky," which he disliked, for the way he walked and ran; and "Ducky Wucky," the favorite of many sportswriters, which he detested. Medwick's teammates rarely used any of these nicknames. He was traded to the Dodgers in June 1940, reuniting him with his former Cardinal teammate Durocher, both of whom harbored resentment over having been, in their view, unceremoniously banished from Bird land. A few weeks after the trade, Medwick was hit in the head with a pitch by Cards pitcher Bob Bowman, an act that Dodger president Larry MacPhail thought was premeditated. MacPhail threatened legal action against Bowman. Medwick recovered physically, but seemed mentally wary of inside pitches thereafter and was not the same hitter he had been. In June 1942, however, he was on a hitting tear and looked like the Medwick of old.

When the game resumed, Camilli returned to the plate and drew a walk. Lanier got a second out, but Billy Herman and Mickey Owen singled to tie the score. Beazley took over and retired the Dodgers without further scoring, then shut them out in the seventh as well. But in the bottom of the eighth, with one out, Camilli drew another free pass to first and went to third on a single by Johnny Rizzo, who had replaced the injured Walker. Herman followed with a perfectly placed squeeze bunt that Beazley fielded, but not in time to get either Camilli scoring from third or Herman racing to first. The Dodgers led by one. A bad situation became worse when French lined a double over the head of right fielder Enos Slaughter to drive Rizzo and Herman home with two more runs. French returned to his pitching duties in the top of the ninth and retired the Redbirds for a 5–2 Brooklyn win. The Cardinals had managed only eight hits off the Dodger southpaw, two of them by Lanier. It was not the start to the series for which St. Louis had hoped, as they were now five and a half games behind Brooklyn.

The next day, the Cardinals and Dodgers played a tranquil game devoid of fisticuffs, made more peaceful perhaps by a Ladies Day crowd that included more than ten thousand of the reputedly gentler sex. The ladies, however, were full-throated and not so gentle in voicing their conviction that it was the Cardinals who were to blame for the fight that put one of their favorites, Dixie Walker, on the bench nursing his wounds. Billy Southworth chose Ernie White, making his first start since his injury in late May, to face Brooklyn ace Whitlow Wyatt. Southworth also juggled his lineup to get more lefthanded hitters into the game, starting Harry Walker in center instead of Moore and Ken O'Dea behind the plate rather than Cooper. The Dodgers drew first blood in the otherwise bloodless contest, scoring twice in the second inning when Johnny Rizzo, a Cardinal reject, smacked a two-run homer into the left-field seats. In the fourth, Pete Reiser led off with a single to center but went all the way to third base when Walker threw wildly in returning the ball to the infield. With no one out and a runner on third, White bore down to strike out Medwick and Camilli, then got a first strike on Rizzo. As a southpaw, with his back to third base, White was concentrating on the hitter when Reiser took off for home and slid safely across with a clean steal for a third Brooklyn run. White struck out Rizzo to end the inning.

The Cardinals finally got to Wyatt for a run in the sixth on a Walker double and Slaughter single, but the Dodgers came back with one of their own in the eighth on a safe bunt by Owen, a sacrifice by Wyatt, and a single by Arky Vaughan. White pitched well in a losing effort, working through seven innings and giving up seven hits before leaving for a pinch hitter in the eighth. Gumbert took over to hold Brooklyn scoreless in the bottom of the eighth. In the ninth, the Redbirds rallied as Slaughter led off with a single and Musial followed with a double. Wyatt got the next hitter out with no advance by the runners, but O'Dea lifted an outfield fly deep enough to score Slaughter, and Jimmy Brown kept the game going with a single to score Musial. But George Kurowski, who entered the game in the eighth after Marion was lifted for a pinch hitter, made the last out by becoming Wyatt's sixth strikeout victim. It was Wyatt's seventh win and moved Brooklyn six and a half games ahead of St. Louis.

Southworth sent the veteran Lon Warneke to the hill for the third game to face nine-game winner Curt Davis. The Cardinals jumped on Davis quickly for two runs in the second inning on a double to center by Brown, a double to right by Marion, and a single to right by Crespi. The Dodgers responded in their half of the second. With one out, Camilli walked and Augie Galan lined a single to center, sending Camilli to third. Billy Herman bounced sharply to Warneke, who tried to catch Camilli in a rundown between third base and home, but Camilli managed to get back to third and everyone was safe. With the bases loaded, catcher Mickey Owen promptly shot a single to center to tie the score. The Cards went up again by two in the third. With one out, Musial sliced a double just inside the left-field foul line. After a second out, the inning was extended when Vaughan fumbled a grounder from Ray Sanders for an error. Brown followed with a booming double to left, scoring both Musial and Sanders. But in the fifth, Brooklyn got consecutive singles from Reese, Vaughan, Reiser, and Medwick to plate two runs and tie the score once more.

Brooklyn broke the game open in the sixth when Herman led off with a two-base hit to right. Owen followed with a drive to right that Slaughter, after a long run, dropped for an error, putting runners on second and third. That was it for Warneke, who handed the ball over to Harry Gumbert with nobody out. Gumbert fared no better. Dodger pitcher Hugh Casey, who had taken over for Davis in the third, singled up the middle, driving in both runners. Reese followed with another single to center. Vaughan bounced out, with both runners advancing. Pete Reiser was walked intentionally to fill the bases, bringing the hot-hitting Medwick to the plate. "Muscles" smacked Gumbert's first pitch into center, bringing home two more runs, but Reiser was cut down trying to advance to third on a strong throw by center fielder Terry Moore. Brooklyn had taken an 8–4 lead. The Dodgers' assault continued against Redbird relievers Howard Krist and Murry Dickson as Brooklyn scored single runs in the seventh and eighth while the Cardinals could do nothing against the Mighty Casey, who turned in his best effort of the season. The Redbirds were now seven and a half games behind.

In three days, the Cardinals' dreams of gaining significant ground on the Dodgers had been shattered. As they prepared for the Sunday doubleheader, all the Cards could hope for was to recover some of the ground lost in the first three games of the series. Their ace Mort Cooper took the ball in the opener, and on a scorching-hot day he chilled Brooklyn's bats, throwing a five-hit shutout for his ninth win of the season. Cardinal batsmen were as hot as the day as they hammered two rookies, Ed Head and Les Webber, and veteran Lynwood "Schoolboy" Rowe for eleven runs on fourteen hits, six of them for extra bases. Sanders had two of the hits, one a round-tripper, and drove in three runs; Musial drove in two with a home run and a triple; and even light-hitting Frank Crespi chipped in with his first extra-base hit of the year, a double that drove home two runs. In the nightcap, fortunes reversed as Kirby Higbe pitched the Dodgers to their fourth win in the five-game set, besting the Cardinals and Howard Pollet 5–2. The Redbirds led off the scoring on third-inning singles by Crespi, Slaughter, and Musial, but the Dodgers tied the game in the fourth on a Medwick single following a Reiser double. The Dodgers sent Pollet to the showers in the sixth when they took advantage of a Crespi error and some timely hitting to score three times. As the day ended, the disappointed Cardinals left the field to the sad strains of "St. Louis Blues" played by Ebbets Field organist Gladys Gooding, herself a native of St. Louis.

Having arrived in Brooklyn with a seven-game winning streak and trailing the Dodgers by only four and a half games, St. Louis departed seven and a half games out of first place. Almost gleefully, John Kiernan of the *New York Times* wrote, "Durocher's Dandies beat the Cardinals four out of five, which was a rude shock to Little Billy Southworth and his hired hands in St. Louis uniforms . . . So instead of hauling the Dodgers back," he continued, "the Cardinals themselves were knocked down and trodden upon and the strange situation today is that the Dodgers have a larger lead in the National League than the Yankees have in the American League."[40] Many thought the Dodgers' lead would prove insurmountable. For more than a decade, National League races had been dogfights, hotly contested from start to finish. Brooklyn's lead was the largest any team had enjoyed over that period. The ever-upbeat Southworth conceded that the challenge before "his boys" was now greater, but tried to sound optimistic, noting that the Redbirds were off to play the slumping Braves and the futile Phillies while the Dodgers had to face the more powerful western teams. Tommy Holmes of the *Brooklyn Eagle* also cautioned against a rush to judgment. "St. Louis clubs traditionally are hungry ball clubs and the current team is one of the hungriest," Holmes reminded readers. "Branch Rickey thinks that's the way ball clubs ought to be, that hungry athletes are capable of overcoming tremendous odds through hustle born of sheer desperation." "There is enough behind that theory of 'the Brain,'" he concluded, "to make it likely that the Cards will be back in the fight again."[41]

CHAPTER 6

Fireworks in July

The Cardinals had a day off following the series with the Dodgers, and as they headed north to Beantown to engage Casey Stengel's Braves, pundits were busy writing them out of the pennant race. "The Brooklyn Dodgers have erased virtually all question of their retaining the National League pennant," an Associated Press writer asserted, adding that the only thing to be decided was which Dodger would win the league's Most Valuable Player award.[1] The Redbirds were also subjected to the all-too-familiar explanation of their plight: the trade of Johnny Mize. Paul Scheffels of the United Press, purporting to speak for his fellow scribes, wrote it was "generally acknowledged" that the trade of Mize would most likely cost St. Louis the pennant since the team had "failed to click for one big reason—lack of long-range punch."[2] Sid Keener of the *Star-Times* contrasted the 1942 productivity of Big Jawn, who had a .320 batting average, eleven home runs, and fifty-three runs batted in, to that of Sanders and Hopp, who combined were hitting .230 with seven home runs and thirty-two RBIs. Keener attributed the trade to Mize's failure to get along with Southworth. Mize had gained weight, was not in top shape, and had tailed off offensively and defensively. Hopp, on the other hand, had impressed his manager in 1941 with his hustling play and a .303 batting average.[3]

The Monday open date was followed by a rainout on Tuesday, forcing the travel-weary Redbirds to play a midweek doubleheader with the Braves on Wednesday. They lost both games. "The Cardinals hopes of reducing the Dodgers first place margin," the *Sporting News* reported in vivid wartime imagery, "were bombed, machine-gunned and torpedoed when the Braves administered a double setback to the Redbirds."[4] It might have added that the Cardinals largely surrendered in the opener as their three pitchers—Gumbert, Krist, and Dickson—handed Boston ten free passes to first base. Meanwhile, St. Louis batsmen touched the Braves' soft-tossing knuckleballer Jim Tobin for eleven hits but only two runs. Ken

O'Dea's two-run homer in the seventh was the only clutch hit a Cardinal delivered, and Murry Dickson promptly gave the runs back in the bottom half of the
inning as the Redbirds went on to lose 6–2. In the nightcap, Ernie White pitched
well enough to win, whiffing five, walking one, and giving up only six hits. Two of
the hits were bunts, but two others were home runs, a two-run blast in the fourth
by Frank Demaree and a solo shot in the eighth by Chet Ross. Southpaw Willard
Donovan baffled St. Louis hitters, retiring the first fourteen in a row before Sanders singled with two out in the fifth. In the end, the Birds managed only five hits
off the rookie hurler and did not score until the ninth as the Braves prevailed 3–1.
It was the Cardinals' thirteenth loss to a lefthander.

There were dark skies and drizzling rain in Boston the next day, but the game
was played despite the inclement weather. It was the Braves' Army-Navy relief
game, and the crowd of 25,093 was treated to a gigantic display of military
personnel and materiel, as well as to a stirring air spectacle. Whatever warlike
tendencies the Braves themselves may have harbored were quickly subdued by
Mort Cooper, who went into the breach once more for the Redbirds and tossed
a two-hit shutout. Cooper carried a no-hitter into the sixth, when Braves left
fielder Ross ducked to avoid an inside pitch and had the ball hit his bat, loop
toward right field, and fall between Crespi racing out from second and Slaughter charging in from right. The other hit was also accidental: Ernie Lombardi
tried to check his swing, could not, and hit the ball fair just beyond the infield.
Cooper had never been more dominant, posting his tenth win and running his
streak of scoreless innings to thirty-two. The strapping righthander had given up
only one run in his last five games, and it seemed that he alone was keeping the
Cardinals' pennant hopes alive. The Cards managed only eight hits off a trio of
Boston pitchers, but bunched several to score three times in the third, then added
another to win 4–0. When the game was over, the Braves auctioned off home
plate for two hundred dollars to add to the military relief fund. "They can't be
accused of selling damaged goods," one fan quipped, "the Braves never stepped
on it."[5]

The Cardinals' brother battery, Mort and Walker Cooper, came into its own
in 1942. The two Missourians were products of the St. Louis farm system, Mort
arriving at the end of the 1938 season and Walker late in 1940. Mort had been
in the starting rotation since 1939 and seemed on the cusp of stardom in 1941
until he was felled in June by elbow surgery.[6] At 6'2"and more than two hundred
pounds, the hard-throwing righthander was an imposing figure on the mound
and could blow his fastball by most hitters. He experimented with various
off-speed pitches, including a screwball, then in 1941 developed a forkball to go
with his bread-and-butter fastball and an assortment of curves he could throw at
different speeds. He could be temperamental, was a sharpshooter with a rifle, was
quite superstitious, and for a time had a pet alligator named Elmer. But he was a

good-hearted fellow, well-liked by his teammates, who especially enjoyed being in the game when he pitched. "It was a pleasure to play behind him," Stan Musial recalled, "because he knew where he was going to pitch the hitters and you could play them accordingly."[7] Unlike his younger, more straight-laced teammates, Mort was something of a throwback to an earlier age in baseball. He was known to bend the rules at times, had a taste for the bubbly, loved to eat, and struggled to stay in top shape, but he always told Southworth, "I'll be ready when you need me." The manager acknowledged, "He was always ready."[8]

Mort and Walker had been a brother battery since they were kids, but at first Walker was the pitcher and Mort the catcher. "We were doing all right," Mort recalled, "until one afternoon a foul tip hit me on the elbow. It hurt like blazes, and after hopping up and down and using some language, I ripped off the chest protector and mask and said I was finished." Walker put on the catching gear and Mort took the mound, "and it's been that way ever since."[9] Two years younger than Mort, Walker had seen part-time duty as a catcher with the 1941 Cardinals, then became the team's primary receiver in 1942. Walker was built much like his brother, though an inch taller, but the two were unlike one another in many ways. Mort had thick, dark hair, a round, reddish face, and was somewhat on the fleshy side, whereas Walker had blond hair that was thinning a bit, was rather pale but was tall and lean, a powerful hitter and a very fast runner in his early years. "Mort is nervous, restless, and quick tempered," one reporter noted. "He is a ready talker and sociable, and likes to go places and do things. Walker is quiet and unemotional, talks rarely, and smiles even less often."[10] His mother said it was a "great event" in their home when Walker smiled. There was another difference as well: Walker was a prankster. He would nail a teammate's shoes to the clubhouse floor, give him a "hot foot" while sitting in the dugout, or light a match to his newspaper if he caught him reading in a hotel lobby. If Walker had been drinking a little, Terry Moore remembered, "he'd grab your necktie and either cut it in two or tie it into knots."[11]

⌇

From Boston, the Cardinals moved to Philadelphia for a four-game weekend series where they were met yet again by heavy skies and gloomy, wet weather, which hung around for two days and caused the Friday and Saturday games to be canceled. The dismal weather seemed a reflection of the team's disappointing road trip. After two days of inactivity in the City of Brotherly Love, the Redbirds were finally able to get back to baseball in a Sunday doubleheader.

The first game went fifteen innings, and at times the players must have felt that it would never end. Johnny Beazley, who had pitched well in relief, was given his third start of the season, and for twelve agonizing innings he pitched into and out of trouble. The Phillies twice had a runner on third with only one out, but came away with just one run. With two on and no outs in the thirteenth, Beazley gave way to Howard Krist, who wiggled out of the jam, but in the fifteenth Krist gave up the run that made the Phils a 2–1 winner. It was Krist's first loss in two years after thirteen straight wins. Tommy Hughes went all the way for Philadelphia, scattering ten hits through fifteen innings in one of the best outings of his career. Hughes survived a scare in the tenth inning, but it did not come from the Cardinals. Returning to the bench after running from first to third, he collapsed, but was revived and then returned to the mound to throw five more innings of shutout ball. In the nightcap, Lon Warneke went the distance for the Cards, holding the Phillies to five hits and only one run to end the road trip with a 3–1 win. The game "marked the finish of a journey," a St. Louis writer observed, "which may ultimately prove to have been the finish of St. Louis pennant hopes."[12]

A trip that had begun with two victories over the Giants ended with the Cardinals losing seven of their next ten games. Losing four of five to the Dodgers had been bad enough, but losing three of five to the second-division Braves and last-place Phillies was worse, more so because Brooklyn had gone 5–2 after playing the Cardinals. St. Louis entered the Brooklyn series four and a half games behind, left it seven and a half behind, and ended the road trip nine games behind the front-runners. Despite Southworth's persistent optimism, there was in fact almost nothing in their eastern swing that gave reason to be optimistic. Mort Cooper accounted for three of the team's five wins, all of them shutouts. Warneke had the only other complete-game victory, and Beazley the one win in relief. White and Pollet had each failed twice as starters; Lanier, Gumbert, and Beazley had all failed once; and as a kind of exclamation point, Howard Krist had lost his first game in two years. Redbird hitters shared in the blame, as the offense continued to be spotty at best. Only Musial, who hit .414, and Walker Cooper, at .300, had provided consistent punch during the trip. The average for the rest of the team was under .230, with Moore, Slaughter, Marion, and Crespi below that mark. Ironically, the Redbirds outscored their opponents in the twelve games 50–49, but tallied more than a third of their runs in the three Cooper shutouts. In the other nine games, they plated only thirty-two runners while their opponents were chasing home forty-nine.

The road trip, however, was not quite over for the sagging Redbirds, who stopped in Columbus, Ohio, for an exhibition game with their Double A club. Columbus had won the American Association championship in 1941; the system's two other Double A clubs and the Single A affiliate in Houston had won league championships as well. It would mark 1941 as the pinnacle of success for the farm system built by Branch Rickey. Three of the 1942 Cardinals—Ray Sanders, Harry Walker, and Murry Dickson—had played for Columbus in 1941. Exhibition games were largely a reward to minor-league affiliates and especially to their fans, who could see their former favorites as well as their big-league teammates take on the hometown farm club. It was also a chance for Southworth and Rickey to size up prospects for the future. For the big-leaguers, however, these games were always an annoying add-on to an already long season, the more so at the end of a long and disappointing road trip. The players no doubt would have much preferred to have the day off at home to rest and prepare for their next National League opponent, the Pittsburgh Pirates.

~

War news from the Western fronts in early July continued to tell of Axis advances. In the Soviet Union, Germany reopened its offensive, but instead of Moscow, their primary target shifted south toward the Russian oil fields in the Caucasus and southwest toward the Volga River and the industrial city of Stalingrad. After a fierce engagement in eastern Ukraine late in May, Nazi forces advanced rapidly across a broad front while Soviet troops retreated toward Stalingrad to avoid the German strategy of encirclement that had been so costly to them in men and materiel the year before. On July 1 the Germans captured the fortress of Sevastopol with its naval base on the Black Sea; two days later they took the city of Voronezh on the Donets River. With air superiority and fast-moving tanks, the Nazis rampaged across the open countryside of the Ukraine and before the end of the month had captured the city of Rostov on the Don River, which brought them to within two hundred miles of both Stalingrad to the east and the Maikop oil fields to the south. The front pages of St. Louis newspapers carried almost daily accounts of the fighting, often with maps to chart German advances and current lines of battle.

In North Africa, Erwin Rommel's Afrika Korps had swept across the Libyan desert to reach El Alamein on July 1. There were heavy casualties on all sides. With his army exhausted and his supply lines stretched to the limit, Rommel paused briefly to rest and resupply his forces. This gave the Allies time to add fresh men and new equipment. The United States increased shipments of the Grant tank that had proved so effective, while American airmen joined the British in regularly bombing Nazi strongholds in rearguard areas to make resupply more difficult for the enemy. Rommel renewed his offensive in the second week of July, but the newly fortified El Alamein line held and the battle became a stalemate. At the time Tobruk fell, Winston Churchill was in the United States conferring with Franklin Roosevelt on plans for opening a second front in Europe. The British defeats in North Africa led to strident calls from London for him to return home immediately and produced a challenge to his hold on the office of prime minister. A vote of "no confidence" in Churchill's government was defeated in the House of Commons, but it was a political shot fired across the bow of the British ship of state.

In the Pacific, fighting had become sporadic following the American victory at Midway. The United States continued its buildup of ships, planes, and troops in the region, mainly in Australia, while Japan, despite failures to capture Port Moresby or Midway, continued to seek a more perfect defensive perimeter in the southwest Pacific. In late July, they turned their attention to the Solomon Islands and began constructing an airfield on Guadalcanal, a strategic location from which to attack U.S. ships bringing reinforcements and armaments to Australia and also from which an invasion of the Land Down Under might be launched. At the same time, the United States, which had not taken back any of the territory the Japanese had captured, began planning for offensive operations of its own.

On the home front, the nation was close to full war mobilization by the summer of 1942, with several hundred thousand men and women in military service and half the nation's manufacturing capacity converted to production of warships, airplanes, tanks, guns, and ammunition. The everyday lives of Americans had changed in ways large and small. A ceiling was placed on wages; prices were frozen on most food items and wearing apparel; a system of rationing was instituted for staples like meat, sugar, and butter. Gasoline and tires were also rationed, a national speed limit was instituted, and daylight savings time was introduced. Protest demonstrations disappeared and were replaced by victory rallies and war-bond sales. To save fuel, many businesses, including bars and restaurants, reduced their hours of operation, and stores cut back on home deliveries of groceries and other goods. The *St. Louis Post-Dispatch* reported that the shopping bag had become a symbol of patriotism, a "wartime necessity" for carrying groceries and other goods home, adding that designers were making bags that were smart as well as practical. Shopping bags were no longer the "homely paper model" associated in comic strips with "a woman whose weight was hefty or a man of the hen-pecked variety," but were now a stylish accessory that complemented the attire of women.[13]

Changes in family life were often dramatic, especially for women who had to adjust to separations from husbands gone to the military or moved great distances to find war-related employment. As the war effort gobbled up available manpower, more and more women replaced men on production lines in war industries and other areas of employment. In addition, a Women's Army Corps was formed that, for the first time, took women into the military to serve in roles other than as nurses: women took jobs as clerks, dieticians, hygienists, pharmacists, and accountants, and worked in other jobs as well to release more men for combat duty. Recruitment of officers for the new WAC began in St. Louis in late May, followed by a more general recruitment of women to fill the ranks. The press reported that women would wear dark olive-drab uniforms, the same color as army men.[14]

Americans on both coasts continued to live in fear of direct attack by Germany or Japan. There seemed no end to the U-boat attacks on shipping along the Atlantic seaboard, though submarine chasers and armed escorts for convoys were reducing this threat. On the West Coast, residents were unnerved in late June when a Japanese submarine lobbed five nine-inch shells from several miles offshore that landed near Fort Stevens at the mouth of the Columbia River in Oregon. No damage resulted, but Colonel Carl Doney, commanding officer at the fort, told reporters they "came close—too damn close."[15] For the most part, St. Louisans felt safe from enemy attack, but in July the director of civilian defense for the region, Joseph Sholtz, advised them to be prepared for "token" raids, and the *Post-Dispatch* obliged by publishing a map showing that it was physically possible for Germany or Japan to bomb the Mound City.[16]

The threat of German sabotage was of greater concern than aerial bombing to St. Louis and to the nation in general. Throughout the first half of the year, newspapers across the country featured stories about individuals in the hundreds arrested as German agents, spies, or propagandists, many of them U.S. citizens, women as well as men. The most sensational case was of eight German saboteurs who landed in the United States by submarine in early June, four on Long Island near the Hamptons and four in Florida near Jacksonville. They came with plans, money, and materiel for a two-year campaign of terror aimed at a variety of targets including the Pennsylvania Railroad terminal in Newark, New Jersey, power plants at Niagara Falls, locks on the Ohio River near Cincinnati, and several aluminum manufacturing plants, one of them in East St. Louis. All eight had lived in the United States (two were U.S. citizens), and all had friends and relatives in the country. They were captured after one of the eight got cold feet and turned the others in to the FBI. All were promptly arrested and at the direction of President Roosevelt tried before a military tribunal, found guilty, and sentenced to death. It was the first use of a military tribunal since the assassination of Abraham Lincoln.

Baseball continued to face uncertainties about its future. The two league presidents, Ford Frick and Will Harridge, saw "dubious times" ahead for the game. Minor-league baseball was especially at risk; their losses to the draft in 1942 were far heavier than those of the majors because their players were younger. At the same time, polls taken of servicemen reported that 95 percent opposed canceling the major-league season and wanted baseball to continue. Attendance, which was down in the first weeks of the season when war news was bad, improved as the news got better. Jack Zeller, general manager of the Detroit Tigers, ignited a firestorm among baseball executives with the suggestion that the 1943 season be shortened by two months, eliminating games in April and September. Owners rejected the idea summarily. The question persisted of how men physically fit to play a demanding sport could be unfit for military service; with this question went another, more often implied than asked: Were major-league players being given preferential treatment? Johnny Pesky, a rookie with the Boston Red Sox in 1942, recalls people stopping him on the street to ask, "What the hell are you doing out of the service?" But it was Pesky's teammate Ted Williams whose draft status became the most controversial of any player when he successfully appealed his 1A classification, making him the poster boy for the press of the major-leaguer more concerned with baseball and himself than with the war and his country.[17]

$\sim$

The Cardinals finally made it home from their eastern tour on the last day of June for a week of games before the major leagues took their annual three-day break for the All-Star Game. Mort Cooper got the home stand off to a winning start with a 4–2 complete-game victory over the Pittsburgh Pirates. Cooper's streak of thirty-two consecutive scoreless innings ended in the first when Pittsburgh first baseman Elbie Fletcher, who had looked bad swinging at the first two pitches, connected on a hanging curve to lift a fly ball just inside the foul pole onto the pavilion roof for a home run. The Cards tied the game in the bottom of the first; Slaughter then untied it with a two-run double in the fifth. Pittsburgh tallied again in their half of the sixth, but Brown got the run back with his first home run of the season in the seventh. A tiring Cooper struggled into the ninth inning, when the Pirates put two runners aboard. But he retired Maurice Van Robays on a long drive into deep right center and fanned former Cardinal Stu Martin on a three-two pitch to end the game and earn his eleventh win.

The next day, Ernie White gave the Cards a good start on July, pitching a six-hit shutout of the Pirates, his first win since late May. The Redbirds tagged their nemesis Ken Heintzelman with the loss, stinging him with a succession of singles and a sacrifice bunt to take the lead with two runs in the third, then adding two more on doubles by Ray Sanders and Walker Cooper in the fourth and eighth. The Cardinals won again the next evening behind the five-hit pitching of Johnny Beazley. It was a tight game as Pirate starter Bob Klinger held St. Louis to one run in the first seven innings while Beazley was blanking the Buccaneers. Lloyd "Dutch" Dietz took over for Klinger in the eighth and the Birds quickly added two runs with a display of the opportunistic baserunning that had become the team's trademark. With Moore and Musial on base, Ken O'Dea ripped a sharp single to right, hit so hard that it looked as if Moore might be thrown out at home. But the hurried throw was wide and skipped past the catcher, permitting Moore to score easily. Turning the corner at third base, Musial saw Dietz chasing the errant throw, and he headed for home. He and the ball arrived together, and Musial crashed into the Pirates' 6'2", 225-pound catcher, Babe "Blimp" Phelps, who dropped the ball as Musial tagged the plate for a second run. Pittsburgh avoided a second shutout with a run in the ninth but lost 3–1.

Lon Warneke went to the mound the next day hoping for a sweep of the series, but it was not to be. Fletcher again got Pittsburgh on the board with a first-inning home run, after which the Pirates added single markers in the second and fourth and two more in the eighth. Trailing 5–2, the Redbirds rallied in the ninth, scoring twice. But with two out and the tying run on base, Dietz, the losing pitcher the day before, took over for starter Johnny Lanning to get the last out, and last laugh, in the 5–4 Pittsburgh win.

Chicago followed the Pirates into St. Louis for the traditional Independence Day doubleheader plus a Sunday twin bill the next day. The Redbirds split the doubleheader on the Fourth. Facing Mort Cooper in the opener, the Cubs touched off the first explosion of the day with a five-run outburst in the fifth inning, ignited by a two-run blast from Lou Novikoff. Jimmie Foxx, acquired by the Cubs several weeks earlier from the Boston Red Sox, followed one hitter later with a rocket into the left-field seats. This ended the day for Cooper, who had been uncharacteristically wild from the outset. The Cards fought back but lost 6–5 as second baseman Lou Stringer made a sensational diving stab of a Musial line drive to snuff out a ninth-inning Redbird rally. The Windy City crew began the second game with another explosion of three runs in the first inning against Howard Pollet, whose afternoon ended early. The Cardinals, however, had some pyrotechnics of their own, blasting four Chicago pitchers for thirteen hits and nine runs. Slaughter led the St. Louis attack with four hits, two of them doubles, and two runs batted in. Moore, Hopp, and Crespi all chipped in with two hits apiece. After pitching two and two-thirds innings in the first game, Murry Dickson returned in the nightcap to go eight and a third innings in relief of Pollet for a 9–3 win.

On Sunday, the Cards took both ends of the doubleheader. Bill Lee and Harry Gumbert hooked up in the opener, in which the Redbirds prevailed 5–3. St. Louis rolled out the heavy artillery as five of their eleven hits were for extra bases. Crespi and O'Dea, who were feasting on Cubs pitching, led the attack with two hits apiece, each driving in two runs. In the second game, the Cardinals wasted no time in grabbing the lead, scoring five times in the first inning when their first six hitters reached base against the Bruins' young lefthander Johnny Schmitz, who walked two, hit a third, and threw a wild pitch in addition to serving up three hits. But the Cubs were not dead. They roared back to tie the game at five in the fifth against Ernie White, who needed help to get the last out. Still, the Cardinals were not to be denied. In their half of the fifth, they rang up their second five-run inning of the game, beating up on another lefty, Vern Olsen. Walker Cooper had a pair of hits, including a triple, and drove home three runs, while Jimmy Brown had a double and a single and two runs batted in. Beazley, who pitched to only one man in the fifth before leaving for a pinch hitter, was the beneficiary of the

Cards' five-run fifth, getting credit for the 11–6 win, while Max Lanier labored through the final four innings to preserve it.

~

The 1942 All-Star Game was played in New York's Polo Grounds, moved from Ebbets Field so that more people could attend. A share of the revenues was designated for military relief. The Cardinals, with five players—Terry Moore, Enos Slaughter, Jimmy Brown, Walker Cooper, and Mort Cooper—and the Dodgers, with six, dominated the National League All-Star roster, while the Yankees alone had nine players on the American League squad.[18] The Cards' Mort Cooper was tapped to be the starting pitcher for the National League. In his July 4 start against the Cubs, Cooper had not worn his usual jersey with the number 13 on the back. The team wanted him to look "spic and span" for the All-Star Game, so they had his white home uniform cleaned and shipped to New York.[19] Sartorial splendor, however, did not impress the American Leaguers, as leadoff hitter Lou Boudreau, the Cleveland Indians' shortstop, drove Cooper's second pitch deep into the left-field seats. The Redbirds' ace retired the next two hitters, but Yankee outfielder Tommy Henrich then lashed a double off the right-field wall and Detroit first baseman Rudy York followed with a mighty blast into the upper deck in right to give the American League a 3–0 lead. The only National League score came in the eighth, on a home run by the Dodgers' Mickey Owen. Both Walker Cooper and Enos Slaughter had singles in the contest, but American League pitchers made the first-inning runs stand up for a 3–1 win. As the winners, the American League All-Stars played the next day in Cleveland against a team of major-leaguers in military service. With former Detroit great Mickey Cochrane as manager, the military All-Stars included Bob Feller and Hank Greenberg. The American Leaguers again struck in the first inning, as Joe DiMaggio and Rudy York reached Feller for hits that drove in two runs on the way to a 5–0 victory. The game drew 62,054 spectators, and all proceeds went to military relief.

The day after the All-Star Game, the Cardinals made a surprising move, selling Lon Warneke to the Chicago Cubs in a waiver deal. Signed originally by St. Louis, Warneke had been released, then signed by the Cubs, with whom he came to the majors in 1930. He was dealt to St. Louis after the 1936 season and won eighty-three games, including a no-hitter, in his five and a half years as a Cardinal. A fan favorite, his sale conjured memories of other popular Redbirds sent away solely for money. "We have so many young pitchers that it's impossible to give them enough work, and without work they're not effective," Sam Breadon explained to a skeptical audience of reporters. Seemingly in agreement, Southworth added, "We felt it was necessary to dispose of one pitcher and Warneke became the man on the basis of his record this year. He is getting up in years and, in my judgment, has lost some of his pitching stuff."[20] But Vernon Tietjen of the *Post-Dispatch* thought that while Southworth said the deal was fine, "his tone indicated he was hardly pleased."[21]

Breadon's explanation of the sale did not end with the need to give younger pitchers more work. He went on to say, "You can't have a pitcher of Warneke's class and salary around if you can't work him regularly, and we believe the younger men are more valuable to us, particularly for next year."[22] Some construed the remark to mean that the Cardinals were conceding the 1942 pennant to the Dodgers. "I don't know whether the Cardinal front office has given up or not," Tommy Holmes of the *Brooklyn Eagle* opined, but "the sale of Lon Warneke . . . certainly didn't look like the move of an outfit that expects to win a pennant." Holmes could not resist tweaking St. Louis officials by adding: "For people that resent charges of cheapness, the Cardinals front office has the strangest way of disproving the allegation."[23] Joe King of the *New York World-Telegram* saw the sale as "primarily a move by Sam Breadon to balance the budget, to get rid of Lon's $12,500 salary and help make up for the estimated $60,000 the Cards lost when the last Brooklyn series was washed out."[24] Breadon heatedly denied that the team was giving up on the 1942 season and rejected as well the suggestion that the team's financial situation was behind the move.

~

The Cardinals went back to work on July 9 in a night game against the visiting New York Giants. Johnny Beazley, now in the rotation in place of Warneke, made the St. Louis decision to go with youth look good as he shut out the New Yorkers on six hits. The Cards turned the tables on one of their lefty tormentors, Dave Koslo, hammering him for nine runs on nine hits in the first six innings on their way to a 9–0 win. All-Stars Enos Slaughter and Terry Moore hit home runs to account for four of the Redbird runs, and even Beazley, known affectionately as "the Weazel," joined the hit parade with a three-run triple. The Birds backed their rookie hurler with sterling defense, turning double plays in the early innings to kill the Giants' scoring threats. After the game, New York manager Mel Ott lamented that his team had been treated "shamefully" by the Cardinals all year. "We've won only three out of a dozen games with them. It seems like they always have good pitching when we play 'em," he groaned. "When we make mistakes they take advantage. It just seems we can't beat 'em."[25]

Mort Cooper started the next day, but was outpitched by Bob Carpenter, whose off-speed pitches dizzied Cardinal hitters through eight innings of shutout ball. In the ninth, Carpenter retired the first two Redbirds easily and got two quick strikes on Whitey Kurowski, but lost him when the Cards' third baseman singled to left. Walker Cooper pinch-hit for Marion and lashed a double to left. With the tying runs on base, Ott replaced the weary Carpenter with Ace Adams.

Billy Southworth countered by sending Coaker Triplett up to hit for Max Lanier, who had pitched two scoreless innings in relief of Cooper. Triplett hit Adams's first pitch for a single to left to score both runners and tie the game. Having used all his reserves, Southworth had to put a makeshift defense on the field for the tenth, moving Moore from center to third base, Kurowski from third to second, and Musial from left to center. Murry Dickson came in to get through the top of the tenth, despite an error by Moore. In the home half, Moore and Slaughter led off with singles. Musial laid down a sacrifice bunt that Adams grabbed, whirled, and threw to third to get the lead runner, but no one was covering the bag, and Moore sprinted home with the winning run as the ball bounced toward the grandstand.

Fortune, however, fled the Cardinals in the final game of the series. Howard Pollet started for the Redbirds and again could not make it out of the first inning, as the Giants jumped on him for three runs on two doubles and a pair of singles. Dickson came on to pitch through the sixth inning, giving up two runs, one a solo home run by left fielder Babe Barna. Lanier followed and gave up a home run to Johnny Mize, completing the scoring in an 8–3 New York victory. Carl Hubbell was the winning pitcher. The Cardinals collected nine hits off the Giants' veteran, but King Carl stayed ahead of batters, got outs when he needed them, and went the distance for only his second win of the season.

The Braves followed the Giants into St. Louis for a three-game series beginning with a Sunday doubleheader. The Cardinals won both games. In the opener, the Redbirds jumped on Lou Tost in the first inning, scoring three times, then added another run against the Boston lefty who had beaten them twice earlier in the season. This was more than enough support for Harry Gumbert, who gave up only two hits in going the distance for a 5–1 win. Cardinal outfielders made only five putouts as Gumbert had the Braves pounding the ball into the dirt throughout the game. In the nightcap, Ernie White started for the Cards, but ran afoul of the long ball. Right fielder Chet Ross launched a White pitch into the bleachers in the first inning with no one on base; third baseman Nanny Fernandez hit another in the fourth with one runner aboard to put the Braves three runs ahead. The Cards struck back in their half of the fourth, scoring six times against southpaw Bill Donovan, another early-season tormentor. Aggressive baserunning paid off in the big inning, as both first baseman Max West and second baseman Tony Cuccinello threw the ball away for errors while trying to cut down Redbird runners. Krist came on to pitch five innings, while the Cardinals added three more runs to go with fourteen hits in the 9–3 win.

Monday was an open date, but a costly one for the Redbirds. Terry Moore tore the nail off the little finger of his throwing hand while trying to disentangle the bumpers of two cars.[26] He said nothing about it and started the next day, but Southworth saw immediately that something was wrong with his swing and benched him after one time at bat. Moore would remain on the sidelines for the next four days.

The Cards and Braves finished their series with a Tuesday night game that had a storybook finish. Cooper started for the Cardinals and again struggled, giving up eight hits and five runs in five innings. The Cards fought back with three runs in the sixth, knocking out Boston starter Al Javery. They narrowly escaped falling farther behind in the seventh when Pollet was ineffective in relief, but Krist came on to put out the fire. In the bottom of the eighth with one on, Kurowski pulled a Lou Tost fastball into the left-field seats for a two-run homer to tie the score. The game went to extra innings, with Krist pitching nearly perfect ball into the eleventh, giving up a walk but no hits or runs. In the bottom of the eleventh, Stan Musial, who already had three hits in the game, belted a Dick Errickson fastball onto the pavilion roof for a dramatic home run, his seventh of the season, giving the Cardinals a 7–5 win.

The Cardinals had picked up their pace in the first half of July, winning ten of thirteen, but gained only half a game on the Dodgers, who had won nine of twelve. The Birds would, however, have a chance to cut into the Dodgers' lead in the upcoming weekend series of back-to-back doubleheaders between the teams. But first they had four games with last-place Philadelphia. The series began with a doubleheader that was part of the annual Tuberculosis Day. The pregame program had a decidedly military character as several bands, a drum and bugle corps, and a Navy marching unit paraded around the field, in addition to which fifty-two recruits from St. Louis formed on the infield to be sworn into the Navy. This show of military force may have awed the Phillies, who were subdued twice with relative ease.

In the opener, Beazley went the distance, walking six and giving up nine hits but only three runs in a 7–3 win. The Cardinals pounded three Philadelphia pitchers for eleven hits, including doubles by Brown, Kurowski, and Harry Walker and triples by Slaughter and Beazley, who was proving to be almost as skilled at the plate as on the mound. Murry Dickson received the call in the second game and responded with a seven-hit complete-game victory. The Redbirds collected another eleven hits against three different Philadelphia pitchers, winning 9–4 as Harry Walker, substituting in center for the injured Moore, led the way with two singles, a double, and two runs batted in. Musial continued his hot hitting with a pair of singles, knocking in two runs. Any concerns the Cardinals might have had in March and April about Musial's hitting "have been allayed," Roy Stockton of the *Post-Dispatch* commented, adding that Musial now looked like "the brightest star the Cardinals have unveiled lately."[27]

On Thursday, the Birds met up again with Tommy Hughes, the second-year righthander who had beaten them in a fifteen-inning game at the end of the June road trip. Once again the game went into overtime, and once again Hughes pitched a complete-game victory, as the Phillies scored in the tenth to win 4–3. Gumbert started for the Redbirds and gave up three runs in five innings. He was succeeded by the seldom-seen Whitey Moore, who turned in a strong four innings before weakening in the tenth. Moore walked Stan Benjamin to start the tenth and had a two-ball, no-strike count on shortstop Al Glossop when Southworth went to his bullpen and signaled Mort Cooper into the game for his first relief appearance of the season. Glossop reached Coop for a hit that sent Benjamin to third, from where he scored on Danny Litwhiler's high infield bounder. As had been so often the case, the Cardinals had numerous chances to score, getting ten hits and five walks, but they stranded twelve runners. O'Dea alone left seven runners on base.

Playing their seventh game in five days, and facing a pair of doubleheaders over the weekend with Brooklyn, Southworth reached into his bag of hurlers and plucked Howard Krist, who had not started a game all season. Known to his teammates as "Spud," the rangy righthander turned in a complete game in the series finale, setting the Philadelphians down on five hits and one run. On defense the Redbirds turned four double plays, while the offense battered three of the visiting pitchers for thirteen hits and ten runs. Slaughter had a big day with three hits, a double and triple among them, and two runs driven home. Walker Cooper and Jimmy Brown drove in two runs each as well. Winning three of four from the Phillies kept the Cardinals on a hot pace, but moved them no closer to the Dodgers, who were taking three of four from the Cubs.

～

The Dodgers arrived in St. Louis at the end of a long, successful, and tempestuous road trip. They had won twelve of sixteen games, but stirred controversy at almost every stop. In Pittsburgh, Leo Durocher banned all but two reporters from the clubhouse because the others had criticized him for throwing a wet towel at an umpire. This inflamed Dan Daniel, the dean of baseball writers, who denounced the action: "this wet-towel, sweat shop Caesar stuff is as out of date as the horse car."[28] Two days later in Chicago, with Brooklyn comfortably ahead, the Cubs' Lou Novikoff and Jimmy Foxx hit home runs, after which Kirby Higbe started "dustin" and a full-fledged beanball war broke out. Furious Cubs manager Jimmie Wilson fumed to reporters, "Here we were trailing 5–0 and we get two homers, so they start to throw at us. Well, when anybody throws at us that way, by gosh, we're going to throw at them." "They call them the Bums," Wilson growled. "Well, I have another name for them."[29]

Durocher and Wilson had been teammates on the Cardinals for part of the 1933 season, but there was no love lost between them, nor between their teams. An Associated Press reporter called their mutual hostility "one of the most vicious feuds in baseball annals." Brooklyn's bench jockeys were also in full voice

in Chicago, heckling and taunting to the extent that as Cubs reliever Hi Bithorn
was being removed from the game, he wheeled and fired a fastball aimed at
Durocher's head on the Dodgers' bench. When Casey Stengel heard about the
game, the Braves' manager said the Dodgers were getting "awful" in their "rough-
housing" and that "all National League teams are going to throw everything they
got against the Bums."[30]

The importance of the weekend Dodgers-Cardinals series could hardly be
overstated, at least from the perspective of St. Louis, as *Brooklyn Eagle* writer
Tommy Holmes recognized. "It's just about the last shot in the barrel for the ever-
charging Cardinals and they know it. Unless they can knock the Dodgers down
to something near their own size," he continued, "it is doubtful that the Brooklyn
leaders will ever again be within range of their artillery." Only a St. Louis sweep
of the four games, Holmes added, could hurt the Dodgers.[31] Cardinal fans across
the region agreed on the importance of the games, as St. Louis hotels reported
a rush of reservations for the weekend. In anticipation of huge crowds, parking
lot owners near Sportsman's Park announced their prices would double, from a
quarter to half a dollar. Both Southworth and Durocher had managed their
pitching staffs to have their preferred starters ready for the four games. The
only thing hotter than the series was the St. Louis weather. The rains of June
had turned into the sauna of summer, with high humidity and temperatures
that weighed more and more heavily on the players in their sweat-soaked flannel
uniforms.

The pitching matchup for the first game was between two southpaws, Ernie
White for the Cardinals and Larry French for the Dodgers. Brooklyn drew first
blood with two runs in the third inning and one in the fourth. St. Louis scored
in their half of the fourth when Walker Cooper singled, Kurowski was hit by a
pitch, both moved up on a sacrifice by Hopp, and Marion drove in one with a
sacrifice fly to the outfield. The Dodgers got that run back in the top of the fifth,
but the Redbirds answered with two of their own in the bottom half of the inning. Terry Moore, still not fully healthy, led off the fifth with a double to left, and
Slaughter looped a Texas League single to center on which Moore was unable to
score. The next hitter, Coaker Triplett, singled to center to bring Moore home
and send Slaughter to third. Cooper got the handle of his bat on an inside pitch
and lofted a high, twisting pop foul down the left-field line. Third baseman Arky
Vaughan chased it down in foul territory to make a running catch with his back
to the plate. Slaughter broke for home; Vaughan spun around and threw toward
the plate. French cut the throw off, pivoted, and heaved the ball wildly to catcher
Mickey Owen as Slaughter slid across with the run.

With the Cards trailing by one, Marion led off the sixth with a single, went to
second on a sacrifice by Ernie White, and scored to tie the game when Jimmy
Brown drilled a sharp single to right. French, going for his eleventh win of the

season against no losses, was removed in favor of Hugh Casey, Durocher's bull-pen ace. Harry Walker pinch-hit for the ailing Moore and popped out, but Slaughter walked and Musial, hitting for Triplett, lined a drive off Casey's hand. The Dodgers' pitcher pounced on the ball but threw late and wildly to first. With the ball bouncing down the right-field line, Brown and Slaughter scored to put the Redbirds ahead. Musial's line drive, which was scored a hit, ripped the nail off the little finger of Casey's pitching hand, and he gave way to Ed Head. St. Louis scored again in the seventh when Kurowski looped a two-base hit into short right, then moved to third on a passed ball. As Head released his next pitch, Kurowski broke for home and scored on a perfectly executed suicide squeeze bunt by Marion. For the game, the Cardinals collected sixteen hits in the 7–4 win. Ernie White, who had suffered much of the season with what was described as a "lame arm," went the distance for his fourth win, while French suffered his first loss.

The second game featured another duel between lefthanders, both of whom were named Max: Lanier for St. Louis and Macon for Brooklyn. The Dodgers played long ball with Lanier, posting a single run in the second inning that hinged on a Camilli triple, another in the fourth on a Reiser double, and a third in the sixth on Camilli's thirteenth home run of the season. They scored a fourth run in the seventh inning on Macon's third hit of the game, a triple off Howard Pollet, the third Cardinal pitcher. Through it all, Macon was making quick work of the Redbirds, shutting them out on three hits over the first six innings. In the bottom of the seventh, however, Billy Southworth's "boys" flexed their muscles to play some long ball of their own. In succession, Triplett doubled, Cooper tripled, and Kurowski hit his third home run of the season into the sun-drenched bleach-ers in left to pull the Birds to within one run. But it was as close as they would get. Curt Davis took over for Macon with one out in the seventh and retired the next eight Cardinal hitters in order for a 4–3 Brooklyn win. The split in the double-header left the Cardinals no better off than when the day began.

Sunday was another bright, sunny, steamy, muggy St. Louis summer day as 34,896 fans poured into Sportsman's Park for the second doubleheader of the weekend. It was the largest crowd of the season. Several hundred spectators were perched on the roofs of buildings across Grand Avenue beyond the right-field pavilion, and hundreds more were turned away at the gate. Tickets had gone on sale at 8:30 that morning, and when sales were shut off there were scuffles among disappointed fans as dozens pressed forward, hoping to get in one way or an-other. A security guard was knocked down, but no one was seriously injured, and the disappointed were soon dispersed. Wartime gas shortages notwithstand-ing, parking lots around the stadium were packed with cars from surrounding states—Illinois, Iowa, Kansas, even Kentucky and Oklahoma.

Mort Cooper drew the starting assignment for St. Louis in the first game of the twin bill, once more going against Whitlow Wyatt. The Birds' ace struggled through the first four innings, but held Brooklyn in check until the fifth, when Dixie Walker drove Pee Wee Reese home with the first run the Dodgers had scored against Cooper all season. By then the Cardinals had a seven-run lead. In the second inning they scored twice, largely on their speed. Musial got a scratch hit off Wyatt's glove, beating the pitcher's throw to first. Walker Cooper legged out a hit that went off the glove of third baseman Lew Riggs. Hopp was hit with a pitch, and Marion followed with a single, scoring Musial and Cooper. In the third, the Redbirds battered the Dodgers' ace as Slaughter led off with a sharply hit single that Musial followed with a double high off the right-field screen. Wyatt walked Walker Cooper, then hit Kurowski with a pitch to force Slaughter in with a run and leave the bases loaded. Hopp cleared them with a triple down the right-field line, knocking Wyatt out of the game. The new pitcher, Les Webber, unleashed a wild pitch that enabled Hopp to score the fifth run of the inning. In the sixth, the Dodgers scored two more runs against Cooper, bringing the score to 7–3. Cooper shut Brooklyn out in the seventh, but could retire only one batter in the eighth before his right elbow became so inflamed that he could not continue.

Harry Gumbert took over and got one out in the inning. He was followed by Max Lanier, who got the third out, stranding two Brooklyn runners, but the Dodgers had narrowed the Cardinals' lead to two runs. In the bottom of the eighth, George Kurowski, who had been hit twice in the game by Wyatt pitches, connected with an Ed Head fastball and lined it into the center-field seats for a home run and an 8–5 St. Louis lead, which was the score when the game ended after Lanier retired the Dodgers in order in the ninth, striking out Reiser and Camilli. The game was marred by more beanballs. Wyatt threw at several Cardinals in addition to hitting Kurowski twice. There was no immediate retaliation. But in the fourth inning when Les Webber, pitching in relief, threw two fastballs high, inside, and near his head, Stan Musial left the batter's box and started menacingly toward the mound, bat in hand. Home plate umpire Al Barlick quickly intervened to stop Musial and prevent a fight, but both benches emptied, and while no punches were thrown, a lot of insults were hurled in both directions. Later, Cooper retaliated when Webber came to the plate, plunking him with a payback pitch. Not all St. Louis fans approved, and Cooper heard some boos from the hometown crowd. Not to be outdone, Webber tried to even the score by throwing at Cooper but missed.

Cardinal rookie Johnny Beazley took the mound in the nightcap against the veteran Kirby Higbe. Both were wild. Beazley walked six before leaving with two out in the fifth inning, while Higbe handed out five free passes in just over two innings. The Dodgers got off to a fast start, scoring twice in the first inning, and they would have scored more had not Enos Slaughter thrown Joe Medwick out at the plate as he tried to advance on Billy Herman's fly to right. The Cardinals got one run back in the second inning on Kurowski's third home run of the series and sent Higbe to the showers with five runs in the third to take a 6–2 lead. Higbe had opened the inning by filling the bases with consecutive walks to Slaughter, Musial, and Ken O'Dea. An infield out sent one run home, after which Ray Sanders singled to bring in another. Sanders stole second, which led Higbe to walk Marion intentionally to get to the pitcher, Beazley. But Beazley foiled the strategy with a double and Higbe headed for the bench, replaced by Ed Head, who was making his second appearance of the day and third in the series. Jimmy Brown greeted Head with a run-scoring single.

But Beazley could not stand prosperity. He continued to walk Dodger hitters, and in the fifth inning they capitalized on his generosity. After Head had singled against him, Beazley could not find the plate against Walker and Reese, walking both to load the bases. Medwick beat out an infield hit for one run. This was followed by yet another walk to Camilli, sending home a second run. Billy Herman seized the moment with a two-run single to tie the score and drive Beazley from the premises. Lanier, making his third appearance in the series, came into the game with two men still on base and struck out Owen to end the inning. The game then became a pitcher's duel. Curt Davis relieved Head with one out in the fifth inning and tossed five innings of shutout ball through the tenth, while Lanier was doing the same to the Dodgers. Brooklyn had a chance to go ahead in the tenth when Reiser singled to center with one out and raced around to third as Harry Walker fumbled the ball for an error. After Lanier walked Medwick intentionally, Camilli hit a high-bounding ball to Frank Crespi, who was playing shortstop after Marion had gone out for a pinch hitter in the ninth. Crespi made a quick throw to Brown at second. Making the pivot on double plays was always a problem for Brown, but this time he was perfect and his throw nipped Camilli at first for the final out of the inning.

In the bottom of the eleventh, after five and a half hours of baseball and with almost all the fans still in the stands, Johnny Allen took over the pitching chores for Brooklyn to face Enos Slaughter, who was hitless in the game. Allen worked the count to one ball and two strikes, then gave the Cards' right fielder a pitch he could hit. Slaughter drove it on a line toward the 405–foot marker in the deepest part of the park, just to the right of dead center field. Pete Reiser knew it would be a leadoff triple if not caught. He raced back, heedless of the wall, leaped high on the dead run, and just as the ball hit his glove, his head and arm collided with the concrete barrier. Reiser collapsed, and the impact caused the ball to bounce away. Dazed and staggering, he managed to retrieve it and throw to the cutoff man, but the relay to the plate was late. Slaughter had circled the bases with an inside-the-park home run to win the game 7–6 for St. Louis and pull the Redbirds to within six and a half games of the league leaders.

Meanwhile, Reiser had collapsed again after his throw and lay in a heap on the field, barely conscious. "It was like a hand grenade had gone off inside my head," he said later.[32] Right fielder Frenchy Bordagaray was the first to reach him and helped him to sit up. He recognized that Reiser was badly injured. Pee Wee Reese, Reiser's best friend on the team, dashed from his shortstop position to the side of his fallen teammate, followed by Leo Durocher, the team trainer, and other players who gathered quickly around Reiser. While Reiser lay slumped on the ground, delirium had erupted in Sportsman's Park. Hundreds of jubilant fans jumped onto the field, as was permissible then, and were running around, leaping and cheering for joy, bombarding one another and the Dodgers' players with seat cushions. The St. Louis players celebrated briefly, then retreated to their clubhouse. After several minutes, Reiser got to his feet, and with the assistance of Durocher and others walked slowly, groggily off the field through now thousands of milling spectators. Reaching the bench, he collapsed again and sat for an extended period of time before retiring to the Brooklyn clubhouse.

After showering, Reiser was taken by ambulance to St. John's Hospital, where the Cardinals' physician, Dr. Robert Hyland, examined him. Hyland told the press that Reiser had sustained a "slight brain concussion" and that he advised him to stay in the hospital for a week.[33] Privately, Hyland knew it was worse. Reiser later said Hyland told him that he had suffered a "severe concussion and a fractured skull" and recommended that he "not play anymore that year."[34] When Dodger president Larry MacPhail heard that recommendation, he fumed that Hyland just wanted to keep Reiser out of the lineup to help the Cardinals. The next morning, Reiser was feeling better, so he checked himself out of the hospital and went to his parents' home in St. Louis to rest for a few days. He returned to action six days later on July 25 in a game against Pittsburgh. He went two for four at the plate, and all seemed normal. It would prove to be anything but that.

The 1942 St. Louis Cardinals. Top Row: Frank Crespi, Coaker Triplett, Ray Sanders, Terry Moore, Howard Pollet, Mort Cooper, George Kurowski, Lloyd Moore, Walker Cooper. Middle Row: Harrison Weaver (trainer), Ernie White, Johnny Beazley, Harry Walker, Howard Krist, Murry Dickson, Jimmy Brown, Johnny Hopp, Butch Yatkeman (trainer). Bottom Row: Marty Marion, Enos Slaughter, Stan Musial, Mike Gonzalez (coach), Billy Southworth (manager), Clyde Wares (coach), Max Lanier, Sam Narron, Ken O'Dea. Front: Bobby Scanlon (batboy). Courtesy of the National Baseball Hall of Fame Library, Cooperstown, New York.

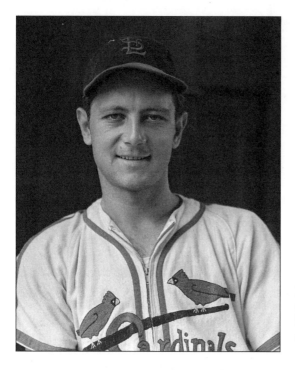

Johnny Beazley won twenty-one games as a rookie, two in the World Series. Courtesy of Allied Photocolor.

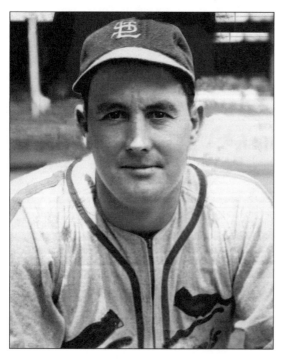

Mort Cooper won twenty-two games and was named the National League's Most Valuable Player. Courtesy of the National Baseball Hall of Fame Library, Cooperstown, New York.

Harry Gumbert had five wins as starter, four more as a reliever, and five saves. Courtesy of Allied Photocolor.

Max Lanier, the Dodger killer, won thirteen games, five of them against Brooklyn. Courtesy of the National Baseball Hall of Fame Library, Cooperstown, New York.

Howard Krist won five games as a starter and eight more in relief. Courtesy of the National Baseball Hall of Fame Library, Cooperstown, New York.

Ernie White fought through injuries to win seven games, then shut out the Yankees in the World Series. Courtesy of Allied Photocolor.

Murry Dickson, the rubber-armed rookie, pitched in thirty-six games as a starter and reliever. Courtesy of Allied Photocolor.

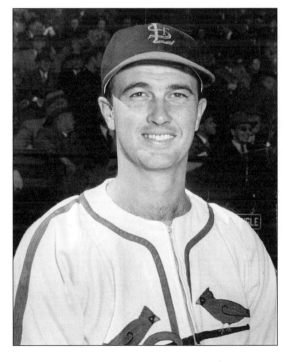

Howard Pollet won seven games as a starter, but suffered arm problems during the season. Courtesy of the National Baseball Hall of Fame Library, Cooperstown, New York.

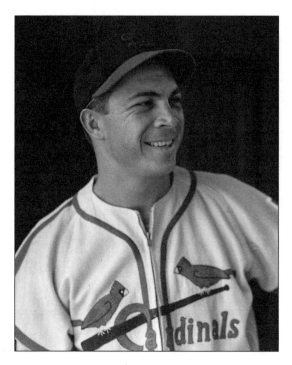

Speedy Johnny Hopp won the first-base job at midseason and provided a hot bat in the stretch run. Courtesy of Allied Photocolor.

Marty Marion, "Mr. Shortstop." A premier defender, he also led the majors in doubles in 1942. Courtesy of the National Baseball Hall of Fame Library, Cooperstown, New York.

George "Whitey" Kurowski, the rookie third sacker, delivered game-winning home runs against the Dodgers and Yankees. Courtesy of Allied Photocolor.

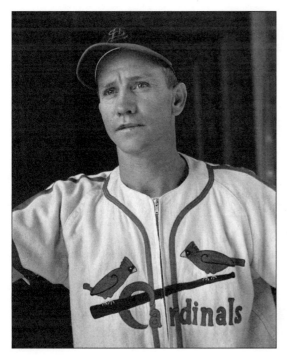

Jimmy Brown, sparkplug lead-off hitter and second baseman, was a clutch hitter for the 1942 team. Courtesy of Allied Photocolor.

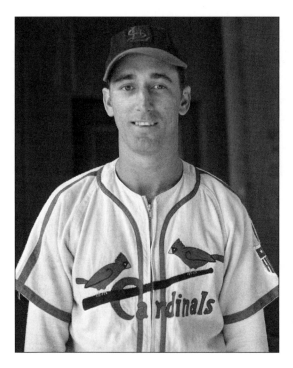

Harry Walker, a rookie out-fielder, filled in well when Terry Moore was injured. Courtesy of Allied Photocolor.

Enos "Country" Slaughter, an outstanding defensive right fielder, led the team in hitting, homers, and RBIs. Courtesy of the National Baseball Hall of Fame Library, Cooperstown, New York.

Coaker Triplett platooned with Stan Musial in left field, starting against lefthanders. Courtesy of the National Baseball Hall of Fame Library, Cooperstown, New York.

Stan Musial, the National League Rookie of the Year in 1942. The speedy left fielder hit for average and power. Courtesy of the National Baseball Hall of Fame Library, Cooperstown, New York.

Ken O'Dea, reserve catcher, was
a lefthanded hitter with power.
Courtesy of Allied Photocolor.

Walker Cooper, the starting
catcher. Brother of pitcher
Mort, he was fast and hit for
average and power. Courtesy
of Allied Photocolor.

Ray Sanders, a rookie in 1942, started the season as the regular first baseman, but eventually lost the job to Hopp. Courtesy of Allied Photocolor.

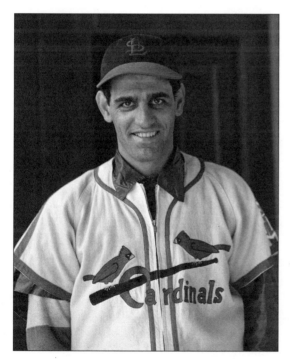

Frank "Creepy" Crespi, utility infielder at second base and shortstop, was a line-drive singles hitter and an excellent fielder. Courtesy of Allied Photocolor.

Terry Moore, the team captain and leader of the young Cardinals. He was an outstanding center fielder and a solid hitter. Courtesy of Allied Photocolor.

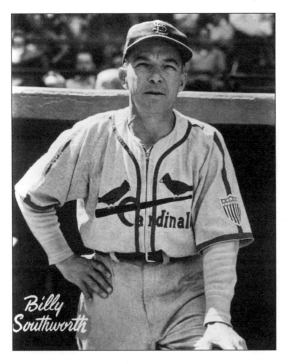

Billy Southworth was named National League Manager of the Year in 1942. Courtesy of the National Baseball Hall of Fame Library, Cooperstown, New York.

Branch Rickey, vice president, general manager, and architect of the Cardinals' farm system. Courtesy of the National Baseball Hall of Fame Library, Cooperstown, New York.

Sam Breadon, owner and team president. Courtesy of the National Baseball Hall of Fame Library, Cooperstown, New York.

Brooklyn president Larry MacPhail (left) and manager Leo Durocher (right), whose stormy personalities combined to make the 1942 Dodgers the most hated team in the National League. Courtesy of the National Baseball Hall of Fame Library, Cooperstown, New York.

Stalwart Dodger pitchers Whitlow Wyatt (left), a nineteen-game winner who lost three times to Mort Cooper in magnificent duels, and Hugh Casey (right), who won six games and saved thirteen out of the Brooklyn bullpen. Courtesy of the National Baseball Hall of Fame Library, Cooperstown, New York.

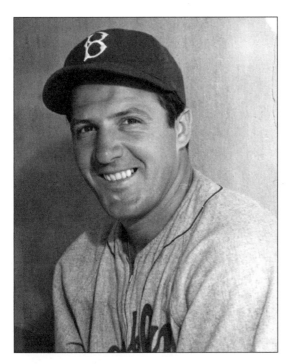

Joe Medwick, the Dodgers' slugging left fielder, was one of many former Cardinals on the Brooklyn team. Courtesy of the National Baseball Hall of Fame Library, Cooperstown, New York.

Pete Reiser, the sensational young center fielder whose midseason injury hurt the Dodgers' chances. Courtesy of the National Baseball Hall of Fame Library, Cooperstown, New York.

Fred "Dixie" Walker was a fan favorite in Brooklyn and the brother of the Cardinals' Harry Walker. Courtesy of the National Baseball Hall of Fame Library, Cooperstown, New York.

Dolph Camilli, the Dodgers' slugging first baseman, led his team in home runs and RBIs. Courtesy of the National Baseball Hall of Fame Library, Cooperstown, New York.

Harold "Pee Wee" Reese, Brooklyn's speedy young shortstop and leadoff hitter, solidified the Dodgers' infield defense. Courtesy of the National Baseball Hall of Fame Library, Cooperstown, New York.

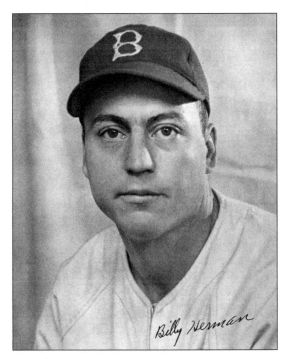

Billy Herman, veteran second baseman and good hitter, was a professional's professional. Courtesy of the National Baseball Hall of Fame Library, Cooperstown, New York.

Larry French, a veteran lefthander, won fifteen games for the Dodgers in 1942 and was a torment to the Cardinals early in the season. Courtesy of the National Baseball Hall of Fame Library, Cooperstown, New York.

Curt Davis, veteran righthander, former Cardinal, and a fifteen-game winner for the 1942 Dodgers as a starter and reliever. Courtesy of the National Baseball Hall of Fame Library, Cooperstown, New York.

Charlie "King Kong" Keller, the Yankees' left fielder, hit for power and average. Courtesy of the National Baseball Hall of Fame Library, Cooperstown, New York.

Joe DiMaggio, the "Yankee Clipper," was New York's star center fielder. He led his team in triples and RBIs in 1942. Courtesy of the National Baseball Hall of Fame Library, Cooperstown, New York.

Charles "Red" Ruffing, veteran righthander and big-game pitcher, threw a near no-hitter in the first game of the World Series against the Cardinals. Courtesy of the National Baseball Hall of Fame Library, Cooperstown, New York.

Joe Gordon, the Yankees' second baseman, led his team in hitting and was named the American League's Most Valuable Player. Courtesy of the National Baseball Hall of Fame Library, Cooperstown, New York.

Yankee manager Joe McCarthy (left) and Cardinal manager Billy Southworth meet before the start of the 1942 World Series. Courtesy of the National Baseball Hall of Fame Library, Cooperstown, New York.

The Cardinals celebrate their World Series win. George Kurowski (left) hit the game-winning homer in the fifth game as St. Louis closed out the series, Enos Slaughter (center) played a key role throughout the series, and Johnny Beazley (right) was the winner of the final game. Courtesy of the Associated Press.

CHAPTER 7
Darkness before the Dawn

The doubleheader win on July 19 brought the Cardinals to within six and a half games of the Dodgers, the closest they had been in a month. Moreover, Brooklyn was leaving St. Louis with its star center fielder Pete Reiser in the hospital and its ace reliever Hugh Casey nursing a damaged finger. The Dodgers seemed less concerned about Reiser's injury than Casey's. Musial's line drive had broken his little finger as well as torn the nail off, and it was clear that he would be unable to pitch for several weeks, including when the Cardinals visited Brooklyn on July 28 and 29. The Cardinals also had injury concerns. Terry Moore had not recovered fully from his bruised finger. He had started both games of the Saturday doubleheader, but left the games early, and he did not play in either of the Sunday games. There was also growing concern about Mort Cooper. It had been just over a year since Cooper's elbow surgery, and the big righthander was suddenly struggling, in pain, and fearful that the bone chips which necessitated the surgery had returned. So long as the team was still in the pennant race, he vowed not to have any surgery. But Cooper finally relented and let Dr. Hyland examine his arm, who found the problem to be a strained ligament and advised a week to ten days of rest.

Whatever else troubled Southworth, he had to be pleased with the overall performance of the team while at home. The Cards had won eighteen of the twenty-three games played since returning to Sportsman's Park on June 30, a .783 winning percentage, and they had beaten the Dodgers three times out of four and cut their lead from nine games to six and a half. Most encouraging perhaps was that the team—the whole team—was finally hitting as had been expected. Each of the everyday players, except Jimmy Brown at .276, was over .300 for the home stand. The middle of the batting order—Slaughter, Musial, and Walker Cooper—had hit .333, .320, and .382 respectively. The number-two hitter,

Terry Moore, had a .310 average, while Kurowski, batting sixth, was at .344. In the seventh and eighth spots, Hopp had hit .317 and Marion a remarkable .352. The reserves had also done well, especially Harry Walker, who filled in for the injured Moore and posted a .412 mark. Yet nothing about the offense pleased Southworth more than that Stan Musial had begun to hit with consistency and authority. Of his performance in the early months of the season, Musial told Robert Morrison of the *Post-Dispatch*, "For some reason or other, I had fallen into the habit of trying to get all the power from my arms," and thus he failed to get his wrists and his weight fully into his swing.[1] That corrected, he was now among the top hitters in the National League.

The Redbirds' offensive display, combined with the season-long woes of Ernie White and Howard Pollet, led John Wray of the *Post-Dispatch*, who seemed to revel in the role of contrarian, to argue that the Cardinals' problem was now pitching, not hitting, and he served up numbers to show that, while trailing in total hits, the team was ahead of the Dodgers in doubles, triples, home runs, and total bases.[2] Billy Southworth disagreed. Of Brooklyn's fast start, he said, "There's nothing mysterious about it. Look at the batting averages. There's your answer." Ticking off the Dodgers' lineup, Southworth pointed out that everyone except first baseman Dolph Camilli was hitting better than in 1941. "In contrast, virtually every man on our team is hitting far below his 1941 level." By contrast, "our pitching," he continued, "is the best in the league. Our pitchers have been yielding very few earned runs in a game." He concluded, with the voice of authority, "It's the batting."[3]

Southworth thought the pitching staff most impressive for soldiering through Mort Cooper's struggles. The Cards' ace had launched the home stand with a complete-game victory, but he had only one other win and no complete-game wins in five subsequent starts. Beazley had stepped forward with three complete-game victories, and Ernie White showed signs of returning to his 1941 form with two route-going wins in addition to a well-pitched game for which he got no decision. Gumbert turned in solid work as a sometimes starter and sometimes reliever, posting two complete-game wins and appearing twice in relief. Dickson, Lanier, and Krist had become a solid relief corps, and each of them could also start when needed. Only Pollet continued to be a disappointment. In four outings, two as a starter and two in relief, he pitched a total of just five and a third innings and was hit hard in all of his appearances. Southworth would continue to spot him in games in the hope that he, like White, could recover his previous form.

The Cardinals left St. Louis immediately after the Sunday doubleheader, but instead of an open date on Monday, July 20, they had another exhibition game that night against the club's Double A affiliate in Rochester, the Red Wings. The team that had sent Stan Musial to the Cardinals the year before had no one like him in 1942. Erv Dusak, an outfielder and sometimes third baseman, had an impressive spring training with the Cards and was generally thought to be the best prospect at Rochester, but a slick-fielding young shortstop, Joffre Cross, just up from A ball, had caught the eye of some in the organization. Both men would join the Cardinals in September when big-league rosters expanded. There were no pitching prospects of note. Max Surkont, who went to spring training highly touted, encountered arm problems in Florida that stayed with him throughout the season and stalled his advancement. In the exhibition game, the Cardinals continued their winning ways, defeating the Red Wings 7–5, after which they left for Philadelphia.

~

In July, while the Cardinals were at home trying to make up ground on the Dodgers, a controversy erupted over the absence of African American players in the major leagues. In 1942, professional baseball was a house divided by the skin color of the players. There were two sets of professional leagues in America, one in which all players were white or light-skinned Latinos like Cardinal coach Miguel Gonzalez, and another in which all were African Americans or dark-skinned Latinos. Agitation to desegregate baseball had begun in the latter half of the 1930s, led by Lester Rodney, a white sportswriter for the *Daily Worker*, the official newspaper of the American Communist Party. He was joined by African American sportswriters at black newspapers, primarily Sam Lacey of the *Washington Herald* and Wendell Smith of the *Pittsburgh Courier Journal*.[4] A number of other white sportswriters—including Jimmy Powers, Shirley Povich, and Bill Corum—had urged the major leagues to open their doors to players of color. For several years, major-leaguers like Bob Feller had organized teams of white players from various big-league clubs to play postseason exhibition games against black All-Star teams, and most of the white players on Feller's teams said they would be comfortable having African American teammates. Questions were always raised about whether any black players were good enough to play in the majors, which evaded the larger question. When asked which pitcher was the toughest he had faced in his first year as a big-leaguer, Joe DiMaggio, who had played with Feller against the black All-Stars, replied without hesitation, "Satchel Paige," naming the great righthander from the Negro Leagues who usually organized the black squads for games against the white teams.

Major-league officials, owners, and managers had been reluctant to speak out about bringing black players into white baseball, but by 1942 several current and past managers—Bill McKechnie of the Cincinnati Reds, Casey Stengel of the Boston Braves, Ray Blades formerly of the Cardinals, Jimmy Dykes of the

Chicago White Sox, and Leo Durocher of the Dodgers—had voiced the opinion that desegregation would surely happen. Yet they always qualified their remarks by saying it would depend upon the fans being ready for it. All agreed that they had seen African American players capable of playing in the majors. By the early 1940s, more and more players, including a number of former Cardinal greats like Dizzy and Paul Dean and Pepper Martin, shared the view that blacks would eventually play in the majors and that there were plenty of them good enough to do so. There were also owners like Clark Griffith of the Washington Senators who said publicly that desegregation of the major leagues would come, a sentiment with which National League president Ford Frick agreed, calling the entry of black players into the majors inevitable. All of them, however, were careful to pass the buck to the fans, saying it was dependent upon their acceptance of black players.

There were of course owners and players who opposed the idea, as well as those who preferred to say little or nothing on the subject. The Dodgers' Larry MacPhail observed that the entry of African Americans into the majors would most likely kill off the Negro Leagues, which were the third-largest black-owned business in the country. He also waxed indignant over the nature of the controversy that had arisen: "Unfortunately the discussion of the problem has been contaminated by charges of racial discrimination," he gruffed, "most of it vicious propaganda circulated by professional agitators who do not know what they are taking about."[5] The *St. Louis Star-Times* asked the owners of the Cardinals and Browns whether their clubs would give a black player a trial if one came to a tryout camp. Both owners were noncommittal. Sam Breadon declined to comment, while William DeWitt replied that the Browns did not conduct open tryouts but relied instead on recommendations. As to whether they would use a black player, DeWitt replied, "I haven't given the matter much thought."[6]

The controversy arose in 1942 from a comment by Leo Durocher. After his team had been shut out by a black pitcher in Havana, where the Dodgers took part of their spring training, the "Lip" was quoted as saying, "I wouldn't hesitate a minute to sign up some of those great colored players if I got the OK." For years it had been believed that major-league baseball had a rule against signing black players. But by the early 1940s it was more generally thought that there was no such rule, that instead a "gentleman's agreement" existed among the owners to exclude African Americans. As more and more owners denied this, the focus of responsibility (and blame) fell on Commissioner Kenesaw Mountain Landis. Lester Rodney published a long and blunt open letter in the *Daily Worker* addressed to Landis, accusing him of being the only impediment to the entry of black players into the world of white baseball. Against the backdrop of war, Rodney began with an appeal to American patriotism: "Negro soldiers and sailors are among those beloved heroes of the American people who have already died for the preservation of this country and everything this country stands for . . . including the great game of baseball." Rodney wrote that he would not mince words, and he surely did not, telling Landis: "You, the self-proclaimed 'Czar' of baseball, are the man responsible for keeping Jim Crow in our national pastime."[7]

Landis responded by summoning Durocher to a meeting and demanding an explanation of his springtime remark. Durocher denied the quote attributed to him, whereupon Landis declared emphatically that there was no rule, either "formal or informal, or any understanding unwritten, subterranean, or sub-anything" that prevented the hiring of black players. "I told Durocher," the commissioner continued, "that he could hire one Negro or 25 Negro ball players just the same as whites."[8] Most major-league owners remained silent about Landis's pronouncement, but Pittsburgh's William Benswanger made a point of publicly agreeing with the commissioner. "There is not and never has been, to my knowledge, anything to ban Negroes from baseball," he said, adding, "I know nothing of any agreement in the major leagues to ban Negroes." James Gallagher, general manager of the Chicago Cubs, told reporters, "Our scouts have never recommended a Negro player." Then, striking his own patriotic pose, he opined, "I think everyone in the country should be doing something of more value to the nation as a whole than stirring up racial hatred. That's my personal opinion and has nothing to do with baseball."[9]

Near the end of July, at the request of "some paper," Benswanger announced that the Pirates would give black players a tryout. "Colored men are American citizens with American rights," he explained. "I know there are many problems connected with the question, but after all, somebody has to make the first move." Benswanger assured Pirate fans and baseball followers in general that "anything I do will be calculated to help our team and our game," adding that he supposed if he signed a black player and then dropped him, he would be accused of discrimination. "But I have a clear conscience in the matter," he asserted, "and I intend to keep it." Pittsburgh manager Frankie Frisch dismissed the whole thing, saying he did not believe there was anything to it.[10] The *Daily Worker* applauded Benswanger and reported that the tryout was scheduled for August 4 and would include three players: pitcher Dave Barnhill of the New York Cubans, and catcher Roy Campanella and second baseman Sam Hughes of the Baltimore Elite Giants. Benswanger immediately denied that a tryout date had been set or players chosen. "We would not raid any Negro club," he said, "and would require the written consent of the owner of said club before tryouts."

In early August, the *Sporting News* weighed in to defend the division of professional baseball into black and white realms. In its editorial, "No Good from

Raising Race Issue," the argument was made that blacks and whites preferred their own leagues and that bringing so many different races together might produce riots. Like MacPhail, the editorial writer argued that integrating baseball would undermine the Negro Leagues, and blamed the controversy on "agitators" who "have sought to force Negro players on the big leagues, not because it would help the game but because it gives them a chance to thrust themselves into the limelight as great crusaders in the guise of democracy."[11] African American columnist Joe Bostic, writing for the Harlem newspaper *People's Voice*, announced that he was "lukewarm" to the idea of blacks in the majors for reasons that were "purely mercenary." The "net results," he argued, "would be written in red ink on the ledgers of the Negro National and American Leagues." Even one black player in the white leagues, he continued, will "hurt the 'million-dollar' annual business of organized Negro professional ball," because that player "would monopolize the attention of the followers of Negro professional baseball." The "large revenues" earned by the Negro Leagues "would all evaporate with the diversion of interest and patronage as a result of a few Negroes going to the majors."[12]

Other African Americans also had reservations about desegregating white baseball, including Satchel Paige, who doubted that all the problems could be worked out successfully. "You might as well be honest about it," the veteran of seventeen years in the Negro Leagues said. "There would be plenty of problems, not only in the South where the colored boys couldn't be able to stay and travel with the teams in spring training, but in the North where they couldn't stay or eat with them in many places." "All the nice statements in the world from both sides," he concluded, "aren't going to knock out Jim Crow." Moreover, Paige said, he doubted that any major-league team would be willing to match the $37,500 salary he had earned in the previous year.[13] Nevertheless, Benswanger moved ahead with plans for a tryout, announcing that Wendell Smith at the *Pittsburgh Courier Journal* would pick some players. Catcher Josh Gibson of the Homestead Grays and shortstop Willie Wells and pitcher Leon Day of the Newark Eagles were among those mentioned, with the tryout to be held after the regular baseball season concluded. In the end, whether owing to pressure from the baseball establishment or simply to a change of heart, Benswanger never carried through with plans for a tryout, and it would be five more years before the color line was crossed by Jackie Robinson and the Brooklyn Dodgers.

~

The Cardinals started their second swing through the East in Philadelphia on July 21. With Mort Cooper ailing, Billy Southworth opted for Howard Krist to start the first game. In only his second start in 1942, Krist responded with a complete game, scattering six hits to pick up his seventh win of the season and twentieth in twenty-two career decisions. It was not an elegant performance by the slender righthander, who was constantly behind hitters in the balls and strikes count, but he walked only three and managed to wiggle out of numerous tight spots. Two double plays helped. The Phils scored in the first, but were shut out the rest of the way, while the Cardinals banged out twelve hits and six runs against Tommy Hughes, who had beaten them twice previously. Every Redbird batter got at least one hit, including Krist. Walker, Musial, and Slaughter picked up two each in the 6–1 win.

Johnny Beazley took the mound the next day, and despite walking three, giving up ten hits, and hitting a batter, he did not permit a Phillies runner to cross home plate, leaving twelve of them stranded on the base paths during the 7–0 Cardinals victory. The Redbirds collected fourteen hits against three Philadelphia pitchers, and everyone in the lineup except Musial got at least one hit, including doubles by Walker, Kurowski, and Marion and a triple by Crespi. St. Louis went for the sweep the next day but failed, blowing two leads as Harry Gumbert took the 4–3 loss. The Birds failed to capitalize on one opportunity after another against the Phils' 6'5" righthander Frank "Rube" Melton, who had been plucked from the St. Louis farm system the year before.

The Redbirds moved on to Boston, where Max Lanier opened with a six-hit shutout of the Braves. St. Louis hitters pounded Boston starter Jim Tobin and rookie Jimmy Wallace for sixteen hits and eight runs. It was again a team effort as all the regulars joined in the hit parade, with Slaughter, Musial, and Sanders collecting three apiece. The team's speed and Southworth's style of play were also on exhibit as St. Louis laid down eight bunts, three for base hits and two successful as sacrifices. The next day, the Braves broke on top with a run in the first inning against Krist, who was making his second successive start. The Braves' lefty Lou Tost had his way with Cardinal hitters through the first four innings. In the fifth, Slaughter hoisted a long home run with two men aboard, and the Cards added three more runs in the sixth as Brown and Marion led the way. Krist weathered one threat after another, laboring into the ninth, then needing help from Gumbert to clinch the 6–3 victory. His work had rarely been a thing of beauty, but Krist was filling in capably for the ailing Cooper.

On Sunday, July 26, the Redbirds split a doubleheader with the Braves. In the first inning of the opener, they jumped all over starter Al Javery, who gave up two runs without getting anyone out. Boston manager Stengel turned to his bullpen and summoned Tom Earley, who had just returned from a five-day suspension for breaching team rules. Earley ended the first with no further scoring and then held the Cardinals scoreless the rest of the way on only one hit. The Braves came back in the second inning, scoring four times against Johnny Beazley to take the lead. They pushed across another run against Howard Pollet in the seventh for a 5–2 win. St. Louis took the nightcap 5–3. The Birds scored three runs in the fourth inning to grab the lead, but starter Murry Dickson could not hold it. He was hit hard and left in the fifth with the game tied. The versatile Gumbert came to his rescue, shutting out the Braves on one hit the rest of the way. The Redbirds scored the winning runs in the sixth on a double by Coaker Triplett, a single by Walker Cooper, and two wild pitches.

From Boston, the Cardinals headed south to Brooklyn for three games with the Dodgers. The Redbirds had won five of the seven games played so far on the road trip, but nonetheless had fallen another game farther behind the league leaders, who had rebounded from their series in St. Louis to win six of their next seven games. The Cardinals were getting no help from the rest of the league in their pursuit of the Dodgers. Pitcher Larry French, a veteran of thirteen big-league campaigns whose career was resurrected with the Dodgers in 1942, gave Leo Durocher credit for the club's success, calling him "the first real leader I have worked for in my whole baseball career." Durocher, he declared, "makes the Brooklyn club tick. He is dynamic. He yells hardest, has the most pepper, the most life on the bench. With him around, the Dodgers cannot possibly go into a serious slump." Moreover, French enthused, "Durocher's judgment is splendid, and yet he is in a baseball sense a gambling fool. He takes these long chances at the right time."[14] Durocher meanwhile was looking forward to getting some revenge for his team's losses a week earlier in St. Louis. The series was scheduled to start on his thirty-seventh birthday, and he told reporters that all he wanted was three wins over the Cardinals.

The Redbirds arrived in Flatbush for what the press called a "now or never" series, a description that had become a cliché in describing Cardinal-Dodger engagements in the 1942 season. But instead of being greeted by Durocher and his Dodgers, they were met again by rain. Postponement of the first game required a doubleheader the next day. The skies were still threatening when the Cardinals arrived at Ebbets Field on July 28 to find it filled with 33,212 boisterous Brooklynites, the Dodgers' second-largest weekday crowd of the season, all of them ready to celebrate Durocher's birthday albeit a day late. The Cards broke on top with an unearned run in the first inning of the opener, but the lead was short-lived as they handed the Dodgers five unearned runs in the bottom half of the inning. An error by Marty Marion with two men out opened the door, and Durocher's men walked through with their bats blazing, hammering starter Ernie White and driving him from the premises before he could register another out. St. Louis scored a run in the third, but Howard Pollet, in relief of White, gave it back in the bottom of the fourth. Still, the Redbirds fought back against French, scoring two in the fifth and two more in the sixth to tie the game and ending the day for the Dodgers' lefty. Pollet breezed through the Brooklyn lineup after the fourth in his best outing in weeks, but in the bottom of the eighth he hung a curve to former Cardinal Johnny Rizzo, who drove it far back into the left-field seats for a home run that gave the Bums a 7–6 win.

Rain returned to delay the start of the second game for ninety minutes. The heavy skies seemed to some like a portent of the Cardinals' pennant prospects as the Dodgers took the field with the hope of delivering the knockout blow. The game quickly became a pitchers' duel as Max Lanier and Kirby Higbe worked through six tense innings with the score tied 1–1. Then in the seventh the Redbirds exploded. Marion led off with a double, Lanier drew a walk, and Brown bounced a grounder to Dodger third baseman Arky Vaughan, who booted the easy chance for an error that enabled Marion to score. Harry Walker then bunted for a hit to score another run; Slaughter followed with a single, driving home two more. That was the last pitch for Higbe, who was replaced by rookie Ed Head. As lightning pierced the black skies and thunder echoed throughout the park, the Dodgers went into a slowdown, clearly hoping that the rain would return, wash away the Cardinals' runs, and leave the game a tie that would have to be replayed. But Musial and Sanders greeted Head with singles to drive home runs, and O'Dea followed with a bounder to Dolph Camilli on which Musial tried to score but was out at the plate. Kurowski singled to keep the rally going and end the day for Head. Schoolboy Rowe trudged to the mound, accompanied by more apparent stalling by the Dodgers. Lanier, up for the second time in the inning, stroked a single to add another run, but at this point Kurowski went out of his way to get caught in a rundown to end an inning that one reporter called "a farcical race against time." The gods fouled Durocher's birthday wish as the rains stayed away and the game continued, and with another run in the ninth, St. Louis won 9–1 for a split in the twin bill.

The following day, the Cardinals welcomed Mort Cooper's return to the mound for the first time in ten days to face his frequent rival Whitlow Wyatt in a twilight game. Weather continued to be a problem. The start of the game was delayed twenty minutes until 7:05 p.m., but 26,682 of the Flatbush faithful ignored the threat of a storm to watch their Bums and the Birds go at it in the rubber game of the series. It was quickly apparent that the Cards' ace was not in command as he had been in previous outings against Brooklyn, giving up four runs on six hits in five innings. Cooper left trailing 4–1 after the Dodgers scored twice in the fifth, an inning in which the St. Louis defense also let him down. What proved to be the winning run scored on an error by first baseman Ray Sanders, who muffed a hurried throw by George Kurowski on Joe Medwick's swinging bunt toward third. But the greater frustration for the Redbirds was their inability to take advantage of repeated opportunities to score against Wyatt, who gave up six hits and four walks over the first six innings. The Cards threatened in almost every inning, but left eight runners stranded on base, five of them in scoring position. In the seventh, they mounted another charge as Brown led off with a single, Walker doubled, and Slaughter doubled to drive them both home. After Musial fouled out, Walker Cooper bounced a ball back to Wyatt, who trapped Slaughter off second base for the second out of the inning. Sanders followed with a single that would have tied the game had Slaughter still been at second. Kurowski walked to fill the bases and Terry Moore came up as a pinch hitter for Marion. But the Redbird captain lofted a soft fly to right fielder Dixie Walker to end the inning with St. Louis trailing 4–3.

In the bottom of the seventh with one out, the game was ended abruptly at 9:14 as umpire "Beans" Reardon waved the teams off the field, enforcing the New York City wartime "dim-out" regulations that forbid stadium lights from being on for more than an hour after sundown. This gave Brooklyn the win and added a game to their lead over a frustrated St. Louis club. It was the first major-league game cut short by the dim-out rule, and the first time the Dodgers had beaten Mort Cooper all season. Dodger fans reacted to stopping play as if it were lights-out on the Cardinals' pennant chances as well as on the game, and according to Tommy Holmes of the *Brooklyn Eagle*, the Dodgers seemed to agree: "There was a lot of yip-yap going on in the clubhouse with the Dodgers making like crazy as though the 1942 National League pennant race had been won." The odds now, Holmes conceded, were heavily against the Cardinals.[15]

With July coming to an end, the Redbirds now trailed Brooklyn by eight and a half games. More and more commentators agreed that the race was probably over. "Fans probably won't pay a great deal of attention to the baseball standings these days," an Associated Press reporter opined, "because the New York Yankees and Brooklyn Dodgers are making runaways of the major league pennant races."[16] Even Roy Stockton of the *Post-Dispatch* groaned that "the remainder of the season doesn't look too bright for the Cardinals [whose] pennant hopes have faded to a point where even die-hard fans are having their doubts." "It's been a long time," Stockton sighed, "since the [senior] circuit had such a poor race."[17] Dan Daniel of the *World-Telegram* was more tentative, suggesting that there might still be time for Southworth to get his "machine" running well, but he added that "from now on," Durocher's "most worrisome task" may be "the maintenance of an alert against overconfidence."[18]

～

After meeting with President Roosevelt in Washington in late June and surviving a no-confidence vote in London in early July, Winston Churchill set off to consult with his commanders and rally the troops at El Alamein. In Africa, as July drifted into August, Alan Moorehead writes, "the British could at least claim that they had emerged from their blackest hour."[19] For the time being, Egypt was safe. The stalemate that resulted from blocking Rommel's Afrika Korps at El Alamein continued into August as the two sides played a tit-for-tat game of advance, withdraw, advance, and withdraw again, all the while building up their supplies of men, equipment, and fuel in anticipation of the next free-for-all. While in Africa, Churchill named General Bernard Montgomery to head the British forces and then took off for Moscow to meet with Soviet leader Josef Stalin. In Washington, Churchill and Roosevelt had decided against opening a second front in Europe in 1942, choosing instead to build up American troops in North Africa. U.S. and British forces were to join in attacking Europe through its underbelly on the Mediterranean once Rommel was defeated in Africa.

With his nation under siege—the Germans were at the doorstep of Moscow as well as closing in on Stalingrad and the Caucasus—Stalin was anxious to have a second front opened in Europe and very much preferred an invasion in the north of the continent that would force Hitler to transfer some of his military muscle to the defense of the homeland. As Churchill arrived, the Soviet Union was setting the oil wells in the Maikop and Grozny fields on fire to prevent this critical resource from falling into enemy hands, denying Hitler the prize he so wanted. Shortly after the British prime minister departed, the Germans reached Stalingrad and began a furious assault on the city.[20] During his several days in the Soviet capital, Churchill persuaded Stalin that it was impossible for the United States and Britain to mount a successful invasion of the continent in 1942 and that a southern invasion of Europe was more practicable than one in the north. Reluctantly, Stalin agreed. Meanwhile, British and American fliers continued to bomb German cities and other targets in Western Europe. These attacks had reached a new peak of destruction at the end of July, when fifteen two-ton bombs hit the Rhineland industrial city of Dusseldorf and left massive destruction behind. The American press was upbeat in reporting on the Russian talks and the fighting at El Alamein.

Churchill returned to Africa after leaving Moscow, only to be greeted by news that North Africa was by no means his only worry. India was in turmoil. The Free India movement led by Mahatma Gandhi and his supporters in the All India Congress Party had been calling for independence for months. During the summer, British emissary Stafford Cripps had discussions on the future of India with Gandhi and others and finally put forward a plan by which India would gain its freedom, but not in a time of war. There were fears in Britain that an independent India might negotiate a separate peace with Japan, though Indian leaders repeatedly pledged to fight on the side of the Allies if granted independence. Gandhi and his followers found the Cripps proposal unacceptable and demanded immediate independence. Public protests followed. In Calcutta, anti-British rioting was met with force, several protesters were killed, and on August

9 Gandhi and other All India Congress leaders were placed under house arrest. Three days later, mobs in New Delhi stormed the city hall and set it aflame. Order was restored, but an uneasy truce followed. Through it all, the United States maintained a hands-off policy.

While Churchill was commuting between London, Moscow, and El Alamein, the United States was making final plans for its first offensive excursion in the Pacific. The offensive was aimed at capturing the airfield on Guadalcanal that the Japanese had been building since early July. On August 9, the same day that Gandhi was arrested in India, U.S. Marines invaded Guadalcanal as well as smaller islands nearby and easily captured the poorly defended airfield. The Japanese responded by attacking U.S. forces by air, but with little effect. The same was not true for a naval engagement that followed, during which the United States lost a number of warships and was forced to withdraw its naval forces, leaving the Marines on Guadalcanal vulnerable to counterattack.[21] The invasion was of course front-page news in St. Louis papers, though the precise location of the conflict was veiled in secrecy, with reports saying only that there was heavy fighting in the Solomon Island chain.

The same vagueness characterized news reports two weeks later when the Japanese counterattacked, landing a sizable force nearby at Milne Bay on New Guinea that was beaten back after fierce jungle fighting. Air and naval battles, none of which were conclusive, continued through the remainder of August and into September. In mid-September, the Japanese landed a yet larger force to reclaim the airfield, which had been renamed Henderson Field to honor a hero of the Midway battle. In a series of furious nighttime attacks, the enemy launched one assault after another, but American Marines, now well dug in and fortified with artillery, foiled each of them. The Japanese took heavy casualties and quit the assault. Henderson Field was safe, although fighting on Guadalcanal would continue until February of 1943, and for the first time the United States had reclaimed territory, however modest, that had been under Japanese control, a triumph heralded in the American press.

At home, attempts to subvert the war effort competed with news from abroad for headlines and front-page coverage. In late July, a soldier at Jefferson Barracks in St. Louis, Prescott Freese Dennett, was arrested on a federal warrant that charged him with conspiring to undermine the morale of the armed forces. A native of Bangor, Maine, and a graduate of the Columbia University School of Journalism, Dennett had taken part as a newspaperman before the war in a campaign against U.S. intervention in Europe. One of twenty-eight indicted, he claimed to be a "victim of the hysteria of the times."[22]

His arrest was part of a Department of Justice sweep to corral subversive activists nationwide by taking isolationists, anti-Semites, and Nazi sympathizers into custody. Among those arrested were George Otto Brennerman of Chicago, an artist whose work was said to be injurious to the American defense; Herman Max Schwein of Los Angeles, a German-American Bund leader; Gerald Winrosh of Wichita, publisher of the *Defender*, which expressed anti-Semitic and pro-Nazi views; William Griffin, publisher of the *New York Enquirer*, which was isolationist, anti-Roosevelt, and anti-British; Colonel Nelson Sanctuary, an Army Reserve officer said to be anti-Semitic and isolationist; William Dudley Pally of Noblesville, Indiana, head of the Silver Shirts and one of the nation's most militant Fascist leaders; and Elizabeth Dilling, author of anti-Semitic and anticommunist books and a leader of mothers' groups protesting the war. Among the organizations named in the indictments were German-American Bunds, the Silver Shirts, America First Committees, the Friends of Progress, and the Ku Klux Klan. All were linked to a conspiracy to violate laws forbidding interference with the armed forces and with sedition, which together carried a penalty of thirty years in prison.[23]

Frightening as stories of subversion from within may have been to some Americans, the message delivered in the nation's press was that of an ever-vigilant government ready to deal quickly and severely with any and every threat. The point was made dramatically in early August when six of the Nazi saboteurs who had slipped into the United States by submarine in New York and Florida earlier in the year were sent to the electric chair. After their conviction by a military tribunal in July, President Roosevelt reviewed all eight cases, decided that the two who cooperated with authorities should receive thirty-year jail sentences instead of death, and approved the death sentence for the others.[24] As elsewhere, the executions were front-page news in St. Louis, where the press retold the story of their capture while reporting on their deaths. The coverage included biographies of convicted men and photographs of those executed and of the electric chair in which their lives ended.

For all the unpleasant news from home and abroad, there were also humorous stories about the efforts of ordinary Americans, many of them children, to support the war effort. In St. Louis, seven-year-old Michael Warren set out to volunteer for the Navy and wound up in a police station, where the bag he carried was found to contain a toy cannon and a bug spray with insecticide with which he planned to kill Japanese. The police called his parents and sent him home with instructions to kill Japanese beetles.[25] In Little Rock, Arkansas, a budding scientist, nine-year-old Kennard Clark, sliced a piece from his belt, melted it with sulfur, and produced a rubberlike substance. He sent it to President Roosevelt in the hope that it might solve the rubber shortage.[26] In Massachusetts, a twenty-five-year-old Braintree resident, Paul Revere, a descendant of the Revolutionary War hero, was sworn into the Army, then mounted a horse and reenacted his ancestor's historic ride to thunderous applause from the assembled troops.[27] A 385-pound shipbuilder in San Pedro, California, wrote to Roosevelt, saying he needed overalls of a special size and could not get them. He told the president that he had voted for him three times, presumably in different elections, and needed the overalls to avoid becoming the "California Mahatma Gandhi." The War Production Board assured him that he would get his pants.[28]

~

Following the series with the Dodgers, the Cardinals at last had an open date, but the team remained in New York for a four-game weekend series with the Giants. It was four days of listening to a growing chorus of pundits singing the praises of the Dodgers and awarding them the National League flag. The rain that had hung over the games in Brooklyn continued to fall on Gotham, causing the first game against Mel Ott's crew to be canceled and giving the Cardinals an unwanted second full day to reflect upon both the Brooklyn series—one game lost for want of a timely hit, another lost to wartime regulations—and the growing number of obituaries being written for them. Applauding the Cardinals' players as "good, game guys" who "kept in there," Tommy Hughes of the *Eagle* pointed out that, despite winning twenty-two of thirty-one games played in July, the Redbirds had gained no ground whatsoever on the front-running Dodgers. The Cardinals had been eight and a half games behind Brooklyn on July 1, and they remained eight and a half games behind on August 1. Worse yet, Holmes added, the toughest part of the Dodgers' schedule was behind them, while the most difficult part for the Cardinals lay ahead.[29]

New York writers were like a Greek chorus chanting the name of Johnny Mize incessantly, his trade the tragedy that led to all of St. Louis's problems in 1942. A hot-hitting July had raised the St. Louis team batting average to the top spot in the National League, but twenty-one of their thirty-six losses had come by one run, due, their critics endlessly suggested, to the absence of consistent slugging that Mize would have provided. The cruelest cut may have come from John Wray of the *Post-Dispatch*, who went beyond the Mize trade to earlier deals with the Dodgers, noting "the evident smiles on the mugs of Curt Davis, Joe Medwick, and Leo Durocher, all sold down the river by the Cards as excess baggage" and who were now "putting the Dodgers over in a big way."[30] But for many the surest evidence that the race was over came from New York oddsmaker Jack Doyle, who quit taking bets on the pennant races in both leagues, declaring that the Yankees and Dodgers were sure things.

The skies over Coogan's Bluff cleared for the Saturday doubleheader with the Giants, and Billy Southworth sent Max Lanier to the mound to face lefty Tom Sunkel, yet another former Cardinal banished from Birdland. The Cards got all the runs Lanier needed in the first inning when Brown walked to lead off and, one batter later, Slaughter hit his tenth home run of the season to put St. Louis ahead 2–0. Lanier was masterful, striking out five, walking only one, and holding the Giants' sluggers to five singles. The Redbird defense was equally masterful, turning five double plays as the men from Missouri took the opener 3–1. In the nightcap, the Cards fell behind early when New York scored single runs in the first, third, and fifth innings, hammering Johnny Beazley for nine hits, including a solo home run by shortstop Dick Bartell, who crossed home plate pointing and wagging his finger at bench jockeys in the St. Louis dugout. Meanwhile, the Cards could do nothing against the soft slants of Bob Carpenter, who held them scoreless through the first seven innings. But in the eighth, the Cardinal offense came alive. Trailing 2–0 and with one out, Slaughter singled, and Musial followed with a home run. Sanders then singled, and a tiring Carpenter walked O'Dea. Ace Adams came on to relieve Carpenter with the two runners on base and was greeted by George Kurowski's line-drive single to left to tie the score. Marion fanned, but Terry Moore, hitting for the pitcher, singled home Kurowski with the go-ahead run.

The lead was short-lived. Pollet took over mound duties for St. Louis in the bottom of the eighth, struck out the first two batters, and got two strikes on first sacker Babe Young, only to have him turn on an inside pitch and line it just inside the foul pole down the short right-field line for a game-tying home run. Ironically, Young was in the lineup only because Johnny Mize was injured. The game went into extra innings with the fourth St. Louis pitcher of the game, Howard Krist, on the mound working against former Redbird "Fiddler Bill" McGee. In the bottom of the eleventh, the Birds infield, which had been sensational all afternoon, imploded while trying to field bunts. New York center fielder James "Buster" Maynard opened the frame with his third single of the afternoon. Catcher Harry Danning bunted for a sacrifice, but when first baseman Johnny Hopp tried to cut Maynard down at second, his throw was too late. The next hitter, second baseman Mickey Witek, bunted down the third-base line. Kurowski and Krist got tangled together trying to field it, and Witek was safe with a hit to load the bases. Babe Barna came off the bench to bat for McGee and lofted a fly ball to center that Harry Walker caught, but it was deep enough for Maynard to scurry home from third with the winning run. It was another one-run loss for the Birds, and another half-game lost to the Dodgers, who had won against the Cubs.

On Sunday, the Giants had their aces, Carl Hubbell and Hal Schumacher, ready for the Cardinals. St. Louis came away with a split in the twin bill and was lucky to get that. Hubbell shut them down on one run in the first game in one of his best performances of the season. Mel Ott supplied all the runs the Giants' southpaw needed with a solo homer in the first and a grand slam in the fifth as the New Yorkers won 7–1. Mort Cooper started the second game and appeared to be recovered from the ailments of July. New York scored twice against him in the first inning thanks to an error by Cooper himself, after which the Redbirds' ace held the Gothamites scoreless on four hits. The Cardinals tied the game with two runs in the sixth, then won it in the ninth without the benefit of a hit. Musial got aboard safely on an error by shortstop Bartell, whose low throw skipped past first sacker Young, enabling the St. Louis outfielder to reach second. Sanders bounced a grounder to the right side of the infield that moved Musial to third. The Giants walked O'Dea intentionally, but Kurowski spoiled their plans with a successful squeeze bunt to Young at first, whose hasty throw to the plate could not get Musial flying down the line from third for a 3–2 Redbird win and a split in the series.

There was no rest for the road-weary Redbirds, who left immediately after Sunday's second game for a trip to the upstate New York village of Cooperstown and an exhibition game with the Philadelphia Athletics in the fourth annual Hall of Fame Game. Played at historic Doubleday Field, then said to be the birthplace of baseball, the game was part of the festivities surrounding induction ceremonies in which former Cardinal great Rogers Hornsby would be enshrined with the game's immortals. Despite wartime travel restrictions, almost seven thousand fans jammed the small ballpark, spilling over onto the outfield grass from one foul line to the other to watch the teams battle through eight innings tied at 2–2. In the ninth, Musial led off with a long drive well over the head of A's center fielder Mike Kreevich and easily circled the bases. But the baseball had gone into the crowd, and the umpires called it a ground-rule double. The Cards went on to load the bases for Walker and Marion, both of whom singled, bringing three runs home for a 5–3 St. Louis win.

While the Cardinals were in Cooperstown, the Dodgers moved into the Polo Grounds to play the Giants in another of the games scheduled for armed forces relief. A crowd of 57,035 turned out for the twilight affair that started at 6:45. Brooklyn held a 7–4 lead going into the bottom of the ninth inning, but the Giants rallied. Billy Werber led off with a single, followed by a walk to Mel Ott. As the tying run in the person of slugger Babe Young strolled to the plate and with the heart of the New York batting order to follow, home plate umpire George Magerkurth abruptly waved his arms to indicate that the game was over, again enforcing New York City's dim-out rule. As the floodlights at the Polo Grounds were extinguished, the huge crowd, surprised by the umpire's action, began to boo lustily and became frenzied in its anger. The organist tried to quiet them by playing the National Anthem, but there was no silencing the raucous gathering, which almost drowned out the organist with its booing. The fans' outrage of course had no effect on the outcome of the game, which was a Dodgers victory, their second dim-out win within the week.

Leo Durocher had chosen Whitlow Wyatt to pitch the game. National League umpire-in-chief Bill Klem blamed Wyatt, a slow and deliberate worker, for having caused delays throughout the game, noting especially the time consumed in the walk to Ott immediately preceding the abrupt ending. National League president Ford Frick publicly deplored the stalling tactics and confronted Durocher about why he had saved Wyatt for another twilight game after the experience of the previous week. Giants president Horace Stoneham told reporters that the Army had denied permission to keep the lights on until 9:30 if necessary and also announced that after the next day's game, which was also scheduled as a twilight affair, there would be no more twilight games played at the Polo Grounds. For the Dodgers, it was another controversy in an already controversy-laden season, but one that increased their league lead by a half game.

The Cardinals had been on the road for fifteen days, in which time they had played fourteen regular games and two exhibition games; another ten days and eleven games, all against western teams, stood between them and home. This final phase of the trip began in Cincinnati, where Cardinal killer Johnny Vander Meer was ready and waiting. The lefty, called the "Dutch Master" after the cigar of that name, was on his game through the first six innings, holding the Cardinals to two hits and no runs, striking out five, and permitting only one runner to advance beyond first base. Howard Krist made another start for Southworth and was no puzzle to Cincinnati hitters, who rocked him for five hits and three runs in his two innings of work. The Reds added three more hits and a run against Krist's replacement, Harry Gumbert.

In the seventh, Vander Meer suddenly could not find home plate as he crossed that fine line between brilliance and wildness. He gave up a leadoff single to Ray Sanders, walked two batters, and served up a two-run single to Jimmy Brown. Terry Moore followed with a drive into left center that carried into the enclosed folding steps of an exit gate. One run scored, but instead of being a triple that would have sent a second run in to tie the score, Moore's wallop was declared a ground-rule double, which meant the tying run was left at third base. Right-hander Joe Beggs took over mound duties for the Reds and walked Slaughter intentionally to load the bases. Stan Musial, hitting for Coaker Triplett, then lashed a long drive to the deepest part of Crosley Field, but center fielder Eric Tipton raced back and on the dead run made the catch for the final out of the inning. Beggs proceeded to hold the Birds scoreless and hitless over the last two frames to secure a 4–3 Cincinnati win, leaving the Redbirds to think about Moore's "double" and wonder if the fates were indeed against them.

Meanwhile, the Dodgers played a second straight dim-out game in New York that ended in a 1–1 tie. The St. Louis loss thus dropped them another half game behind Brooklyn. The Cards rebounded the next night behind the strong right arm of Johnny Beazley, who had struggled in recent outings but was dominant in this one as he struck out eight and gave up only three singles. The rookie right-hander faced only thirty batters and was never in trouble as Cincinnati hitters beat the ball into the ground all night. St. Louis outfielders registered only five putouts for the game. The Cardinals' hitters got to Bucky Walters for five hits and four runs in his three innings of work, sending the team on its way to a 5–0 win. Enos Slaughter continued his torrid hitting with two singles, and the Redbirds were helped by a porous Cincinnati defense that committed four errors. Over his last thirty-three games, Slaughter had hit .423 with eleven doubles, eight triples, and five home runs.

The Cardinals had a day off for travel to Pittsburgh for a four-game series that would turn out to be five. They stumbled badly in the opener as the Pirates routed Max Lanier with an eight-run second inning. The stubby southpaw gave up five hits and a walk before leaving with only one out, to be followed by Harry Gumbert, who gave up two more hits and a walk. Bob Elliott had a double and single in the big inning, while Vince DiMaggio had two singles and Elbie Fletcher a single and a walk. The Cardinals came back in the top of the third, knocking Pirate starter Hank Gornicki out and scoring three times. But the Buccaneers retaliated with two runs in their half of the third and then five more in the fifth inning as they pounded five St. Louis pitchers for sixteen hits. While it was a bad day for the pitching staff, it was not so for the hitters, who collected eleven hits, including three doubles and two triples. But it was not enough as Pittsburgh went on to a 13–6 win, handing the Cards their worst defeat in weeks, made more painful by an injury to second baseman Jimmy Brown.

Mort Cooper took the mound the next day in the Saturday afternoon tilt, and the Pirates picked up where they had left off the day before, hammering the big righthander for six hits and five runs in the first three innings. Cooper was wild, walking four before leaving with two out in the third, and leaving behind renewed concerns about his arm. Faced with an uphill battle, the Cardinals came back with two runs in the fourth, single tallies in the fifth and seventh, and finally tied the score in the eighth on a single by Frank Crespi, who was subbing for Brown, and a long double by Terry Moore, who was pinch-hitting for the pitcher. The game remained tied at the end of regulation play and went to extra innings, in which neither team so much as threatened to score. Finally, at the end of the sixteenth inning, the game ended in a 5–5 tie when in umpire Jocko Conlan's judgment it became too dark to continue. The Cardinals' bullpen had taken over in the third inning and turned in a Herculean performance as three pitchers—Krist, Gumbert, and Dickson—held Pittsburgh scoreless on five hits over the final thirteen and one-third innings. But after tying the score, the Redbird offense also disappeared, as they got only one hit in the final eight innings of play. Now it would all have to be done over again.

There was no joy in the St. Louis clubhouse after the long afternoon of no decision. The Birds had won only three of seven games since the Brooklyn series, missing an opportunity to gain ground on Brooklyn, which had won four and lost four over the same stretch. The Birds found themselves nine full games behind the league leaders with fewer and fewer games to left to play. Roy Stockton of the *Post-Dispatch* had earlier employed the cliché of it being darkest before the dawn, and surely this was the darkest hour for the 1942 Cardinals, who could not have imagined that the next day would be the dawn of a historic drive over the last third of the season in which they would win forty-three of their final fifty-one games to rip the National League pennant from the grasp of the Dodgers and claim it as their own.

CHAPTER 8
The Cardinals Take Wing

August was traditionally the month for vacations in America. In 1942, with the nation at war, most St. Louis families were "vacationing" at home in their back yards, sunbathing and gardening, entertaining themselves in make-shift pools, and with badminton, neighborhood barbecues, and picnics that commonly included balloon-busting contests and "wheelbarrow" races. Some, mainly men, found recreation in softball, golf, handball, and fly casting, while wealthier St. Louisans had tennis and croquet courts and real swimming pools in their back yards. For children, George Vierheller, director of the St. Louis Zoo and Sam Breadon's springtime buddy, organized shows of performing elephants, orang-utans, and other animals, while the Muny Opera presented the political satire popular as a children's show, *The Wizard of Oz,* and the colorful saga of life on the Mississippi River, *Show Boat.* The latter, the highlight of the season, featured Sammy White and Norma Terris as Frank and Magnolia, roles they created in the original Ziegfeld Theatre production. Proceeds from one performance were given to military relief.

For professional baseball players, August was anything but a vacation; it was the "dog days" of summer. Four months of hard, almost continuous toil can wear physically and mentally on players. The almost daily bumps and bruises, the scrapes and scratches, strains and sprains from which they recover fairly quickly in April and May grow into distracting aches and nagging pains by August, made more debilitating by the mental fatigue of the long season with its ups and downs, and more exhausting by the searing heat of summer afternoons. For a young and more resilient team like the Cardinals, August posed fewer threats, but to an older and more vulnerable one like the Dodgers, it was an ominous time, even for a team with a nine-game lead. For a team with so great an advantage, it was too easy to slip into the mind-set of coasting on its lead, to lose the sharpness, the edge, the focus that had got them to where they were.

~

Following the deeply frustrating fourteen-inning tie with the Pirates, the Cardinals met Pittsburgh in a Sunday doubleheader and won both games. Stan Musial enjoyed a great day playing before friends and family from his nearby home of Donora, Pennsylvania. In the first inning of the opener, he tripled after singles by Kurowski and Moore to give the Cards a two-run lead, then trotted home on a single by Walker Cooper to make it a three-run advantage. Staked to this early lead, Johnny Beazley calmed the Pirates' bats through the first five innings, but the hometown team broke through against him in the sixth, scoring three times to knot the game and end the day for the Redbird rookie. After taking over for Pittsburgh starter Rip Sewell in the first, Johnny Lanning held the Cards scoreless over the next six innings. But in the eighth, Musial struck again, doubling home Enos Slaughter with what proved to be the winning run in a 4–3 decision that went to Murry Dickson.

Musial was not done. In the nightcap, he followed Harry Walker's first-inning double with a double of his own to put the Birds up by one, which became two in the second when they added a run on a Pittsburgh error, a sacrifice bunt, and a single by Frank Crespi. St. Louis starter Ernie White was literally knocked out of the box in the bottom of the second when a line drive off the bat of Elbie Fletcher ricocheted off his groin. White was helped from the field and taken immediately to a local hospital. He was replaced by Howard Krist, who gave up a run-scoring fly to Frankie Gustine but then blanked the Pirates on five hits for the remainder of the afternoon, one that ended early when umpires called the game after the eighth inning because Pennsylvania's "blue laws" forbade play after 7 p.m. on a Sunday.

Rather than a day off on Monday, the Cardinals had to replay the tie game from Saturday. Mort Cooper made the start and was again hit hard. But despite six hits in the first four innings, the Pirates could score only once. In the fifth, the Redbirds put together a Marion double and three singles, scoring twice to take a 2–1 lead. Cooper's day ended in the bottom half of the inning when Pittsburgh scored four times, three on a bases-loaded triple by third baseman Bob Elliott. Cooper's outing did nothing to allay concerns about his physical condition. Meanwhile, St. Louis hitters continued to enjoy Pirate pitching, collecting eleven hits on the day, but they also bounced into three double plays that ended scoring threats. The Birds lost 6–4. The Cardinals had gained a full game with their two wins on Sunday while the Dodgers were rained out, but gave it back in their loss to the Buccos while Brooklyn was shutting out the Phillies.

For their part, the Dodgers found themselves embroiled in yet another controversy. Their Saturday game in Boston had become a beanball contest between

Whitlow Wyatt and the Braves' Manuel Salvo, with each pitcher hitting the other in the course of the contest. National League president Ford Frick fined Wyatt seventy-five dollars and Salvo fifty, the difference due to Wyatt having thrown his bat. Frick also issued a directive that, in the future, managers would be held responsible for beanballs and fined five hundred dollars for their occurrence.[1] Dodgers president Larry MacPhail was furious that Wyatt drew a larger fine, blustering that it made it look as if his team was more to blame. His words fell on deaf ears around the league as most teams no doubt thought the Dodgers were most likely the aggressors.

The Cardinals moved on to Chicago, where they took the first of four games against the Cubbies. In a battle of lefthanders, Max Lanier and Chicago's Vern Olsen had similar games through the first five innings. The Redbirds scored twice in the top of the third when Olsen issued walks to Terry Moore and Johnny Hopp that were followed by run-scoring singles from Enos Slaughter and Coaker Triplett. The Cubs tied the score in the bottom of the inning without getting the ball out of the infield. Lanier returned Olsen's gift by walking the first two hitters, the third bunted safely to load the bases, and two infield outs produced two runs. The Cards went ahead with one run in the sixth when Kurowski walked with two outs, Marion beat out a slow grounder to deep shortstop, and Crespi lined a crisp single to left to send the Redbird third sacker home. The Birds put the game away with four runs in the ninth for a 7–2 win.

The next day, the Cardinals met the Cubs in an unusual midweek double-header to make up for a game canceled earlier due to weather. St. Louis put on an offensive display in both games, getting eleven hits in the opener, three for extra bases, and thirteen in the nightcap, including a Slaughter home run. Beazley started the first game and was no mystery to Windy City batsmen, who reached him for ten hits in six and one-third innings of work. Still, the Cards had a 5–4 lead when Beazley departed in the seventh, after which his team-mates' bats boomed against Cubs reliever Hi Bithorn for a 9–4 win, with Beazley getting credit for his thirteenth victory of the season. St. Louis took the lead early in the second game and was in command all the way behind the eight-hit, complete-game work of Harry Gumbert. The Redbirds put twenty-one men on base against three Cubs hurlers and scored eight of them to win 8–3.

While the Cardinals were winning both ends of the twin bill from the Cubs, the Dodgers were downing the Phils 1–0 behind the shutout pitching of Larry French. Brooklyn had not been hitting well in its last seven games, having been blanked twice and held to only one run in three other contests. Pete Reiser had been experiencing recurrent headaches and dizziness from his encounter with the center-field wall in St. Louis and was left at home for more tests at the Johns Hopkins Medical Center when the club left for Boston on August 7. It was more and more apparent how important he was to the Dodgers and how much they missed his bat. Still, even with Reiser hurting, Brooklyn had been able to maintain its eight- to nine-game lead over the Redbirds.

Larry MacPhail continued to stew about the beanball incident in Boston and became convinced that everyone was against him and his team. "We have a bad press," he fussed. "The rest of the league hates us. Do you think Ford Frick wants to see us win the pennant? They're all taking pot shots at us."[2] The Dodgers' recent lackluster play added to his frustration. He believed that a lack of focus and intensity was behind their puny offense, and after the 1–0 win over the Phils he decided to speak his mind as only he could. He summoned Leo Durocher, his coaches, and all the players to the press box after the game and, with sportswriters present, he lashed out first at Ford Frick for the unfair ways in which the team had been treated by the league office, then blasted the press for covering the Dodgers as if they had already won the pennant. Finally, he erupted at Durocher and the team for lethargic and lackadaisical play. Ever volatile, MacPhail rarely hesitated to vent his views, however incendiary they might be, and in this extraordinary setting he was most fierce in faulting the Dodgers themselves, declaring that only Mickey Owen, Pee Wee Reese, Pete Reiser, Joe Medwick, Curt Davis, and Hugh Casey were "carrying gloves" to every game. With a final flourish, he predicted that the Cardinals could and likely would win the pennant if the Dodgers continued to play as if the season were over. Incensed, Dixie Walker offered to bet the Dodgers' president a hundred dollars on the spot that Brooklyn would win. MacPhail demurred.

Like a jockey astride a tiring thoroughbred rounding the clubhouse turn and heading into the stretch, MacPhail had applied the whip to the Dodgers. His effort received no sympathy from the press, one wag quipping that the only place MacPhail would find "sympathy" was in a dictionary. The press not only failed to applaud his action but instead accused him of accomplishing nothing but making his team "mad." "I hope I did," MacPhail responded, "and I hope they stay mad if that's what they need to play winning ball in every game. They ought to be mad. I know I'm mad." Recalling that the tight race to the wire in 1941 had not given his team time to prepare for the Yankees, he added, "I want to win this pennant and as soon as possible. Hell with winning it on September 20 or 18. Let's win it on August 28 if we can. We want to win it quickly because the sooner we win it the better chance we'll have to win the World Series."[3]

Whatever effect, if any, MacPhail's outburst had on the Dodgers was not immediately apparent as bad weather postponed their next game. The Cardinals, wrapping up their series with the Cubs and their long twenty-five-day road trip, probably wished they had shared in the Dodgers' fortunes, as the Birds were pummeled by the Chicagoans 13–5. Murry Dickson started and lasted only four innings, giving up six hits and five runs. He was followed by Pollet, Krist, and the rarely seen Whitey Moore, who together gave up eight more runs. Claude

Passeau held the weary Redbirds to five runs, four of them coming in the ninth inning long after the outcome had been decided. As the Cards headed home, they were eight and a half games behind the Dodgers, having won fourteen and lost ten during their travels. They had finished the trip winning five of their last seven after the extra-inning tie in Pittsburgh and would be at home for the rest of the month. Southworth's crew knew it really was now-or-never time for them.

~

The Cardinals had continued to hit well on their swing around the league. They and the Dodgers were the best hitting clubs in the Senior Circuit. Enos Slaughter had a Hall of Fame–worthy road trip: a batting average of .406 with five triples, four home runs, and twenty-two runs driven in. Both of his outfield partners—Terry Moore and Stan Musial—hit over .300, as did Harry Walker, who played more than usual owing to Moore's injury. It was, however, shortstop Marty Marion who was the most pleasant surprise. While the other infielders struggled in the mid-to-low .200s, Marion hit .363 away from home. "It's Slugger Marion Now!" the *Globe-Democrat*'s Bob Burnes proclaimed. The Cards' shortstop was hitting .188 on June 1, but came home in mid-August sporting a .283 average. In almost 150 times at bat since early July, Marion had hit at a .340 pace. Mr. Shortstop was beginning to look like Mr. Slugger.

Billy Southworth was no doubt pleased that his young pitching staff had performed well during the struggles of Mort Cooper. Coop started four times during the trip, won only once, lost twice, had a no-decision, and was hit hard in all but one of his outings. Max Lanier and Johnny Beazley led the staff in meeting the challenge of Cooper's ineffectiveness. Lanier started five times and turned in four wins, all of them complete games. At age twenty-seven, the stocky southpaw was one of the "veterans" of the pitching staff, having been with the club for two full seasons and parts of two others. As both starter and reliever, he won ten games for the 1941 team and had begun the 1942 season in the bullpen. But as Ernie White and Howard Pollet struggled with tender arms and were often unavailable or ineffective, Lanier moved more and more into the starting ranks and became the team's most dependable lefthanded pitcher.[4]

On the mound, Lanier had a high leg kick, not ideal for a reliever, and threw almost directly overhand, though he would drop down sidearm against lefthanded hitters. He was a powerful pitcher with a "booming" fastball, sharp-breaking curve, and decent changeup. He was also an intelligent pitcher who thrived on steady work, which he believed helped his control.[5] A North Carolinian, he had turned down a scholarship to Duke University to sign with the Cards when offered a contract by Branch Rickey's brother Frank. Lanier proved especially effective against Brooklyn in 1942, beating them five times in seven tries. He later attributed his success against the Dodgers to Leo Durocher's shouting at him all the time. "He thought it was going to upset me, but the madder I got, the better I could pitch."[6]

Johnny Beazley made six starts on the trip, won three, two of them complete games, and had a no-decision in a fourth game that the Redbirds went on to win. At twenty-three, he had bounced around the minors for four years, first in Cincinnati's farm system and then with the Cardinals before landing in New Orleans in 1941, where with the help of manager Ray Blades and various Cardinal coaches he learned how to pitch. "My idea was to try to fog the ball past batters," Beazley explained. "It didn't work, but thought I knew it all."[7] He came to St. Louis near the end of the 1941 season in time to impress with a complete-game win against the Chicago Cubs. Tall and handsome, Beazley, whose home was in Nashville, Tennessee, began the 1942 season in the bullpen, where his excellent work combined with strong performances in occasional starting opportunities led the Cardinals to sell veteran Lon Warneke to make room for him to be a regular starter. He had not disappointed them. A bit cocky and somewhat temperamental, Beazley was the classic power pitcher with a "whistling fastball" and a "snappy curve," as one observer described his pitches.[8] Like many hard throwers, he had to battle wildness, and the intensity of his pitches was such that his hand and fingers would quiver while on the mound and for a time after a game, though not when he gripped the ball for a pitch. For a change of pace, Beazley would simply take something off his fastball, or sometimes his curve, and that was all he wanted: "None of those screw ball pitches for me," he told an interviewer. "I don't want no part of 'em."[9]

Howard Krist became the swing man of the staff in Cooper's absence, picking up three wins in three starts and four relief appearances. Tall, lean, lantern-jawed, Krist bore a resemblance to the dancer Fred Astaire, though he worked in a baseball cap and flannels, not a top hat and tails. A hard thrower with good control, he was well suited for relief work. Krist had moved through the St. Louis farm system to reach the Mound City in 1937, only to have a succession of injuries send him back to the minors for three years. Among the injuries was a chipped bone in his elbow that required surgery by Dr. Robert Hyland, pairing Krist with Mort Cooper as Hyland's contributions to the Redbird pitching staff. In 1941 and 1942, Southworth had used Krist primarily out of the bullpen, but he never hesitated to use him as a starter when needs dictated. With Cooper on the shelf, Krist had gotten the Cardinals off to a winning start on the now-completed road trip with a complete game victory over the Phillies and followed that four days later with a win over Boston in which he pitched into the ninth inning.

The veteran Harry Gumbert and rookie Murry Dickson were the other swing men on the staff. On the recent trip, they had worked mainly in relief—Gumbert appearing six times, Dickson seven—but both made two starts as well, and between them they picked up three wins. Gumbert was the only Cardinal hurler to be with the team for the entire season who was not a product of the St. Louis farm system, other than the seldom-used Whitey Moore. A breaking-ball specialist, his fastball had improved with time, as had his changeup, but it was his versatility that made him most valuable. The rangy righthander would appear in thirty-eight games in 1942, nineteen as a starter, nineteen in relief.

At 5'10" and 157 pounds, Murry Dickson was the smallest pitcher on the St. Louis staff and easily the most versatile in his repertoire of pitches. Dickson threw seven pitches—a fastball, curve, sinker, slider, knuckleball, screwball, and forkball—in addition to which he would throw overhand, underhand, and side-arm and also vary both his position on the mound and his windup. Stan Musial recalled that teammates called him the "Thomas Edison of the mound" because he was always experimenting with pitches. Branch Rickey thought him simply a "scatterbrain" with a scatter-arm who would inevitably have control problems.[10] Easygoing and seemingly unworried about anything, the twenty-five-year-old righthander came of age as a major-league pitcher as the road trip progressed.

The disappointments among the pitchers continued to be southpaws Ernie White and Howard Pollet, from whom so much had been expected after their strong work the year before. White made an early exit in each of his three starts during the road trip, the last due to an injury that had him on the shelf as the club returned to St. Louis. He was also unimpressive in two relief appearances. Neither White nor Pollet registered a win on the trip; each picked up a loss. Lloyd "Whitey" Moore, the ninth member of the staff, made two appearances on the trip, discounting exhibition games, both in relief, and was of no consequence in the scheme of things.[11] Southworth had managed to have the team play at an almost .600 pace in the twenty-four games with what amounted to a five-man pitching staff. Heroic, perhaps, but it was clear that a serious run for the pennant required that Mort Cooper return to form and that White and Pollet make some contribution.

~

In mid-August, with the Dodgers seemingly a sure thing for the National League pennant, baseball was displaced briefly in the bars of Brooklyn by talk about that other national pastime: politics. A fractious fight had developed within the New York Democratic Party over its 1942 gubernatorial nomination. The opposing sides were headed by the state's heaviest political hitters: James A. Farley, former postmaster general and national party chair, on one side, and his former boss, President Franklin Roosevelt, on the other. Farley's candidate was John J. Bennett, the state attorney general, while Roosevelt backed the state's junior U.S. senator, James M. Mead. Bennett was a Brooklyn native, and the state party convention was to be held in the borough, which made the high-profile bloodletting up close and personal for Flatbush Democrats. There was a soap opera quality to the affair that only heightened interest. Initially, Farley had courted Roosevelt on behalf of Bennett, but the attorney general was not a New Deal liberal or a reliable friend of labor unions, and FDR demurred. Eventually the president chose to support Mead, but when his candidacy failed to generate much enthusiasm, Roosevelt hinted darkly that another candidate might enter the race. None did.

For days, the Democrats' family feud was front-page news in all the New York papers, but nowhere more than in the *Brooklyn Eagle,* where support for the candidacy of the homegrown Bennett was strong. With rumors of plots and counterplots and talk of conspiracies abounding, the nomination battle no doubt reminded some of Larry MacPhail's "us-versus-them" view of the Dodgers in relation to their National League foes. Farley had broken with Roosevelt after the national party's 1940 convention, where his presidential ambitions were crushed by FDR's nomination for a third term. Some analysts saw the fight as political payback by Farley; others thought it a battle for control of the New York delegation to the 1944 national convention.[12] The melodrama ended happily for Farley and the *Eagle* as Bennett won the nomination easily, but with a divided party he was defeated in November by Republican Thomas E. Dewey. By then, however, a far greater defeat would haunt the Dodger faithful.

＄

As Winston Churchill met with Josef Stalin in Moscow and the Nazis closed in on Stalingrad, the Cardinals opened a three-week August home stand against the Cincinnati Reds. Mort Cooper started the first game and eased some worries with a two-hit shutout, displaying the mastery he had shown in the first three months of the season. The fast-paced contest, played in one hour and thirty-one minutes, was his seventh whitewash of the year and third two-hit game. Cooper, who wore the number 13 on his jersey, had been stuck on thirteen wins for more than two weeks and had never won more than thirteen games in a season in either the major or minor leagues. Among the more superstitious of the Redbirds (Terry Moore ranked high in that regard as well), Cooper decided to switch his jersey number to 14, and thus, on August 14, he won his fourteenth game. The Cardinals also welcomed back second baseman and leadoff hitter Jimmy Brown, who had missed the previous week with a chipped bone in a toe and a wrenched back. Brown celebrated his return with a single to drive in the second run in the 4–0 win.

Weather forced postponement of Saturday's game, and the gloomy day was not brightened by John Wray's column in the *Post-Dispatch.* Wray was almost always the newspaper's glass-half-empty guy. He noted that the Cardinals had "played even with the Dodgers over the last forty [games]" but had made up no ground. It was "too bad," he lamented, that they had "let themselves fall back in the first half of the campaign. . . the Dodgers have only to continue at their current pace to force the Redbirds to perform a miracle to finish first."[13] Had he waited a day to write his column, Wray might have added that all the miracles in 1942 appeared to be happening in Brooklyn. As St. Louis was soaking in a steady rain, Flatbush was aglow in a dramatic come-from-behind Dodger win over Boston. Trailing 4–3 in the bottom of the ninth with two outs, two strikes on the hitter, and fans streaming for the exits, Braves ace Jim Tobin tried to slip a fastball past Dolph Camilli, who blasted it high over the right-field wall for a two-run home run that instantly turned a one-run loss into a one-run win and transformed Ebbets Field from deathly silence to bedlam. The win also moved the Dodgers nine and a half games ahead of the Cardinals.

The skies in St. Louis cleared for the Sunday doubleheader. Harry Gumbert strode to the mound to begin the first game, only to leave it in the second inning with no one out and four runs on the scoreboard for the Reds. But the resilient Redbirds, who had scored once in the first against Cincinnati starter Bucky Walters, came back with two in their half of the second and two more in the third to take the lead and send the Reds' righthander to join Gumbert on the sidelines. Murry Dickson took over for Gumbert and blanked the visitors through the seventh inning, but ran into trouble in the eighth, when Cincinnati tied the score before Max Lanier could end the frame. In the bottom of the inning, the Cards went back to work, putting runners on second and third with Stan Musial coming to the plate. Reds manager "Deacon" Bill McKechnie ordered that Musial be intentionally passed for the second time in the game, loading the bases. Walker Cooper foiled the strategy with a ringing single on which left fielder Eric Tipton unleashed an errant throw that enabled all the base runners to score. The Cardinals put more runners on, and Lanier drove two of them home. The two-hour, thirty-eight-minute donnybrook had seen twenty-five hits, twelve walks, four Cincinnati errors, and seven pitchers before the Redbirds claimed a 10–5 win.

In the nightcap, lefthander Johnny Vander Meer was set to go against the Cardinals. He had baffled them repeatedly in four encounters, two of them shutouts. Through four innings of one-hit pitching it appeared that he would notch a fifth win, but in the fifth, the Redbirds drove their nemesis from the game with a seven-hit, five-run uprising. Johnny Beazley went the distance in the 6–3 win despite giving up seven hits and five walks. Walker Cooper, who caught both games of the twin bill, had a big day at the plate, stroking five hits in nine tries and producing two runs. Marty Marion continued his strong hitting with a four-for-eight day, driving in a run and scoring three. Terry Moore collected hits in both games to extend his consecutive-game hitting streak to sixteen. Sweetening the victories was the Dodgers' 3–0 defeat in a rain-shortened game with Boston, which enabled St. Louis to pick up a game and a half on Brooklyn for their afternoon's work.

Chicago followed Cincinnati into St. Louis for a brief two-game series and had their ace, Claude Passeau, ready to go. The Cardinals jumped on him in the first inning, scoring twice thanks to the bat of Walker Cooper. The Redbirds added two more runs in the third and another in the fourth to build a five-run lead. Meanwhile, Max Lanier kept the Cubbies off the scoreboard, scattering seven hits and stranding eight Chicagoans on the base paths as he threw his second shutout, the fourteenth for the team. Moore extended his hitting streak and Marion remained hot. The running game was on display, with the Birds flying around Sportsman's Park: aggressive baserunning forced hurried throws, including an errant one by Chicago first baseman Rip Russell, while Musial and Slaughter stole bases against Chicago's rookie catcher, Chico Hernandez. The following day Mort Cooper returned to the mound, once again under the lights, in search of his fifteenth victory, wearing his brother's jersey with its number 15. He was in command all the way, holding the Bruins scoreless until the eighth inning, when they scored their only run. Lon Warneke, who had been a Cardinal six weeks earlier, started for the Cubs in his first appearance against his former team. Where speed had been the Redbirds' game the day before, this time it was power. Enos Slaughter and Walker Cooper led a twelve-hit attack with home runs, while Johnny Hopp stroked two doubles as St. Louis prevailed 5–1 and Cooper notched his fifteenth win.

The Cards had an open date following the two games with the Cubs. Many of the players lived at the Fairgrounds Hotel, which was three blocks from the ballpark, and on off days they would get together with their families. Most of the players found housing in hotels because baseball players still suffered an unsavory reputation as rowdies, ruffians, and drunkards. Marty Marion remembered how many of his teammates had trouble finding housing. "The kids love you," he recalled. "The grown people didn't."[14] Nonetheless, the players liked St. Louis and especially the support of its fans at Sportsman's Park. The 1942 Cardinals, as Max Lanier and others attest, were a close team, a young team with young families, and the players enjoyed being together off the field as well as on. They liked to picnic in grassy areas near the Mississippi River where their kids could run and play together while the players and their wives lounged and chatted about pleasantries and plans. At other times, the Laniers would invite teammates and their families to their apartment in the evening for sandwiches and watermelon. They entertained themselves with music and in other ways. "We really enjoyed it," Lanier recalled, "had lots of fun."[15]

With no game to cover, Robert Morrison of the *Post-Dispatch* addressed a new and troublesome question for players in 1942: when they were to eat and sleep. Players had traditionally looked forward to a steak dinner following an afternoon game, but with wartime, games now started at various times—1:30, 3:00, 4:30, 5:15, 6:45, 8:30—whatever was the whim of the "brain in the front office." Night games were bad enough as a disruption in player routines, but now there were twilight games as well. Billy Southworth explained the new "routines" of the Cardinals. For night games, the heavy meal was at 4 p.m., with a late breakfast around 9 a.m. and possibly a light lunch. For twilight games, the heavy meal was either early in the afternoon or after the game, with breakfast at the regular time.[16] It was not a problem for players alone: Morrison added that it created a quandary for "Mrs. Fan" as well, who had to plan family meals.

Having rested for a day (and presumably eaten at normal times), the Cardinals went back to work with a weekend series against the Pittsburgh Pirates, who would be followed into St. Louis by the Brooklyn Dodgers for another all-important series. The temptation to look ahead must have been great, but Southworth insisted, as he had all season, that his team focus on the day at hand, on playing one game at a time. In the series opener, Johnny Beazley was matched against Larry Dietz. After both teams put up runs in the first inning, neither could score again until the fifth, when the Pirates took a 2–1 lead. This seemed to awaken the Bird bats, which produced four runs in the fifth, two in the sixth, one in the seventh, and two more in the eighth for a 10–2 St. Louis win. The Cardinals' power was on display as Stan Musial hit his ninth home run and Walker Cooper bashed his seventh. Johnny Hopp had a double to score two runs as he collected three hits for the second game in a row and seemed at last to be coming out of his season-long slump. Beazley struggled with his control throughout the game, but held Pittsburgh to only six hits in going the distance for his fourteenth win.

Both teams came geared for offense on Saturday in what proved to be a sloppy game. Each team got eleven hits, in addition to which the Pirates drew six walks from four Redbird pitchers and were helped by three St. Louis fielding errors. Howard Krist started and was not sharp. He walked three and gave up seven hits before leaving after the fourth inning, but he departed with the Cards on top 5–4, a lead to which they added two runs in the bottom of the fourth. Howard Pollet took over and was gone quickly after he gave up a run on a walk and two hits. Southworth turned to Beazley, who had thrown nine innings the day before. He stopped the Buccos in the fifth, but gave up a run in the sixth and was gone. Max Lanier came on to protect the rapidly shrinking lead, which he did with one-hit pitching over the final three innings to get credit for the 7–6 win. Enos Slaughter and Jimmy Brown were the hitting stars for the Redbirds with three apiece, each with a two-bagger. Walker Cooper also doubled to drive in two runs. It was not the kind of baseball the Cardinals were accustomed to playing, but they survived.

Their luck ran out in the first game of the Sunday doubleheader against lefthander Ken Heintzelman, who was 2–1 against them on the season. The game went back and forth. The Cardinals scored in the second inning; the Pirates responded with two runs in the fourth to take the lead and added another in the sixth. Harry Gumbert started for the Birds but was finished after the sixth, and for the second day in a row Southworth chose one of his primary starters for help. With Mort Cooper making a rare appearance in relief, the Cards tied the game with single runs in the sixth and seventh, but the Redbird ace was not at his best. He twirled a scoreless seventh, but was touched for two runs in the eighth on a home run by Elbie Fletcher, a triple by Frankie Gustine, and a single by catcher Al Lopez. Heintzelman hurt his arm in the sixth and was replaced by Bob Klinger, who gave up four hits and a run but held on for a 5–3 Pirate win that ended St. Louis's eight-game winning streak. Terry Moore's twenty-game hitting streak came to an end as well.

The Cardinals recovered in the second game behind the brilliant pitching of Murry Dickson, who took a two-hit shutout into the ninth inning. In the ninth, Pittsburgh rallied for two runs on two hits before the young righthander got three outs to end the game. Hitless in the first game, Terry Moore collected three hits, including a double, in the nightcap. Stan Musial had a two-run double and Whitey Kurowski drove in another run with a double. The Cardinals had come home to win nine of ten games, but at the same time the Dodgers had won eight of ten. Despite playing at a .900 clip, the Redbirds had gained only one game on the league leaders. "The bums of Leo Durocher have had a disheartening way of refusing to collapse when it would mean the most to the Redbirds," Robert Morrison of the *Post-Dispatch* wrote, noting that the Dodgers had won their Sunday doubleheader while the Cardinals were splitting theirs. "Tain't so bright an outlook, eh, Bud?" he asked rhetorically.[17] The oracle of gloom, John Wray, weighed in as well: "You couldn't blame Manager Billy Southworth for grousing a bit at his bad luck. For two seasons he has been chasing the Dodgers and he hasn't caught up with them yet. Last year and this one Billy has felt that he had the better team. But for this or that reason the boys can't make the grade."[18] Joining the prophets of doom, New York bookies were now quoting 5–1 odds against the Cardinals winning the pennant.

~

"Railroad wheels rolled jingle, jangle, jingle as our guys rode merrily along," Tommy Holmes of the *Brooklyn Eagle* wrote en route to St. Louis, adding that "it was a laughing, boisterous gang of Dodgers that Leo Durocher led toward the old fur trading post on the west bank of the Mississippi River." Durocher, looking ahead to the St. Louis series, had gambled with his starting pitching in the just-completed four-game series with the New York Giants and won every game. Now, Holmes told his readers, the Dodgers' manager "heads for old St. Louis today with the four pitchers he pointed at the Cardinals more than a week ago ready for action."[19] Larry French, Curt Davis, Max Macon, and Whitlow

Wyatt would be the starters for Durocher's Dodgers. Billy Southworth countered by announcing that Max Lanier would pitch the first game, but refused to say who would start the others. "That's just the sort of thing Leo Durocher and the Dodgers would like to know," the cautious skipper hedged, sounding as if he were a spokesman for the War Department.[20]

The train carrying the Dodgers from their Sunday games in New York to the Monday encounter in St. Louis was making a historic journey. It was the first time a team would play one day on the East Coast and the next in the league's westernmost city. It was a twenty-two-hour train trip that brought Durocher's men to St. Louis in midafternoon for the night contest. At Sportsman's Park, the Dodgers found the largest crowd ever for a night game in the Mound City as 25,814 showed up for the showdown between the league's two best and hottest teams. The Dodgers also found four umpires assigned to the series, rather than the customary three, which seemed a clear signal from the league office that another beanball contest between the teams would not be tolerated.

The tension in the ballpark was palpable. The Cardinals appeared to be a relaxed ball club, but appearances were deceiving. Harry Walker took a liking to a popular Spike Jones tune, "Pass the Biscuits, Mirandy," and during the August home stand it became the team's victory anthem. A clubhouse "band" formed, much like the Mudcat Band of Gashouse days, led by the mandolin of Doc Weaver, the team's trainer. Musial, Lanier, Walker, and others joined in on harmonica, slide-whistle, and coat-hanger drumsticks to add an entertaining dimension to postgame revelry and relaxation.[21] Before the games, the players were serious, although pregame conversation was relaxed and casual with easygoing talk, joking around, and laughter common among men who were teammates and who genuinely liked one another. But before the first game of this series, Bob Broeg, then a young reporter for the *Post-Dispatch*, went to the Cardinal clubhouse, which few writers did, and found the players grim and silent. "I went up to the pressbox," Broeg later reported, "sat down next to [Roy] Stockton, and shook my head" and whispered "P-r-e-s-s-u-r-e." "The Dodgers," he added, "were feeling it too."[22]

As promised, lefthanders French and Lanier were matched against each other in the opening contest of the four-game set. The Cardinals drew first blood in the first inning when Terry Moore doubled and Enos Slaughter brought him home with a sharp single to right field. The Redbirds added another run in the third inning and three more in the fourth. Meanwhile, Lanier was masterful, holding the Dodgers hitless until Mickey Owen doubled with two outs in the fifth. Brooklyn finally scored in the top of the eighth, which snapped Lanier's streak of twenty and one-third innings of scoreless ball. St. Louis responded with two runs in the bottom half of the eighth, after which Lanier finished the job in the ninth, a four-hitter, beating the Dodgers for the fourth time in five tries. Moore had a big evening with three hits including a double, four runs scored, two driven in, and a stolen base. Slaughter and Musial also had doubles and Marion a triple in the Cards' twelve-hit assault on three Brooklyn pitchers.

Onetime St. Louis favorite Joe Medwick had a particularly unpleasant evening, being subjected to verbal harassment in left field throughout the game. In the second inning, after he popped out to second baseman Jimmy Brown, the bleacher crowd rose en masse to "welcome" him back to his position with taunts and catcalls. In the fifth, Medwick provoked a torrent of boos from the grandstand crowd when he bounced a ball toward center that Marion fielded but followed with a high throw to first for an error. Medwick thought it should have been ruled a hit and made gestures at the official scorer to show his irritation. He was quickly erased in a double play and heard it again from the big crowd when he pointed at the official scorer and thumbed his nose while trotting back to the Dodgers' bench. That Medwick, like Durocher and Pete Reiser, made his home in St. Louis in the off-season made no difference to the fans, nor did the fact that he had not asked the Cardinals to trade him to the Dodgers. He was forever treated like a "traitor" to the Cardinal cause.

"This old trading post," Tommy Holmes wrote in his game report, "continues to be the outstanding plague spot in the National League for the Brooklyn Dodgers, the one city . . . where the championship talents of Leo Durocher and his men are unrespected. . . . Their record against the Cardinals at Brooklyn," he continued, "is pleasing enough—six victories in nine games—but out here the sight of Billy Southworth's athletes dashing around like so many jackrabbits appears to freeze our league leaders into a sort of panic." The long train ride might have taken something out of the team, he speculated. French had pitched well enough, but "there were those moments when the Cardinals' speed seemed to throw the Dodgers into the aforementioned trances."[23] Still, Holmes comforted his readers that the Cardinals really had to sweep the series to turn the pennant race into a dogfight.

There were long lines outside Sportsman's Park before the second game, another night game that drew a new record crowd of 33,527, breaking the old record set twenty-four hours earlier. Mort Cooper, wearing jersey number 16, went against Whitlow Wyatt in what had become the familiar matchup of the teams' aces. For those expecting a classic pitchers' duel, Cooper and Wyatt did not disappoint. Through twelve tense innings the two righthanders set the other side down without a run, often three-up, three-down, with almost no serious threat to score. The closest call came in the ninth, when Dolph Camilli lofted a high drive headed for the roof of the right-field pavilion, only to have a steady wind from the southeast knock it down. The ball hit high on the screen covering the front of the right-field stands and was fielded cleanly by Slaughter, who fired it to Marion, who in turn relayed it to Kurowski at third to get the Dodgers' first baseman trying for a triple, giving the huge crowd an opportunity to release a great cheer.

At the plate, the Cardinals were a study in futility. In twelve innings they managed just five hits, got only two runners as far as second base, and advanced no one to third. The Dodgers were little better, though they did get one runner as far as third. Fans broke the tension by booing Joe Medwick at every opportunity and treating Leo Durocher to the same when he was tossed from the game in the twelfth for arguing ball-and-strike calls. In the thirteenth, Brooklyn broke through. Mickey Owen led off with a single and went to second on Wyatt's sacrifice bunt. Cooper retired Pee Wee Reese for the second out, but Lou Riggs singled to bring Owen home.

In the bottom of the inning, Moore was first up and hammered a line drive to center straight into the glove of Pete Reiser, who barely had to move to catch it. But Slaughter worked Wyatt for a walk, the sixth the Dodger hurler had given up, and Musial followed with a single to left center, shallow enough that Slaughter had to stop at second. With the tying run in scoring position, Walker Cooper lined a crisp single to center that sent Slaughter racing around third and sliding home to tie the score just ahead of a strong but hurried throw. The pent-up emotions of the crowd broke as they cheered wildly and rained seat cushions, scorecards, and straw hats on the field. "The roar of the jam-packed St. Louis stand," Tommy Holmes wrote, "must have awakened the long-dead Indians in their mound cemeteries" across the Mississippi River in Illinois.[24] Play was halted while the grounds crew with the aid of several fans cleared the field. The Dodgers used the interruption to change pitchers, bringing the previous day's starter, Larry French, into the game. When action resumed, Coaker Triplett, pinch-hitting for Hopp, sent a shot back up the middle. The Dodgers' second baseman Billy Herman raced toward the second-base bag, speared the ball with a brilliant backhand grab, stepped on second, and fired to first for a game-saving double play.

Cooper retired the Dodgers quickly in the fourteenth inning. French returned to the mound for the Dodgers. Kurowski led off the bottom half of the fourteenth with a bunt single that just eluded the Dodgers' lefty. French departed and Les Webber came on to pitch. Marty Marion laid down a sacrifice bunt along the first-base line that was fielded by Camilli, who threw to second to get Kurowski, but the throw was late and both runners were safe. Mort Cooper, hitting for himself after fourteen innings of work (unusual, but not unprecedented), also laid down a bunt to move the runners along, but Webber snapped it up, whirled, and fired a strike to third base to cut down the sliding Kurowski. Jimmy Brown was given an intentional pass to load the bases and create a force play at every base. Terry Moore was the next batter. With the count two balls and two strikes and the clock reaching midnight, the Redbirds' captain hit a bounder toward left between third and shortstop. Third baseman Riggs lunged for the ball, caught it, slipped, recovered, and whipped it to the plate, where catcher Mickey Owen stretched out like a first baseman to catch it, but the ball arrived a split second too late. Marion raced across home with the winning run, and the crowd, almost all of which was still present, went crazy. "We had to win it," a jubilant Mort Cooper told the press after the game, "and we did, and we're going to give the Dodgers a tussle from here on out." [25] The next day's headline in the *New York World-Telegram* concurred: "Dodger Flag Hopes in Greatest Peril of Season."

Johnny Beazley faced Max Macon in the third game of the series. It was a twilight affair, and fewer fans were in attendance. With the Dodgers still in the doldrums offensively, Durocher juggled his lineup, benching the struggling Reiser in favor of Augie Galan, replacing shortstop Pee Wee Reese, a righty hitter, with lefthanded-hitting Arky Vaughan, and moving Lou Riggs to leadoff and Dixie Walker into the third spot. Both teams scored early, the Cards in the second inning and the Dodgers in the third. The Redbirds missed an opportunity to take charge of the game in the second when they had a run in and the bases loaded with none out, but Macon struck out one batter and got the next to hit into a double play. The Dodgers' run in the third came on a freak play. With one out, Vaughan hit a high bouncer behind the mound that looked like an easy out, but Beazley, blinded by the late-afternoon sun coming through the grandstand, let the ball drop behind him for a hit. Vaughan subsequently came around to score.

After the second inning, Macon set Bird batters down with ease, giving up no hits from the sixth through the ninth. Beazley, on the other hand, was in and out of trouble—"in more jams than a bunch of kids in a kitchen pantry," as Bob Burnes of the *Globe-Democrat* described his performance. A brilliant play by Marty Marion saved him in the eighth, as the lanky shortstop raced far to his left to grab Medwick's sharply hit grounder headed for center field and, running full speed toward right field, slipped the ball to Jimmy Brown at second, who caught it bare-handed just in time to retire the hard-charging Dolph Camilli. The hometown crowd roared its approval. In the ninth, the Dodgers tried a bit of psychological warfare on the Cards that was more comical than effective. With one out, Owen singled and went to third on Macon's single. Apparently intent on rattling the high-strung Beazley, Leo Durocher strolled to home plate to speak with umpire Al Barlick. When the conversation ended and Durocher returned to the bench, Owen on third called time to tie his shoelaces, at which point the runner on first, Macon, could not be found. He finally emerged from the Brooklyn dugout to take his position as the runner on first base. As play was about to resume, Beazley called time and gave the Dodgers some of their own medicine by calmly kneeling on the pitcher's mound to tie his own shoelaces.

When the game at last resumed, lefty-swinging Lou Riggs sliced a ball into shallow left and the Cardinals' defense took over. Left fielder Coaker Triplett, playing toward center, raced to his right barely in time to reach the ball inside the left-field foul line, and made a quick throw to the infield to hold Owen at third. The next hitter, Arky Vaughan, sent Triplett in the opposite direction, into deep left center to haul in his long drive for the third out. For the second straight day the contest went into extra innings. Beazley retired the Dodgers without incident in the top of the tenth. In the bottom half, Jimmy Brown, who had twice ended innings by hitting into double plays, drew a walk. Terry Moore followed with his only hit of the day, a single to left on which Brown could advance no farther than second. This brought the heart of the Redbird batting order to the plate. Enos Slaughter dug into the batters box and, with a mighty swing, topped the baseball down the third-base line, where Macon grabbed it and threw the Redbird right fielder out at first by a whisker, Brown and Moore advancing to third and second. Triplett was the next batter; like Slaughter, he took a home-run swing at a curve-ball and dribbled it down the third-base line. Macon again rushed to field the ball, but this time he slipped as he reached it, had no play at first, and tried desperately to scoop the ball to Owen at home plate. With two outs, Brown was off from third as soon as the ball was hit, stormed down the line, and crashed into the Dodgers' catcher, who went one way and the ball another as the determined Brown slid home for a 2–1 St. Louis win.

Following the collision, Owen lay sprawled on the ground, seemingly injured, but the only Dodger to come to his aid was coach Freddy Fitzsimmons. Owens had to be helped from the field by three Cardinals, Brown, Triplett, and Billy Southworth, who was coaching at third. St. Louis fans were ecstatic with the third straight triumph over the Dodgers, which brought the Redbirds to within four and a half games of first place. St. Louis sportswriters shared the fans' enthusiasm, Bruce Bohle writing that the Cards had "out-hustled and out-played the cocky Dodgers."[26] Brooklyn writers were more circumspect. "The spirit of our Dodgers is willing enough," Tommy Holmes observed, "but the flesh is woefully weak." Holmes noted that the Dodgers had scored only three runs in the thirty-three innings played in St. Louis.[27] *Brooklyn Eagle* columnist Harold Parrott reflected on the meaning of it all. "It could be," he wrote, "that the Dodgers have been traveling over their heads, and are now being debunked by a team that has been slighted all along. It could be that the Cards, hanging onto the Dodgers' coattails all season when other teams would have been discouraged and folded, have too much innate class." It could be, he concluded, "but I don't believe it."[28]

Going for the sweep, Southworth gambled and lost. He chose Max Lanier to start game four just two days after Lanier had pitched nine innings to win the first game of the series. Lanier responded well in the early innings, throwing four hitless frames, but almost every hitter made him work, taking him deep into pitch counts, two of them drawing walks. The Cardinals scored first, in the third inning, but missed the chance for a big inning when, with two on, Slaughter launched a long drive to right center that looked like a home run. Instead, the ball hit off the top of the wall and dropped directly into the hands of Pete Reiser, whose strong throw back to the infield was relayed home to catch a Redbird runner trying to score the team's second run.

In the fifth inning, the Dodgers changed strategy. Instead of taking pitches, they began to swing at Lanier's first-pitch strikes. With one out, Mickey Owen looped a single that went off the glove of a leaping Jimmy Brown at second. Arky Vaughan followed with a grounder between first and second that looked like a possible double play, but a miscommunication between Brown and first baseman Johnny Hopp, each of whom thought the other would field the ball, permitted the ball to roll past them into right field for a single. Owen, a slow runner, lumbered around second base, headed for third, and looked to be an easy out, but Slaughter's throw was wide of the bag and Owen was safe, with Vaughan moving to second.

Dodger pitcher Curt Davis, known affectionately as "Coonskin," came to the plate, and Southworth brought his infield in for a possible play at home. But Davis punched a single into center field through the drawn-in infield to drive in the two runners. Pee Wee Reese kept the Brooklyn rally going with a soft single to center. Billy Herman followed with a solid single to left center that scored Davis with the third run. Lanier departed and Ernie White entered to face Pete Reiser. He got Reiser to foul out, but Joe Medwick followed with a line-drive single to center that brought Reese home with the fourth run of the inning. White finished the fifth without further damage and pitched hitless and scoreless ball in the sixth and seventh innings. Howard Pollet followed him to do the same in the eighth and ninth innings. But the Cardinals could do nothing against the side-arming Davis who was impressive in distributing eight hits, all singles, and walking none. The 4–1 loss dropped the Redbirds back to five and a half games behind the Dodgers.

It was now hand-wringing time for St. Louis sportswriters. "The road is steep and time is running out," Roy Stockton wrote, "but the Cardinals still are in the race for the National League pennant."[29] Bruce Bohle, bullish twenty-four hours earlier, now anguished: "Brooklyn's Dodgers are gone and so, it seems, are the Cardinals chances for winning their first pennant since 1934." "There is no doubting the courage of the Cardinals," he continued, "and no one who has followed the club this season will have the slightest suspicion that they will give up their fight to overtake the Dodgers."[30] But like Stockton, Bohle clearly thought the road was perhaps too steep. The Cardinals were five and a half games back with thirty to play, only two of them with the Dodgers, both in Brooklyn. Moreover, St. Louis would be playing mainly against the stronger western teams while Brooklyn would be matched against the weaker eastern clubs. Harold Parrott of the *Brooklyn Eagle* added a third consideration: "Beyond Cooper and Wyatt, it is a veteran Dodger staff against a very young Cardinals staff."[31] Clearly, he believed that experience would prevail.

~

Billy Southworth, ever the calming optimist, shared none of the reservations voiced in the press. He knew his Redbirds needed help from other teams if they were to catch Brooklyn's Bums, but he also knew that his team had come together with Hopp and Kurowski playing every day and with the young starting pitchers having grown up behind Mort Cooper. They stood at 12–2 on their home stand and had a week to go before hitting the road again. That week began with three games against the last-place Phillies, starting with a Friday doubleheader. Murry Dickson went against Frank Hoerst in the first game. The Cards treated the Philadelphia hurler rudely with five hits and four runs in the first two innings, by which time Hoerst was gone in favor of Sam Nahem. But the "Quakers," as writers often dubbed the Philadelphia nine, did not go peacefully. Dickson struggled with his control from the outset, enabling the Phils to score twice in the third inning and rid themselves of the little righthander with two more runs in the sixth to tie the score. In the seventh, facing a fourth Philly pitcher, the aptly nicknamed "Boom-Boom" Beck, the Cardinals erupted for three runs, with George Kurowski's two-run triple the inning's big hit. Harry Gumbert, who took over for Dickson, gave up five hits and a walk in his three-plus innings of work but allowed no runs to score, and thus received credit for the 7–4 win.

In the nightcap, the Redbirds faced righthander Rube Melton, who had beaten them earlier in the City of Brotherly Love. They showed Melton neither love nor mercy in St. Louis, hammering him for six hits and six runs in the first four innings. The Cards added another in the fifth against first-game starter Hoerst to take a 7–0 lead. Johnny Hopp, whose bat had come alive on the home stand, led the St. Louis attack with a home run and three runs driven home. Stan Musial also drove in three with two singles. Howard Krist started for the Cardinals and snapped off five scoreless innings before the Phils battered him for five runs in the sixth. He left with no one out, turning mound duties over to Ernie White, who quieted the Philly uprising and went on to save the win. White, returning from a groin injury, had thrown two solid innings the day before against the Dodgers and now turned in an impressive four-inning, one-hit performance in relief of Krist. Southworth could hope that his lefthander, who had won seventeen games for the 1941 Cardinals, was now fully recovered from the arm and other ailments that had slowed him in 1942.

The Redbirds defeated Hans Lobert's Philadelphians the next day behind Mort Cooper, who picked up his seventeenth win wearing a jersey with that number. Cooper was in control throughout, but never in command as he had been against the Dodgers earlier in the week. The visitors took a brief lead with a run in the fourth inning. The Cards came back immediately with two in their half of the inning to move ahead, only to watch the Phils knot the contest with a run in the fifth. After the fifth, Cooper pitched scoreless ball, while the Cardinals went on to tally two in the sixth and one in the seventh for a 5–2 win. The bottom of the batting order stood tall for the Birds as Kurowski and Marion had two doubles apiece and drove in four runs between them, while Hopp had two hits and drove in the other run. The sweep of the Phillies gave Southworth's band of determined warriors a 15–2 record on their home stand and a 20–4 record since the fourteen-inning tie at Pittsburgh on August 9. St. Louis also got help from Chicago, which took one of two games from the Dodgers, enabling the Cards to gain a game and a half on Brooklyn and close to within four games of the league leaders.

The Cardinals were not the only St. Louis team playing good baseball. The Browns were the surprise team in the American League, moving into third place with steady pitching and the outstanding play of rookie shortstop Vernon Stephens. In addition, the city's American Legion team from the Stockham Post had played its way into the national semifinals behind their standout player Lawrence Berra, known to later generations of baseball fans as "Yogi." On the lighter side, the Associated Press published a photograph of Cardinal hitters that included Marty Marion posed with Enos Slaughter and Stan Musial, prompting the Redbird shortstop, best known for his defensive abilities, to quip that it was "the first time I have been photographed with a bat in my hands."[32] The reality of war also hit home at the end of August when Slaughter announced that he had enlisted in the armed forces as an aviation cadet. It raised anew concerns that Slaughter might not finish the season with the Cards, but alarms were quieted when the Redbirds' right fielder reported that he would be permitted to do so. "Country" Slaughter, as he was known, was the team's best hitter, standing near the top of the league in batting average and leading the club in home runs and runs batted in.

Following the three-game sweep of the Phils, the Cards ended August by winning a Sunday doubleheader from Boston. In the opener, both starters, Johnny Beazley and lefthander Lou Tost, struggled from the outset. Beazley labored through six innings, giving up seven hits, three walks, two wild pitches, and three runs. Tost was touched for seven hits, three walks, two wild pitches, and three runs before leaving with two out in the fifth, turning hill duties over to Johnny Sain. In the top of the sixth, Sain helped himself with a single to drive home the tying run, but in the bottom of the inning he gave it back and then some as the Redbirds scored five times. The big hit was a bases-loaded triple by the cadet-in-waiting Enos Slaughter. Harry Gumbert delivered three scoreless innings to secure the win for Beazley.

In the nightcap, Ernie White rewarded Southworth's patience with a nine-inning, five-hit, two-run performance. The Cardinals' hitters, however, were able to score only twice against Will Donovan and Jim Tobin, and the game went into extra innings. After saving the first game for Beazley, Gumbert came on in relief again, was perfect through two innings, and won the game with his bat. After Hopp singled and was sacrificed to second by Marion in the bottom of the eleventh, Gumbert, hitting for himself with the winning run in scoring position, lashed a double to right to bring Hopp home. The Birds had collected eight hits before the winning rally in the eleventh, including a double by Triplett and a triple by Moore, but three Boston double plays erased scoring threats.

As the Cardinals were taking two from Boston, the Dodgers, still struggling on offense, were splitting a twin bill in Pittsburgh. "After coasting along in the comparative safety of a lengthy lead through most of the National League campaign," an Associated Press story observed, "the Dodgers found themselves separated from the threatening Cardinals today by nothing more than three short games."[33] In St. Louis, the mercurial Bruce Bohle of the *Star-Times* revised his view once again: "They've already been counted out more times than a punch-drunk pugilist, but today finds the Cardinals still in there scrounging."[34] In Brooklyn, the confidence of three weeks earlier had turned into anxiety. "On this Black Monday," Tommy Holmes of the *Eagle* wrote, "it is evident that the Dodgers are in dog-gonned serious trouble." Noting that they had blown a Saturday game in Chicago before splitting a Sunday doubleheader in Pittsburgh, Holmes added: "Our guys look tired and, without getting panicky about it, there is a growing fear that the Cardinals may have too much youth and vitality if the campaign resolves into a neck-and-neck drive down the September stretch."[35]

The Dodgers beat the Pirates in eleven innings on Monday, August 31, ending the month three and a half games (four in the loss column) ahead of St. Louis, who had the day off. Among the concerns of Durocher and the Dodgers, none worried them more than the condition of Pete Reiser. The Dodgers could not be at their best without Reiser contributing as he had in 1941 and the first half of 1942, Tim Cohane of the *Herald Tribune* observed. But "Reiser does not look good," Cohane wrote. "He is pale and drawn . . ."[36] Reiser had started the August 28 game against the Cubs but after one inning asked to come out and was sent again to Johns Hopkins, this time, the team said, for treatment of a torn ligament in his left thigh. "Strange part of it is that no one knows exactly what the trouble is," Tommy Holmes wrote, doubting that a pulled leg muscle was the whole story.[37] Like Cohane, he told his readers what they most likely already knew without being told: "The Dodgers simply aren't the Dodgers without Reiser in there cutting and slashing."[38]

CHAPTER 9
Flying High into the Stretch

As September arrived, fighting on all fronts of the war had moved to a new level of intensity, nowhere more so than at Stalingrad. The race for the National League pennant might provide a distraction from the war for some Americans, but there was no distraction for the hundreds of thousands of Soviet soldiers digging in to defend Stalingrad. In the final week of August, German aircraft launched a massive and relentless two-day bombing of the city, leaving it an inferno and almost wholly destroyed. Because the Luftwaffe had no night-flying capacity, the Russians, under cover of darkness, could move reinforcements and war-making materiel into the city and civilians and industrial equipment out. The Nazi ground assault that followed the bombing met with ferocious resistance, and by mid-September the struggle had become what the Germans had sought always to avoid: urban street warfare. Fighting was fierce, often hand-to-hand, and casualties were enormous on both sides, but the Russians, though outnumbered four to one, refused to lose.[1] Because of the pennant race, the scores of the Cardinals' games began appearing on the front page of the *Post-Dispatch* after mid-September, but they were always placed well below the headlines, maps, and stories of the great battle news which topped every edition.

On the other side of Europe, the British Royal Air Force maintained its steady bombardment of German cities. For the first time, the U.S. Eighth Air Force saw action, hitting targets along the French coast and in the Low Countries to the north. Near the end of August, fighting became heavy once again in North Africa as Rommel renewed his desert offensive, driving forward at El Alamein. In the ensuing battle, some U.S. soldiers fought alongside those of Britain and the Commonwealth countries, especially American airmen who continued with the British to bomb the German and Italian tanks and troops. Initially, Rommel was successful in pressing the fight against the Allies, but ultimately his drive stalled and he found himself again in a costly stalemate. In early September, he decided that enough was enough and withdrew. By the middle of September it was again relatively quiet in North Africa as both sides paused to resupply their forces, which was time-consuming and costly for both sides as British warplanes destroyed about one-third of the German ships in the Mediterranean carrying fuel, equipment, and men, while German U-boats along the west coast of Africa played havoc with U.S. merchant ships.

In the Pacific, Japan struck repeatedly at Guadalcanal, trying to drive U.S. forces from the island and regain control of the airfield. There were ongoing land and sea battles throughout August, but Henderson Field remained in U.S. hands. In the latter part of the month the United States won a major sea engagement in the eastern Solomon Islands in which the Japanese lost several ships, including a carrier, while U.S. losses were minimal.[2] The battle had again been fought mainly in the air, with planes launched from carriers and the fleets themselves removed from direct contact. In September, another large Japanese invasion force tried to reclaim Guadalcanal, but it too was repulsed. There was renewed fighting on New Guinea as well. Having failed to take Port Moresby by sea, the Japanese chose to attack by land, crossing the treacherous Owen Sydney mountain range in early September. Conditions were awful for both sides, but the Allies again mounted a successful resistance.

In Washington, Franklin Roosevelt sought to rally greater support for the war effort with a speech intended primarily for youth at home and abroad, assuring them that they would inhabit a better world when the war was over. The battle is "going to be long and hard and bitter," the president told them, but "this time we shall know how to make full use of victory" to build a better world. Roosevelt deplored the "little men of little faith" who "mock and smear at the Four Freedoms and the Atlantic Charter," denouncing "these puny prophets," as he called them, who "decry our determination to implement our high concepts and sound principles."[3] Earlier Roosevelt had delivered a harsh, unforgiving, and uncompromising message to the leaders of the Axis powers. The only acceptable surrender was unconditional surrender, he told them, after which the political and military leaders responsible for the brutal and deadly treatment of civilians during the war would be tried in an international court of justice for their crimes against humanity.

Nine months after Pearl Harbor, war had become a fact of life for Americans at home. More and more women were working on the production lines in the war industries. Among the patriotic images that appeared in September 1942 was the poster of "Rosie the Riveter," a testament to the new role of women in the war effort and one that would resonate in the postwar world as the social and economic status of women underwent dramatic changes in American life. Women also filled many military-related jobs, ferrying planes across the country and testing equipment such as the new nylon parachute. Housewives who stayed at home also found themselves doing war work. Typical was a two-day drive in St. Louis to collect tin cans. It produced around 250 tons of metal, with an estimated 73 percent of households participating by cleaning cans and putting them curbside for pickup.

Drives to collect scrap metal for salvage seemed to be everywhere. Junkyards in Missouri collected more than ten tons of metal in the month of September alone. At Jefferson Barracks in St. Louis an old fence made of Civil War rifle barrels that stood in front of the General Ulysses Grant house was torn down for scrap metal, though a few of the rifle barrels were saved as historic relics. The most unusual scrap collection, however, was (where else?) in Brooklyn, where in the last week of the baseball season any fan who brought ten pounds of scrap metal to a special gate was admitted free to a Dodgers game. Metal piled up in a street alongside Ebbets Field until it looked like a junkyard.[4]

Campaigns to sell war bonds were many. In September, the U.S. Treasury Department announced "Salute to Heroes" month in which movie theaters were enlisted to sell war bonds and stamps to their patrons. In a matter of weeks, St. Louis movie houses reported almost four hundred thousand dollars in sales. Members of the movie community in Hollywood became especially active in selling war bonds. Committees were organized in the various studios, and a friendly competition among them brought in five million dollars over the next few months. Movies themselves also took on an increasingly patriotic character. The film *Desperate Journey,* about five commandos in Germany and starring Errol Flynn and Ronald Reagan, was featured in St. Louis movie houses as the Cardinals were playing their final September series in Brooklyn. St. Louis fans might well have thought the film was about the Redbirds.

~

August ended with all the pennant contenders adding players to strengthen their rosters. The world champion Yankees acquired outfielder Roy Cullenbine from the Washington Senators to replace Tommy Henrich, whom they had lost just days before to military service. The Dodgers also dealt with the Senators to acquire veteran righthander Louis Norman "Bobo" Newsome. The Cardinals instead drew on their farm system, recalling outfielder–third baseman Erv Dusak. Cullenbine had started the season with the St. Louis Browns but fell into disfavor with manager Luke Sewell for not being an aggressive hitter. Browns vice president William DeWitt called him the "laziest human being you ever saw" who "wouldn't swing a bat," preferring a walk.[5] In 1942, Cullenbine hit .193 for the Browns and .286 for the Senators, but he would hit .364 in twenty-one games for the Yankees. Newsome was one of baseball's great characters and one of its best pitchers as well, though he received scant recognition for the latter. He won 211 games in a twenty-year career during which he changed teams fifteen times and worked for some of the era's worst ball clubs. Loud, colorful, and never short on self-confidence, Bobo, upon learning of the deal, wired congratulations to Leo Durocher, saying that the Dodgers had just "bought pennant insurance" and "ain't got nothing to worry about now."[6] Dusak, who had come close to winning a job with the Cardinals in spring training, brought a promising righthanded bat as well as versatility to the club.

At the start of September, the Cardinals had three games remaining on their home stand, a final one with Boston and then two with the New York Giants. Mort Cooper, who liked to pitch at night, volunteered for the Tuesday night finale with the Braves, though he had thrown a complete game against Philadelphia only two days earlier. It was not a premier performance. Big Coop gave up nine hits, including three each to Paul Waner and Ernie Lombardi, but held Boston to three runs. Redbird hitters battered Braves starter Al Javery for eleven hits over the first seven innings but could score only three runs, two of them coming on a double by Walker Cooper in the fourth. In the bottom of the eighth, with the score tied, the Cardinals pulled off a trick play that led to the winning run. Johnny Hopp singled to open the frame, was sacrificed to second by Whitey Kurowski, and went to third on an infield hit by Marty Marion. The Cards then executed a "phantom" squeeze play. As Javery released his pitch, Hopp broke for home. Mort Cooper bunted toward third base. Javery rushed to the ball, fielded it with his back to third base, spun around, and fired it home, not realizing that Hopp had stopped and returned to third. Cooper was safe at first, which loaded the bases. Jimmy Brown followed with a fly ball hit far enough to score Hopp with what proved to be the game-winning run. Cooper struggled but came away with his eighteenth win while wearing jersey number 18.

In the *Post-Dispatch*, Roy Stockton took the win as an opportunity to laud the work of St. Louis manager Billy Southworth. "Despite all the bad breaks and the discouraging lead the Dodgers took early and have held tenaciously," he wrote, "the Cardinals have kept their morale high. That is where Southworth had shown his managerial ability. It would have been easy for the Cardinals to lose heart," but they had not, for which the credit went to Billy the Kid, who had clearly matured as a big-league manager. Lavishing praise on the Redbird skipper, Stockton concluded: "Southworth stands as one of the most skillful keepers of morale that the game has known."[7]

St. Louis had won six straight since losing the last game of the Brooklyn series, but the New York Giants brought the streak to an abrupt end. Johnny Mize, whose name had fallen out of local sports pages once the Cardinals began to win, led the Giants' assault upon Max Lanier with a perfect day at the plate—three hits and two walks—and was responsible for driving home two of New York's eight runs. In just over three innings of work, Lanier gave up six hits and walked five in his first outing since doing double duty in the series against the Dodgers. In all, the Giants pounded four Redbird hurlers for fourteen hits, including three doubles. The Cards got eight hits but only two runs. The 8–2 loss was only their fourth in twenty-five games, but it dropped them another game behind Brooklyn, who edged Cincinnati 3–2 in twelve innings. The Cardinals' loss, combined with the emotional win over the Reds, produced a loud postgame celebration in the Dodgers' clubhouse. "With the Cardinals beaten on the scoreboard," a happy Leo Durocher chortled, "I wanted to win this one if I had to use every pitcher on the club." [8] With Brooklyn now four and a half games ahead, Joe Williams of the *Herald Tribune* thought the race was over: "the Cardinals' prospects get no brighter as the days run on and it's our notion they are already whipped."[9]

The Redbirds ended their home stand the next day with a 7–0 win. In a match-up of lefthanders, twenty-one-year-old Howard Pollet outpitched the venerable thirty-eight-year-old Carl Hubbell. Striking out four and walking one in going the route, Pollet won for the first time since June 7 and looked like the pitcher the Cards had expected after his late-season heroics in 1941. In scoring seven runs, the Cards registered nine hits, five of them for extra bases. They also got help from an outside source as strong winds played tricks with fly balls all day. In the third inning, with the bases loaded, Erv Dusak lifted a high pop fly just beyond the reach of shortstop Billy Jurges that the wind tossed and twisted away from left fielder Babe Barna as well. It fell in for a double, scoring all three runners and giving St. Louis a 3–0 start toward the win.

As the Cardinals packed their bags for a road trip that would keep them away from home cooking until the last week of the season, they could look back on a home stand that would have been thought an impossible dream three weeks earlier. They had won twenty, lost only three, taken three of four from the Dodgers, and cut the Brooklyn lead in half. Concerns about their pitching that returned to St. Louis with them in mid-August were all but forgotten by early September. Fifteen times the starting pitchers had gone nine innings or longer. Staff ace Mort Cooper, on whom much of the concern had centered, led the staff with five complete-game wins, followed by Johnny Beazley with five wins and four complete games. Max Lanier had two complete-game victories; Howard Krist had two wins in two starts, one a complete game; Murry Dickson and Howard Pollet added complete-game wins; while Ernie White had gone nine innings in an extra-inning game in which he got no decision. The apparent recovery and promising work of White and Pollet was gratifying to Southworth, who had stayed with them through sore arms and other injuries that dogged the two lefties during the season.

Pitching had been the big story, but the impressive mound work had been backed by solid hitting and a steady, often sparkling defense. Enos Slaughter led the team with a .372 average for the home stay, but it was the hitting of Johnny Hopp at .362 that brought the biggest smile to Southworth's weathered face. It solved the manager's season-long question about who to play at first base and also stabilized his batting order. Hopp had been hitting in the eighth spot, but with a suddenly hot bat he was moved to seventh for the second game of the doubleheader on August 23 and then eventually to sixth in the order. This gave Southworth a lefthanded hitter between two righthanded swingers, Walker Cooper and George Kurowski. Against southpaws, Hopp would drop back to seventh and Kurowski would hit sixth. When Hopp moved up in the batting order, Marty Marion, who had remained hot with the bat at home, dropped from seventh to eighth, where his speed and ability to bunt and hit behind runners was more valuable.

Southworth made little use of his bench during the three weeks at home. The same lineup was on the field almost every day, with the principal exception being that Coaker Triplett continued to platoon with Musial in left. Ken O'Dea got a couple of starts behind the plate, and Frank Crespi started at shortstop the last two games at home after Marty Marion jammed his ankle jumping into a base in the September 1 game. Harry Walker and Ray Sanders were used as pinch hitters, while Whitey Moore saw no action whatsoever as Southworth went with an eight-man pitching staff. It was a determined Redbird squad that left for Cincinnati to, as one sportswriter quipped, "open a second front"—one that would decide the outcome of the pennant race, much as Roosevelt, Churchill, and Stalin expected a second front in Europe would decide the outcome of the war, though it was by no means clear to St. Louisans that the "good guys" would prevail in the "war" between the Cardinals and Dodgers.

～

The Cardinals moved into Cincinnati as the Dodgers were departing after taking two from the Reds. Southworth sent Johnny Beazley to the mound against the Redlegs. It was not his finest hour. He was wild, walking five batters and surrendering six hits. He was also saddled with uncharacteristically sloppy defensive play by the usually reliable Terry Moore and Marty Marion. Though almost constantly in trouble, Beazley pitched through jams and had given up only three runs before leaving with one out in the seventh. The Cards hammered the veteran Paul Derringer for five runs in the early innings as Musial tripled, Kurowski homered, and both Slaughter and Marion doubled. Speed was a critical factor in the team's scoring. Musial's third-inning triple was a line drive down the left field-line, a legitimate double that his fleetness of foot turned into a triple. Hopp followed by legging out an infield hit to drive Musial home. Howard Krist relieved Beazley in the seventh and took over the game with an explosive fastball, retiring eight straight Cincinnati hitters, striking out three, and preserving the 5–3 win for the Beaze.

Speed was again a decisive factor in the Redbirds' 3–2 victory the next day. Ray Starr shut the Cardinals out until the sixth inning, when the Birds scored twice to take a 2–1 lead. Terry Moore started the rally with a looping fly just over the infield into center field that shortstop Eddie Joost got his glove on but could not catch as it fell for a single. Slaughter flied out, but Musial singled sharply to center field, sending Moore galloping to third. Ken O'Dea, in the lineup to give Walker Cooper a day off, sliced a single into short left–center field as three Reds raced in vain to reach the ball. When all were slow to recover, Musial, running at the crack of the bat, came all the way around from first to score the go-ahead run. Veteran umpire Lee Ballanfant later called it the greatest single piece of baserunning he had ever seen.[10] Cincinnati tied the game in the bottom of the sixth, but in the ninth Johnny Hopp, who had a perfect three-for-three day at the plate, lined an ordinary single to center that he stretched into a double with some daring baserunning to beat Eric Tipton's hurried throw. Whitey Kurowski followed with a single to drive him home with the winning run. Krist got credit for the 3–2 win with five innings of brilliant work in relief of starter Harry Gumbert.

Mort Cooper, wearing Gumbert's uniform with its number 19, started the final game of the Cincy series, and except for a second-inning home run by rookie outfielder Frank Kelleher, he was in control for an easy 10–2 win, his nineteenth of the season. The Cardinals struck early and often with two runs in the first, single runs in the second and third, and pairs of runs in the fifth, seventh, and eighth, scoring ten runs on eleven hits and six walks. Five of the St. Louis hits were for extra bases, including a triple by Hopp and another home run by Kurowski to go with doubles by Brown, Moore, and Marion, the latter registering his major-league-leading thirty-fourth two-bagger. The Birds again flew around the bases with abandon, forcing three Cincinnati errors.

With Brooklyn having just played in Cincinnati, comparisons of the Cardinals and the Dodgers were inevitable. "The verdict of this [Cincinnati] jury," Tom Swope wrote in the *Star-Times*, "is that the Cardinals . . . were a better ball club than were the Dodgers. . . . They showed more speed and power than did the Dodgers, and more of the old hustle," and "if they continue to slash into good pitching and tear around the bases the way they did here . . . they will either win or give the Dodgers an even greater scare."[11] But more important than the judgment of the "jury" in Cincinnati was that while St. Louis was thumping the Reds, Brooklyn was splitting a doubleheader in Boston, moving the Redbirds to within two and a half games of the front-runners.

From Cincinnati, the Cardinals went to Pittsburgh for a Labor Day doubleheader. Max Lanier started the opener and cruised through the first five innings, scattering five hits and permitting no runs. Meanwhile, the Cards piled up a 5–0 lead, with the bats of Musial and O'Dea leading the way. In the sixth inning with two outs and a runner on third, the Pirates exploded. Seven hits, three walks, an error, and three pitchers later, they had scored eleven runs. St. Louis added a run to make the final score 11–6, but it was a game that Cardinal pitchers—Lanier, Dickson, and Pollet—let get away. Dickson took the loss, but it was Lanier about whom most questions were asked, as this was his second failed start since making the two appearances in four days against Brooklyn in St. Louis. Adding to Southworth's worries, Marty Marion had to leave the game when he aggravated his sore ankle. The Cardinals came back to win the nightcap, however, on the strong right arm of Johnny Beazley. Ironically, Frank Crespi, subbing for Marion, was the star of the 6–4 win with a triple, two singles, a run scored, two driven in, and a stolen base.

In their Labor Day twin bill in Boston, the Dodgers took a three-run lead in the first inning of the first game on a Dolph Camilli home run, then sent Boston's starter to the showers with a six-run fourth on their way to an easy 11–4 victory. Early in the second game the scoreboard reported the St. Louis loss to Pittsburgh, which meant that Brooklyn had picked up a game on the Cards with their first-game victory. They were, at the time, struggling in their second game against the teasing and tantalizing stuff of Jim Tobin. Bobo Newsome, who had thrown a shutout in his first outing with his new club, was on the mound again for the Dodgers and held the Braves to one run over the first four innings. But in the fifth and sixth Boston got to him for three runs to take a 4–0 lead. Brooklyn came back with three in the top of the seventh, only to have the Braves add another in the bottom of the inning. That was it; the Dodgers could do no better than a split for their day's work.

After the game Dolph Camilli voiced the frustration that he and others on the team felt: "Damn it, we miss what they call golden opportunities. If we'd taken that second game . . . we'd be three and a half in front and we could look back and laugh at the Cardinals as we get back home. Now, we've got to dig in some more." Leo Durocher put up a stiffer front: "We've got 'em, I think. The Cards don't play today and we get a free roll against the Pirates. . . . We win that and we're three in front. We should be at least three in front when they come to Brooklyn [this] Friday. They won't beat us then."[12] The Dodgers did win the next day, with rookie Ed Head pitching a complete-game shutout, putting Brooklyn three games up just as Durocher had hoped. Neither team played the following day. It was an open date for Brooklyn, while the Cardinals' game was rained out. Both teams played on Thursday, September 10, as they prepared to meet in Brooklyn for games on Friday and Saturday.

The Cardinals were in New York to play the Giants, with Howard Pollet again matched against Carl Hubbell. The outcome, however, may have been decided before the game ever started. As St. Louis was finishing its pregame fielding practice, an errant throw from Stan Musial sailed over the head of the Cards' catcher and hit Hubbell behind the right ear just as he began to warm up. "King Carl" wanted to continue but was wobbly and had to be helped from the field. In his place the Giants substituted "Prince Hal" Schumacher, who was given extra time to warm up fully. Nonetheless, Schumacher got off to a poor start, walking Jimmy Brown on four pitches. Terry Moore followed with a perfectly placed bunt along the third-base line for a hit. With two men on, Slaughter lashed a single to right, scoring Brown. Mel Ott fielded Slaughter's hit quickly and rifled a throw that beat Moore to third base, but no one was covering the bag, permitting Moore to score and Slaughter to reach third. Slaughter then scored on Walker Cooper's fly to the outfield. The three runs were sufficient for Pollet, who gave up a seventh-inning home run to Ott but allowed no other scoring while the Cards added two more runs on a home run by Moore for a 5–1 win.

In Brooklyn, the Dodgers met the Chicago Cubs, with Kirby Higbe paired against former Cardinal Lon Warneke. The Cubs scored three times in the first inning, ending Higbe's day, and added three more in the second to dispatch Hugh Casey as well. The Windy City crew continued their assault with four runs against Larry French and Johnny Allen while Warneke, the old "Arkansas Hummingbird," was humming. Except for Arky Vaughan's two-run home run in the third, Warneke held the Dodgers scoreless to register a 10–2 complete-game victory, which brought the Cardinals to within two games of the Dodgers on the eve of their weekend showdown. "At no time this year have the boys looked as bad as they did yesterday," Tommy Holmes of the *Eagle* lamented. "Our heroes seemed dead on their feet and slow between the ears from the very first pitch." Holmes noted that Pete Reiser left the game after two innings, adding, "the kid just isn't right."[13]

～

"What P. T. Barnum would give, were he alive, to have the opportunity of staging this grand melodrama!" James Murphy of the *Brooklyn Eagle* wrote on the eve of the final Cards-Dodgers encounter, adding that Barnum had a worthy successor in Larry MacPhail.[14] Immersed in controversy much of the season, MacPhail had another fracas going, though on a somewhat lighter side than the others. For weeks, he had been in a running controversy with a retired Brooklyn music teacher, Reid Spencer, who deplored the organ at Ebbets Field (he called it a "calliope") and wanted its use discontinued as a public nuisance. The Dodgers' organist, Gladys Gooding, came to MacPhail's defense, saying she got the job because "Larry MacPhail plays the piano and is a lover of fine music."[15] MacPhail offered no self-defense, but instead resorted to the familiar strategy of getting even with his detractors. Deciding that the Dodgers needed a victory march, he chose for that purpose Spencer's own composition, said to be the musician's pride and joy, a "Canzonetta" in E flat major. Gooding rendered it with gusto, and Spencer apparently decided to leave bad enough alone.[16]

As the Cardinals arrived at Ebbets Field on September 11, they were playing good baseball and they knew it. "We've been making up for lost time because we have a club full of youngsters," Billy Southworth told reporters. "Now that we're going full speed we don't expect to stop until after we've played the Yankees in the World Series." He was confident that having a younger ball club would "tell in the final reckoning."[17] Enos Slaughter was blunt in voicing the team's confidence: "We can lick the Dodgers. They're just another club to us." Terry Moore, on the other hand, chose to marvel at how popular the Cardinals were away from home. "In eight years with the Cards, I never saw a St. Louis club so popular as we are now." The fans in Cincinnati, Pittsburgh, Chicago, and even (and perhaps especially) those in New York's Polo Grounds "wanted us to win," the Redbirds' captain continued. "It's a strange feeling, I'll tell you. But it gives a club a big lift, and makes a fellow feel like sin when he loses."[18] With his usual braggadocio, Dizzy Dean simply took winning the pennant for granted and announced that the Redbirds were the only National League team that could beat the Yankees. *Brooklyn Eagle* columnist Harold Parrott dismissed Dean's remarks, deriding him as "Lord Haw-Haw of St. Louis."

In the same column with his Dean aside, Parrott published a lengthy interview with Branch Rickey about the Cardinals. "This you can be sure of," the sage of St. Louis observed, "the Cardinals will go on winning right down to the wire. Brooklyn has the lead, and a break on the schedule from here in. But if the Dodgers stub their toes, we will win, as sure as you sit there." Pointing out that the Redbirds had won twenty-six of their last thirty-one games, Rickey continued: "Right now there is little doubt that the Cardinals are stronger than the Dodgers." This is "no freak," Rickey added, "but a regular phenomenon. Look at 1926, 1930, 1931, 1934, all years we won pennants. We started slowly, but did not jell until late, and then really went to town." "This is an organizational peculiarity of mine," Rickey reflected. "I build a bit too much perhaps on the kid side and it takes my teams time to develop. But it's a better failing than to have too many veterans." Shifting to the Dodgers, Rickey asserted, "The Brooklyn club is sitting on a volcano of sudden disintegration," adding, "I will give you a word of warning, young man. Win the pennant in Brooklyn this year, for if you do not you will find the Cards will win easily in 1943."[19]

There was nothing cocky about the Dodgers, who came stumbling into the series having lost four of their last seven games. Theirs was a grim determination, touched perhaps by a bit of fatalism. The latter seemed clearly the case with Larry MacPhail. "When the ball club was eight and one-half games ahead, I warned it that it would blow the pennant unless it played better ball. Some of them thought I was seeing things, and maybe were unimpressed. Now, I doubt if we can win."[20] For the first time all season, the press found some faults with Leo Durocher's managing, though it was always couched in a politeness unlikely to provoke an explosion from the Dodgers' boss. Dan Daniel of the *Herald Tribune* was typical in suggesting that Dodger pitchers were not being handled well and urged Durocher to "husband his pitching" so as not to "wear out his hurlers now."[21]

Brooklyn's veteran staff was showing evidence of wear from the long season. The starters had been impressive from opening day through most of August. From August 3 to the St. Louis series on August 24, Dodger hurlers had finished what they started in twelve of the seventeen games played. But from the series in St. Louis to the one about to begin in Brooklyn, they had completed only four of fifteen games. There was, moreover, little pattern to Durocher's use of his starters. Whitlow Wyatt and Kirby Higbe worked on a more or less regular schedule every fifth or sixth day, but there seemed to be no similar schedule for Larry French, Curt Davis, Johnny Allen, Max Macon, or Ed Head. All of the starters were used in relief, including Wyatt and Higbe, though less often in their cases. In the extra-inning win on September 2, Durocher used five pitchers, three of them starters, including Wyatt. He then held Wyatt out of action for eight days, saving him to start the "pot-o-gold" series with the Cardinals, as the *Eagle's* Tommy Holmes labeled it. The July injury to Hugh Casey no doubt created some disarray to the Dodgers' pitching staff, but age and perhaps a touch of panic contributed as well.[22]

The two-game set began on September 11, a dark and gloomy day, full of ominous forebodings for the almost thirty thousand Dodger fans in attendance to support their Bums in this final showdown with St. Louis. Wyatt faced off against his personal nemesis Mort Cooper in the first game. It was their third meeting of the season, and Cooper had triumphed in the first two, a 1–0 two-hitter in May and the fourteen-inning 2–1 win in August. Both pitchers normally wore uniform number 13, as Wyatt did when he took the mound, but Cooper, as had become his practice, wore number 20 in a bid for his twentieth win. Durocher had anguished over whether to start Wyatt against Cooper or save him for the second game against a lesser Cardinal pitcher. Overnight, however, he settled on his ace righthander in what he hoped would be a reprise of a meeting between the two the previous September in St. Louis in which Wyatt outpitched Cooper in a 1–0 win that triggered Brooklyn's final surge to the National league pennant. This time, the two warriors matched one another for the first five innings, putting zeros on the scoreboard, each giving up only one hit—a line-drive single to center by Johnny Hopp for the Cards, and a grounder to deep shortstop that the Dodgers' Pee Wee Reese legged out for a hit.

In the sixth, the Cardinals took the lead. Mort Cooper led off with a bouncer up the middle into center field that a diving Reese almost reached but missed. Jimmy Brown sacrificed him to second. After Terry Moore made the second out of the inning, Enos Slaughter, who had been slumping, smashed a drive that just tipped the outreached glove of first baseman Dolph Camilli and went into right field. Camilli had slowed the ball enough that Cooper was able to score from second. In the eighth, Cooper again ignited a Redbird rally when he dribbled a roller toward shortstop that Reese charged and juggled ever so slightly, but enough for Cooper to reach first before the throw arrived. It was ruled a hit. Batting from the left side, Jimmy Brown followed not with the usual Southworth sacrifice, but instead swung at an off-speed pitch that he hit for a double down the left-field line, sending Cooper scurrying to third. Moore, who had failed in the sixth, did not do so again. Wyatt got ahead in the count two strikes and no balls, then whipped a fastball six inches inside off the plate and high at the letters. Moore hammered it barely fair down the left-field line into the corner for a long single that scored both runners. Wyatt later said he got the ball exactly where he wanted it. "I'll never know why he swung," he said, "and still less how he ever hit the pitch that hard."[23]

Meanwhile, Cooper was handcuffing Brooklyn's batters. He allowed only four base runners. After Reese's infield hit in the third inning, Augie Galan singled in the sixth, Billy Herman walked in the eighth, and Arky Vaughan singled in the ninth. The game ended when Joe Medwick lined out to Johnny Hopp. Medwick quit running when he saw the ball headed directly at the Birds' first baseman. But the ball was spinning with a great deal of English and Hopp dropped it, whereupon Medwick made a mad dash for the bag and slid, only to be out by an eyelash. The three-hit, 3–0 win was Cooper's twentieth of the season, his seventh straight victory and eighth shutout, three of which had come against the Dodgers at Ebbets Field. There were other Cardinal fans at the game, but the happiest was probably Mort and Walker Cooper's younger brother Jim, who was stationed nearby at the Brooklyn Navy Yards and attended in his military uniform, seated in a box next to the St. Louis dugout.

The heretofore confident tone of the New York press changed after the Cardinals' win. In fact, it transformed the views of *Herald Tribune* columnist Joe Williams, who for weeks had dismissed any thought that the Cardinals posed a threat to the Dodgers. Indeed, the day before he had again declared that "in our book, the race is over," adding a backhanded compliment to the Cardinals for having given it the "old college try" against "almost impossible odds."[24] But after the epiphany of Cooper's shutout, Williams became a convert: "Right now, Billy Southworth has the best ball club in the major leagues. It's riding a high wave of momentum, punch, pitching, and spirit."[25]

Both Southworth and Durocher puzzled over who to start in the second game. Billy the Kid had either Johnny Beazley or Max Lanier ready to go. Beazley had pitched well against Brooklyn in the recent St. Louis series, but he was high-strung, and the Dodgers' bench jockeys had been loud and merciless in riding him throughout the game, making taunts that, Harold Parrott reported, featured "ultra-personal remarks by Durocher."[26] Beazley had kept his cool then, but the game in St. Louis was not the pressure-cooker that a game with a first-place tie at stake would be. Lanier, on the other hand, had not been pitching well. He had beaten the Dodgers four times earlier in the year but lost on his second try in the four-game August series, a Southworth decision that some were calling a "boner." For Durocher, meanwhile, the choice was between veteran righthander Curt Davis or young lefthander Max Macon. Davis had pitched well against the Cardinals in previous meetings, but he would be working with only four days' rest. Macon was the pitcher Durocher had projected for use against the Redbirds. Durocher thought the southpaw would be more effective against lefty hitters like Slaughter and Hopp and would most likely take Musial out of the game altogether. But Macon had no experience pitching with the pressure of a big game like this one. In the end, Southworth opted for the more experienced Lanier, and Durocher for the rookie Macon.

As the clubs were running through their pregame drills, Tommy Holmes of the *Eagle*, who had covered the Dodgers all year, thought there was an obvious difference between the two teams. "The veteran Dodgers were grim and obviously thoughtful while the younger Red Birds were smiling and sure of themselves although not overconfident." Moreover, many among the almost twenty-seven thousand Flatbush faithful who filled the grandstand struck Holmes as fatalistic, believing that the Dodgers had to win or the season was over. Mort Cooper mirrored the more relaxed mood of the Cardinals. Reporters asking about his three-hit shutout found the happy-go-lucky Cooper wanted to talk instead about his two base hits to start the two rallies that won the game. Like many pitchers, Cooper took pride in his hitting and liked to talk about it, and he was a good hitter, as were many of the Cardinals' hurlers. When asked about the team, Cooper glowed: "It has the finest spirit of any St. Louis club during the four years I've been with the Cards. It's a great all-around team."[27]

Macon worked a scoreless first inning, with the Cards going down in order. In the Dodgers' half of the first, Stanley Bordagaray, playing center instead of Reiser, led off with a single, stole second, but was out trying to swipe third. In the second with one out, the Cardinals' Walker Cooper singled to left to bring George Kurowski to the plate. Macon teased him with three slow curves, all of which were hit hard but foul, the third just two feet to the left of the left-field foul pole. Macon tried one more off-speed delivery, which Kurowski again pounded to left on a line ten feet fair into the lower stands for his ninth home run of the season and a 2–0 Redbird lead. The Dodgers came right back in the bottom half of the inning. With one out, Camilli stroked a single to center. Mickey Owen followed with a sharp grounder to Hopp at first, who threw high to second. Marion managed to spear the ball to force out Camilli but had no play at first. Reese, with two out, laced a double over the head of Coaker Triplett off the left–center-field wall to score Owen from first. But Vaughan ended the inning with a pop foul down the left-field line on which Kurowski made a nice running catch with his back to the infield.

After the second inning, the game became a scoreless duel between the two southpaws, with the tension mounting inning by inning. Lanier put two Dodgers on base in the fourth, but Slaughter bailed him out by racing in to grab Reese's short fly just beyond second base to end the threat. In the seventh, Brooklyn presented the best theater of the day. Down 2–1, Owen led off with a grounder to the right of Hopp that the first baseman could not reach, but second baseman Jimmy Brown, ranging far to his left, fielded the ball and snapped a throw to Lanier covering first to nip the heavy-footed Owen. In almost the same motion, first-base umpire Al Barlick called Owen out and threw first-base coach Charlie Dressen out of the game, igniting an arm-flailing, jaw-to-jaw discussion of the call between coach, player, and umpire. A livid Leo Durocher leaped from the Dodgers' dugout to join in challenging the umpire's decision with all of his customary vigor. It was, the New York Times reported, "one of his bitterest argumentative exhibitions" of the season. Durocher followed Barlick into right field and "gave a bit of shouldering" to the umpire as league president Ford Frick and chief of umpires Bill Klem "watched in grim silence from the press box."[28] "What Dressen said," Bob Burnes of the Globe-Democrat observed, "must have been plenty, even for Brooklyn."[29]

Lanier soldiered on, aided by excellent outfield play. In the eighth, Musial, in the game as a late-inning defensive replacement for Triplett, raced into left center to grab Bordagaray's bid for extra bases leading off the inning. In the ninth, with one out, Billy Herman drew a walk and stayed at first when Slaughter went into deep right center to take an extra-base hit away from Johnny Rizzo that would have tied the game. Joe Medwick followed with a single to right that sent Herman to third and brought Dolph Camilli to the plate with the tying run ninety feet from home. But Lanier fooled Camilli, who topped a harmless grounder to Brown for the third out in what Roscoe McGowan of the New York Times called "the most important time at bat for a Dodger this year."[30] Lanier had made the two runs from the second inning stand up for nine innings. It had been a struggle. He had given up just five hits but had walked five and made a wild pitch. At several points, it appeared that Southworth was ready to go to his bullpen, but Lanier weathered the storms and brought the Cardinals into a dead heat with the Dodgers for first place in the National League.[31]

⁓

"Flatbush fandom's worst fears today are a woeful reality" was the verdict of Roscoe McGowan of the New York Times. "These irrepressible St. Louis Cardinals are tied with Brooklyn's Dodgers for the National League lead." In St. Louis, Roy Stockton of the Post-Dispatch assured readers "it is true," the Cardinals "share the top National League position with the Dodgers," while Bob Burnes at the *Globe-Democrat* waxed melodramatic: "From the depths of oblivion, almost hopelessly out of the pennant race, the Cardinals have fought their way up into a tie for the National League lead." A bullish Sam Breadon chortled, "I think we're in," adding that it was probably time to start printing World Series tickets. In Brooklyn, a caustic Leo Durocher was having none of this. "It took those guys five months to catch us," he growled. "Now it's a new season." Billy Southworth, no longer facing questions about catching Brooklyn, was asked whether his team might now succumb to the jitters that seemed to have afflicted the Dodgers. "Nerves? Jitters?" Southworth responded rhetorically. "These boys won't get them. Why should they? They've finally gained what they've been trying for all season. That should make them happy, not nervous." One thing was for sure, Joe King of the *Herald Tribune* observed: win or lose, the Cardinals' drive since mid-August was "one of the most thrilling and productive stretch runs in the history of baseball."[32]

The Cardinals may have taken time after the game to join in singing their victory song, "Pass the Biscuits, Mirandy," but they had little time for celebrating their climb to the top of the National League. They had to pack their bags and catch a night train to Philadelphia for a Sunday doubleheader the next day. Before boarding at New York's Penn Station, Terry Moore held an informal meeting with the players. "We've got about two weeks of this fight left," Moore said to them. "Let's agree that nobody stays out late until this thing is over. We will give all we have and anyone who breaks our own rules—well, we'll know how to treat him." His teammates cheered their captain and agreed to do as he suggested.[33]

On arriving in the city of Brotherly Love, Johnny Beazley got into an altercation with one of the porters at the train station. The red cap asked to carry his bag, but Beazley declined, after which Beazley said the fellow cursed him. Beazley threw his bag at the porter, who in turn pulled a knife and slashed Beazley's right thumb. While his teammates could see their pennant chances disappearing with the injury, the rookie righthander, sliced thumb and all, took the mound the next day to face the cellar-dwelling Phillies in the first game of the afternoon. A crowd of slightly more than twenty thousand fans turned out for the contest, many of whom watched the scoreboard as intently as the game, and a cheer went out every time a run was put up for Cincinnati against Brooklyn. Beazley had rarely been in better form. He had good command of his fastball and curve, walked only one, and pitched one of his best games of the season. At the same time, Philadelphia starter Tommy Hughes was holding the Redbirds in check save for a single run in the fifth inning brought home by Marty Marion's double.

Beazley nursed his 1–0 lead into the ninth inning, only to have the defense let him down. Danny Litwhiler started the trouble with a short fly ball down the right-field line on which Slaughter, Hopp, and Brown converged. All three hesitated, then Brown lunged to make the catch but missed the ball. It went for a double. Beazley got the next hitter to pop out, but rookie shortstop Bill Burich lined a single to center. Litwhiler rounded third and headed for home with the tying run. Terry Moore made a perfect throw to the plate in time to get the runner, but Walker Cooper dropped the ball for an error. Second baseman Danny Murtaugh then hit an easy grounder that Marion charged but fumbled for another error. Catcher Mickey Livingston followed with a sharp single to drive Burich in with the run that gave the Phillies a 2–1 victory. In Brooklyn, when the "2" was posted on the scoreboard showing a Philadelphia win, the crowd of more than thirty-three thousand erupted in loud and sustained applause and shouts of joy. "The cheering lasted nearly three minutes," Roscoe McGowan reported, "and the Brooklyn game was held up until it subsided."[34]

St. Louis managed only three hits in the first game and would not do much better in the second against Rube Melton. Through the first three innings, the former Cardinal farm hand gave up only a bunt single to Marion. Howard Krist, the St. Louis starter, flirted with trouble through the first three innings as the Phils put runners on base in each of the frames but could not score. In the Cardinals' fourth, with one out, Slaughter worked a walk. Musial followed with a long, high drive into right–center field that went for a triple, sending Slaughter home with the first run. O'Dea failed to get Musial home, but the hot-hitting Johnny Hopp came through with a two-out double to give the Birds a two-run lead. The Phils came right back as Danny Litwhiler and Nick Etten led off the home half of the inning with back-to-back line drives, followed by Burich beating out a slow infield roller to load the bases. Murtaugh then made it four straight hits with a single that drove in two runs. That ended Krist's day. He was replaced by Bill Beckmann, recently promoted from Rochester, who stanched the bleeding with the game tied. In the top of the fifth, Terry Moore connected for his sixth home run of the season, a line drive into the upper deck of the left-field stands. Beckmann, who had won his last six games in the minors, pitched brilliantly, holding the Phils to three hits and no runs in his six innings of work to earn the 3–2 win and a split in the doubleheader.

A Philly fan, Theodore Gotwalt of York, Pennsylvania, became ill at the ballpark and was rushed to a local hospital, where physicians diagnosed his problem as "acute hysteria." At the same time, something akin to acute hysteria was afflicting Dodger fans at Ebbets Field, where the Flatbush faithful "died slowly in their seats [as] the Dodgers dropped both games of a double header to Cincinnati."[35] The Cardinals now stood alone in first place. After 148 days on top, Durocher's "once carefree and high-riding athletes," the *Eagle's* Tommy Holmes wrote, "lost command of the situation for the first time with the loss of that Sunday double header to the vengeful Reds of Cincinnati." The slide of the Dodgers, he added, had become something of a "civic tragedy" in Brooklyn, where "on every street corner fans are asking each other what's wrong with the ball club and getting no kind of answers that help." Holmes offered an explanation: "The Dodgers . . . haven't had anything like a break in a long, long while." He offered hope: "There isn't anything in the constitution which says that St. Louis must continue to do everything right while their opponents continue to do everything wrong."[36]

Bucky Walters won the opener for Cincinnati against Bobo Newsome, who had won his first start in Dodger blue, but failed for the second time since. Adding insult to injury, he was driven from the game in the fourth by a bases-clearing double by Walters. Brooklyn tried to crawl back into the game but lost 6–3. In the nightcap, Curt Davis was ineffective, giving up seven hits in eight innings and allowing four Cincinnati runs. Meanwhile, the Dodgers' hitters, still mired in a team-wide slump, got only five hits and one run against Ray Starr. Brooklyn collected a total of eleven hits in the twin bill, ten of them singles. The Dodgers had now lost five straight games and eight of their last eleven. They were clearly a tired team. After the Sunday losses, Durocher conceded that it had "been a long time since our guys have been themselves." With the next two days off, the Dodgers' skipper wanted his players to do anything that would take their minds off baseball. "I hope our guys will go to the movies or any place that will keep them out of radio earshot," he said, adding, "I'll tell you Wednesday night whether or not we're going to win this pennant. It all depends on what we show against the Pirates. If we come back with the old vinegar and a few base hits, we'll win it."[37]

The *Brooklyn Eagle* decided to do what it could to revive the Dodgers' fortunes by forming a Booster's Club so fans could show their support for the team in its time of peril. Addressed to "Brooklyn Baseball Fans," it read in part:

> Are we going to let the Dodgers make their gallant fight for the pennant alone? Are we going to sit back and give up, or are we going to show Manager Leo Durocher and his men that we are with them, down to the last game . . . ?
>
> The pennant race is still that—a race. It isn't over by any means, but thousands of fans in Brooklyn are giving up; fair weather fans are now rooting against the Dodgers . . .

Fans were invited to send their names to the *Eagle,* and for the next ten days the newspaper published more than three thousand names of fans who backed their Bums.

〜

Baseball on the playing field had to share the stage in September with baseball on the silver screen. As the Cardinals-Dodgers showdown was about to start,

Hollywood released Samuel Goldwyn's *Pride of the Yankees*, about the life and death of Lou Gehrig, the great New York Yankees first baseman. Gary Cooper had the starring role, while two of Gehrig's old teammates, Babe Ruth and Bill Dickey, appeared as themselves. The American League took out a large ad in the *Sporting News* to celebrate the occasion and express gratitude to Goldwyn. "Baseball has a very small part in the picture," W. J. McGoogan observed. "Cooper is very carefully kept covered when it comes to the baseball parts but he does a swell job of helping to make the picture a grand tear jerker." He noted also that Ruth and Dickey did "all right."[38]

A few days after *Pride of the Yankees* was released, as if on cue, the Yankees clinched the American League pennant on the strong right arm of Ernest "Tiny" Bonham, who won his twentieth game, aided by the booming bat of Joe DiMaggio, who contributed three singles and a home run. It was the thirteenth pennant the New Yorkers had claimed since 1921 and the seventh pennant for their manager, Joe McCarthy. The Bronx Bombers had moved into the lead on May 6 and never relinquished it, though there was a moment before the All-Star game when their lead dipped to just three games over the second-place Boston Red Sox. But they went to Boston, beat the Olde Towne Team two games out of three, moved four games ahead, and were never threatened thereafter.

CHAPTER 10

Down to the Wire

The fight for the National League pennant had become intense by mid-September and may have been first in the minds of many in St. Louis, Brooklyn, and perhaps elsewhere in the country. But the real battle at the time was half a world away in the Russian city of Stalingrad, one that a Swedish reporter called the "greatest battle in world history."[1] No one who so much as glanced at a St. Louis newspaper could miss reports on the fighting. Large black headlines in all of the city's daily papers guided readers to stories about the fury of the German assault and the ferocity of the fighting, street by street, building by building, back and forth, as casualties mounted on both sides. In one five-day period, the Stalingrad railroad station changed hands fifteen times. The Germans had captured the southern and central areas of Stalingrad, and as the Cardinals and Dodgers were meeting for the final time in the season, the Nazis launched what they hoped would be their final assault on the northern, industrial section of the city. Stalingrad sat against the Volga River, and to prevent the Germans from surrounding the city the Russians had destroyed all of the bridges crossing the river. It made the battle a fight to the death for the Soviet troops, who had no escape route, and it became much the same for the Germans when Hitler ordered that the burned-out and ruined city be taken at any cost. His order took on a greater urgency when snow began falling in the western Caucasus Mountains in the middle of September. The deep snows of the Russian winter had stalled the German war machine in 1941, and now in 1942 snow had come more than a month ahead of schedule.

～

During the two off-days in which the Dodgers hoped to regroup and rearm, the Cardinals were wrapping up their visit to Philadelphia by winning two, though not without some difficulty. On Monday, September 14, the Redbirds jumped on Phillies starter Ike Pearson for a run in the first inning on a walk to Terry Moore and a double by Enos Slaughter. But Moore, who had been nursing a sore leg for some time, aggravated it in his race around the bases and had to leave the game. Neither side could score again until the sixth, when the Phils pushed across a run, but they then handed the lead right back to the Cardinals when their porous defense committed three errors. Undaunted, the Philadelphians ended starter Harry Gumbert's day in the seventh with four hits good for two runs and a 3–2 lead. Johnny Podgajny took over mound duties for the home team and threw a scoreless eighth, but he could not match that in the ninth. Four St. Louis hits, including a triple by Harry Walker, in the game replacing Moore, and a double by Musial, together with three more Philly errors, enabled the Birds to score four times and gain a 6–3 win. Stan Musial's nineteen-year-old brother, Ed, on leave from the Sixteenth Field Artillery at Ft. Riley, Kansas, was in the stands to cheer his brother's heroics.

Mort Cooper started the final game of the series against the veteran Si Johnson. The Cardinals again took the lead with two runs in the third, but the Phils got one of them back in the same inning and added another in the eighth to even the score. Cooper was no mystery to Philadelphia hitters, who reached him for ten hits before he departed with one out in the ninth. Murry Dickson took over, kept the Phils off the board, and took the game to extra innings. Johnson held the Redbirds in check through the thirteenth inning, but in the fourteenth, with two out, Dickson doubled and Jimmy Brown singled to put the Cards up 3–2, after which Dickson tossed a sixth scoreless inning for the victory. Cooper had worn jersey number 21 for the game and, for the first time since he began the practice, he did not get the corresponding win. The three-hour, nineteen-minute game ended on a sour note when Philadelphia's manager, Hans Lobert, charged into the grandstand to confront a spectator who had been heckling him. The altercation ended quickly without any violence.

After the Dodgers dropped both ends of the Sunday doubleheader with Cincinnati and began their two-day sabbatical, they became a punching bag for other clubs with hard feelings toward them—a measure of the enmity they had engendered around the league. Larry MacPhail suggested that Cincinnati was not trying as hard against other teams as they were against Brooklyn, provoking Reds traveling secretary Gabe Paul to accuse the Dodgers of having a "persecution complex." "We're not trying to beat them any harder than we're trying to beat any other team in the National League. But they think we are, and that's what's getting 'em down." With touch of sarcasm, he added, "It's a wonder they haven't gone running to the league president about the way everybody's picking on them." With evident satisfaction, Paul concluded: "You know the old saying, something about reaping what you sow, don't you? Well, that's what's happening to the Dodgers right now. All year they've been hollering 'teacher' every time something happened they didn't like. Some of them, like coach Chuck Dressen, have said some pretty mean things to rival players, too. They're getting it all back now."[2]

Eddie Brannick, Paul's counterpart with Brooklyn's archrival New York Giants, could not restrain himself in an interview with John Kieran about the Dodgers' fall from first place. With unvarnished sarcasm, he told the *Times* writer, "Yes, the report is true. I nearly died laughing. But I'm able to sit up and take nourishment now. Ho, Ho, Ho! Ha, Ha, Ha! Excuse it please. Just a slight relapse. I wonder how Arsenic and Old Lace [Brannick's nicknames for Durocher and MacPhail] are feeling now. It must have been a terrible shock to them watching their Brooklyn bubble dancers and seeing the bubble burst . . . Who ever called that a ball club? It's a circus with a calliope." As for MacPhail, Brannick asked, "Where is the Vanishing American now? When [the Giants] went over to Brooklyn, he went to Canada to catch fish. He came back when he thought it was safe for him in Flatbush again. When the Cardinals went to Brooklyn for that crucial series," Brannick continued, "MacPhail turned up in Washington. . . . They tell me he's in the Army. Maybe he thinks he'll be safer in a world war than he would be in Brooklyn when the Cardinals clinch the flag." With one last jab, Brannick concluded: "I think I'll phone Sam Breadon now and get my St. Louis tickets for the series."[3]

The two wins in Philadelphia while the Dodgers were idle moved St. Louis two full games ahead of Brooklyn. The Cardinals had ten games left to play, six of them at home; Brooklyn had twelve, ten at home. From Philly, the Cards moved to Boston for their final visit. To face the Braves, Southworth tapped Ernie White, who had shown signs of having recovered from his arm woes. Jim Tobin got the call from Boston manager Casey Stengel. St. Louis scored in the first and third innings, the latter run coming on Slaughter's thirteenth home run. The Cardinals added four more in the sixth on five hits and two Boston errors. The speed of the young Cardinals was once again telling as Redbird runners hurried the Bostonians repeatedly into fielding and throwing errors. The Braves' only score came on a sixth-inning home run by Ernie Lombardi after they were already behind by six runs. The "Schnoz," as the big catcher with the large nose was affectionately known, had recently taken over the National League batting lead. With both Pete Reiser and Joe Medwick fading, Lombardi would claim the batting title at season's end.

While the Cardinals were in Boston, the Dodgers were home against Pittsburgh in the game that Leo Durocher said would tell him whether his team could get back into the race. Before the game, Durocher acknowledged that the Cardinals were "better than we thought they were" and that "their fighting spirit is remarkable," but he was quick to add that they "aren't as good as their long winning streak," which he called "just plain unnatural for any ball club." He thought it unlikely they could sustain that pace.[4] The Dodgers certainly came out fighting even before the game with Pittsburgh began. When four spectators got into a fistfight with ushers about an hour before game time, Dixie Walker and Mickey Owen jumped into the stands to join the brawl. Police arrived, arrested the four combatants for disorderly conduct, and hauled them off the jail. The team took out the rest of its aggression on six Pirate pitchers, pounding them for nineteen hits and ten runs and making both Whitlow Wyatt, who held the Buccos to three runs for his eighteenth win, and manager Durocher feel better.

The Cardinals finished their two-game set in Boston with a come-from-behind win. Beazley started for St. Louis but was hit hard and departed in the third with one out after a succession of singles, the last of which was off his kneecap. Howard Pollet entered and retired the Bostonians, but not until three runs had scored. The Redbird lefty then kept the Braves off the scoreboard through the eighth. At the same time, the Cards could score only once off Al Javery, on a Marion triple and Pollet single in the fifth. In the ninth, the Cards rallied. Walker Cooper dribbled a slow roller toward third base that he beat out for a hit. Johnny Hopp then drew a walk, advancing Cooper to second. Kurowski tried to sacrifice, but instead forced Cooper at third.

Southworth summoned O'Dea to pinch-hit, but before he could send him to the plate, Hopp called time to meet with his manager to suggest he use Ray Sanders instead. Sanders had not had a base hit in weeks, but Hopp had noticed that he had been hitting the ball on the nose in batting practice. Southworth sent Sanders to the plate, and on the second pitch he lined a single to right to score Hopp and send Kurowski to third. O'Dea was used next to hit for Pollet. He took a fearsome swing on the first pitch, then crossed up the Boston defense by putting down a perfect squeeze bunt to score Kurowski with the tying run. The Cardinals added three more for a five-run inning. Max Lanier took over for Pollet but faced only two hitters and left with both aboard and none out. Harry Gumbert entered, gave up a run, got an out, and faced Ernie Lombardi with the game on the line. Handsome Harry got the Braves' catcher, a notoriously slow runner, to hit into a game-ending double play, sealing a 6–4 Birds win. After the game, Terry Moore called attention to Hopp's suggestion of Sanders. "I point that out," he said, "because Hopp and Sanders are rivals for that first base job," adding, "that's the team spirit that has been winning for us."[5]

Following the loss, Casey Stengel was rapturous about the running Redbirds. "It's one of the few clubs I ever saw that gets its extra base hits out of its ankles," the Boston manager told Joe Williams of the *New York Herald Tribune*. "They aren't a ball club, they are a track team," he continued. "They take very mean advantage of you. When they should stop at first they go to second, when they should stop at second they go to third, and most of them are 'home-minded.' Personally, I think they are merely lazy. It wearies them to stay out there on second or third. They like to sit on the bench. They must all be Southerners," he joked. "You get a moral victory when you can even make them slide." Then, getting serious, Stengel added, "This is the fastest ball club I've ever seen in my life; they're a bunch of Cobbs all rolled up into one." William agreed: "It seems to us this is a 'get on' ball club and once on, a 'don't stop' ball club. Even their best hitters bunt . . . they sacrifice, they hit and run, they squeeze . . . Their theory seems: 'What difference does it make how you get the runs as long as you get them?' And up to now they have been getting them."[6] Williams dubbed their style of play "mid-Victorian, the kind of stuff the old Orioles used to pull," and he began to call the Cardinals the "St. Louis Swifties," while his colleague at the *Herald Tribune*, cartoonist Willard Mullin, depicted them famously as riverboat gamblers.[7]

Welcome as the opinions of Stengel and Williams may have been, more welcome to the Cardinals was the news that the Pirates had beaten the Dodgers 3–2. St. Louis now held a three-game lead. Dropping another game behind was bad enough, but the loss itself was deeply painful for the Brooklynites. They had numerous opportunities to score throughout the game, but could never get the timely hit. As they left the field, the Dodgers were downcast, almost lifeless. They walked "with the tread of the condemned," Jack Mahon wrote. "They didn't speak, they looked at the ground [and] not at each other."[8] Tommy Holmes of the Eagle thought them "a beaten team unless a miracle intervenes." But after seeing "their gloomy deadpans down in their clubhouse dungeon," Holmes did not expect a miracle.[9] Dan Daniel of the *Herald Tribune* later identified this game as the day the pennant was lost.

~

Friday was a travel day on which the Cardinals moved to Chicago for their last two road games of the season. With eight games to play, they had a three game lead. For all the satisfaction everyone associated with the club must have taken in its drive to the top, no one was more pleased than the Cardinals' general manager, Branch Rickey. "This is the club I've always dreamed about," he told Joe Williams of the *Herald Tribune*. "It has the college spirit. There isn't a man on the team who considers himself a star. That's why they play so well together, why they have been able to come from so far back to take the lead—and now that they're taken it they aren't going to relinquish it, either." They were Rickey's boys, almost every one of them a product of his farm system. Rickey loved younger players, hungry players, team players, and the 1942 Cardinals embodied all of his ideals. "As for selling our stars, I plead guilty to having been too impetuous on one or two occasions," he conceded. "I thought our youngsters were ready to carry on, but it turned out I placed too great a burden on them. But these are chances you must take, if you hang on to your veteran stars too long you retard the development of your youngsters."[10]

But it must have been a bittersweet moment for the Mahatma, whose twenty-six-year tenure with the Redbirds was coming to a close due to his strained relationship with owner Sam Breadon. Speculation was that Rickey might return to the St. Louis Browns, with whom he had been employed before moving to the Cardinals. There was even talk that he might move to Brooklyn if Larry MacPhail joined the military. A prominent law firm in St. Louis made it known that it would welcome Rickey as an associate, and Republican Party leaders were trying to recruit him to run for the U.S. Senate. Rickey had long been a popular speaker at Republican fund-raisers. John Wray of the *Post-Dispatch* reported that Colonel Isaac Hedges was trying to sell party leaders on Rickey as a candidate. "Branch is a natural," Hedges said, adding that "his proper sphere is something bigger than baseball. He has everything it takes to make a great statesman."[11] Rickey was non-committal, no doubt realizing that politics is a very different game from baseball and probably realizing too that rookies can be treated even more harshly in it than they are in the game he loved.

It was, however, manager Billy Southworth, not Branch Rickey, who drew the most accolades for the Cardinals' success. Roy Stockton of the *Post-Dispatch* acknowledged that not many had thought St. Louis could catch Brooklyn, and while several factors had contributed to the team's rise to the top, he pointed to Southworth as the one who "deserves a tremendous portion of praise. His great contribution was keeping up club morale, making the team play at top speed even when first place seemed impossible to reach . . . Few managers," Stockton told readers, "could have done what Southworth did, calmly and without any fiery rhetoric, to keep the boys plugging away day after day."[12] Joe Williams of the *Herald Tribune* agreed: "The St. Louis Cardinals are not only a red-hot ball club but they are being directed by a red-hot manager. Their Mr. Southworth apparently can not do anything wrong." As a strategist, Williams added, Southworth looked like "a combination of Napoleon, MacArthur, and Houdini."[13] Rickey joined in the applause for Southworth, calling him a "great manager" and saying that his achievement "stands out as one of the greatest in the sports and athletic world in our memory."[14]

～

In Chicago the Cardinals were welcomed by rain that led to the postponement of their Saturday meeting with the Cubs and necessitated a doubleheader the next day. While the Redbirds were lounging around their hotel, the Dodgers were defeating Philadelphia in extra innings, 5–4. Brooklyn scored the winning run in the eleventh on a bases-loaded walk to Pete Reiser as Si Johnson, who had pitched impressively against the Cardinals a few days earlier, imploded. Pee Wee Reese drew a walk to lead off the inning and was moved to second on a sacrifice by Billy Herman. After Hugh Casey popped out, Johnson threw only one strike to the next three Dodger hitters, walking Dixie Walker, Arky Vaughan, and Reiser to bring in the winning run. With the win, Brooklyn picked up half a game on St. Louis in the standings.

Mort Cooper was matched against his former teammate Lon Warneke in Sunday's first game, played before the largest crowd of the season at Wrigley Field. The Cardinals managed only one run against long, lean Lon, and they had to steal it. In the fourth inning, Hopp drew a walk. Kurowski then bounced a single into left, and when the Cubs' left fielder, Lou Novikoff, did not charge the ball aggressively, Hopp sprinted around second and headed for third, where he eluded the tag with a nice hook slide. With two outs and Mort Cooper batting, the running Redbirds pulled off a double steal. Kurowski waited until catcher Chico Hernandez was about to return the ball to the pitcher, then broke for second. Surprised, Hernandez hurriedly threw to shortstop Bobby Sturgeon, but Kurowski stopped halfway to second, inviting a rundown. As Sturgeon moved toward Kurowski, Hopp broke off third, stopped, and looked as if he could be picked off. Sturgeon wheeled and threw to Stan Hack at third, but as the throw went to Hack, Hopp raced for the plate and slid under Hack's hurried and high throw home. The Cards had several variations of the double steal; this one was called "Kansas City Lou."[15]

One run was all Cooper needed as he set the Cubs down on four hits and no runs for his ninth shutout of the season. Southworth exulted in the way the game was won: "Did you see how the boys used their speed and dash and made those Cubs throw that ball—and the ball game—around?" "It was speed and daring all right," Harold Parrott told his Brooklyn readers. "Almost foolhardy it seemed. But it has been paying off for these Cards."[16] In the nightcap, the Cardinals' speed did not come into play because they had few opportunities to use it against Cubs ace Claude Passeau, who shut them down completely, scattering five hits and tossing a shutout for his nineteenth win. The Redbirds had split a doubleheader without anyone on the team batting in a run.

In Brooklyn, the Dodgers missed another opportunity to gain ground on St. Louis as Brooklyn split a doubleheader of its own. The Phillies unleashed seldom-seen power against Whitlow Wyatt, who gave up round-trippers to Litwhiler and Etten in losing 7–3. The crowd at Ebbets Field vented its frustration and disappointment by booing their beloved Bums, who, Roscoe McGowan wrote, "folded like an accordion."[17] Bobo Newsome salvaged the afternoon with a six-hit win in the second game. Tommy Holmes of the Eagle was especially downcast after the twin bill. "It was the sort of Sunday afternoon that made you think of a funeral—bleak, gray, and never a hint of sunshine." The Dodgers "had all the appearance of fellows attending their own wake." Durocher, however, was in no mood to start hanging crepe and scolded the press. "It isn't over yet! . . . The Cardinals are feeling the strain now, and you can tell it," he claimed, pointing to the single run the Redbirds had scored in two games with the Cubs.[18]

Before the Sunday games in Chicago, Cubs officials received a telegram from an unknown source in Brooklyn. "We think you members of the other teams have quit to the Cardinals," it read. "We cannot believe that it is an accident which has caused so many of you to make the poor selections of pitchers and pinch hitters. We cannot do anything but appeal to your sporting blood." Chicago general manager James Gallagher was sure that one of MacPhail's "stooges" had sent it, while Cubs manager Jimmy Wilson snarled, "they cannot 'take' it in Brooklyn." "By the way," he sneered, "where is all that smart Durocher and Dressen baseball that was winning for Brooklyn when they were ten games on top?"[19] The *Eagle's* Harold Parrott, covering the games in person, seemed skeptical of Brooklyn's complaint: "I can tell you that 30,000 people in Chicago yesterday saw their Cubs who hate the Dodgers like Poison, make life miserable for the St. Louis league-leaders."[20]

The *Brooklyn Eagle* sent Parrott west to cover games on a daily basis, and he acknowledged that the trip had been a "revelation" to him. That the Cardinals were almost daily winning games in improbable ways was one thing, but the antipathy toward Brooklyn was even more astonishing to him. "In Cleveland and Detroit, where they never see the Dodgers, the citizens went into a happy tumult whenever it was announced that Brooklyn was being beaten again." In Chicago, the loudest cheers of the afternoon came when the Dodgers' first-game loss was posted. Out here, Parrott wrote, "Durocher is a bully, a swaggering menace to baseball." But the "birds," he added, had come home to roost on the Dodgers' manager. By "birds" he did not mean the Cardinals, but rather "the Bronx version of invective that Lippy Leo has been spraying all over the league this semester." The season, Parrott concluded, has been a "vendetta." "Old timers will tell you that never before was so much venom pumped into a 154-game schedule."[21]

∼

The Cardinals finished their final road trip of the season having won thirteen and lost only three, continuing the hot pace they set during their August home stand. When they left St. Louis on September 4, they trailed the Dodgers by four games. Upon their return on September 21, they were two and a half games ahead of Brooklyn. Their final six games would be on friendly turf. Arriving from Chicago by train at Union Station that evening, the players were welcomed by their wives and fifteen assorted but devoted fans. At Sportsman's Park the next day, a disappointing crowd of 4,891 showed up for the afternoon contest with the Pittsburgh Pirates, but the small gathering had "star" quality as it included former

Cardinal great "Sunny Jim" Bottomley, who had played for four St. Louis pennant winners and hoped to cheer the 1942 Redbirds on to similar glory.

Southworth opened the series with Ernie White, who had pitched a complete-game win against Boston five days earlier, while Pittsburgh manager Frankie Frisch, a teammate of Bottomley on three of those pennant-winning Cardinal clubs, countered with Hank Gornicki. Both hurlers posted zeroes through the first four innings. In the fifth, it was again Cardinal speed that put the first run on the board. Marion beat out an infield hit and went to second on a White sacrifice. Brown bounced a grounder up the middle that second baseman Frankie Gustine reached, but his throw to first was late. Without breaking stride, Marion rounded third and raced for home, sliding across before first baseman Elbie Fletcher's hurried throw could reach the surprised catcher, Al Lopez, at the plate. Pittsburgh tied the score in the seventh, and the game went to the ninth with the score 1–1. In the bottom half of the inning, Marion drew a walk with one out and stole second. Following an out, Brown bounced a ball just beyond Gustine's reach into short right field and Marion raced home with the winning run. "Those guys make you play bad baseball," Frisch lamented. "You gotta hustle to get 'em out and in hustling you kick the ball around."[22]

All of the big bats that slumbered in Chicago continued to snooze in St. Louis, but the Redbirds found a way to win on Marion's speed and Brown's contact-hitting. Harold Parrott continued to be amazed, reporting that "this gambling, galloping outfit" won a game "that no other team in baseball would have been able to make come true," adding that the Cardinals "have the opposition jittery with these surprise tactics."[23] John Drebinger of the New York Times agreed. He concluded, tongue no doubt in cheek, that the Redbirds had "reduced the art of winning airtight ball games to an exact science." They had beaten the Pirates with only "one blow" that "really amounted to anything."[24] Marion and Brown got the plaudits, but Southworth was probably happiest with the work of Ernie White, who walked four but struck out seven and surrendered only six hits. With the win, St. Louis kept pace with the Dodgers, who beat the Phillies 3–1 behind an outstanding pitching performance by Kirby Higbe.

With five games left, Southworth chose Howard Pollet to start the Tuesday game against the Pirates. Pollet's season had paralleled that of White: both had loomed large in the team's pitching plans at the start of the year; both had been tormented throughout by arm problems; and now both were showing signs of regaining their old effectiveness. In the previous week, Pollet had pitched well in two relief appearances, getting a win in Boston and pitching three strong innings in the loss to the Cubs. But Pollet did not have it this day. He gave up three runs on six hits and a walk and departed with two out in the third inning, turning mound duties over to Harry Gumbert, who, with help from Murry Dickson, held the Pirates scoreless over the last six innings. Meanwhile, Pittsburgh starter Truett "Rip" Sewell kept the Redbirds' bats on ice through the first four innings and would have made it five if the Pittsburgh defense had not frayed again.

In the fifth, Kurowski lofted a high fly that should have been caught but instead dropped for a hit between two Pirate outfielders, each of whom thought the other would catch it. Marion followed with an easy grounder to third baseman Bob Elliott, who threw to Gustine for a force play, but the second sacker juggled the ball for an error. After an out, Brown bounced a ball to Gustine, who fell as he fielded it, recovered, and threw to second too late to get Marion. Sewell was livid, arguing vociferously that Marion had been out. With the bases now loaded, Harry Walker bounced to Fletcher at first, who flipped the ball to the still-fuming Sewell, but the Pirates' pitcher failed to tag the bag, an error that allowed a St. Louis run. Slaughter followed with a sharply hit ball to Fletcher that looked like a double play, but it squirted off his glove for a hit and another run. Sewell, still badgering the umpires, then threw an inside slider to Stan Musial, who smacked a towering drive to the back screen of the pavilion roof for a grand slam and four more runs. The Cardinals added another four runs against several other Pittsburgh pitchers, aided by more errors and a hit batsman, to win 9–3, with all but one of their runs unearned.

The Dodgers kept pace, beating the Giants, but it took them eleven innings. The game marked the reappearance of Larry MacPhail at Ebbets Field after ten days of suffering in silence. To Tommy Holmes, this "leant a certain backstage piquancy to the events of the day." It also gave MacPhail a stage for his theatrical fulminations as one Brooklyn misplay after another helped the Giants build a 4–0 lead. The Dodgers came back to take the lead, only to have the Giants rally to reclaim it with three runs in the ninth when Dixie Walker banged into the right-field wall trying unsuccessfully to catch a long drive by Johnny Mize. "Five thousand bucks at stake," MacPhail groused, referring to the share a player would get from World Series money, "and he can't hold a ball he's caught."[25] The Dodgers came back to tie the game in their half of the ninth on a pinch hit by Lew Riggs, sending MacPhail into ecstasies over the managerial genius of Durocher, and won it in the eleventh when Dolph Camilli launched one out of the park. The next day, MacPhail announced that he had accepted a commission in the Army and would end his association with the Dodgers at the close of the season. Sobbing, he told reporters, "the five years I spent in Brooklyn were indeed happy ones. I don't think I'll ever again have a baseball connection."[26]

With their wins over Pittsburgh, the Cardinals moved to within two games of clinching at least a tie for the pennant. But W. J. McCoogan of the *Post-Dispatch* found the word "pennant" was taboo with the team. Terry Moore had forbidden its use. "We've never won one of those things since I started here in 1935. And believe me I'm not saying anything now." Moore recalled the 1935 season in which the Cubs won twenty-one straight games to nose out the Redbirds. "They beat us out that year and we didn't go into a tailspin. . . . So the thing to do is saying nothing until you're really in."[27] There were those who thought the Cardinals were in. As St. Louis was beating Pittsburgh for a second time, Arthur "Happy" Felsch, a forty-year-old upholsterer from Milwaukee and baseball comedian, took up residence at the pavilion gate on Grand Avenue to be the first in line to buy World Series tickets. He brought a packing case with a borrowed mattress—his "cardboard abode"—in which he planned to live for the next six days. Felsch had been doing this for fourteen years and only once, in 1941 in Brooklyn, was he second in line, although in 1934 he was beaten out for first in line for the pavilion in St. Louis and had to settle for being first in line for the bleachers.[28]

∽

As the Cardinals prepared for their next opponent, the Cincinnati Reds, they seemed less affected by the pressures of a tight pennant race than by the physical demands of the long baseball season. With games almost every day for six months and half of their time spent moving from city to city, there is little time for players to rest and recover from the daily wear and tear. By September, every player is hurting in some way. Pain is a constant companion as legs grow heavy, arms weary, and mental fatigue makes concentration on the game more of a challenge. Being a younger team, the Cards may have withstood these difficulties better than other teams, but they had their walking wounded, though nothing like the year before. Terry Moore continued to nurse a sore leg, had not played in ten days, and was not ready to play against the Reds. Harry Walker, known affectionately as "Needle Nose," had played well in his place, hitting .333, but he was no match for Moore in center field, nor did he provide the leadership Moore offered as the team's captain. Marty Marion continued to play with a heavily taped ankle from a three-week-old injury. It did not affect his baserunning, but it bothered him on the quick moves required on defense, especially when planting his foot to throw from deep shortstop. Johnny Hopp was fighting a cold that had hung on for days; George Kurowski seemed simply to be worn down as a rookie playing his first long major-league season; both Hopp and Kurowski had fallen into hitting slumps. The good news for Southworth was that the pitching staff was healthy. It had carried the team since the September showdown in Flatbush; the Redbirds had scored three or fewer runs in six of their last ten games but had lost only two.

Billy Southworth had Johnny Beazley and Mort Cooper ready to pitch the two games against Cincinnati, while the Reds were armed with Bucky Walters and Ray Starr. Johnny Vander Meer, who had pitched so well against the Cards all season, was not available because he had pitched in Chicago the day before. This again lit Larry MacPhail's short fuse: "How about that McKechnie," he grumbled about the Reds' manager. "Vander Meer is the best pitcher in the league against the Cardinals and this is the second time in succession that he's pitched the day before the Reds play the Cardinals."[29] Harold Parrott agreed with MacPhail, dubbing McKechnie "a charter member of the 'Down With Durocher' chowder and marching club." Noting that Vander Meer had beaten St. Louis repeatedly during the season, Parrott complained, "If McKechnie plays to win, as he said recently, his best bet tonight against the Cardinals certainly would have been Vander Meer." Instead, the Reds' southpaw had pitched in "a meaningless game" the day before.[30]

As the Cardinals took the field for the night game with Cincinnati, they knew Brooklyn had beaten Philadelphia 6–0 that afternoon behind the near perfect pitching of Larry French, who allowed one hit but faced the minimum of twenty-seven hitters when the one Philly base runner was erased in a double play. The Cardinals' Johnny Beazley, going for his twentieth win of the season, was close to perfection as well after allowing the Reds two first-inning runs. In the third inning, the Cards scored three times against Reds starter Bucky Walters. Harry Walker got a gift double when second baseman Lonny Frey and right fielder Mike Marshall collided trying to catch his short pop fly. After Slaughter grounded out, Musial poked a soft single into left that scored Walker. Walker Cooper followed with a sharply hit double-play ball to third baseman Bert Haas, who rifled a throw to second, but Frey could not hold the ball and both runners were safe. Ray Sanders, in the game for the slumping Hopp, sent a low line drive to center on which Gee Walker tried to make a shoestring catch but missed. Both runners scored to give St. Louis a 3–2 lead. The Birds added an insurance run in the seventh on a Musial double, while Beazley held the Reds to just one hit after the first inning.

"Time was running out on the Dodgers," Parrott told his Brooklyn readers, "and luck was still running in like a flood for these Cardinals. I wouldn't believe these dispatches I'm sending . . . if I didn't see these freak things happen . . . I've seen the Cardinals play five ball games in the last four days," he continued. "They won four—and yet with a single break here or there—they would have lost all five."[31] As Parrott was preparing the Flatbush faithful for the worst, Larry MacPhail was venting in a telegram to Reds manager Bill McKechnie, known as the "Deacon" for his strong Methodist convictions. "All the deacons and choir singers in the Methodist organization," it read, "appreciate your sportsmanship in not pitching Vander Meer against St. Louis." McKechnie chuckled, "That's the first time in all my baseball experience I ever heard of the president of one club trying to tell the manager of another who to pitch."[32] Deacon Bill replied to MacPhail the next day: "Congratulations on your appointment as Lieutenant-Colonel in the Army. Please accept this as my application for the job as your orderly . . . Believe I could be of great assistance in keeping you orderly."[33]

The Cardinals needed one more win to clinch a tie for the pennant, and Mort Cooper delivered it on a chilly afternoon with a two-hit shutout of Cincinnati in which he struck out six, walked none, and retired the last fourteen Reds in order. It was his twenty-second win, his tenth shutout, and the eighteenth for the staff. The Redbirds scored in the first inning, added two more in the fifth, one in the sixth, and two in the seventh for the 6–0 victory. Stan Musial led the Cards' attack with his second straight three-hit game, driving home two runs. Jimmy Brown also had three hits and a run batted in, while Walker Cooper drove in the other two runs for his brother. Musial also turned in an acrobatic catch on the first play of the game as he raced into deep left center to make a somersaulting grab of leadoff hitter Eddie Joost's bid for an extra-base hit. Brooklyn also won, with Whitlow Wyatt besting Jim Tobin and the Braves 5–3. The Dodgers had 101 wins, but they now could hope for nothing more than a tie.

"Durocher looked pale and drawn," Tommy Holmes reported. "This season had been easy on him until a little more than a month ago when the Dodgers began to show advance signs of a slump and the Cardinals had launched their terrific winning jag. But recent weeks have taken a heavy toll on the fiery little skipper," Holmes continued. "Sleepless nights, loss of appetite, jagged nerves—they're part of the price that must be paid by almost every manager of a ball club in a tight pennant race."[34] Harold Parrott provided the benediction: "I guess it's only right and just that the Cardinal organization should win this National League pennant . . . in Branch Rickey's last year here in St. Louis. The preacher-like Rickey and the wild and wooly MacPhail, whom Branch brought into the game, are the two most amazing men I've ever met in baseball."[35]

～

Following the games with Cincinnati, the Cardinals had an open date. Nothing could have been more welcome. Billy Southworth stayed in bed with a cold, while the players met in the clubhouse to decide how World Series shares would be divided. Tickets for the Series had gone on sale a week earlier for three of the games scheduled in St. Louis—the first, second, and sixth games of the series. A set of three tickets cost $17.50, with a limit of two sets to a customer. Sales were brisk. Ticket manager Joseph Goldsmith added eight people to handle the deluge of applications from four mail deliveries a day. One unusual request was for a seat in the middle of a row because, the applicant wrote, "I am a very fat man" who did not want to block people getting in and out. Applications far outstripped supply, and after only a few days Sam Breadon announced that no more ticket requests would be accepted.[36] Breadon also met with architect William Levy to discuss adding temporary box seating on the field and expanding the press box. In addition, lodging was scarce, even on the east side of the Mississippi River in Illinois. Three national conventions had been scheduled for St. Louis months earlier and had taken many of the hotel rooms. The Redbirds' front office was frantically trying to make as many arrangements as possible for visitors to stay in private homes or rooming houses.

While the Cardinals had the day off, the Dodgers were in action against the Boston Braves. Twenty-five thousand fans were at Ebbets Field for the Dodgers' final home game of the season, seventeen thousand of them gaining admission by bringing a donation of scrap metal for the war effort. The game was a free-swinging affair that went back and forth. Brooklyn took an early lead on Dolph Camilli's twenty-sixth home run, but Boston fought back, with Max West hitting two round-trippers. Tied at the end of nine innings, the game went to the eleventh. The Dodgers loaded the bases with one out. Billy Herman then bounced a routine grounder to Sibby Sisti for what should have been an easy force play at the plate, but the second baseman's throw home was so high that catcher Ernie Lombardi did not even bother to jump for it. The error gave Brooklyn a 6–5 win that kept hope alive for Dodger fans.

The Birds got a second day off when rain forced postponement of their game with Chicago. The Dodgers moved to Philadelphia for their final two games. Despite poor field conditions, they won the first game, bringing their season win total to 103. Bobo Newsome was the starter in what was a close game until Brooklyn broke it open with six runs in the sixth inning. Camilli, with two hits, including a double, and four runs-batted-in, and Pee Wee Reese with triple that knocked home two led the Dodgers' attack. The 8–3 win maintained the possibility of the season ending in a first-place tie. The pennant race thus came down to the last day of the season. The Dodgers would play one game, while the Cardinals would play two. The National League pennant would go to St. Louis unless Brooklyn won and the Cardinals lost both of its games, in which case the season would end in a tie and there would be a one-game playoff in St. Louis to determine the league championship.

It was a sunny but chilly September Sunday in St. Louis, with temperatures in the mid-fifties and the field still damp from the rains of the previous day, but more than thirty-one thousand fans filled Sportsman's Park, ready to cheer the Redbirds to the victory that would secure the pennant. Ernie White got the call from Southworth in the first game. The Cubs answered with former Redbird Lon Warneke. Chicago drew first blood with a run in the fourth inning, but the Cards answered with four in the fifth. Kurowski led off with a walk. Marion bounced to his counterpart at shortstop, Len Merullo, who in rushing to make a throw fumbled the ball for an error. White followed with a single to tie the score. Brown sacrificed, moving Marion to third and White to second, and then Terry Moore, playing his first game in almost two weeks, lined a single to center to drive both runners home. Slaughter singled to center to drive Warneke from the game, who left to the polite applause of St. Louis fans. Hi Bithorn took over and got Musial to force Slaughter at second, but Moore scored on the play.

White held the Cubs to one run until the seventh, when they added a second run, but in the bottom of the inning St. Louis put the game away with another four-run rally on three singles, a walk, and two Chicago errors. The Cardinals added a meaningless run in the eighth, and the game went to the ninth. White, who had given up only five hits, struck out the first two Cub hitters, Bill Nicholson and Dominic Dallessandro. Kurowski moved to the mound to return the ball to White and later said he told him, "Get this guy quick, I'm about to break down and cry," to which White replied, "I'm about ready to bawl."[37] Cubs catcher Clyde McCullough, hitless on the day, stepped to the plate and lashed a long drive to left. But Musial ran the ball down and caught it for the third out, and St. Louis had won the pennant. The crowd was in a frenzy of joy, cheering wildly, some tossing straw hats onto the field as the Cardinals rushed to hoist White and Southworth onto their shoulders and carry them off the field in triumph.

The players trooped into the clubhouse, where at first no one said anything. Bob Burnes of the *Globe-Democrat* reported that one would have thought it was just another game, but trainer Doc Weaver put the Notre Dame Victory March on his phonograph and Kurowski, usually a quiet fellow, yelled, "Why doesn't somebody say something? We just won the pennant!" For the next thirty minutes, it was pandemonium as players, munching on chocolate bars and sipping bottles of soda, congratulated one another, mingling with family members and club officials. Photographers and reporters crowded into the room. Coach Buzzy Wares, Harry Walker, Max Lanier, Ken O'Dea, and Frank Crespi began to sing, "killing several songs beautifully," as one reporter described their harmony. Southworth came in, was immediately mobbed, and told everyone, "This is the finest bunch of boys I've ever had the happiness to be with. They've followed orders perfectly and now they're getting their reward." He called it "easily the happiest day of my life," though he admitted that "the biggest thrill of all came the day we licked the Dodgers for the second straight afternoon and drew even with them."[38] Sam Breadon came in, grabbed Southworth to congratulate him, then went around the room congratulating each of the players.

For the players, the strain and pain of the season seemed washed away by the win. They were ecstatic. Johnny Hopp said it was the "realization of a boyhood dream." Marty Marion felt "swell." George Kurowski sighed, "We sure didn't win it the easy way." Stan Musial added, "I'm so happy I don't know what to say." The triumph was perhaps sweetest for the Redbirds' captain, Terry Moore, who grinned, "Boy, this means a lot to me," and kept repeating, "This is nice." He also said that players had received dozens of "jinx" letters telling them to give up. "I never saw so many letters," he said. "We pinned 'em up and laugh at them." Ernie White told reporters the game was "the biggest victory of my career," adding that after the Cards scored four runs in the fifth inning, he went back to the mound and "didn't have a thing on the ball." But he got through the inning and "my stuff came right back the next inning and I had it the rest of the way."[39]

Dizzy Dean, the great Cardinal righthander from the Gas House Gang, took his place in the middle of the clubhouse to declare to any who would listen that the 1942 Cardinals were a better team than the 1934 Cardinals. Dean had returned to St. Louis to broadcast Redbird games on one of the two local stations that carried their contests and proved to be by far the most popular announcer, one survey showing that he commanded 82 percent of the audience for Cardinals games. He was not popular, however, with the city's Board of Education, which complained that his abuse of the English language—"slud" for slid, "throwed" for throws, "them" for the—was leading school children to speak the same way. Diz had earlier told his radio listeners, "Folks, I'm broadcasting to you about the greatest team in baseball, and they will run them Yankees right out of the ballpark." Now, his voice rising above the bedlam, he shouted, "Boys, I knowed you could do it all the time, and I'm as proud of you as if I wuz playing with you myself. And I wanna tell you something else," he added, "the people's going to remember this team as long as baseball is played."[40] Eventually the umpires stuck their heads into the room to remind everyone that there was another game to play.

Beazley asked to pitch the nightcap that was sure to be anticlimactic. The Cardinals' lineup featured a number of reserves and a couple of the September call-ups from the farm system. Working rapidly and well, Beazley permitted the Cubs a run in the first inning and nothing thereafter, giving up seven hits, all of them singles, in a game played in less than two hours. Facing Claude Passeau, the Redbirds matched the Cubs' first-inning run with one of their own, then added two more in the second and a single marker in the sixth for a 4–1 win. It was Beazley's twenty-first victory of the season and gave the team 106 wins, the most for any National League team since Pittsburgh's 110 wins in 1909. The Dodgers won their finale against the Phillies to finish with 104 wins, the most in a single season for any club in Brooklyn history.[41] The Dodgers had thundered down the stretch, winning all their games in the final week of the season, but the hard-driving Cardinals had matched them win for win.

～

Leo Durocher was gracious in defeat, wiring congratulations to the Cardinals, saying, "We have been beaten by a great ball club and we'll all be pulling for you in the World Series." But the loss was a bitter pill for the Brooklyn players. "I've lost some tough pennant races before," a dismayed Billy Herman said. "I was with the Cubs when we were nosed out of three or four championships. But this is the hardest thing I've ever gone through. When you win 104 games and finish second there isn't anything to say."[42] Dolph Camilli echoed Herman: "It's pretty tough to lose the pennant, particularly after winning 104 games." Dixie Walker was more philosophical: "You've got to give the Cardinals credit for a drive like that. There isn't anything you can take away from a bunch that can come from far behind when they should have known they were beaten." "Remember," he added, "they won it. We didn't lose it."

As the Yankees boarded a train for St. Louis and the start of the World Series, Joe DiMaggio asked the question everyone in Brooklyn was asking: "What happened to the Dodgers? I thought we were going to play them in the series."[43] The question haunted Brooklyn. Tommy Holmes of the *Eagle* conceded that it was not easily answered. "Obviously," he wrote, "this is not the same ball club that was way out front by itself not so long ago." He speculated that "perhaps there are too many older players in the Dodger ranks." Whatever the explanation, it was clear that there had been "a let-down all the way along the line" as the team had gone into a batting slump in mid-August from which it never really emerged.[44] Holmes did not mention the injury Pete Reiser suffered against the Cardinals in July, which often kept the team's best hitter out of the lineup and rendered him largely ineffective when he did play. Reiser had been leading the league with a .346 batting average when he collided with the center-field wall in St. Louis; he hit more than a hundred points below that afterwards.

Former St. Louis manager Charles "Gabby" Street, who led the Cardinals to championships in 1930 and 1931, had a different explanation, namely, Leo Durocher. After the St. Louis series in late August, Durocher made frequent changes in his lineup instead of staying with the team that had built the big lead. Changes like that, Street explained, weaken team play and work on players' nerves, causing them to tighten up.[45] Street might have added that Durocher seemed to handle his pitchers differently as well after the four-game August series with the Cards, showing less patience with his starters and becoming more dependent on his bullpen.

Joe Williams of the *Herald Tribune*, however, offered the simplest explanation: the Dodgers were beaten by a better team. "No team ever put on such a spectacular and dramatic finish" as the 1942 Cardinals, he wrote. "The team didn't back into the championship as so many teams do in these characteristic National League climaxes. They went out and won it the hard way." The Redbirds had trailed the Dodgers by ten games in early August, by nine in mid-August, and were being counted out by all the pundits, including Williams, who went on to say that no one should belittle the Dodgers: "They won enough games to win the pennant in any normal race." In short, he concluded, "the Cardinals had a good team to beat and did it."[46]

CHAPTER 11
On the Big Stage

The war intruded upon the World Series before it could begin. Travel restrictions made it impossible for the Yankees to reach St. Louis from New York in time for the opening game scheduled for Tuesday, September 29. The first game was pushed back a day. On September 30, the day the series began, Adolf Hitler spoke to the German people for the first time in five months, telling them that the Reich would hold its gains in the coming year, attacking where necessary, and assuring them that Germany would never "capitulate but would emerge victorious." In London, the speech was interpreted to mean that Hitler was more concerned about the home front than had previously been the case, and that he had become reconciled to the inevitability of a long war. In Washington, U.S. Secretary of State Cordell Hull saw it much the same way, saying that Hitler was "desperately preparing his people for still greater hardships."[1] For the most part, Hitler's speech was seen by the Allies as a favorable sign. But with a long war ahead, major-league baseball would continue its financial support for military relief agencies. A substantial portion of World Series revenue would be donated to the United Service Organizations to benefit all men and women in uniform. ·

St. Louis was quiet on the eve of the series. Large, happy, orderly, but rather undemonstrative crowds turned out in the downtown area after the Cardinals beat the Cubs to clinch the pennant. It was unlike the boisterous outpourings in 1926, when the Redbirds won their first pennant, or even in 1931 after the team had upset the heavily favored Philadelphia Athletics in the World Series. It was wartime, but it was also Sunday, and taverns were closed. Indeed, the bigger and rowdier celebration occurred across the Mississippi River in East St. Louis, Illinois, where taverns were open on Sundays. The public temper in St. Louis remained restrained as the first game of the World Series neared.[2] Locals said the city had worn itself out rooting for the Redbirds during their September drive to the pennant. City hotels were also full of conventioneers, many of whom had only passing interest in the series. Much of the remaining hotel capacity, however, had been taken by fans who came for the Sunday doubleheader and were staying for the series. Baseball officials and sportswriters were scattered about the city, many of them doubling up where they could find rooms. It took "both a reservation and a willingness to argue to get any kind of room," the Associated Press reported.[3] In the absence of large common gathering places like hotel lobbies, baseball officials, newsmen, and fans packed bars and restaurants as their meeting places.

The 1942 World Series attracted the largest press, radio, photography, and newsreel contingent in years, a corps of 451 mass media professionals in all, including almost a dozen from outside the United States. The Mutual Broadcasting Company purchased radio rights for one hundred thousand dollars, with Gillette as corporate sponsor and Bill Corum, Red Barber, and Mel Allen as announcers. Two Mutual affiliates would also carry the World Series to the world: Don Dunphy would call the play-by-play via shortwave to the British Broadcasting System for broadcast to American soldiers in England and elsewhere, while Renee Canizeras would do the same in Spanish for Latin American fans. The World Series predictions of sportswriters were predictable: they picked the Yankees to win. Al Horwitz, president of the Baseball Writers Association, believed the veteran Yankees would sweep the kiddy Cardinals in four straight. Almost all the rest took the Bronx Bombers in five games, or at most six. But a few went with the Cards, including two from Boston, John Trohan of the *Traveler* and Gerry Moore of the *Globe,* whose choice of St. Louis may have rested less on conviction than on vengeance—they were Red Sox correspondents hoping to see the Yankees defeated.

Lines formed in earnest at Sportsman's Park on the afternoon of September 29 as fans queued up to purchase bleacher and pavilion tickets. Pavilion seats sold for $3.45, those in the bleachers for $1.15, and by early morning of game day the lines snaked along Grand Avenue, around the corner, and down more than a block on Spring Avenue for the pavilion, and along Sullivan Avenue the full length of the stadium for the bleachers. Many of those in line were from out of town: a produce worker from Terre Haute, a construction worker from Utah, five farmers from Kansas, six high school kids from Indiana, a preacher from Tennessee, two African Americans from Kentucky, and a maintenance man from Denver among them. One St. Louisan near the head of the line was Tommy Ryan, a fourth grader at the Adams School, who arrived immediately after class on the twenty-ninth. His mother came by several times during the night to check on him, and he told everyone that he had permission to miss school for the first game. It was for the most part an orderly crowd that passed the time by playing cards, shooting craps, telling stories, or trying to sleep, all under the continuous gaze of St. Louis policemen. Vendors did a good business selling hot coffee, and eventually scalpers appeared doing business primarily in grandstand seating: $50 for a $6.50 box seat and $20 for reserved seats.[4]

The outfield gates swung open at 7:30 a.m. and were closed by 10 as the twenty-eight hundred pavilion and thirty-nine hundred bleacher seats sold out in just over two hours, leaving hundreds of disappointed fans on the outside unable to get in. The grandstand opened at 10, and those with standing-room tickets began to flood into the park with here and there a skirmish among fans anxious to get in before these doors closed as well. The new field boxes and the standing-room areas increased the capacity of Sportsman's Park to around thirty-five thousand, but this was nowhere near sufficient to meet demand. Fans could be seen on the rooftops of buildings across the street from the park, trying to see what they could of the contest. Even the players were displaced by the crowd as the temporary field boxes forced both teams to sit on benches in front of their dugouts. Everyone associated with the Cardinals had been hounded for tickets. Billy Southworth complained publicly that fans had been "running my players ragged" with ticket requests.[5]

At ten o'clock Benjamin Rader's twenty-five-piece brass band took up seats behind home plate and began to entertain the early arrivals. At 10:30 the Cardinals took the field for their pregame practice, forcing the band to move several times. It was customary for teams to purchase new uniforms for the Series, but St. Louis did not do so. Southworth said it was because they did not want to change their luck; the more cynical thought it was because the ownership was too cheap. A host of former Cardinal stars were in attendance: Jesse Haines, Rogers Hornsby, Jim Bottomley, Johnny Mize, Joe Medwick, Leo Durocher, and Dizzy Dean, all of whom would eventually find a place in baseball's Hall of Fame. The pregame ceremonies were simple: a squad of Marines in dress uniform marched to the center-field flagpole and saluted as Old Glory was raised and Rader's band played the National Anthem. Flanked by National League president Ford Frick and American League boss Will Harridge, baseball commissioner Kenesaw Mountain Landis, who was delayed a few minutes by heavy traffic, threw out the first ball, and the contest was ready to begin.

~

To the surprise of no one, Billy Southworth chose twenty-two-game-winner Mort Cooper to open for the Cardinals. Yankee manager Joe McCarthy, however, passed over his big winner, Ernest "Tiny" Bonham, in favor of thirty-eight-year-old Charles "Red" Ruffing. A native of Granville, Illinois, Ruffing had appeared in seven World Series and was a seven-time winner in those games. Veteran sportswriter Grantland Rice was impressed that he had "never seen two teams as sure of winning, nor any two world series teams better matched," to which he appended the thought that Cooper might be the "winning factor" in the Series.[6]

Tommy Holmes of the *Brooklyn Eagle* also saw Cooper as the key, saying that if he lost the first game the Yankees would win in five. Cooper started well, setting down the first two Yankees easily in the first inning, then walked Roy Cullenbine and gave up a hit to Joe DiMaggio before getting Charlie Keller on strikes. In a bit of psychological warfare, McCarthy went to home plate in the first inning to question the big righthander's delivery. It was the first of many arguments the New Yorkers would have with the arbiters throughout the Series. In the bottom of the first, after retiring Brown easily, Ruffing walked both Terry Moore and Enos Slaughter, which brought McCarthy out again to argue with the home plate umpire about the strike zone. Ruffing settled down and retired the next two Cardinals without difficulty.[7]

The game was scoreless until the fourth inning, when the Yankees pushed across a run with two out. DiMaggio led off with a sharp single to left between third and shortstop. Cooper retired the next two hitters, but then walked catcher Bill Dickey. With two on and two out, first baseman Buddy Hassett punched an inside fastball into left field to bring DiMaggio home. The Yankees added another run in the fifth when, with one out, third baseman Robert "Red" Rolfe dropped a single into center and went to third on Cullenbine's double off the right-field wall. DiMaggio pulled a sharp grounder to Kurowski, who tried for a double play, tagging Cullenbine coming into third base, but his throw to first was too late to retire DiMaggio and Rolfe scored. Meanwhile, Ruffing set the Redbirds down inning after inning with no hits, their only base runners after the first coming on walks in the third and sixth innings.

Cooper ran into more trouble in the eighth. DiMaggio led off with his third hit of the game, after which the Cards' righthander struck out the next two hitters and seemed safely through the inning. But Dickey pulled a single to right, sending DiMaggio to third, from where he scored when Hassett lifted a low curve just over the outreached glove of a leaping Jimmy Brown at second base. With runners at first and third, Ruffing hit a line drive toward right center that was playable for Slaughter, but it scooted out of his glove for a two-base error and both runners crossed the plate for a 5–0 New York lead. Harry Gumbert took over for Cooper to get the last out. In the bottom of the eighth, Ruffing, who was working on the first no-hitter in World Series history, got the first two Cardinals, only to have Terry Moore hit an outside pitch into right field for a single to end Ruffing's quest for glory. Slaughter followed with a lazy fly to DiMaggio in center for the final out of the inning.

Max Lanier came on to pitch the ninth for St. Louis and found himself in immediate trouble, all of his own making. Rolfe led off with a single to right. Playing for an insurance run, Cullenbine laid a bunt down the third-base line that Lanier grabbed, but he threw to first well over the head of Johnny Hopp. As the ball bounded into the right-field corner, Rolfe scored and Cullenbine raced around to third base. Lanier retired DiMaggio on a smash back to the pitcher, holding the runner at third. Charlie Keller then drew a walk, and Lanier tried unsuccessfully to pick him off first base. When Hopp returned the ball to Lanier, he muffed it. As the ball rolled slowly toward Kurowski at third, Cullenbine took off to score the second run of the inning.

Trailing 7–0 and with only one hit to show for their afternoon's work, the Redbirds came to life in the bottom of the ninth. After Stan Musial led off by fouling out to catcher Dickey, Walker Cooper pulled a hard drive toward left that third baseman Rolfe knocked down, but the Cards' catcher beat his throw to first for the second St. Louis hit. Hopp lofted a harmless fly to Keller in left for the second out, after which Ray Sanders was sent in to pinch-hit for Kurowski, who had struck out three times against Ruffing. Sanders drew a walk. Marty Marion followed with an opposite-field triple into the right-field corner that scored Cooper and Sanders for the first St. Louis runs of the game. Ken O'Dea came off the bench to hit for Lanier and singled to center, scoring Marion. Brown followed with a single into short center on which Frank Crespi, running for O'Dea, had to hold at second.

That was the day for Ruffing. He was succeeded by Spurgeon "Spud" Chandler, who was greeted by Terry Moore with a single to left that scored Crespi with the fourth Redbird run of the inning. Slaughter next hit a grounder to shortstop Phil Rizzuto that took a bad hop off the hard St. Louis infield and hit the diminutive Rizzuto in the face. It was scored a hit and loaded the bases. With the tying runs on, Musial came to the plate again. Having made the first out of the inning, he proceeded to make the last one as well, pulling a grounder wide of first that Hassett fielded and tossed to Chandler covering the bag to give the Yankees a 7–4 win in the first game.

The Cardinals were disappointed by the result but not discouraged. The four-run ninth buoyed their confidence that they could win. After all, they had won the spring series in Florida against these same Yankees. Southworth had little to say to the press after the game, other than that he thought the four runs scored with two out would be a "tonic" for his boys. Mort Cooper was among the most disappointed by the loss and was especially dismayed by the hitting of Hassett. "Boy, that Yankee uniform sure must do something to you," Cooper lamented. "That's better hitting than I ever saw Buddy do in the National League." Hassett had played for six years with Boston and Brooklyn before joining the Bronx Bombers in 1942.[8]

McCarthy also had little to say, other than that Ruffing had "pitched a swell game . . . was fast and strong until the ninth . . . too bad he couldn't finish [but] that's baseball." For "Marse Joe," as the Yankees' skipper was known, it was business as usual: he had never lost a World Series as manager of the Yankees, and he did not expect to lose one now. Ruffing, who would later call his performance "the best Series game I pitched," acknowledged that he had simply run out of gas in the ninth: "I was tired all over and didn't have a thing."[9] John Drebinger of the *New York Times* mirrored the matter-of-fact attitude of the Bronx Bombers: "the years roll on [and] so apparently do Ruffing and the Yankees. . . . The mighty McCarthy machine is one up in its quest of another world championship [and] again off to their customary commanding lead."[10] Tommy Holmes of the *Brooklyn Eagle*, however, once again heard familiar footsteps, noting that the "Cardinals exhibited that abysmal ignorance of which they were guilty throughout the entire National League season. They did not know they were beaten."[11]

The lines outside Sportsman's Park for the second game of the series were shorter, but the bleachers were full by noon and the pavilion filled soon thereafter. It was more of a hometown crowd in the bleachers; few of the out-of-towners had stayed around for the second game. It was also a noisier crowd, clanging cowbells and at times breaking into song. There were as well some self-appointed entertainers in addition to the great Cardinals fan Mary Ott, decked out in a red hat and black coat, who was ready to raise her shrill voice in support of the Redbirds. Asked to demonstrate her familiar jeering half-cackle, half-laugh, she declined, saying, "I'm saving that for DiMaggio." Seventy-four-year-old Harry Thobe, a bricklayer from Oxford, Ohio, who had missed only one World Series, was there with his battered straw hat, red-striped trousers, red and white parasol, and old tin horn, sporting a Cardinal emblem on his back. The police also stopped a man wearing white underwear who was admitted only after proving that he had on street clothes underneath. Once inside, he busied himself by helping young women find seats, much to his delight and their embarrassment. Meanwhile, the A. J. Martini band entertained in left field with one eye on their music and the other on fly balls. One ball rolled up to a trumpet player, who stuck it in his pocket and kept playing.

The day was hazy but clear with a slight breeze. The starting pitchers were no surprise: the sensational rookie, Johnny Beazley, for the Cards, who unbeknownst to anyone carried a rabbit's foot to the mound for good luck, and for the Yanks, Tiny Bonham, their leader in wins during the regular season. Beazley had bouts of wildness and pitched from behind in the count all afternoon. He began the game by walking the leadoff hitter on five pitches. Immediately, Southworth had Howard Krist begin to warm up in the bullpen, but Krist was not needed as "Johnny the Beaze" retired the next three Yankees in order. In the bottom of the first, the Cardinals jumped to an early lead. Bonham, who gave up only twenty-four walks all season, walked leadoff hitter Jimmy Brown. Playing for one run, as he had all year, Southworth had the second batter, Terry Moore, lay down a sacrifice bunt. Bonham fielded it, but he misjudged Brown's speed and threw late to second in a failed attempt to cut him down. With two on, Bonham bore down, getting Slaughter to slice a fly to left that was chased down by Charlie Keller and Musial to foul out down the right-field line to first baseman Buddy Hassett. But just as it appeared the Cards might squander a scoring opportunity, Walker Cooper lined a Bonham pitch into right center that rolled to the wall for a double, scoring Brown and Moore to put St. Louis up by two.

Beazley and Bonham posted goose eggs from the second through the sixth innings. In the seventh, the Redbirds struck again. With one out, Johnny Hopp singled sharply into right and made a wide turn at first, taunting Cullenbine to throw behind him, but the New York right fielder did not take the bait. George Kurowski followed with a line drive barely fair down the left-field line that ticked off the glove of a diving Keller and rolled to the wall for a triple, scoring Hopp. The Yankees were incensed that the ball was ruled fair and protested vehemently. Keller and third baseman Red Rolfe charged umpire George Magerkurth to make their case loudly and were joined by McCarthy, who was even more vigorous in his disagreement with the call. Magerkurth had been the target of the Yankees' ire in the first game about his strike zone, and after the game they hinted that a National League umpire might do anything to help St. Louis win.[12] From the third-base coach's box, Southworth had a good view of the ball and was certain that it had been fair. Kurowski stayed at third but was unable to score as Marty Marion bounced out and Beazley struck out.

Though hit hard at times, Beazley rolled along into the eighth inning with a 3–0 lead. He breezed through the first two hitters in the eighth as well, but Cullenbine then beat out an infield hit. DiMaggio came to the plate, and on a one-ball, no-strike count Cullenbine surprised the Birds by stealing second base. DiMaggio followed with a single that brought him home. Annoyed, the hot-tempered Beazley fired a first-pitch curveball that failed to break to Charlie "King-Kong" Keller, who was ready for it and silenced the St. Louis crowd by launching a Ruthian blast that cleared everything in right field and landed on Grand Avenue for a two-run homer to tie the game. Beazley got the next hitter for the third out, but it looked as if momentum was now with the New Yorkers.

In the bottom of the eighth, the youthful Cardinals showed they were no more impressed with the Yankees' momentum than they had been by a ten-game Dodger lead. After Brown made the first out, Moore hammered a long drive to center that looked promising, but was caught by DiMaggio, who made a fine running catch. With two down, Enos Slaughter lashed a drive into the right-field corner that he stretched into a double with a head-first slide into second as short-stop Phil Rizzuto misplayed Cullenbine's throw. The ball rolled a few feet away. Without hesitation, Slaughter popped up and scampered to third before a play could be made on him. The next hitter, Stan Musial, followed with his first hit of the series, bouncing a grounder up the middle over the second-base bag and into short center field to bring Slaughter in from third with the go-ahead run.

In the Yankees' ninth, Dickey led off with an infield hit. George "Tuck" Stainback, a reserve outfielder and former Cardinal, went in to run for him. Buddy Hassett continued his hot hitting with a single into right field. Slaughter, who played the outfield like an infielder, fielded the ball on the bounce and fired on a line to Kurowski at third. Stainback, with good speed and running all the way, tore around second and headed for third, but Slaughter's throw reached Kurowski while Stainback was still two strides from the bag, and he was an easy out. Leading the cheers, Dizzy Dean told his radio listeners, "Slaughter throwed a better strike from right field to third than I ever did." Dean, of course, had never thrown a strike from right field, though he threw quite a few from the pitcher's mound. His audience knew what he meant. Slaughter later said the throw was the single greatest thrill in his baseball career.[13] As the inning continued, McCarthy chose Red Ruffing, the winner of the first game and a very good hitter, to bat for Bonham. Beazley got him to loft an easy fly to Slaughter, who hung on to the ball this time. Rizzuto then bounced to his counterpart at shortstop, Marion, who threw him out to retire the Yanks, give the Cardinals a hard-fought 4–3 win, and even the series at one game apiece.

It was a "nerve-racking dramatic struggle," John Drebinger of the *Times* wrote, in which the "amazing young Cardinals put on another of their electrifying finishes" to send "an exhausted but tremendously happy crowd dancing jubilantly through the exit gates, confident that Billy Southworth's astonishing infants would acquit themselves well in the next three games" in New York.[14] Tommy Holmes believed the Yankees had never played a team quite like the Cardinals, adding that "the notion is slowly beginning to dawn that there never was an outfit like this St. Louis bunch before."[15] The Cardinals were in high spirits after the game, including owner Sam Breadon, who made a rare visit to the locker room to congratulate the players. The joy of the Redbirds contrasted sharply with the sour mood of the Yankees. "No quieter, sadder band of players ever trooped off a baseball field than the Yankees today," James Dawson observed.[16] No photographs were permitted in the Yankees' clubhouse, where McCarthy attributed the St. Louis win to "breaks." "They got the breaks, that's all there was to it. When you get the breaks you win. We didn't get them." There were plenty of photographs in the St. Louis locker room, with players insisting that a perpetually smiling Southworth be in all of them. A grinning Slaughter was hailed for his perfect throw in the ninth, while Beazley said he felt "great" after beating that "tough bunch." "My boys proved themselves today," a confident Southworth told reporters, adding, "We're going [to New York] to beat the Yankees and we will."[17]

~

Both teams departed for Gotham immediately after the game. Due to wartime restrictions, they had to travel on the same train, though there was no fraternizing between them. It was the first time since World War I that rival teams in the World Series had been on the same train. Sportswriters were also aboard, and for them it was nirvana to have access to all the players on both teams. Frederick Lieb recalled later that the Yankees "were dumbfounded, even annoyed, at the thought of having lost a Series game . . . that was a thing that just wasn't done."[18] The train arrived in New York around 2 p.m. on Friday, October 2. A crowd of around two thousand was waiting at Grand Central Station to show their support for the Bronx Bombers, but almost all of the Yankees got off at the 125th Street stop. The disappointed crowd was left to welcome the high-flying Redbirds, few of whom they recognized. The temper of the Cardinals continued to contrast with that of the Yankees, described by John Drebinger of the *New York Times* as "grimly determined." "They offered no excuses for the loss of the second game," he wrote, "but seemed perplexed by it and not convinced that it was simply the result of the breaks going the other way."[19]

A huge crowd of 69,123—a record for a World Series game—greeted the players at Yankee Stadium for game three. In St. Louis, the crowd had featured a host of former Redbird stars. In New York, the "stars" were politicians: Governor Herbert Lehman, Mayor Fiorella LaGuardia, gubernatorial candidate Thomas E. Dewey, former mayor James J. Walker, and former postmaster general James A. Farley. A large contingent of police was assigned to the stadium, patrolling it on foot, horseback, motorcycle, and in plain clothes, the latter on the alert for pickpockets. There were a number of firemen on duty as well. Fans unable to get into the stadium found locations from which to watch the game on the rooftops of many nearby buildings, some as far away as the Bronx County Courthouse four blocks from the field. Yankee Stadium was dressed with red, white, and blue banners on each of its several levels, and the opening ceremonies had the now-familiar patriotic tone, with a military unit marching to center field for the raising of the Stars and Stripes to the accompaniment of "The Star-Spangled Banner."

None of the St. Louis players had ever seen the inside of Yankee Stadium, much less played there, having only viewed the "House That Ruth Built" from the heights of Coogan's Bluff, where the New York Giants' Polo Grounds overlooked the distant Yankees' home. A breeze from the northeast on a crisp day unfurled the large world championship banner on the center-field flag pole as if to remind St. Louis of the challenge before them. The unfamiliarity of the players with the stadium was evident early when Frank Crespi led the Cardinals onto the field before the game and into the wrong dugout.

Righthander Spud Chandler, a sixteen-game winner in 1942, took the mound for the Bronx Bombers, dressed in their pin-striped home uniforms. Chandler was matched against southpaw Ernie White, who had pitched effectively in September after months of frustration.[20] McCarthy tried to get more righthanded punch into his lineup by starting Jerry Priddy at third base instead of Rolfe and moving Joe Gordon into the fifth spot in the batting order ahead of Keller. The Cardinals went down in order in the first as Chandler struck out both Moore and Slaughter. In their half, the Yankees threatened when Rizzuto beat out a bunt for a leadoff hit. Buddy Hassett, also trying to bunt, was hit on the left thumb, retired to the dugout briefly, returned with the thumb heavily taped, tried again to bunt, and popped a foul behind the plate to Walker Cooper. As the next hitter, Roy Cullenbine, was striking out, Rizzuto stole second and continued to third when Cooper's throw skipped past Marty Marion into center field. But Rizzuto got no farther as White struck out DiMaggio to end the inning. The Yanks not only failed to score but also lost Hassett for the rest of the series with a broken thumb. Priddy moved from third to first, while the veteran Frank Crosetti, another right-handed hitter, took over at the hot corner.

The Cardinals scored first, in the third inning, without the benefit of a hit and without getting the ball out of the infield as their speed continued to be their greatest weapon.[21] Kurowski led off with a walk, and Marion followed with what appeared to be a successful sacrifice bunt to move Kurowski to second. But New York manager Joe McCarthy challenged the umpire's call arguing not only that the ball had gone into foul territory but also that Marion's bat had hit it twice and he should be out. After a conference, the umpires gave the Yankees' skipper half a loaf, ruling the bunt had gone foul. With New York's corner infielders charging hard, Marion swung away at the next pitch and topped a roller past the third baseman but close enough to the mound for Chandler to field. He grabbed the ball and threw to second baseman Joe Gordon covering first, but the throw was too late to get the Cards' speedy shortstop. The Yankees once more disputed the call. White followed with yet another bunt that moved the runners to second and third. Jimmy Brown then bounced a ball high over the pitcher's head that Gordon fielded, but his only play was at first, permitting Kurowski to cross the plate with the first run of the game.

White returned to the mound and from the third inning through the eighth held the Bronx Bombers to just three singles. He was aided greatly by the superb play of his team's outfield. In the sixth, DiMaggio hit a tremendous drive into deep left center that seemed certain to be an extra-base hit. Musial and Moore broke toward the ball. At the last second, Musial slid under Moore, who dove headlong above him to make a sensational backhanded catch of the sinking line drive a few inches off the ground. DiMaggio pulled up abruptly between first and second and stood frozen for the better part of a minute, staring at Moore in apparent disbelief that anyone could have caught his long drive, while the Redbirds' captain trotted impassively off the field to be embraced joyfully by everyone in the St. Louis dugout. In the seventh, Musial raced back to the left-field wall to grab Joe Gordon's drive that seemed destined for the seats. The next hitter, Charlie Keller, connected on a long drive to right center that had home-run distance, but Slaughter sprinted from his position in right field to the wall in right center. As he reached the wall, an orange thrown from the stands whizzed by, narrowly missing his face, but with unbroken concentration Slaughter leaped, shot his glove hand above the wall as fans grabbed at him, and returned with the ball firmly in his grasp.

In the ninth, the Cardinals added an insurance run that provoked not one but two more Yankee arguments. Marv Breuer came in to pitch for New York, and Brown singled on his first pitch. Moore bunted. Breuer fielded the ball, whirled, and threw to second, where Brown was initially signaled out, but almost immediately the call was reversed because Breuer's throw, which was high and a bit wide, had pulled Rizzuto off the bag. Once again the Yanks came after their bête noire Magerkurth to protest the call, but to no avail. Slaughter followed with a single to center that scored Brown and sent Moore racing around second and toward third. DiMaggio fired a strike to Crosetti at third. Ball and runner arrived together, but with a fadeaway slide Moore avoided the tag and reached back to grab the bag. Third-base umpire Bill Summers, an American Leaguer, called him safe, and the New Yorkers erupted once more. Crosetti threw the ball to the ground, charged Summers, and, as the *Times* reported it, "plowed both hands into the arbiter's ample stomach by way of emphasizing his points of argument." The report added that "Summers being a man of large and substantial proportion pushed the trim Yankee infielder right back and sturdily held his ground against the onslaughts of all the other Yankees, including a thoroughly enraged McCarthy."[22] All of the bluster came to nothing. Moore remained at third base, and during the argument the Yankees failed to call time, allowing Slaughter to move up to second. But the Yankees' "fireman," relief pitcher Jim Turner, entered the game to put out the blaze without further runs or furor.

The Yanks went quietly in their half of the ninth. DiMaggio got a one-out single, but White induced Gordon, still hitless in the series, to foul out to Kurowski, and Keller hoisted an easy fly to Slaughter for the final out. White's six-hit, 2–0 win was the first time the Bronx Bombers had been shut out in a World Series game since October 5, 1926, when Jesse "Pop" Haines of the Cardinals had blanked them 4–0 on the way to an earlier Redbird championship. After losing to the Cardinals in 1926, the Yankees had won the next eight World Series in which they appeared—1927, '28, '32, '36, '37, '38, '39, and 1941—over which time they had lost only four games and never more than one in any of these series. But history was the last thing on the mind of anyone in the boisterous Cardinals' clubhouse after the game as the players cheered their success. Ernie White whooped, "Boy I feel gooder as hell," adding that it was "the greatest game I ever hope to pitch."[23] Southworth was happy but cautious, warning, "We've still got to win two ball games."[24] The Yankees' locker room was again quiet as the players, "grim-faced and weary," trooped in. As if in a daze, McCarthy went directly to his office without a word. Most players showered and dressed, but Dickey, Keller, and DiMaggio sat in front of their lockers, still in uniform, staring into space.[25]

Tommy Holmes continued to marvel at Southworth's style of play, asking, "since when has it become good baseball to play for one run in the first inning?" But most newspaper commentary focused on the constant bickering and complaining of the Yankees about the umpiring, which seemed out of character for the team. It amazed Bob Burnes of the *Globe-Democrat* that "the once proud and haughty Yankees [were] crying and cringing, begging for help from the umpires, sobbing over each little thing that doesn't go quite their way." John Drebinger of the *Times* mused that "there must have been moments in that stirring ninth with the Yanks storming the arbiters all over the field, when the Cards most likely thought they were still battling the Dodgers." Billy Southworth thought it was all tactical. "They're complaining about everything, trying to rattle a young club. . . . it won't be so easy," he added, because "my boys are confident." But Jack Malaney of the *Boston Post* had another explanation. He thought it was because this New York team lacked the old Yankee self-assurance. When the Yanks and Red Sox had played a four-game series at the end of the season with nothing at stake, he recalled, "the Yanks even then complained about every little thing. It was so obvious that everyone noticed it and we felt then that the Yankees weren't sure of themselves. The way they've carried on in this series, we're convinced."[26]

Southworth had planned to save Mort Cooper for the fifth game, but the Redbird ace lobbied hard to start game four. Billy the Kid trusted Cooper to know when he was ready to pitch and sent him out for the fourth game. Joe McCarthy countered with his outstanding rookie, Hank Borowy, who had won fifteen games in his first tour of duty with the world champs. The Yankees got out of the gate quickly against Cooper, scoring a run in the first when Red Rolfe, first-pitch hitting, looped a double just inside the left-field foul line and Roy Cullenbine lined sharply into left center to score him. Cullenbine was held to a single by the swift fielding and strong throw to second by left fielder Musial. The Cardinals had some impressive at bats against Borowy in the first four innings and made the young righthander throw a lot of pitches, but nevertheless they had only a double and an infield single to show for their efforts. In the fifth, however, they put together their biggest inning of the series, scoring six times in another display of their speed.

Stan Musial got the inning started with a bunt toward third base on which he beat Borowy's throw on a close play at first that provoked yet another Yankee protest about the umpiring. Walker Cooper followed with a hot shot between

Borowy's legs into center field. Musial, challenging DiMaggio's arm, tried for third. Once again ball and runner arrived together, but Musial slid hard into Rolfe, who failed to field the throw cleanly. Musial was safe, while Cooper took second. Hopp walked to fill the bases, after which Kurowski sizzled a drive just beyond the reach of third baseman Rolfe for a single scoring two runs and sending Hopp to third. No doubt rattled by the explosion, Borowy walked Marion on four pitches to again fill the bases, after which Mort Cooper blooped a single to right that sent two more Redbird runners home.

That was it for Borowy, who had retired no one in the fourth inning. Atley Donald took over and got Jimmy Brown on a short fly to DiMaggio in center, but Terry Moore smacked Donald's next pitch into left for a single that scored Marion. The second out came when Slaughter hit an infield bouncer that led to a forceout of Moore at second. But the Cardinals were not done. Musial slashed a line drive past first baseman Priddy down the right-field line that went for two bases, scoring Slaughter with the sixth run of the frame. The inning ended when Walker Cooper hit a line drive toward right that second baseman Joe Gordon speared.

With a 6–1 lead and Cooper on the mound, the odds of a Cardinal win seemed good, and they got better as the big righthander retired the New Yorkers in the fourth and fifth innings, with a huge assist from Terry Moore in the fourth, who raced back to the 457-foot sign in left center to haul in another tremendous drive by DiMaggio. It was a different story for Cooper in the sixth, however, as he suddenly ran out of gas. Rizzuto slapped his first pitch to left for a single; Rolfe worked a full count before walking; and Roy Cullenbine followed with a sharply hit single to center to score Rizzuto. DiMaggio popped up to Marion at short, but Charlie Keller picked him up by pulling an outside fastball high and deep into the right-field stands for a three-run homer.

Harry Gumbert took up mound duties for the Cards, replacing the no doubt disappointed Cooper, and got Joe Gordon to bounce to third, only to have Kurowski throw the ball into the dirt at first for an error. With Hopp holding the runner at first, Bill Dickey bounced a ball toward the usual position of the first baseman. Second sacker Jimmy Brown, ranging far to his left, fielded it, and from the outfield grass he threw the slow-moving Yankee catcher out at first, with Gordon moving to second. With the tying run at second base, Gumbert bore down on Jerry Priddy, but could not get a fastball past him. Priddy's double to right field evened the score. Howard Pollet became the third Redbird pitcher of the inning, and with one pitch he got Donald to bounce to Brown for the third out.

For the second time in the series, the Yankees had come from behind to tie the Cardinals, and for the second time the Redbirds came right back to regain the lead. Slaughter led off the top of the seventh with a walk. Musial worked the count full and, with Slaughter running, took a pitch very close to the strike zone. When the umpire was slow in calling it a ball, Dickey began to throw to second, then hearing the umpire's call tried to hold up and instead threw the ball over the head of shortstop Rizzuto and into center field, enabling Slaughter to move on to third. Walker Cooper followed with a humpback liner to shallow center for a single that brought Slaughter home and moved Musial to second. This ended Donald's day, and Bonham came on to pitch. Hopp welcomed him with a bunt and danced along the first-base line, forcing Priddy to tag him while the runners advanced to second and third. After fouling off several pitches, Marion flew out to DiMaggio in center whose throw to the plate was high and up the line toward first, permitting Musial to score easily with the second run of the inning. Ray Sanders came to the plate as a pinch hitter and popped to Rolfe to end the inning with the Birds holding an 8–6 lead.

Max Lanier became the fourth Cardinal pitcher of the afternoon, and after Rizzuto led off the inning with his third hit of the game, he retired the Yanks without further difficulty. In the eighth, the Cardinals threatened again, but did not score, while Lanier set down the middle of the New York batting order—Keller, Gordon, and Dickey—on two lazy flies to the outfield and a pop fly near the pitcher's mound on which Kurowski stumbled, fell, and caught the ball sitting down. The Redbirds added an insurance run in the ninth when Hopp singled to center, went to second on Kurowski's sacrifice, took third on Marion's come-backer to the pitcher, and scored on Lanier's single to right. In the bottom of the ninth, Lanier got the first hitter on a grounder to Marion. Buddy Rosar, a backup catcher, pinch-hit for Bonham and singled over Marion's head to keep the flame of hope alive for the New Yorkers. But it was quickly extinguished as Rizutto flew out to Slaughter and Rolfe bounced out to Brown. With the 9–6 win, the Cardinals took a commanding lead in the series. Lanier got the win and said it was a birthday present for his son Hal, who was three months old that day and who would grow up to have a ten-year big-league career as an infielder.

The Yankees' locker room was again somber, but the team was visited by Babe Ruth, who tried to pep the players up. "Keep your chins up, boys, you're not licked," the Bambino told the quiet Bombers. "You're never licked. We'll get 'em yet. There's always tomorrow."[27] It was a scene of joy again in the St. Louis locker room. Hopp and Frank Crespi were talking nonstop, with nothing complimentary to say about the Yankees. In the showers, Ernie White was leading some teammates in a rendition of the tender hillbilly ballad, "Willie, My Toes Is Cold." Terry Moore circulated around the room, speaking quietly to all of his teammates, while Billy Southworth was all smiles in telling reporters, "I've always wanted a running ball club. I have one now."[28] Sportswriters lavished praise on the Redbirds for their aggressive baserunning in their big third inning and for their stirring defensive play, especially Moore's catches in center field. A consensus was emerging that the Cardinals' captain was every bit Joe DiMaggio's equal in the outfield. Grantland Rice was impressed by the courage of the Cardinals: "It takes a game team to see its best pitcher, Mort Cooper, driven from the game—and still come swarming back without the least discouragement."[29]

On the lighter side, John Kieran's column in the *Times* announced, "Crime Wave in the Bronx." "They murdered a couple of pitchers in the Bronx yesterday. There were about 70,000 witnesses to the crime, the police have a clue and nothing at all will be done about it."[30] When FBI director J. Edgar Hoover and his sidekick Clyde Tolson showed up the next day for the game, humorists in the press box speculated that they were there to investigate this crime; others thought they had been summoned by Joe McCarthy to check the loyalty of the umpires; while still others were sure they were investigating the theft of World Series money from the Dodgers and Yankees by the Cardinals.

The Yankees, who had been arguing about everything throughout the series, renewed their complaining even before the fifth game started, this time targeting the Cardinals themselves instead of the umpires. When Terry Moore reached home plate for the exchange of lineups, umpire Bill Summers told him, apologetically, that Joe McCarthy, through coach Art Fletcher, objected to the presence of an individual not in uniform being in the dugout with the Cardinals. Incredulous, Moore asked, "You mean Butch?" Morris "Butch" Yatkeman was the team's clubhouse attendant. He had been with the Redbirds for almost twenty years, beginning as batboy in 1924 and serving in his present capacity since 1932. Fletcher, whose facial features resembled those of the comic strip character Dick Tracy, indicated that Yatkeman was who McCarthy meant. "Okay, 'Chisel Chin,'" Moore reportedly replied, "you can go back and tell McCarthy that there won't be any 'tomorrow' in this Series."[31]

As Yatkeman retreated to the clubhouse to listen to the game on radio, the Cardinals resolved to make good on their captain's promise. But it was also a determined group of New Yorkers who took the field on an overcast, foggy afternoon for their now-or-never game with St. Louis. Yankee Stadium was again packed, with 69,052 anxious fans hoping their favorites could get back on track before it was too late. McCarthy went back to his first-game starter and World Series meal ticket, Red Ruffing, while Southworth countered with Johnny Beazley. Feeling some pressure, perhaps, Ruffing began the game with six straight pitches out of the strike zone, walking Jimmy Brown and getting behind in the count against Terry Moore. But he quickly righted himself to strike out Moore and get Enos Slaughter to hit into a double play. In the bottom of the first, leadoff hitter Phil Rizzuto looked at a ball and a strike, then lined the next pitch down the left-field line into the bleachers for a home run to put the Yankees ahead. Both pitchers were flawless through the second and third innings, but in the St. Louis fourth Slaughter led off by smashing Ruffing's first pitch high and deep into the lower right-field stands for a game-tying home run that landed under an air-raid sign that read, "Alert." It was the first Cardinal round-tripper of the series.

It was now the Yankees who came right back, scoring in the bottom of the fourth as Rolfe beat out a drag bunt and went to second on Beazley's wild throw to first. Cullenbine stroked a long drive to right center that Moore raced to the 407-foot sign to haul in, but Rolfe went to third after the catch. Joe DiMaggio whacked Beazley's next pitch into left for a single to score Rolfe, and the Yanks had the lead again. Keller followed with a hard single through the right side of the infield, sending DiMaggio to third. This brought Southworth to the mound to ask his young pitcher if he was all right, to which the cocky Beazley responded, "Sure, but Billy, are you all right?"[32] Beazley proceeded to strike out Joe Gordon and get Bill Dickey to bounce out to Marty Marion, thereby denying the Pin Stripers a big inning.

The Yanks threatened again in the fifth. With one out after Marion robbed Jerry Priddy of a hit, Ruffing dribbled a swinging bunt toward third base and easily beat Kurowski's hurried throw. Rizzuto bounced to Hopp at first, but Hopp's throw to second was in the dirt, Marion could not handle it, and runners were on at first and second. With tensions high, Rolfe hit a routine grounder to second that Brown fumbled for an error, loading the bases with still only one out. Cullenbine left them loaded when he popped up to Marion behind third for the second out. As Joe DiMaggio approached the plate with the crowd roaring, Southworth again visited his rookie hurler but made no change. Beazley slipped a curveball past the Yankees' center fielder for a first-pitch strike, then missed with another curve. On the third pitch, DiMaggio hit a shot on the ground headed for left field. But Kurowski managed to field it, and then he beat Rizzuto in a footrace to the third-base bag for the final out of the inning. St. Louis fans sighed in relief; those for the Yankees groaned in disappointment.

The Cardinals tied the score in the sixth. Moore led off with a single to left and Slaughter followed with a single to right, moving Moore to third. Musial lifted a high pop fly into the growing darkness that had descended on the infield, but Rizzuto caught the ball for the first out. Walker Cooper, swinging late, hoisted a short fly to right that landed just fair. Cullenbine charged and fielded the ball, had a momentary problem getting it out of his glove, then fired toward home plate, where it appeared the Yankees had a play on Moore. Anticipating that the throw would go home, Slaughter broke for second after the catch. Seeing this, Priddy cut off Cullenbine's throw, permitting Moore to score, then heaved the ball wildly trying to get Slaughter at second. Slaughter moved to third on the error, and Hopp followed with a long fly into deep center field that DiMaggio caught after a long run to end the inning.

Beazley was hit hard in the sixth but retired the Yankees in order when Musial made a nice running catch on a slicing line drive off the bat of Charlie Keller and Slaughter went to the right-field wall at the 344-foot sign to haul in Bill Dickey's bid for a home run. Beazley got through the seventh more easily, aided by another long running catch by Slaughter, who took Rolfe's fly just in front of the Cardinals' bullpen gate. He retired the side in order in the eighth as well, the third out coming as Keller with a mighty swing topped a roller between first and the pitcher's mound that Beazley scooped up before outrunning the Yankees' left fielder to the bag.

Ruffing worked through the seventh and eighth with no difficulty, though he was relying more on off-speed pitches than he had earlier in the game. In the ninth, he got two quick strikes on Walker Cooper, but the Cards' catcher rifled the next pitch into right center for a leadoff single. Hopp sacrificed him to second, bringing George Kurowski to the plate. In the darkness that shrouded the field, Ruffing went to his fastball. The Redbird third baseman smacked it hard and deep, but foul, into the left-field stands. Ruffing tried to fool him on the next pitch with an off-speed delivery that seemed to float up to the plate. Kurowski timed it perfectly and ripped into it. The ball sailed through the haze, barely visible from the grandstand, and settled deep in the left-field seats just fair inside the foul pole for a two-run homer. It was Kurowski's first home run since September 12 in Brooklyn, when his round-tripper moved the Redbirds into a tie with the Dodgers for first place. Ruffing retired the next two Redbirds without incident, but St. Louis held a two-run lead as the game moved into the bottom of the ninth.

Beazley got two quick strikes on leadoff hitter Joe Gordon, but lost him as the second baseman lined a single into the left-field corner, his first hit in the Series. The next batter, Bill Dickey, bounced a double-play ball to Brown at second, but in his anxiety Brown fumbled it, and both runners were safe. As New York's hopes brightened and the crowd roared with anticipation, the day grew even darker. The Cardinals' outfielders looked more ghostly than real through the haze that had settled upon the stadium. Walker Cooper went to the mound to speak with Beazley and told Marty Marion, who had joined them, to be alert, while Doc Weaver from the dugout aimed his famed "double whammy" at the Yankees, with his left hand on top of the right, the little fingers pointed at each other, while baring his teeth and snarling. Jerry Priddy stepped to the plate, with the Cardinals expecting him to bunt to get the tying runs into scoring position.

With his first pitch, Beazley fired a fastball high and tight. Priddy pulled his bat away as he fell back. Cooper came up quickly from his crouch, caught the ball, and whipped it to second, where Marion had crept behind Gordon. Anticipating a bunt, Gordon had taken a couple of steps beyond his normal lead at second and could not retrace them before Cooper's throw reached Marion, who slapped the tag on him as he jumped frantically and futilely back toward the bag.[33] The mood of the crowd now matched the day as the pickoff of Gordon took the spirit out of the New York fans as well as out of the Yankees. Priddy popped to Brown for the second out. George Selkirk, pinch-hitting for Ruffing, bounced to Brown, who flipped the ball to Hopp for the third out. In a game played in just under two hours, the Cardinals had completed their sweep of the mighty Bronx Bombers in their own house and claimed their mantle as World Champions.[34]

∼

The St. Louis locker room was bedlam. "Few clubhouses have matched the Cardinals quarters in reckless abandon," James Dawson wrote. "They stormed into their quarters like the champions they are—swaggering, noisy, monarchs of baseball's universe."[35] The celebration began as an uproar and grew into pandemonium as players were screaming, slapping one another on the back, and shouting "We beat the Yankees!" and "We beat 'em in their own back yard!" White, Gumbert, Brown, Crespi, and others broke into singing hillbilly tunes like "Good Ole Mountain Music." Terry Moore walked around as if in a daze, congratulating everyone. Kurowski refused to let go of the bat with which he hit the home run. As cameras flashed, the players hoisted Southworth onto their shoulders, then hugged Kurowski and Beazley and hoisted them as well. Branch Rickey came in, and up too he went, as did baseball commissioner Kenesaw Mountain Landis and National League president Ford Frick. When lowered to the floor, Frick gasped, "I never saw anything like this. Let me out of here."[36]

Joe McCarthy came to congratulate the Cardinals, as did many of the Yankees—Ruffing, Bonham, DiMaggio, Keller, Rolfe, and others. An ecstatic Southworth rambled on, speaking to no one and everyone: "We took 'em, and we took 'em decisively . . . we won in clean, honest, sportsmanlike fashion . . . with dash and youth . . . something that all American boys can be proud of . . . it's just grand. Anytime you can beat a ball club like the Yanks . . . well, I just feel wonderful. If I felt any better I wouldn't be able to stand it. A marvelous bunch of kids!" Pausing briefly, he added, "it's an honor to beat a team like the Yankees."[37] After more than half an hour, some order was restored and the players began to shower, dress, and prepare for their return to St. Louis.

The Yankee clubhouse was again silent as players turned in their uniforms for the last time, then showered, dressed, said their quiet "good-byes" to their manager and teammates. As some left, they could see the big white banner with "World Champions" being hauled down from the flagpole in center field. Long after all the players had left, a solitary figure emerged from Yankee Stadium. A youngster ran over, held out a program, and asked for an autograph. The man obliged. Two reporters recognized Joe McCarthy and extended their condolences about the Yankees' loss. "It ain't so bad," McCarthy replied. "They still want my autograph."[38]

"And so astride the baseball universe there soars today a band of youthful Redbirds," John Drebinger wrote as a postmortem on the World Series for the *New York Times.* "They had come from nowhere to eliminate the swashbuckling, boastful Dodgers in their own league. They were looked upon as 2–1 underdogs as they squared away against the powerful Yanks, who hadn't been vanquished in world series conflict in sixteen years. Yet there they were last night, dashing gaily into the West as victors in a great wartime classic." The consensus among observers was that Cardinal speed had surprised and upset the Yankees and made all the difference. "The kids ran their elders ragged," was John Kieran's assessment. "They were too fast, too lively, too hungry to be halted . . . those dashing Cardinals." The Cardinals won, Leo Petersen of United Press wrote, "because they knew no red light, no `stop' sign on the bases. For them, it was green all the time." Charles Dunkley of the Associated Press agreed: "Speed confused and confounded the Yankees . . . In the face of that speed, a constant haunting thing, the Yankees cracked." The venerable manager of the Philadelphia Athletics, Connie Mack, went further, saying the Cardinals had "invented a new game." "You never know what they're going to do next. If you expect a bunt, they hit. That will unnerve any team in time and it unnerved the Yanks." Tommy Holmes quipped that all clubs looked old and slow compared with the St. Louis Swifties, while his colleague at the *Brooklyn Eagle,* George Coleman, insisted, "It's more than speed . . . It's hustle, hustle, hustle."[39] John Carmichael of the *Chicago Daily News* grew lyrical in agreeing about the running Redbirds, framing his views to the tune of "Three Blind Mice":

> Nine Redbirds. See how they run.
> They run around the gol-dang park.
> They run from morn until it's dark.
> They think this thing is all a lark.
> Nine Redbirds![40]

CHAPTER 12
World's Champion

The Cardinals took the subway from Yankee Stadium to Grand Central Station to board a train for St. Louis. Their celebration, albeit more restrained, continued as they pulled out of New York. Mrs. Sam Breadon bought a round of drinks while her husband leant his voice to the happy singing of players and coaches. The Yankees' catcher, Bill Dickey, was on the train, returning to his home in Little Rock, Arkansas, and visited with the Redbirds as soon as it pulled out of the terminal. He shook hands with all the players and coaches, congratulating them on their victory. "They're gentlemen," he told a reporter. "They play hard. They fight tooth and nail, but you never hear a squawk or a beef. They're so quiet you sometimes forget they're around until it's too late."[1] On the train, the ever modest Southworth talked about his mistakes in the World Series, one of them coming in the fourth game when he told Marion on third base that the squeeze was on, but because Rolfe was watching him he did not signal that to Moore in the batter's box, then yelled to Marion, who did not hear him say that the play was off. Still expecting a bunt, Marion broke for home at the same time that Moore lined a single just past him into left field.[2]

The train reached Union Station in St. Louis shortly after five o'clock the next afternoon. A large platform had been erected at the Twelfth Street entrance between Market and Walnut streets. Fans began gathering more than an hour before the train's scheduled arrival and were packed in front of the stand, blocking Twelfth Street and spilling out onto Market as well. More were jammed inside the terminal, covering the full length and breadth of the station. Police captain Fred Grabbe of the Traffic Bureau estimated that the size of the crowd at its peak was at least twenty-five thousand. It was a noisy mob in a festive mood, mostly adults, many equipped with tin horns, cowbells, and other noisemakers. St. Louis mayor William D. Becker was present, as were Missouri governor Forrest C. Donnell and other dignitaries. Aides to the mayor distributed confetti to the crowd, and Benny Rader's band entertained them while they awaited the arrival of the World Champions.

The train pulled in eight minutes late, and slowly, with police assistance, the players made their way through the throng inside the station and onto the stage outside as the band played "Hail, Hail, The Gang's All Here." Three players had not accompanied their teammates back to St. Louis. Ken O'Dea went directly to his home in upstate New York, while Stan Musial departed in Pittsburgh near his home in Pennsylvania, and Whitey Moore disembarked in Ohio close to his home. Johnny Hopp and his wife were the first to appear on the outdoor platform as aerial bombs were discharged and the happy crowd burst into cheers and applause and pressed forward to be closer to their heroes. The din grew as grinning player after grinning player walked onto the stage, all of them welcomed with a joyful enthusiasm, but the cheering seemed just a bit louder when George Kurowski and Johnny Beazley appeared.

The crowd quieted briefly as Mayor Becker moved to the microphone to introduce Billy Southworth, then burst into sustained applause and cheering. Southworth lauded "his boys" and noted with pride that the Redbirds had beaten the Yankees "decisively" and "without a single kick about umpires' decisions."[3] He introduced Sam Breadon, whose remarks were brief, and then each of the players, who had a few words for the fans. Hopp shouted, "We really let 'em have it, didn't we?" Beazley thanked the crowd; Slaughter drawled, "I sure am happy"; White added, "We're as happy as you are." George Kurowski told the crowd, "I just knew where the ball was and hit it plenty good," while Terry Moore tried to tell everyone that Southworth was the greatest manager in baseball, but cheers for the captain drowned out what he had to say. As a final touch, Mary Ott stepped to the microphone to give one of her ear-splitting cackling laughs, now amplified for all to hear. To a serenade of factory whistles from around the city, the players and coaches left for their homes, but fans, especially the younger ones, continued to celebrate, creating a carnival atmosphere in downtown St. Louis along Washington Street and also in the area of Grand Avenue and Olive Street. Large numbers remained until midnight as revelers paraded the streets cheering and waving pennants, while a stream of gaily decorated cars drove around honking horns and backfiring.

There was no other public celebration—no parade, no introductions at City Hall, no banquets to honor the team. It was wartime, a time for honoring fighting men and women, not baseball players, even if they were world champions. Instead, thirteen of the Cardinals, including Southworth and Breadon, went the next day to give pints of blood at the Red Cross Blood Bank on Olive Street near Tenth. "Didn't know I had a pint of blood," Kurowski joked, then becoming serious, he added, "I got two brothers in uniform. Hope they don't ever need this, but you can't tell." Southworth added that he had a son in the Army Air Corps who would "soon be in the thick of this thing."[4] Breadon quipped that giving blood was more pleasant than having to face the Yankees in a game six. For all the levity, it was a reminder that there was a war going on, a reality that would soon break up the 1942 Cardinals.

~

The baseball season was over, but the war was just beginning. In one of those historical curiosities in which completely unrelated events parallel one another in time, the Redbirds' drive to overtake the Dodgers that began in mid-August coincided with drives by Allied forces in both North Africa and the South Pacific against their foes. August 1942 marked the beginning of the end of Allied retreats in the face of Axis advances and the start of their taking the fight to the enemy. In the Pacific, the turning points were Guadalcanal and New Guinea, where battles begun in August continued into the fall and beyond, but ended with U.S. and Australian forces in control of those strategic locations. Soon a terrible fight would be launched from island to island in the Pacific, pushing the Japanese back toward their homeland. In North Africa, the British and Commonwealth forces held the line at El Alamein in August, and in late October, with General Bernard Montgomery now in command, they launched a relentless drive that pushed Rommel's Afrika Korps out of Egypt and eventually from Libya as well. In November, the United States joined the battle in force, landing troops under the command of General Dwight Eisenhower in French Morocco near Casablanca and in Algeria near Algiers. By early January, American forces had advanced eastward close to Tunis, which Germany had been reinforcing for a last stand. A protracted battle began soon thereafter in which the Axis powers had to defend Tunis against the United States from the north and Britain from the south. It ended in mid-May with the surrender of the Axis forces, clearing the way for the American and British invasion of Sicily in July 1943.

Meanwhile, British bombers continued to punish German cities on an almost daily basis. In August, the U.S. Eighth Army Air Force began flying missions to targets in France and the Low Countries, completing thirty before the end of the year. Early in 1943, American bombers joined with the British for almost continuous attacks on major German cities, with many of the raids including the B-27 Flying Fortress flying in daylight hours.[5] By August, the U-boat threat to American cities and shipping along the East Coast had diminished greatly, though German submarines continued to pose problems for transatlantic shipping. American manufacturers were now turning out war materiel—ships, planes, tanks, and other weaponry—in massive amounts at a rapid pace. Production was no longer a problem; getting the products past German submarines was.

But the biggest reversal of Axis fortunes came in the horrific battle for Stalingrad, where outmanned and outgunned Russian forces hung on tenaciously through August and into October in what had degenerated into vicious urban combat with staggering numbers of casualties on both sides. A final offensive by the Germans in mid-October failed to take the city, after which Nazi forces found themselves running short on bombs and other munitions. In mid-November, with winter at hand, fresh Russian troops that had slowly assembled outside of Stalingrad counterattacked in a pincer movement, encircling German troops and forcing them to fight a bloody retreat to escape from the city. By the end of the year the outcome was no longer in doubt, and on January 31, 1943, the Germans still at Stalingrad formally surrendered. The Third Reich's drive to expand its territory and capture the rich oil fields of the Middle East had been frustrated, denying the Nazi war machine the vital petroleum on which it ran. Stalingrad was a great symbolic victory as well as a military one. "The myth of the invincible Wehrmacht," Pete and Dan Snow write, "was gone." It was a bitter defeat for Hitler, for which he could not escape blame, and it marked "the beginning of a rift in the German High command that would end in . . . a total breakdown in effective leadership."[6] There would be three more years of hard fighting before the war would end in 1945 with the surrender of Germany and Japan, but the corner had been turned.

In St. Louis, baseball and war came together in a large newspaper advertisement by the Alpen Brau brewery following the end of the regular season and before the World Series. It featured the familiar St. Louis logo of a cardinal perched on a bat. The cardinal had a message for Hitler that was drawn from the Redbirds' come-from-behind pennant victory:

Listen to the little Red Bird, Adolf . . . it's telling you
YOUR LEAD ISN'T BIG ENOUGH EITHER!

Sure, Adolf, you got off to a flying start. That foul-play combination, Hitler to Hirohito to Benito, worked like a charm in the early innings.

You banged the ball all over the map . . . because you started playing *your* game before anyone else had a fair chance to warm up and put a team on the field.

That's just what you counted on! But what you didn't count on, Adolf, was the fact that *a fighting spirit can overcome any lead.*

You're starting to realize that now. The United Nations are hitting their stride. They have started smashing your pitchers all over the lot . . . putting men on bases everywhere. Soon they'll be scoring on your home plate.

There's only one flag that you and your teammates are ever going to run up in the game *you* started. It's the white flag of surrender.

In the World Series that lies ahead, we trust it's in the Cards to win, as surely as we know it's in the cards for Hitler, Hirohito, and Benito to lose.[7]

The 1942 World Series had been a great financial success. Despite gas rationing and wartime transportation restrictions, it drew 276,717 spectators, a record for a five-game series, and had receipts of $1,105,249, the third consecutive series to top the million-dollar mark. The winners' share for each of the Cardinals was $6,192.53—more, for all but a few of them, than they had been paid during the regular season.[8] The *Sporting News* lost no time in editorializing on the success of the series as proof of the game's importance to the nation: "The first World's Series since our entry into the second World War again has proved the great hold that baseball has on the American public, that the public wishes to have its baseball, and that baseball has a real, definite purpose as a builder in national morale." The series had been broadcast live by radio to American troops in locations around the world, a point which the magazine noted with its customary patriotism: "This Series means much to American soldiers, sailors, and marines . . . wherever the Stars and Stripes fly in the great global war."[9]

Baseball's financial contributions to the war effort were also pointed to with pride by all in the game. In total, the sixteen major-league games played for military relief had raised more than a million dollars, to which the minor leagues added almost a quarter million more. The annual All-Star Game produced close to ninety thousand dollars that was divided between military relief and a Bat and Ball Fund from which baseball equipment was purchased for members of the armed forces. The second game, between military All-Stars and the American League All-Star squad, contributed another seventy thousand. Of World Series receipts, the shares normally going to the offices of the commissioner and the league presidents, just over $360,000, was turned over to the USO. Baseball also arranged to have 3,150 copies of the *Sporting News* sent to military base libraries, ships at sea, overseas bases, and USO clubs. Beyond this, there was Larry MacPhail's successful scrap-metal promotion in Brooklyn, in which almost sixty thousand of the Flatbush faithful provided around six hundred tons of metal. Albeit more modest, the Cardinals donated various items for auctions conducted after the World Series by sportscasters France Laux and Bob Lyle. Terry Moore's glove sold for a $5,000 war bond, while autographed baseballs, team photographs, and other memorabilia sold in Centralia, Illinois, for more than $100,000 in war bonds.[10]

In 1943, major-league baseball would contribute a great deal more in the way of manpower than it did in 1942, as every team lost numerous players to the military. Players not entering the service found themselves under pressure to find war work in the off-season. The *Sporting News,* ever vigilant in reminding the players of their special patriotic obligations, editorialized:

> Wake up, you players sitting at home, waiting for another season and wondering what is going to happen next year. Wake up to the tremendous responsibilities you must avow as ballplayers.
>
> Wake up to the call to action. Just making a talk once a month at some dinner won't do.
>
> Get into your work clothes, Mr. Ballplayer, and get into a plane or munitions factory or shipyard. Get into something that is WAR.
>
> Wake up and go to some school which will make your service more valuable. But . . . DO WAKE UP![11]

Ironically, several of the Cardinals' players were criticized for heeding this advice and taking jobs in a St. Louis war plant. Their critics said the jobs should have gone instead to workers who were not as well off financially as the players and therefore needed the income more.

∼

Many New York writers were harsh in their judgments on the Yankees' World Series performance. Dan Daniel, dean of New York's baseball scribes, wrote that it was "the most complete and humiliating defeat in the annals of the world series."[12] Many other eastern writers—Frank Graham of the *New York Sun,* Shirley Povich of the *Washington Post,* Cy Peterman of the *Philadelphia Inquirer*—fell back on the cliché "end of an era" to convey their sense of the magnitude of the Yankees' defeat. It would prove to be nothing of the sort. In 1943 the Yankees would win a World Series rematch with the Cardinals, and after the war the team would pick up where it had left off in the early 1940s, dominating the American League from the late 1940s until the mid 1960s.

In St. Louis, October 1942 did bring one era to an indisputable end. After twenty-six years of successful collaboration, Sam Breadon and Branch Rickey parted ways. Never close personal friends, Breadon and Rickey had forged one of the most successful business relationships in the history of baseball. Breadon was willing to finance Rickey's many innovations, from the farm system to the pitching machine, and together they transformed a perennial second-division franchise into a powerhouse. The distance between the two men had grown after an investigation by the commissioner's office in the late 1930s into the propriety of practices in the Cardinals' farm system. Rickey assured Breadon that everything was proper, but Commissioner Kenesaw Mountain Landis found otherwise, determining that the Redbirds were in violation of baseball rules governing the control of minor-league players, and he declared several dozen St. Louis minor-league prospects, including Pete Reiser, to be free agents. Breadon, who had backed Rickey fully, felt his reputation had been stained by the commissioner's action and thought himself misled by Rickey.

The first public rupture came in 1940. With the Cardinals struggling early in the season, Rickey gave public assurances that the job of manager Ray Blades was safe, only to have Breadon, who retained control over managers, fire Blades shortly thereafter and bring Billy Southworth back to manage the team. Breadon and Rickey had differed on other matters over the years, such as beer advertisements in the ballpark and beer sales at Sunday games, which the devout Methodist Rickey opposed but the businessman Breadon accepted. Rickey was also among the highest-paid executives in baseball who was not a team owner, reportedly drawing a salary of fifty thousand dollars plus receiving bonuses and a share of the money from the sale of players, all of which put his annual income from the team at around an estimated eighty thousand. Playing in a small market with two teams, the Cardinals were always strapped for cash, and with war and its uncertainties on the horizon, Breadon, ever the bottom-liner, may have decided that there was too much risk in renewing Rickey's five-year contract after the 1942 season. Though it was not widely known at the time, Breadon informed Rickey before the 1941 season that his contract would not be renewed.[13] During the World Series, he gave Brooklyn permission to speak with the Cardinals' vice-president about replacing Larry MacPhail as president of the Dodgers.

Rickey was in the clubhouse for the team's celebration after their game five victory that brought a world championship back to St. Louis, but he was not on the train that returned the Cardinals to St. Louis. He was instead meeting with the Dodgers' board of directors, and a few days later he joined the Brooklyn baseball club. It was a bittersweet moment for Rickey, who told Harold Parrott of the *Brooklyn Eagle*, "I hate to leave St. Louis. These are my players, my scouts, my executives—this Cardinal organization is my family, it's all of my making."[14] J. G. Taylor Spink, publisher of the *Sporting News,* praised Rickey as the architect of the St. Louis club and "the hero of the World Series."[15]

Shortly before Rickey was named to replace him, Larry MacPhail, who had resigned earlier as president and general manager, quit as a member of the Dodgers' board of directors as well, saying that the demands of his job in Washington made it impossible for him to return for meetings. "When I came down here, I thought of how beautiful Washington would be at this time of year, with the leaves turning and everything. So far, I haven't had time to look at a tree or even listen to a bird," he wrote. "I've been working fourteen to sixteen hours every day."[16] One attraction for Rickey in Brooklyn was being reunited with his son,

Branch Jr., who was director of player development for the Dodgers. Not so attractive was the aging team he inherited with its roster full of veteran players, many of them in their mid-thirties. By 1944, as a result of Rickey's personnel moves and the war, only two everyday players from the 1942 Brooklyn team—Dixie Walker and Mickey Owen—were still regulars, and none of the starting pitchers from the 1942 club remained in the regular rotation, although forty-year-old Curt Davis was still an occasional starter.

In St. Louis, Sam Breadon moved quickly to take command of the Cardinals, and by all reports he had a firm grasp of the problems facing both the game and his team. The club's front office was reorganized, with Rickey's responsibilities parceled out to several individuals. William Walsingham, Jr., Breadon's nephew, was named vice-president; Joe Mathes, a veteran scout, took over as farm director; and Eddie Dyer, a longtime minor-league manager, moved into the front office to assume responsibility for various aspects of player development and evaluation.[17] Breadon met with his staff, including Southworth, after the World Series to review the progress of the minor-leaguers and to lay plans for 1943. He reported that the minor-league clubs had lost one hundred thousand dollars in 1942, as only one returned a profit. Nonetheless, no reduction was planned in the farm system, though Breadon acknowledged that the war made the future of some lower-classification leagues uncertain. At the same time, he was confident that the major leagues would operate in 1943, citing the encouraging recent military success of Allied forces in North Africa. Taylor Spink of the *Sporting News* shared Breadon's optimism and reasoning, writing that "the way things shape up now, with the opening of the African front, and the thrilling naval triumph in the Solomons, baseball is justified in looking forward to a good season" in 1943.[18] Not all in the game shared this view. Many thought the joint meeting of major- and minor-league officials in Chicago in December would have to resolve a number of issues before another baseball season could be a sure thing in 1943.[19]

∼

Breadon and Spink proved correct about 1943, and the Cardinals, much as Rickey had predicted, rolled to a second National League pennant, winning 105 games and finishing eighteen games ahead of second-place Cincinnati. In the World Series, however, the Yankees got revenge for 1942, taking it in five games and sweeping the Redbirds in St. Louis. But while the game was the same, the quality of play was not. Like all of the big-league teams, the Cardinals lost a number of players from the 1942 St. Louis Swifties to the military. Enos Slaughter, Terry Moore, Johnny Beazley, Frank Crespi, Whitey Moore, and rookies Jeff Cross and Erv Dusak were in service from 1943 through 1945. They were joined in 1944 by Jimmy Brown, Harry Walker, Ernie White, Howard Krist, Murry Dickson, and Howard Pollet, and in 1945 by Stan Musial. All of the major-league clubs were forced to restock their rosters with past-their-prime veterans, some of whom, like Pepper Martin with the Cards, had been out of the game for a few years, and with untested rookies. These replacements joined players whose draft classification was 4F, like Marion, Kurowski, and Sanders of the Cardinals.

The Cardinals were hurt less than other teams because their farm system continued to turn out talented youngsters: position players Lou Klein, Al "Red" Schoendienst, Del Rice, Emil Verban, and Augie Bergamo; pitchers Harry Brecheen, George Munger, Al Brazle, Ted Wilks, and Ken Burkhart. All played in the years after the war, and one, Schoendienst, made it into baseball's Hall of Fame. The Cardinals were a very young team in 1942, and Branch Rickey among others thought they would dominate the National League for years to come. In fact, they did. Their success in the 1940s was unrivaled: world championships in 1942, 1944, and 1946, another league pennant in 1943, and five second-place finishes from 1941 through 1949. From 1941 through 1946, they averaged more than one hundred wins a season. Only the Chicago Cubs, who averaged more than one hundred wins a season for nine years from 1904 through 1911, and the New York Yankees, who did the same for seven years from 1936 through 1942, could top the success of the Redbird teams of the 1940s, and none since has enjoyed so sustained a run of success.

The war stole years from the lifetime records of dozens of big-league stars. Much has been written speculating on how many strikeouts Bob Feller might have recorded were it not for his four years in military service, or how many home runs Hank Greenberg or Ted Williams might have amassed had their careers not been interrupted. But little has been written about the teams of that era. The Cardinals' dynasty that might have been—that in fact was—is almost never mentioned among the great dynasties of baseball. Nevertheless, the 1942 St. Louis Swifties have been celebrated by Donald Honig as one of the ten best teams in baseball history. "Few clubs have ever attacked with such baseball sense," Honig writes, "or such splendidly spirited self-confidence."[20]

The 1942 team is generally regarded as the greatest of all Cardinal teams. For Enos Slaughter, who wept shamelessly in the St. Louis clubhouse when told of his trade to the New York Yankees in 1954 and who played six years with the great Bronx Bombers of the Mickey Mantle era, there was no doubt about it: "I don't think I was ever as proud to be with a ballclub as I was to be one of the 1942 St. Louis Cardinals. I've played with other great clubs, but I would have to say that this one topped them all."[21]

CONCLUSION

On Monday, January 11, 1982, members of the 1942 Cardinals were honored at the twenty-fifth annual St. Louis area Baseball Writers' Association dinner at Stouffer's Riverside Towers in downtown St. Louis. The captain, Terry Moore, returned, along with his outfield partners Stan Musial and Enos Slaughter. For that one season in 1942, they may have formed the greatest all-around outfield in National League history, and just possibly the best the major leagues had ever known. They were an exceptional defensive trio. All were fast with good instincts. Moore and Slaughter had two of the strongest and most accurate throwing arms in the game; Musial's had gotten stronger and was more than adequate in left. All were good hitters: Slaughter and Musial led the club in hitting at .318 and .315, as well as in home runs and runs batted in, while Moore hit .288 and was a top base stealer who soldiered through several injuries that took him out of twenty-four games during the summer.

Mr. Shortstop, Marty Marion, anchor of the infield defense, was joined at the reunion by first basemen Johnny Hopp and Ray Sanders, second baseman Frank Crespi, and third baseman George Kurowski. The infield had been a work in progress at the start of the season. Billy Southworth's decision in May to move Brown from third to second and install Kurowski at third resolved part of the puzzle; Hopp taking charge at first base around midseason took care of the other. Kurowski delivered some of the biggest clutch hits of the season; Brown was the team's third-best run producer; and Hopp got hot with the bat as the Cardinals launched their long march to the pennant in August. But of all the infielders, it was Marion, the premier defensive shortstop in the game, who was the biggest surprise at the plate. After two months at the start of the season in which he struggled to hit in the mid-.100s, the lanky Marion went on a tear to finish the season at .276 and lead the major leagues with thirty-eight doubles. Catcher Walker Cooper and rookie sensation Johnny Beazley, who won twenty-one games and with Cooper formed the club's best battery against the Yankees in the World Series, also joined their teammates. Beazley was the only pitcher from the remarkable staff of the 1942 Cardinals in attendance at the dinner. Three members of mound corps had passed away. Mort Cooper, the ace who won twenty-two games, was named the league's Most Valuable Player in 1942, and who with Walker formed the club's brother battery, died young at age forty-five in 1958. Ernie White, the tow-headed lefty who shut out the Yankees in the third game of the World Series, passed away in 1974 at age fifty-eight, and in the same year Howard Pollet, the handsome southpaw who struggled with arm problems through most of the 1942 season but later blossomed into the staff ace after World War II, died at age fifty-three. A fourth member of the 1942 club, second baseman Jimmy Brown, the hard-nosed battler, clutch hitter, and in many ways the sparkplug of the team, died in 1977 at age sixty-seven.

It was a day of reminiscing and storytelling among the old teammates, who with their wives had also gathered for lunch at the Stadium Club in Busch Stadium, which was managed by Marion. The day was crowned by the banquet in the grand ballroom of Stouffer's, where sixteen hundred fans joined with past and present Cardinals, manager Whitey Herzog, and representatives from other teams like Tommy Lasorda of the Dodgers and from other sports like basketball's Magic Johnson for an evening of toasting and roasting. Lasorda lauded the 1942 Cardinals not only for being a great ball club but also for their "determination never to do anything to hurt the reputation of the sport they represented."[1]

∼

The story of the 1942 Cardinals is almost biblical in its proportion, except that, as "David," they slew two giants, not one, and did it with their feet as well as with their "sling-shot" hitting attack. They came from far behind to catch and pass the Dodgers in what J. Roy Stockton called "the most spectacular and surprising dash to diamond glory that anybody cares to remember."[2] The St. Louis drive to the pennant that began on August 10 was, to be sure, "spectacular," but it was more than a mere "dash." It was a long march. It covered fifty-one games, one-third of the season, during which the team won forty-three games and lost only eight, an .843 winning percentage, a pace that is beyond remarkable and approaches astounding. There had been other dramatic late-season dashes to the pennant before the Cardinals in 1942, and there have been some since, but in almost all cases one team faded badly or collapsed while the other swept past. The Dodgers did neither. They played almost .700 baseball against the rest of the National League during the long flight of the Redbirds, good enough to win the pennant against any ordinary challenger.

But the Cardinals were no ordinary team. None had played better over a longer period of time than the St. Louis Swifties. Martin Haley of the *Globe-Democrat* thought the victory march "probably ranks as the most amazing performance in all major league baseball history," adding that only the run of the Miracle Braves in 1914 rivaled it.[3] Those Braves stood in last place on July 18, but they were only eleven and a half games from first in a closely bunched race. After July 18 the Braves went 34–10 (.773) to move into first place on September 8. In comparison, the 1942 Cardinals were ten games out of first on August 5 and then went 44–9 (.830) to claim first place on September 13. The Redbirds went on to defeat the mighty Yankees in the World Series, an upset whose magnitude Frederick Lieb equated with only two others: the defeat of the world champion Philadelphia Athletics in 1914 by the Miracle Braves, and the failure of the 116-game-winner Chicago Cubs in 1906 to defeat the "Hitless Wonder" Chicago White Sox.[4] Taylor Spink of the *Sporting News* added that the St. Louis win "did the game a service [because] the World's Series was in danger of losing its grip as the No. 1 sports event in the very superiority of the Yankees in recent years."[5]

The 1942 Cardinals were built around pitching, defense, and speed. The pitching staff gave up fewer than three earned runs a game, posting a 2.56 earned-run average for the season that was the best in either league. It led the majors in strikeouts, allowed the fewest hits, and tied the New York Yankees for the most shutouts. Led by Mort Cooper's twenty-two wins and 1.77 ERA, the staff included six other pitchers who allowed fewer than three earned runs a game, had a twenty-one game winner in Johnny Beazley, and had two thirteen-game winners in Max Lanier and Howard Krist. Remarkable by today's standards, but not at the time, it was essentially an eight-man pitching staff.

The overall speed of the players (there was not a slow runner on the club) amazed opposing teams and newsmen alike, with some calling them the fastest team in the history of the game. The aggressive and daring baserunning—taking the extra base, forcing defensive misplays—drew regular comments from all who followed the team.[6] Team speed was evident as well in the Cardinals' stellar defensive play, as shortstop Marty Marion and all of the outfielders regularly and routinely turned base hits into outs. "Marion ranged from deep in the hole to the first-base side of second picking up would-be base hits with ease and grace," Honig writes. "Seldom has a shortstop so dominated an infield." As for the outfield, he adds, none "ever closed the gaps on a line drive with more élan than the Musial-Moore-Slaughter trio."[7]

The team lacked home-run power, collecting only sixty for the season (sixth best in the National League). Enos Slaughter with thirteen and Stan Musial with ten were the only Redbirds in double figures. George Kurowski was next with nine, but one of them won a crucial game during the season—the final encounter with the Dodgers in Brooklyn—and he hit another homer that scored the deciding runs in the last game of the World Series in New York against the Yankees. While the Redbirds did not hit many home runs, they did top the National League in slugging percentage, leading both leagues in doubles with 282 and triples with 69 (creating an unusual statistic: few teams hit more triples than home runs). It was also a get-on-base team which drew 551 walks to go with 1,454 hits for an average of more than twelve base runners a game. It was a club that made regular contact with the ball, striking out only 507 times while drawing 551 walks, but in this they were simply typical of a time when power hitting was a less dominant part of the typical team's offense.[8] All five of the top five teams in the National League in 1942 had more walks than strikeouts, as did six of the eight American League teams.

Cardinal players walked off with numerous individual honors. In addition to Mort Cooper being named the National League Most Valuable Player, finishing just ahead of teammate Enos Slaughter, Stan Musial was named Rookie of the Year, beating out teammate Johnny Beazley. George Kurowski joined Musial and Beazley in being chosen for the major-league all-rookie team. Cooper and Slaughter made the Baseball Writers major-league all-star team, while Billy Southworth was named National League Manager of the Year for the second year in a row. Two players from the 1942 team—Musial and Slaughter—would eventually be elected to the National Baseball Hall of Fame and are now enshrined in Cooperstown alongside vice president Branch Rickey and manager Billy Southworth, both of whom were elected posthumously. All of the players honored, like all but a couple of their teammates, were products of Rickey's brainchild, the St. Louis farm system. Never before or since has a pennant winner been built so completely from its minor-league system. Indeed, the 1942 Cardinals represent the pinnacle of the farm system method of player development, a fact not lost on the players at the time. "Cardinal starters were proud that we had all come up through the team's own minor league organization," Enos Slaughter notes, adding that they held it against the Dodgers for not being homegrown.[9]

$\sim$

The 1942 St. Louis Cardinals were something new in baseball. They played the game in an old-fashioned way, winning with speed, daring, timely hitting, strong pitching, and excellent defense, throwbacks, in a way, to the era of "scientific baseball" in which the game was played for one run at a time with pitchers who threw complete games and defenses that could protect slim leads. After World War II, the power game and specialization triumphed as teams in both leagues prized their sluggers who could hit home runs and began to define more specific roles for individual pitchers. At the same time, as a team, the Redbirds were different from those of earlier times in a way that was very important to the future of the game. They were not rowdies or ruffians or drunks. They did not fight among themselves, but played together as friends as well as teammates. Many inside the game itself, from the commissioner to members of the press to opposing players, described the 1942 Cardinals as "gentlemen," and in this they helped to change the image of the professional ballplayer. As the nation moved into World War II, the young Redbirds were often seen as representatives of the best of the nation's youth—spirited, competitive, and of model character, with a sense of fair play and respect for the rules. They were "not only champions," Roy Stockton wrote after the World Series; they were "the sweethearts of the baseball world."[10]

NOTES

Introduction

1. *St. Louis Post-Dispatch,* October 6, 1942, 1B. Joe Williams made the same point, that the Series had been "farm system against farm system." *New York Herald Tribune,* October 6, 1942, 21.

2. For ages, see David S. Neft, Richard M. Cohen, and Michael L. Neft, *The Sports Encyclopedia: Baseball 2007,* 66, 214. For years of service, see *The Baseball Encyclopedia,* 8th ed.

3. *St. Louis Globe-Democrat,* October 7, 1942, 3B.

4. Some owners entered into contracts with their better players that included a bonus if the team drew more than a certain number of fans. Baseball rules forbid bonuses based on individual player performance.

Chapter 1. War Comes to Baseball

1. The one dissenting vote, greeted by boos and hisses, was cast by Representative Jeannette Rankin, Republican of Montana, who in 1917, in her first term as the first woman elected to the House of Representatives, had cast the solitary vote against American entry into World War I.

2. *New York Times,* December 8, 1941, 1.

3. Representative Rankin voted "present."

4. *New York Times,* December 4, 1941, 35, and December 5, 1941, 31.

5. In 1942 the American Association, International League, and Pacific Coast League carried the designation of Double A. This changed before the 1946 season, when they were classified as Triple A. See Leslie O'Connor, *Official Baseball 1946,* 165.

6. Clay Hopper, as manager at Montreal in 1946, would be Jackie Robinson's first manager in white professional ball, while Burt Shotton would be his manager in Brooklyn in 1948, the year after Robinson broke the color barrier in major-league baseball.

7. The major leagues shut down on Labor Day in 1918 in response to the Woodrow Wilson administration's "work or fight" order, that is, engage in an essential wartime occupation or join the military. Several weeks after the season was halted, the Associated Press reported that "the Government informed major league leaders that this had not been intended and that normal plans should be made for the sport in 1919." *St. Louis*

Post-Dispatch, January 14, 1941, 2B. Not all local draft boards appear to have gotten this message. Rogers Hornsby of the Cardinals, for one, was reclassified Class 1 based on the presidential directive. Charles C. Alexander, *Rogers Hornsby: A Biography,* 45.

8. As winter snows shut down the German offensive in late November 1941, Soviet officials acknowledged that their losses included almost half a million dead, more than one million wounded, and another half million missing. They also claimed that Germany had lost more than 15,000 tanks, 13,000 planes, and 12,900 guns. *St. Louis Post-Dispatch,* November 30, 1941.

9. Poll data cited in Winston Groom, *1942: The Year That Tried Men's Souls,* 53.

10. *St. Louis Post-Dispatch,* December 9, 1941, 2B.

11. On St. Louis at the turn of the twentieth century, see James Neal Primm, *Lion of the Valley: St. Louis, Missouri, 1764–1980,* 3rd ed., chaps. 8 and 9.

12. On the effects of the Great Depression on St. Louis, see Richard S. Kirkendall, *A History of Missouri: Volume V, 1919 to 1951,* chap. 5.

13. On St. Louis in 1942, see *Missouri: The WPA Guide to the "Show Me" State.*

14. Quoted in William A. Klingaman, *1941: Our Lives in a World on the Edge,* 421–22. See also William B. Mead, *Baseball Goes to War,* 33–35.

15. At the time, every team played twenty-two games against each of the other teams in its league, divided evenly between home and away dates. Teams made four trips into each city in which they played three three-game series and one two-game series. Neither league made any change in this schedule for 1942, but in 1943, to reduce travel, both leagues scheduled only three visits to each city: two four-game series and one three-game series.

16. In 1939, when the Browns were permitted to play fourteen night games, they drew as many people to those games as they did to all of their sixty-three home day games combined.

17. *St. Louis Post-Dispatch,* December 10, 1941, 2B.

18. The Giants also included first baseman Johnny McCarthy in the deal, but Indianapolis claimed to own McCarthy and Commissioner Landis upheld their claim. The Cardinals received no additional compensation.

19. *St. Louis Post-Dispatch,* December 12, 1941, 2B.

20. Histories of the 1942 season commonly treat it as a war year, but in fact very few major-league players were lost to the military that year. In all, only thirty-two National League and forty American League players from their clubs' protected forty-man rosters were in the military in 1942, and the vast majority of these were minor-leaguers. Few had been everyday players in 1941. All of the star players lost in 1942 were from the American League: first baseman Hank Greenberg of the Detroit Tigers, pitcher Bob Feller of the Cleveland Indians, and shortstop Cecil Travis of the Washington Senators. In addition to Lavagetto, the Dodgers lost veteran backup catchers Herman Franks and Don Padgett, and rookie outfielders Joe Gallagher and Tommy Tatum. The Cardinals lost only two rookies, pitcher Johnny Grodzicki and outfielder Walter Sessi.

21. *St. Louis Post-Dispatch,* December 18, 1941, 3B. Many teams, like the Browns and the Dodgers, used scouts primarily to evaluate players already in the minor leagues, not to find and sign amateurs. The Cardinals, Yankees, and Tigers were among the teams most active in pursuing players not already signed with a professional organization.

22. *St. Louis Post-Dispatch,* January 4, 1942, 1D.

23. *Brooklyn Eagle,* April 14, 1942, 15.

24. For brief descriptions and maps of the December 7 Japanese attacks on Pearl Harbor and across Southeast Asia, see Ronald Story, *Historical Atlas of World War Two,* 78–81.

25. *St. Louis Post-Dispatch,* December 9, 1941, 1. See also Klingaman, *1941,* 424.

26. *St. Louis Post-Dispatch,* December 13, 1941, 1.

27. Bad as the damage was, it could have been much worse. None of the Navy's four aircraft carriers assigned to the Pacific fleet was at Pearl Harbor on December 7; and as the Japanese attack signaled, it would be carriers, not battleships, that would be of greatest importance in the Pacific war. The Japanese raid also did little damage to the repair shops at Pearl Harbor, which allowed the United States to begin work immediately on salvaging what it could of the fleet. In addition, the vast fields of oil tanks were untouched, and most of the planes destroyed were obsolete and scheduled to be taken out of service. See David M. Kennedy, *The American People in World War II,* 91–102.

28. David H. Bercuson and Holger H. Herwig, *One Christmas in Washington,* 230–31.

Chapter 2. Winter of Uncertainty, Spring of Hope

1. *Sporting News,* December 11, 1941, 4.

2. Quoted in Mead, *Baseball Goes to War,* 34.

3. After World War II, Robert Hannegan joined with Fred Saigh to purchase the Cardinals from Sam Breadon.

4. *New York Times,* January 17, 1942, 10. Roosevelt also told Landis that the sentiments in the letter were "a personal and not an official point of view" and that players would receive no special treatment with respect to the draft. See James M. Gould, "The President Says, 'Play Ball,'" *Baseball Magazine,* March 1942, 435–36. Bob Considine suggests that Clark Griffith may have written the "green-light" letter for Roosevelt. "There was a mixed construction in one of the sentences, bordering around the word `got.' Roosevelt's letters are flawless," Considine noted. "Griffith can kick the grammar book around pretty well, and this mixed construction, though it seems a tiny clue in itself, smacked of his wandering pen." *St. Petersburg Times,* February 19, 1942, 12.

5. Mead, *Baseball Goes to War,* 37–38.

6. In 1942 there continued to be a rule that no game begun in daylight could be completed under lights. While still a novelty in the majors, night games had been played for several years before 1935 in both the minor leagues and the Negro Leagues. Their popularity had enabled these teams to survive financially in the Depression years.

7. *Sporting News,* January 22, 1942, 1. See also Mead, *Baseball Goes to War.*

8. National League president Ford Frick was quick to warn that this "wartime measure" should not be taken as a precedent.

9. John Drebinger, "The Increase in Major League Night Baseball," *Baseball Magazine,* April 1942, 497–98.

10. See Bob Hooey, "Billy Southworth," in John P. Carmichael, ed., *My Greatest Day in Baseball,* 180–83. In 2008, Southworth was inducted into the National Baseball Hall of Fame in Cooperstown, New York.

11. Breadon left most player decisions to Rickey, but had always retained control over

decisions about who would be the manager. These decisions had not always been made in consultation with Rickey, but in this case it was made after Rickey had been assuring sportswriters that Blades's job was safe.

12. *Sporting News*, January 1, 1942, 6.

13. Robert W. Craemer, *Baseball and Other Matters in 1941*, 242. The data are drawn from Craemer's work. See also Rudy Marzano, *The Brooklyn Dodgers in the 1940s*, chap. 3; John Snyder, *Cardinals Journal*, 313–20; and Bill Borst, "Showdown in St. Louis," *The National Pastime* (Cleveland: Society for American Baseball Research, 1991), 63–64.

14. In a heated dispute with Sam Breadon during the 1926 season, Hornsby had ordered the owner out of the team's locker room. After the season, Breadon decreed that Hornsby had to go.

15. Jim Hunstein, *1, 2, 6, 9 . . . & Rogers: The Cardinals Retired Numbers & the Men Who Wore Them*, 1.

16. Quoted in Alexander, *Rogers Hornsby*, 115–16.

17. *Sporting News*, January 15, 1942, 10.

18. *St. Louis Post-Dispatch*, February 19, 1942, 3E.

19. The minor leagues in 1942 were organized into a number of different levels from AA through D. On Musial's climb to the majors, see James N. Giglio, *Musial: From Stash to Stan the Man*, 38–56.

20. *St. Louis Star-Times*, March 10, 1942, 21.

21. *Sporting News*, February 5, 1942, 3.

22. *St. Louis Star-Times*, February 6, 1942, 8.

23. *St. Louis Post-Dispatch*, January 14, 1942, 2B; January 17, 1942, 2B.

24. *St. Louis Post-Dispatch*, February 2, 1942, 2E. See also Richard Goldstein, *Spartan Seasons: How Baseball Survived the Second World War*, 65.

25. *St. Louis Post-Dispatch*, February 3, 1942, 4B.

26. Goldstein, *Spartan Seasons*, 65.

27. *St. Petersburg Times*, February 20, 1942, 13.

28. *St. Louis Post-Dispatch*, February 25, 1942, 2B.

29. *St. Petersburg Independent*, February 21, 1942, 2B.

30. *St. Louis Post-Dispatch*, February 24, 1942, 26.

31. *Sporting News*, February 26, 1932, 9; *St. Louis Post-Dispatch*, February 22, 1942, 3E; *St. Petersburg Times*, February 23, 1942, 11–12.

32. *St. Louis Post-Dispatch*, March 15, 1942, 2B. A pepper game is played with several fielders positioned about fifteen feet in front of a batter. The batter hits a ball sharply, the fielder must be quick to field it, tosses it back, and the batter hits the ball again at the fielders, moving the ball around in an unpredictable pattern.

33. *St. Petersburg Times*, February 22, 1942, 11.

34. Lew Bryer, "Meet 'Billy the Kid' Southworth," *Baseball Digest*, December 1942, 37–41.

35. *St. Petersburg Times*, February 22, 1942, 11.

36. *New York Times*, March 10, 1942, 25. In a similar vein, John Kiernan reported that Clark Griffith was having the Washington Senators eat lots of carrots. They had to play more night games than other teams, and pilots in the British Air Force, who flew many night missions in the war, stuffed themselves with carrots to improve their night vision.

Kiernan quoted a physician remarking that the team would be better off taking cod-liver oil.

37. *St. Petersburg Times*, February 26, 1942, 31.

38. *St. Louis Post-Dispatch*, February 23, 1942, 1B; *St. Petersburg Times*, February 24, 1942, 13.

39. *St. Louis Star-Times*, March 9, 1942, 18.

40. The internment of Japanese Americans is now seen as a scar on the Roosevelt record, but not even the American Civil Liberties Union protested the decision at the time.

41. Peter Golenbock, *The Spirit of St. Louis: A History of the St. Louis Cardinals and Browns*, 239.

42. *St. Louis Post-Dispatch*, March 14, 1942, 18.

43. Ibid.

44. *St. Louis Globe-Democrat*, February 21, 1942, 4B.

45. *St. Louis Post-Dispatch*, March 25, 1942, 1B.

46. Before unionization and free agency, players represented themselves in dealing with team owners and had little leverage in bargaining over the terms of their contracts. The reserve clause as it existed then in major-league baseball bound a player to one team and gave that team absolute control over its players, whose options were to either play for whatever the club was willing to pay or retire. There was therefore no rush on the part of clubs to re-sign their players for the next season. Typically, players received one-year contract offers in late January or early February, and most simply signed and returned them, although some players would wait until spring training to sign for the next year. This was the one time when players could negotiate for more money, and there were always some who tried to get a better deal.

47. Living costs in 1942 were such that players could live comfortably on their salaries. A new house could be purchased for less than four thousand dollars, rents averaged about thirty-five dollars a month, a new car sold for less than a thousand dollars, and a gallon of gas cost fifteen cents. Food prices were similar: a gallon of milk cost sixty cents, while a pound of hamburger was half that much, a dozen eggs cost twenty cents, and a loaf of bread only nine cents.

48. *St. Petersburg Times*, February 26, 1942, 31.

49. *New York Times*, March 13, 1942, 25.

50. Donald Honig, *Baseball: Between the Lines*, 99.

51. Ibid.

52. *St. Petersburg Times*, March 18, 1942, 21.

53. *St. Louis Star-Times*, March 18, 1942, 20.

54. Ibid., March 25, 1942, 22.

55. *St. Louis Post-Dispatch*, April 9, 1942, 1E.

56. Ibid.

57. Talbot, Staffer, and Scheffels quotes from *St. Louis Post-Dispatch*, August 3, 1942.

58. Ibid.

59. *St. Petersburg Times*, April 12, 1942, 12.

60. *St. Louis Star-Times*, March 12, 1942, 4B.

61. *St. Louis Post-Dispatch*, March 26, 1942, 2B.

62. Ibid., March 26, 1942, 2B; April 9, 1942, 2E.

63. *St. Louis Star-Times,* April 2, 1942, 22.

64. Musial later blamed his disappointing spring on the poor hitting background at Waterfront Stadium. "They had all the palm trees waving," he explained. "I couldn't pick up the ball very well." See Golenbock, *Spirit of St. Louis,* 240. See also Mel Freese, *The Glory Years of the St. Louis Cardinals,* 104.

Chapter 3. Baby Birds Leave the Nest

1. *St. Louis Post-Dispatch,* April 12, 1942, 2B.

2. See John Morton Blum, *V Was for Victory: Politics and American Culture during World War II,* 54 and 37. Even comic strips contributed to the deception. A study by the Office of War Information found that in most of them "Americans won their battles alone, allies were nonexistent or subordinate [and] the enemy was a pushover."

3. See Kennedy, *The American People in World War II,* part 2, 101–2.

4. Groom, *1942,* 158–59.

5. Ibid. News of the brutal Bataan death march was not generally known to the public until some time later.

6. *St. Louis Post-Dispatch,* April 1, 1942, 1.

7. On the 1942 Browns, see Bill Borst, "A St. Louis Harbinger: The 1942 Browns," in Richard Peterson, ed., *The St. Louis Baseball Reader,* 242–47.

8. *New York Times,* April 16, 1942, 2.

9. *Sporting News,* April 9, 1942, 1.

10. Lon Warneke signed originally with St. Louis but was released by one of their minor-league managers. He subsequently signed with the Chicago Cubs and came to the major leagues with them, then went to the Cardinals in a trade in 1937. His case led to a policy change in the St. Louis farm system to require that any decision to release a player who possessed even one major-league skill (speed, arm, defense, hitting, power) must be made by more than one person. Of the pitchers who began the season with the Redbirds, two others—Bill Lohrman and Clyde Shoun—had come from other organizations, but they were both traded soon after the season began.

11. On the baseball backgrounds of Dodger players, see the *Sporting News,* August 13, 1942, 16.

12. *St. Louis Post-Dispatch,* April 28, 1942, 2B.

13. In the contemporary world of baseball, the thought of being "old" at thirty-five seems a bit odd. On opening-day rosters in 2007, twenty-five players were forty years of age or older. See *USA Today,* April 6, 2007, 2C.

14. See G. Edward White, *Creating the National Pastime: Baseball Transforms Itself,* 181.

15. See Ron Selter, "Sportsman's Park's Right-Field Pavilion and Screen," *Baseball Research Journal* 32 (Cleveland: Society for American Baseball Research, 2004), 77–80.

16. For a humorous feature story on Mary Ott, see the *St. Louis Globe-Democrat,* July 1, 1941, St. Louis Mercantile Library, Ott, Mary, Baseball—St.L.—General Envelope #2.

17. See Maury Allen, *Brooklyn Remembered,* 28–29.

18. There was no office for the manager in the St. Louis locker room. Southworth would take players into the shower room if he wanted to speak with them privately.

19. Peter Golenbock, *Bums: An Oral History of the Brooklyn Dodgers,* 34, 36; Gerald Eskenazi, *The Lip: A Biography of Leo Durocher,* 108, 112. Billy Herman was among the Dodger players who disliked Durocher personally: "He didn't treat all the players the same. He played favorites. He wasn't trustworthy; too often he didn't tell you the truth, and would do everything he could to protect himself, no matter what it did to you." Golenbock, *Bums,* 52.

20. Mead, *Baseball Goes to War,* 44.

21. John Helyar, *Lords of the Realm: The Real History of Baseball,* 44.

22. Murray Polner, *Branch Rickey: A Biography,* 79.

23. On the farm system, see David Quentin Voight, *American Baseball: From the Commissioners to Continental Expansion,* vol. 2, 159–63. On the commissioner's dislike for the farm system, see Golenbock, *Spirit of St. Louis,* chaps. 16 and 26. See too White, *National Pastime,* 287–91.

24. Branch Rickey III, "Forward," in Polner, *Branch Rickey,* 2.

25. *St. Louis Globe-Democrat,* May 11, 1949, St. Louis Mercantile Library, Breadon, Sam, Envelope no. 3.1.

26. Ibid., Envelope no. 2.1

27. J. Roy Stockton, *Saturday Evening Post,* February 22, 1947, File: Breadon, Samuel, National Baseball Hall of Fame, Cooperstown, New York.

28. Klingaman, *1941,* 154.

29. On the tempestuous relationship between Rickey and MacPhail, see Jules Tygiel, *Past Time: Baseball as History,* 91–114.

30. Golenbock, *Bums,* 33, 41.

31. *Sporting News,* April 6, 1942, 1.

32. Roosevelt himself had once been an opening-day replacement under similar circumstances: in 1918 as undersecretary of the navy he substituted for President Woodrow Wilson, who was busy with war work.

33. *St. Louis Post-Dispatch,* April 16, 1942, 1.

34. Ibid., April 21, 1942, 1.

35. In a city of breweries, there were many beers in addition to Falstaff and Hyde Park advertised in the stadium: Stag, Alpen Brau, and Griesedieck among them.

36. *Brooklyn Eagle,* April 16, 1942, 14.

37. Ibid., April 17, 1942, 15.

38. Groom, *1942,* 168–72, 185–94. The apparent discrepancy in dates, April 18 in Tokyo and April 17 in Pittsburgh, is attributable to Japan lying on the other side of the international date line.

39. Kennedy, *American People,* 10.

40. *St. Louis Post-Dispatch,* April 24, 1942, 1. O'Hare was a native of Chicago who had moved to St. Louis before the war. He was later killed in action in the Pacific. It is for him that Chicago's O'Hare Field is named.

41. Estel Crabtree was a valuable outfield reserve in 1941, but early in 1942 he was sent to manage the Rochester club, an assignment that did not work out. He was then declared a free agent. St. Louis wanted to resign him, but Crabtree was unsure about what he wanted to do and sat out for months, essentially missing the 1942 season. In all, he had three hits

in nine at bats for the Cardinals.

42. *Brooklyn Eagle,* April 26, 1942, 2C.

43. *St. Louis Post-Dispatch,* April 22, 1942, 2B.

Chapter 4. The Not So Merry May

1. Unlike today, players did not take the field before the playing of the National Anthem, but instead stayed in the dugout.

2. As news about the war got better, so did attendance, which picked up as the season moved along. Over the four years of the war, attendance at baseball games for the most part remained at prewar levels.

3. The only player of significance lost to the military during the 1942 season was the New York Yankees' right fielder, Tommy Henrich, who left the team in late August but was immediately replaced by Roy Cullenbine, who was acquired in a trade with Washington.

4. Both quotes from the *Brooklyn Eagle,* April 30, 1942, 26.

5. See reports in the *St. Louis Post-Dispatch,* May 4, 1942, 4B, and the *New York Times,* May 4, 1942, 22.

6. Mondays were routinely scheduled as open dates for all teams in 1942, but were often used later in the season to make up games that had been canceled earlier.

7. *St. Louis Post-Dispatch,* May 5, 1942, 2B. Brooklyn writers complained that there were too many rules; see Tommy Holmes, *Brooklyn Eagle,* May 5, 1942, 11. Meanwhile, John Kiernan of the *New York Times,* tongue no doubt firmly in cheek, noted that three players meeting together to challenge an umpire would constitute a "riot" under British law. See *New York Times,* May 6, 1942, 26.

8. *New York Times,* May 7, 1942, 25.

9. *St. Louis Post-Dispatch,* May 11, 1942, 1B.

10. Ibid., May 25, 1942, 21.

11. See Groom, *1942,* 206–13.

12. *St. Louis Post-Dispatch,* May 8, 1942, 1. For an account of the battle, see Groom, *1942,* 198–206 and Harry Gailey, *The War in the Pacific,* 147–52.

13. Groom, *1942,* 202. See also Kennedy, *American People,* 106–7.

14. *St. Louis Post-Dispatch,* May 9, 1942, 1.

15. Kennedy, *American People,* 107. The United States lost one carrier, the *Lexington,* and another, which the Japanese thought had been sunk, was damaged and in need of major repairs. Losses in men and materiel were heavier for the Japanese: ten ships, seventy-seven planes, and more than one thousand airmen and sailors, as opposed to U.S. losses of sixty-six planes and just over five hundred men.

16. Groom, *1942,* 213.

17. Only the Brooklyn Dodgers were adversely affected by this decision, and they later won a modification in it. There were no lights at Yankee Stadium, and night baseball had not been a significant money maker for the Giants. *Sporting News,* April 28, 1942, 4.

18. *St. Louis Post-Dispatch,* May 24, 1942, 25.

19. Players could be placed on an injured reserve list, but when this was done the player had to remain there for two months before he could again be activated. The practice was to keep a player, including sore-armed pitchers, on the roster through the period of re-

NOTES 249

covery. See Original Baseball Research, CliffordBlau@yahoo.com.

20. Hopp, who had been injured, was off to a terrible start at the plate, and the rookie Sanders, who was also struggling with the bat, shared first-base duties for the next month or so until Hopp finally claimed the job full-time.

21. *St. Louis Post-Dispatch,* May 28, 1942, 1B.

22. *Sporting News,* May 28, 1942, 10.

23. Rob Neyer and Eddie Epstein, *Baseball Dynasties: The Greatest Teams of All Time,* 172. Tim McCarver with Phil Pepe, *Few Are Chosen: Defining Cardinal Greatness Across the Eras,* 94. For Kurowski's comments, see Player Box: Terry Moore, center field, Envelope #2, Mercantile Library, University of Missouri–St. Louis. Owner Sam Breadon also admired Moore's "knack" for leadership. "It's an intangible something you cannot put down in so many words," Breadon observed, "but whatever it is, he had it." Ibid.

24. Ibid.

25. Golenbock, *Spirit of St. Louis,* 231.

26. *Sporting News,* May 14, 1942, 3.

27. Moore described his mother as "crazy about baseball" and said she was his biggest fan. "She'd go to a game and when somebody'd criticize me, she'd have an umbrella, and boy, she'd whack them with it! . . . She got in trouble couple of times out there and they put her down in back of Sam Breadon's box so that when she'd come to the game she'd stay out of trouble." Cynthia J. Wilber, *For the Love of the Game* (New York: William D. Morrow, 1992), 223.

28. On Moore's entry into professional baseball, see Rich Westcott, *Masters of the Diamond* (Jefferson, N.C.: McFarland and Co., 1994), 73.

29. Player File: Moore, Terry Blueford, National Baseball Hall of Fame, Cooperstown, N.Y.

30. McCarver and Pepe, *Few Are Chosen.* See too Player Box: Terry Moore, center field, Envelope #2, Mercantile Library, University of Missouri–St. Louis.

31. Player Box: Terry Moore, center field, Envelope #1, Mercantile Library, University of Missouri–St. Louis.

32. Westcott, *Masters.*

33. Player File: Moore, Terry Blueford, National Baseball Hall of Fame, Cooperstown, N.Y.

Chapter 5. The Swoon in June

1. *New York Herald Tribune,* June 3, 1942, 28.

2. *Sporting News,* May 7, 1942, 8.

3. *St. Louis Post-Dispatch,* June 9, 1942, 1B.

4. *St. Louis Star-Times,* June 9, 1942, 16.

5. *Brooklyn Eagle,* June 9, 1942, 16 and 11.

6. Ibid., June 13, 1942, 11.

7. *St. Louis Post-Dispatch,* June 12, 1942, 1E.

8. *St. Louis Star-Times,* June 19, 1942, 16.

9. *St. Louis Post-Dispatch,* June 12, 1942, 2E.

10. Ibid., June 1, 1942, 6.

11. For more on these bombings, see A. C. Grayling, *Among the Dead Cities*, 48–55.

12. Though not reported at the time, Robin Neillands notes that the raid on Cologne had a "political" as well as military purpose, as it was intended to quiet critics of air warfare in both the Parliament and the British Admiralty by showing that it could be effective and was the only way to strike back at Germany at the time. Neillands, *The Bomber War: The Allied Air Offensive against Nazi Germany*, 120.

13. *St. Louis Star-Times*, June 4, 1942, 1.

14. Dan van der Vat, *The Pacific Campaign: World War II, The U.S.-Japanese Naval War 1941–1945*, 181.

15. See Groom, *1942*, 245. Several days after the battle of Midway, the War Department announced that the carrier *Lexington* had not been lost in the Coral Sea engagement; this information had been withheld for strategic reasons. Three months would pass before the War Department announced that the *Yorktown* had been lost at Midway. *St. Louis Post-Dispatch*, September 16, 1941, 1. There was another fortunate outcome associated with the Midway battle. In their diversionary attack on Dutch Harbor, one of the fast and highly maneuverable Japanese fighters, the Zero, crash-landed and was recovered by the United States. American aeronautical engineers used it to design an American fighter plane, the Hellcat, that would prove superior to the Zero in combat. Kennedy, *American People*, pt. 2, 118.

16. Kennedy, *American People*, pt. 2. See also van der Vat, *Pacific Campaign*, 190.

17. Groom, *1942*.

18. Alan Moorehead, *Desert War*, 332, 366.

19. "Red" Schoendienst, who played for Southworth in 1945, credits him with having been "one of the first managers to change pitchers in the seventh and eighth innings." It may have been a case of necessity being the mother of invention. See Rick Hummel, *St. Louis Post-Dispatch*, December 4, 2007, www.stltoday.com/stltoday/sports/stories.naf/cardinals/story/D6C70VC547ED2E608.

20. At the time, most physicians would have agreed with Dr. George Bennett that in most cases surgery was not worth the risk. Bennett, "Physician Studies the Sore Arm," *Baseball Digest*, December 1942, 48–50.

21. Many players from all teams consulted with Dr. Hyland, who had treated Ty Cobb, Babe Ruth, and Dizzy Dean among others in addition to Cooper. He had removed painful growths from both thighs of Johnny Mize, which saved his career, a delicate operation that Hyland regarded as his most difficult. *Sporting News*, August 6, 1942, 4.

22. The 1942 Cardinals led the National League in bunts, and Southworth had his teams bunt more often in the 1940s than any other manager in that decade or than any manager since. St. Louis Cardinals official Web site, November 24, 2007, http://stlouis.cardinals.mlb.com/news/article.jsp?ymd=20071121&content_id=2305805&.

23. Quotes and survey from National Baseball Hall of Fame, Player File: Martin Whiteford Marion.

24. Rick Hines, "Marty Marion: `Mr. Shortstop' Tells It Like It Was," *Sports Collectors Digest*, March 26, 1991, 234–36.

25. Westcott, *Masters*, 51.

26. David Craft and Tom Owens, *Redbirds Revisited: Great Memories and Stories from*

St. Louis Cardinals, 144.

27. Mead, *Baseball Goes to War,* 121.

28. There were three other outstanding shortstops in Marion's time: Pee Wee Reese of the Brooklyn Dodgers, Phil Rizzuto of the New York Yankees, and Lou Boudreau of the Cleveland Indians. All have been elected to the Baseball Hall of Fame except Marion, who literally and figuratively stood head and shoulders above them defensively. John W. Deering, a fan, campaigned unsuccessfully for years for Marion's election. Deering prepared an analysis comparing Marion with Reese and Rizzuto which shows that, offensively, Marion's numbers are comparable to theirs, though Marion was unable to play as long as they did. National Baseball Hall of Fame, Player File: Martin Whiteford Marion.

29. *Sporting News,* September 14, 1942, 5.

30. National Baseball Hall of Fame, Player File: Kurowski, George John.

31. Jerry Lansche, *Stan the Man Musial: Born to Be a Ballplayer,* 32.

32. Craft and Owens, *Redbirds Revisited,* 113.

33. Neyer and Epstein, *Baseball Dynasties,* 172.

34. National Baseball Hall of Fame, Player File: Brown, James Roberson.

35. Cliff Bloodgood, "The Cardinal Called `Creepy,'" *Baseball Magazine,* June 1942, 308. In an era when road games were re-created by means of teletype reports of action, Crespi was known for having the most boring name in all of baseball: seventeen straight dots, no dashes.

36. Lansche, *Stan the Man,* 33.

37. This was unusual, if not unique, at the time. It was forbidden to start games in daylight and end them under artificial lights.

38. *St. Louis Post-Dispatch,* June 18, 1942, 1E. See also Roscoe McGowan's column in the *New York Times,* June 19, 1942, 27.

39. Golenbock, *Spirit of St. Louis,* 200.

40. *New York Times,* June 23, 1942, 25.

41. *Brooklyn Eagle,* June 23, 1942, 9.

Chapter 6. Fireworks in July

1. *St. Louis Post-Dispatch,* June 24, 1942, 4B.

2. *St. Louis Star-Times,* June 25, 1942, 22.

3. Ibid., June 24, 1942, 18.

4. *Sporting News,* July 2, 1942, 8.

5. *St. Louis Post-Dispatch,* June 25, 1942, 2B.

6. Catcher Gus Mancuso said that arm surgery made Cooper a better pitcher because it took something off his fastball and forced him to pitch to spots and also to develop better breaking pitches. National Baseball Hall of Fame, Player File: Cooper, Morton Cecil.

7. Neyer and Epstein, *Baseball Dynasties,* 172.

8. St. Louis Mercantile Institute, University of Missouri–St. Louis, Player File: Cooper, Morton.

9. *Brooklyn Eagle,* June 24, 1942, 11.

10. Bob Rains, *St. Louis Cardinals,* 102–3.

11. Craft and Owens, *Redbirds Revisited,* 186.

12. *St. Louis Post-Dispatch,* June 29, 1942, 1B.

13. Ibid., June 5, 1942, 3B.

14. Ibid., June 7, 1942, 1.

15. *New York World-Telegram,* June 22, 1942, 1.

16. *St. Louis Post-Dispatch,,* June 21, 1942, Pictures Section, p. 3.

17. Bill Nowlin, *Ted Williams at War,* 17–28. Initially, Williams was classified 3A as the sole support for his mother, then reclassified 1A by his local draft board because he was unmarried. An appeal that went finally to the national level resulted in his 3A classification being restored. The controversy surrounding Williams continued to midseason, when he announced that he would enter the military after the season.

18. This was the only year in his long career that Stan Musial did not make the National League All-Star team.

19. In 1942, the Cardinals had one set of home uniforms and one set of road uniforms.

20. *St. Louis Star-Times,* July 8, 1942, 16.

21. *St. Louis Post-Dispatch,* July 9, 1942, 24. A month earlier, the Cardinals had sold veteran catcher Gus Mancuso to the New York Giants. It went largely unremarked in the press, even though Mancuso had been the team's everyday catcher in 1941.

22. *St. Louis Star-Times,* July 8, 1942, 16.

23. *Brooklyn Eagle,* July 9, 1942, 11.

24. *New York World-Telegram,* July 10, 1942, 14.

25. *St. Louis Post-Dispatch,* July 10, 1942, 2B.

26. In the early 1940s, automobile bumpers stuck out from the body of the car. If one car bumped into another, they could get entangled but could then be separated by hand.

27. *St. Louis Post-Dispatch,* July 15, 1942, 2B.

28. *New York World-Telegram,* July 16, 1942, 19.

29. Ibid., 17.

30. *St. Louis Post-Dispatch,* July 16, 1942, 1B.

31. *Brooklyn Eagle,* July 18, 1942, 9.

32. Sidney Jacobson, *Pete Reiser: The Rough-and-Tumble Career of the Perfect Ballplayer,* 118.

33. *New York World-Telegram,* July 20, 1942, 16. See also the *St. Louis Post-Dispatch,* July 21, 1942, 18.

34. Marzano, *The Brooklyn Dodgers in the 1940s,* 82.

Chapter 7. Darkness before the Dawn

1. *St. Louis Post-Dispatch,* July 3, 1942, 7A.

2. Ibid., July 18 1942, 2B.

3. Ibid., July 7, 1942, 2B.

4. Irwin Silber, *Press Box Red: The Story of Lester Rodney, the Communist Who Helped Break the Color Line in American Sports,* chap. 4.

5. *New York World-Telegram,* July 28, 1942, 28.

6. *St. Louis Star-Times,* July 30, 1942, 20. The Negro Leagues were a source of revenue for many major-league clubs that rented their ballparks for Negro League games. Attendance at these games rivaled that for white games. On May 29, 1942, the Black Yankees and

Birmingham Black Barons played a game at Sportsman's Park that drew 11,254 spectators, which was above the *combined* average for Cardinals and Browns games in 1942. Attendance for the 1942 Negro League All-Star Game, played in mid-August in Chicago, was 48,000, the largest baseball crowd of the year in that city.

7. Silber, *Press Box Red*, 69.

8. *St. Louis Post-Dispatch*, July 17, 1942, 1B.

9. Ibid., July 18, 1942, 2B.

10. Ibid., July 26, 1942, 12A.

11. *Sporting News*, August 6, 1942, 4. Edward Moskowitz notes that this issue was the magazine's only one in 1942 that did not have at least one editorial relating in some way to the war. "The irony here is thick," he writes. "These same editors so valiantly trumpeting patriotism and making claims of baseball as a God-given blessing, or baseball epitomizing America's greatness as a land of democracy, and of baseball serving as notice of our stark differences from the dreaded narrow-minded Axis peoples, are also casting their vote for the maintenance of a Jim Crow 'separate but equal' America." Moskowitz, *"The Sporting News* during World War II," *National Pastime* 28 (2003): 52.

12. *St. Louis Post-Dispatch*, August 3, 1942, 2B.

13. *St. Louis Globe-Democrat*, August 7, 1942, 3B.

14. *New York World-Telegram*, July 23, 1942, 15.

15. *Brooklyn Eagle*, July 30, 1942, 9.

16. *St. Louis Post-Dispatch*, July 31, 1942, 1B.

17. Ibid.

18. *New York World-Telegram*, August 1, 1942, 15.

19. Moorehead, *Desert War*, 405.

20. On the initial German assault, see Antony Beevor, *Stalingrad: The Fateful Siege, 1942–1943*, 104–12.

21. Gailey, *War in the Pacific*, 182.

22. *St. Louis Post-Dispatch*, July 24, 1942, 1. Branch Rickey was admired but not warmly embraced by all St. Louis sportswriters.

23. Ibid., August 1, 1942, 1.

24. Ibid., August 9, 1942, 1.

25. Ibid., July 7, 1942, 1.

26. Ibid., July 17, 1942, 1.

27. Ibid., July 10, 1942, 1.

28. Ibid., July 14, 1942, 1.

29. *Brooklyn Eagle*, August 1, 1942, 9.

30. *St. Louis Post-Dispatch*, August 1, 1942, 16A.

Chapter 8. The Cardinals Take Wing

1. In the American League, the rule governing beanballs was that on the first offense umpires issued a warning to the pitcher, and on the second the pitcher was ejected from the game with the possibility of a fine as well. There was no comparable rule in the National League.

2. *New York World-Telegram*, August 12, 1942, 18.

3. *Brooklyn Eagle,* August 14, 1942, 11.

4. As a youngster, Lanier had thrown righthanded until he broke his right arm a couple of times and taught himself to throw lefthanded. The Dodgers' rookie Ed Head had followed the opposite course: he had been a lefthander as a kid who taught himself to pitch righthanded.

5. Craft and Owens, *Redbirds Revisited,* 121–22. As a "thinker" on the mound, see Donald Honig, *Baseball: When the Grass Was Real,* 21.

6. Frederick G. Lieb, *Sporting News,* September 17, 1942, 3.

7. Dick Farrington, *Sporting News,* September 3, 1942, 3.

8. Ibid.

9. Bill James and Rob Neyer, *Guide to Pitchers,* 130. See also John P. Carmichael, "Beazley Strikes 'Em Out," *Baseball Digest,* December 1942, 1–3.

10. James and Neyer, *Guide to Pitchers.*

11. Lloyd "Whitey" Moore was a veteran pitcher who had spent five years with Cincinnati before the Cardinals acquired him early in the 1942 season. A swing man used as both starter and reliever, he had won thirteen games for the 1939 National League champion Reds. With the Cardinals, the thirty-year-old Moore pitched in every exhibition game, but appeared in only nine regular-season games.

12. On the convention fight, see Daniel Scroop, *Mr. Democrat: Jim Farley, the New Deal, and the Making of Modern Politics,* and James MacGregor Burns, *Roosevelt: The Soldier of Freedom,* 277.

13. *St. Louis Post-Dispatch,* August 15, 1942, 2B.

14. Golenbock, *Spirit of St. Louis,* 226–28.

15. Ibid.

16. *St. Louis Post-Dispatch,* August 21, 1942, 3B. This was a question addressed by a number of sportswriters. It was a time without fast-food restaurants when meals were traditionally family gatherings.

17. *St. Louis Post-Dispatch,* August 24, 1942, 4B.

18. Ibid.

19. *Brooklyn Eagle,* August 24, 1942, 9.

20. *St. Louis Post-Dispatch,* August 24, 1942, 18.

21. Freese, *Glory Years,* 118.

22. Bob Broeg, *Memories of a Hall of Fame Sportswriter,* 132. Southworth later told Frederick Lieb that he thought the Dodgers' misplays in the series showed they were "tense, nervous and fretful." Lieb, *The St. Louis Cardinals: The Story of a Great Baseball Club,* 96.

23. *Brooklyn Eagle,* August 25, 1942, 9.

24. Ibid., August 26, 1942, 13.

25. *St. Louis Star-Times,* August 26, 1942, 22.

26. Ibid., August 27, 1942, 23.

27. *Brooklyn Eagle,* August 27, 1942, 11.

28. Ibid.

29. *St. Louis Post-Dispatch,* August 28, 1942, 3B.

30. *St. Louis Star-Times,* August 28, 1942, 12.

31. *Brooklyn Eagle,* August 27, 1942, 11.

32. *St. Louis Post-Dispatch,* August 30, 1942, 14A.

33. Ibid., August 31, 1942, 4B.

34. *St. Louis Star-Times,* August 31, 1942, 18.

35. *Brooklyn Eagle,* August 31, 1942, 9.

36. *New York Herald Tribune,* August 31, 1942, 18.

37. *Brooklyn Eagle,* August 29, 1942, 9.

38. Ibid., August 31, 9.

Chapter 9. Flying High into the Stretch

1. Estimates are from Peter and Dan Snow, *The World's Greatest Twentieth Century Battlefields,* 91ff.

2. News reports of battles in the Solomons, land and sea, consistently emphasized the enemy's losses and minimized those of the Allies. The news media relied on War Department reports, which consistently underestimated U.S. losses for two reasons: to deny information to the Japanese, and to maintain optimism and high morale at home by making victories seem more dramatic than was often the case.

3. *New York Herald Tribune,* September 3, 1942, 1.

4. *Sporting News,* September 24, 1942, 10.

5. David Alan Heller, *As Good as It Got: The 1944 St. Louis Browns,* 15.

6. *Brooklyn Eagle,* September 3, 1942, 11.

7. *St. Louis Post-Dispatch,* September 2, 1942, 2B.

8. *Brooklyn Eagle,* September 3, 1942, 11.

9. *New York Herald Tribune,* September 3, 1942, 11.

10. *St. Louis Post-Dispatch,* September 22, 1942, 5B.

11. *St. Louis Star-Times,* September 5, 1942, 4.

12. Both quotes from the *Brooklyn Eagle,* September 8, 1942, 11.

13. Ibid., September 11, 1942, 13. The *New York Times* shared Holmes's assessment, noting that the Dodgers "did not look good" (September 11, 1942, 27). Reiser blamed his problems on a sore muscle in his upper thigh and groin: "I can't do much real swinging on this leg," he explained. "Batting lefty, it's the pivot leg and most of the weight goes on it." He had switched to batting righthanded against lefthanders to take some pressure off the leg, but it had not helped. *New York Herald Tribune,* September 9, 1942, 35.

14. *Brooklyn Eagle,* September 10, 1942, 13.

15. *New York Times,* August 20, 1942, 13.

16. *Sporting News,* July 30, 1942, 15.

17. *Brooklyn Eagle,* September 10, 1942, 13.

18. *New York Herald Tribune,* September 11, 1942, 17. Moore did not speculate as to whether it was affection for the Cardinals or hatred of the Dodgers that produced this fan response.

19. *Brooklyn Eagle,* September 10, 1942, 13.

20. *Sporting News,* September 17, 1942, 17.

21. *New York Herald Tribune,* September 2, 1942, 32.

22. Larry MacPhail suggested that Durocher had overestimated the capacity of his staff. Before leaving on their long August road trip, the Dodgers' skipper had said he did not

need additional pitching. Before it was over, he was begging MacPhail to acquire another pitcher, which led to the trade for Bobo Newsome. *Brooklyn Eagle,* September 2, 1942, 13.

23. Ibid., September 12, 1942, 9.

24. *New York Herald Tribune,* September 10, 1942, 29.

25. Ibid., September 12, 1942, 17.

26. *Brooklyn Eagle,* September 4, 1942, 13.

27. *St. Louis Star-Times,* September 12, 1942, 4B.

28. *New York Times,* September 13, 1942, sec. 5, p. 1.

29. *St. Louis Globe-Democrat,* September 12, 1942, 2E.

30. *New York Times,* September 13, 1942, 3.

31. For a fuller account of this game, including a box score, see Robert L. Tieman, *Cardinal Classics,* 160–61.

32. *New York Times,* September 13, 1942, sec. 5, p. 1; *St. Louis Post-Dispatch,* September 13, 1942, 17A; *St. Louis Globe-Democrat,* September 12, 1942, 1E; *St. Louis Post-Dispatch,* September 12, 1942, 1B; *Brooklyn Eagle,* September 14, 1942, 9; *New York Herald Tribune,* September 14, 1942, 17.

33. *Sporting News,* September 17, 1942, 13.

34. *New York Times,* September 14, 1942, sec. 5, p. 1.

35. *St. Louis Globe-Democrat,* September 12, 1942, 2E.

36. *Brooklyn Eagle,* September 15, 1942, 11.

37. Ibid., September 14, 1942, 9.

38. *St. Louis Post-Dispatch,* September 11, 1942, 2E.

Chapter 10. Down to the Wire

1. *St. Louis Post-Dispatch,* September 12, 1942, 1.

2. *St. Louis Globe-Democrat,* September 14, 1942, 19.

3. *New York Times,* September 14, 1942, 27.

4. *Brooklyn Eagle,* September 16, 1942, 14.

5. Ibid., September 19, 1942, 9.

6. *New York Herald Tribune,* September 17, 1942, 20.

7. Ibid., September 18, 1942, 22.

8. *St. Louis Star-Times,* September 18, 1942, 13.

9. *Brooklyn Eagle,* September 18, 1942, 13.

10. *New York Herald Tribune,* September 14, 1942, 17.

11. *St. Louis Post-Dispatch,* September 14, 1942, 5B.

12. Ibid., September 16, 1942, 2E.

13. *New York Herald Tribune,* September 19, 1942, 17.

14. *St. Louis Post-Dispatch,* September 20, 1942, 1E.

15. Ibid., September 21, 1942, 4B.

16. *Brooklyn Eagle,* September 21, 1942, 9.

17. *New York Times,* September 21, 1942, 29.

18. Ibid.

19. *Brooklyn Eagle,* September 21, 1942, 9.

20. Ibid.

21. Ibid., September 18, 1942, 13.

22. *New York Herald Tribune,* September 24, 1942, 26.

23. *Brooklyn Eagle,* September 22, 1942, 11.

24. *New York Times,* September 22, 1942, 26.

25. *Brooklyn Eagle,* September 23, 1942, 15.

26. *New York Herald Tribune,* September 24, 1942, 26.

27. *St. Louis Post-Dispatch,* September 223, 1942, 2B.

28. Ibid.

29. *Brooklyn Eagle,* September 24, 1942, 11.

30. Ibid. The Dodgers' Leo Durocher regularly saved pitchers to spot against certain teams, but McKechnie, who had five good starting pitchers, appears to have worked them in rotation regardless of the opponent.

31. *Brooklyn Eagle,* September 24, 1942, 11.

32. *St. Louis Post-Dispatch,* September 24, 1942, 1B.

33. Ibid., September 25, 1942, 1B.

34. *Brooklyn Eagle,* September 25, 1942, 13.

35. Ibid. When Branch Rickey left the Cardinals after the 1942 season to succeed MacPhail as president of the Brooklyn Dodgers, he hired Harold Parrott to work for the team.

36. *St. Louis Globe-Democrat,* September 17, 1942, 3B, and September 19, 1942, 3B; *St. Louis Post-Dispatch,* September 18, 1942, 20.

37. *St. Louis Globe-Democrat,* September 28, 1942, 4B.

38. *St. Louis Post-Dispatch,* September 28, 1942, 20.

39. This account was compiled from the *St. Louis Globe-Democrat,* September 28, 1942, 3B and 5B, and the *St. Louis Star-Times,* September 28, 1942, 20.

40. *St. Louis Post-Dispatch,* September 28, 1942, 17.

41. The Dodgers were not the first National League club to win one hundred games or more and lose the pennant. See Daniel M. Daniel, "Brooklyn's Pennant Failure with 104 Victories Not Without Precedent," *Baseball Magazine,* October 1942, 295ff.

42. *Brooklyn Eagle,* September 28, 1942, 9.

43. *New York Times,* September 29, 1942, 27.

44. *Sporting News,* September 24, 1942, 4.

45. Ibid., 10.

46. *New York Herald Tribune,* September 28, 1942, 17.

Chapter 11. On the Big Stage

1. *New York Times,* October 1, 1942, 1.

2. The Missouri Historical Society celebrated quietly but proudly by mounting an exhibit on St. Louis baseball prepared by curator Marjorie Douglas with some materials dating back to the St. Louis Unions, who won the Missouri baseball championship in 1867.

3. *St. Louis Globe-Democrat,* September 29, 1942, 21.

4. The St. Louis Better Business Bureau filed a complaint with Commissioner Landis about the scalpers because many of its members thought they were being grossly over-

charged for tickets. Scalpers, called "ticket brokers," were required under federal law to register with the Collector of Internal Revenue and pay a tax of 11 percent on the difference between the list price of a ticket and the price at which they sold it. They also had to pay a one-hundred-dollar license fee to the city. Five registered with the city, two from Philadelphia, and one each from New York, Chicago, and St. Louis. Prices for parking also increased from the usual twenty-five cents to a dollar and even two dollars close to the park, in addition to which the stadium concessionaire raised its prices.

5. *St. Louis Post-Dispatch,* September 19, 1942, 4B. There were twenty-six thousand box and reserved grandstand seats, of which seven thousand went to season ticket holders and two thousand to the commissioner's office. The manager, players, and coaches received ten tickets apiece, which was barely enough to take care of family and friends. The sixty-seven hundred bleacher and pavilion seats and two thousand standing-room tickets were sold the day of the game.

6. *St. Louis Globe-Democrat,* September 29, 1942, 3B.

7. The commissioner's office named four umpires for the World Series, two from each league. Throughout the series, New York complained most bitterly about National League umpire George Magerkurth. It was generally believed that the strike zones in the two leagues differed. In the National League, known as a fastball league, the strike zone was a bit higher at the letters on the uniform; in the American League, a breaking-ball league, the strike zone was a bit lower under the letters.

8. *St. Louis Globe-Democrat,* October 1, 1942, 3B.

9. *New York Times,* October 1, 1942, 30. See also Mead, *Baseball Goes to War,* 47.

10. *New York Times,* October 1, 1942, 29.

11. *Brooklyn Eagle,* October 1, 1942, 13.

12. *St. Louis Post-Dispatch,* October 2, 1942, 3B.

13. Carmichael, ed., *My Greatest Day in Baseball,* 216.

14. *New York Times,* October 1, 1942, 1.

15. *Brooklyn Eagle,* October 2, 1942, 13.

16. Ibid., 18.

17. McCarthy and Southworth quotes, ibid.

18. Frederick G. Lieb, *The Story of the World Series,* 182–83.

19. *New York Times,* October 3, 1942, 18.

20. The Yankees had no lefthanders to start against the Cardinals, who had struggled against them through much of the season. Vernon "Lefty" Gomez was at the end of his career and Marius Russo had a sore arm.

21. It appears that the Yankees underestimated the speed of the Cardinals. The *New York Times* reported that before the World Series started, second baseman Joe Gordon poked fun at it, shouting to Charlie Keller in the locker room: "How about it Charlie—shall we bobble one and let that Johnny Hopp run, and then surprise him?" The running Redbirds would prove to be a surprise, but not to Johnny Hopp. *New York Times,* September 29, 1942, 27.

22. Ibid., October 4, 1942, 8. An umpire was not permitted to throw a player out of a World Series game. Only the commissioner was empowered to do that.

23. *St. Louis Globe-Democrat,* October 4, 1942, 3B.

24. *St. Louis Post-Dispatch*, October 4, 1942, 3C.

25. Ibid.

26. *Brooklyn Eagle*, October 3, 1942, 13; *St. Louis Globe-Democrat*, October 4, 1942, G2; *New York Times*, October 5, 1942, 4B; *St. Louis Globe-Democrat*, October 4, 1942, 4B.

27. *New York Times*, October 5, 1942, 22.

28. Ibid.

29. *St. Louis Globe-Democrat*, October 5, 1942, 4B.

30. *New York Times*, October 5, 1942, 22.

31. Bob Broeg, *Redbirds: A Century of Cardinals' Baseball*, 69.

32. Joe Williams, *New York Herald Tribune*, October 6, 1942, 21.

33. Southworth later said this was a planned play, but Marion disagreed. One report was that it was a pitchout. This account follows, among others, that of Lyle Smith, "Marty Marion," in Peterson, ed., *The St. Louis Baseball Reader*, 249.

34. For a brief review of the series, with a composite box score on player performances, see Clifford Bloodgood, "Cardinals Cop the Big Upset," *Baseball Magazine* (November 1942), 533ff.

35. *New York Times*, October 6, 1942, 27.

36. *St. Louis Star-Times*, October 6, 1942, 6.

37. Ibid., 28, and *St. Louis Post-Dispatch,* October 6, 1942, 2.

38. *St. Louis Post-Dispatch*, October 6, 1942, 2.

39. *New York Herald Tribune*, October 6, 1942, 1, 36; *St. Louis Star-Times*, October 5, 1942, 20; *St. Louis Post-Dispatch*, October 6, 1942, 3; *St. Louis Globe-Democrat*, October 7, 1942, 3B; *Brooklyn Eagle*, October 5, 1942, 11.

40. *Sporting News*, October 8, 1942, 10.

Chapter 12. World's Champion

1. *Sporting News*, October 15, 1942, 7.

2. *St. Louis Globe-Democrat*, October 7, 1942, 3B.

3. *St. Louis Post-Dispatch*, October 7, 1942, 1.

4. *Sporting News*, October 15, 1942, 13.

5. Neillands, *The Bomber War*, 183ff. British attacks had been at night under cover of darkness, which was safer but made navigation more difficult. Daytime flights made navigation easier, and they were less dangerous with the B-27, since it flew at an altitude that was above the reach of most enemy artillery.

6. Snow and Snow, *The World's Greatest Twentieth Century Battlefields*, 113, 114.

7. Mead, *Baseball Goes to War*, 11–12. During the war, the term "United Nations" was commonly used to refer to the Allies, as it is here. It does not refer to the international organization that came into being following the war.

8. Sam Narron, acquired late in the season, received a partial share, as did Jeff Cross and Erv Dusak, who had been recalled from the minors in early September. The manager and coaches received full shares, while others like the clubhouse attendant and traveling secretary received partial shares. Lon Warneke, who had been a starting pitcher until sold to Chicago in July, received nothing because baseball rules forbid giving World Series shares to anyone who was a member of another team.

9. *Sporting News,* October 8, 1942, 4.

10. Mead, *Baseball Goes to War,* 6–7.

11. *Sporting News,* October 22, 1942, 4.

12. *New York Herald Tribune,* October 6, 1942, 21.

13. Rickey's contract required that Breadon give notice this far in advance if the contract was not going to be renewed. Presumably, Breadon could have had a change of heart in the interim, but he did not.

14. *Brooklyn Eagle,* October 6, 1942, 11.

15. *Sporting News,* October 15, 1942, 4. On Rickey's move to Brooklyn, including press commentaries, see the November 5, 1942, issue, p. 1ff.

16. Ibid., October 22, 1942, 3.

17. On Breadon taking full control of the Cardinal operation, see ibid., October 8, 1942, 5, and November 19, 1942, 1, and James M. Gould, "Breadon Takes the Controls," *Baseball Magazine* (December 1942), 294ff.

18. *Sporting News,* November 19, 1942, 4.

19. The same issue of the *Sporting News* reported that Larry MacPhail had passed along information from Washington that baseball still had the "green light" to operate in 1943. Ibid., 3.

20. Donald Honig, *Baseball's 10 Greatest Teams,* 101.

21. Enos Slaughter with Kevin Reid, *Country Hardball: The Autobiography of Enos "Country" Slaughter,* 61.

Conclusion

1. *St. Louis Post-Dispatch,* January 12, 1982, 1C.

2. *Sporting News,* October 15, 1942, 1.

3. *St. Louis Globe-Democrat,* October 7, 1942, 3B.

4. *Sporting News,* October 14, 1942, 4.

5. Ibid., October 8, 1942, 4.

6. The stolen base was not a primary weapon in manager Billy Southworth's arsenal, but the team did finish second in the National League in thefts.

7. Honig, *Baseball's 10 Greatest Teams,* 90.

8. Slaughter had almost three times as many walks as strikeouts, Musial and Moore twice as many, while Jimmy Brown remarkably had almost five times as many walks as strikeouts. Only Kurowski had a high ratio of strikeouts to walks, almost two to one.

9. Slaughter with Reid, *Country Hardball,* 61.

10. *Sporting News,* October 15, 1942, 1.

BIBLIOGRAPHY

Books

Alexander, Charles C. *Our Game: An American Baseball History.* New York: Henry Holt, 1991.

———. *Rogers Hornsby: A Biography.* New York: Henry Holt, 1995.

Allen, Maury. *Brooklyn Remembered.* Champaign, Ill.: Sports Publishing, 2005.

Anton, Todd. *No Greater Love: Life Stories from the Men Who Saved Baseball.* Burlington, Mass.: Rounder Books, 2007.

Beevor, Antony. *Stalingrad: The Fateful Siege, 1942–1943.* New York: Penguin Books, 1998.

Bercuson, David, and Holger Herwig. *One Christmas in Washington.* New York: Overlook Press, 2005.

Blum, John Morton. *V Was for Victory: Politics and American Culture during World War II.* New York: Harcourt Brace Jovanovich, 1976.

Broeg, Bob. *Memories of a Hall of Fame Sportswriter.* Champaign, Ill.: Sagamore Publishing, 1995.

———. *Redbirds: A Century of Cardinals' Baseball.* Rev. ed. Kansas City: Walsworth Publishing, 1992.

———. *Stan Musial: "The Man's" Own Story as Told to Bob Broeg.* New York: Doubleday and Company, 1964.

Burns, James MacGregor. *Roosevelt: The Soldier of Freedom.* New York: Harcourt Brace Jovanovich, 1970.

Carmichael, John P., ed. *My Greatest Day in Baseball.* Lincoln: University of Nebraska Press, 1973.

Cohen, Stanley. *Dodgers: The First 100 Years.* New York: Birch Lane Press, 1990.

Craemer, Robert W. *Baseball and Other Matters in 1941.* Lincoln: University of Nebraska Press, 1991.

Craft, David, and Tom Owens. *Redbirds Revisited: Great Memories and Stories from St. Louis Cardinals.* Chicago: Bonus Books, 1990.

Durant, John. *The Story of Baseball.* New York: Hastings House, 1947.

Eskenazi, Gerald. *The Lip: A Biography of Leo Durocher.* New York: William Morrow and Company, 1993.

Finoli, David. *For the Good of the Country: World War II Baseball in the Major and Minor Leagues.* Jefferson, N.C.: McFarland and Company, 2002.

Freese, Mel. *The Glory Years of the St. Louis Cardinals.* St. Louis: Palmerston and Reed, 1999.

Frick, Ford C. *Games, Asterisks, and People.* New York: Crown Publishers, 1973.

Gailey, Harry A. *The War in the Pacific: From Pearl Harbor to Tokyo Bay.* Novato, Calif.: Presidio Press, 1995.

Giglio, James N. *Musial: From Stash to Stan the Man.* Columbia: University of Missouri Press, 2001.

Gilbert, Bill. *They Also Served: Baseball and the Home Front, 1942–1945.* New York: Crown Publishers, 1992.

Goldstein, Richard. *Spartan Seasons: How Baseball Survived the Second World War.* New York: Macmillan Publishing Co., 1980.

Golenbock, Peter. *Bums: An Oral History of the Brooklyn Dodgers.* New York: G. P. Putnam's Sons, 1984.

———. *The Spirit of St. Louis: A History of the St. Louis Cardinals and Browns.* New York: Avon Books, 2000.

Grayling, A. C. *Among the Dead Cities.* New York: Walker and Company, 2006.

Groom, Winston. *1942: The Year That Tried Men's Souls.* New York: Atlantic Monthly Press, 2005.

Halberstam, David. *Summer of '49.* New York: William Morrow and Company, 1989.

Heidenry, John, and Brett Topel. *The Boys Who Were Left Behind.* Lincoln: University of Nebraska Press, 2006.

Heller, David Alan. *As Good as It Got: The 1944 St. Louis Browns.* Charleston, S.C.: Arcadia, 2003.

Helyar, John. *Lords of the Realm: The Real History of Baseball.* New York: Villard Books, 1994.

Honig, Donald. *Baseball: Between the Lines.* New York: Coward, McCann and Geoghagen, 1976.

———. *Baseball: When the Grass Was Real.* New York: Coward, McCann and Geoghagen, 1975.

———. *Baseball's 10 Greatest Teams.* New York: Macmillan Publishing, 1982.

Hunstein, Jim. *1, 2, 6, 9 . . . and Rogers: The Cardinals' Retired Numbers and the Men Who Wore Them.* St. Louis: Stellar Press, 2004.

Jacobson, Sidney. *Pete Reiser: The Rough-and-Tumble Career of the Perfect Ballplayer.* Jefferson, N.C.: McFarland and Company, 2004.

James, Bill, and Rob Neyer. *Guide to Pitchers*. New York: Simon and Schuster, 2004.

Kennedy, David M. *The American People in World War II*. New York: Oxford University, 1999.

Kirkendall, Richard S. *A History of Missouri: Volume V, 1919 to 1951*. Columbia: University of Missouri Press, 1986.

Klingaman, William A. *1941: Our Lives in a World on the Edge*. New York: Harper and Row, 1988.

Kopp, Leonard. *Concise History of Major League Baseball*. New York: Carroll and Graf, 1998.

Lansche, Jerry. *Stan the Man Musial: Born to Be a Ballplayer*. Dallas: Taylor Publishing, 1940.

Leptich, John, and Dave Baranowski. *This Date in St. Louis Cardinals History*. New York: Stein and Day, 1983.

Lieb, Frederick G. *The St. Louis Cardinals: The Story of a Great Baseball Club*. New York: G. P. Putnam's Sons, 1944.

———. *The Story of the World Series*. New York: G. P. Putnam's Sons, 1949.

Marzano, Rudy. *The Brooklyn Dodgers in the 1940s*. Jefferson, N.C.: McFarland and Company, 2005.

McCarver, Tim, with Phil Pepe. *Few Are Chosen: Defining Cardinal Greatness across the Eras*. Chicago: Triumph Books, 2003.

McGee, Bob. *The Greatest Ballpark Ever: Ebbets Field and the Story of the Brooklyn Dodgers*. New Brunswick, N.J.: Rutgers University Press, 2006.

Mead, William B. *Baseball Goes to War*. Washington, D.C.: Contemporary Books, 1999.

Moorehead, Alan. *Desert War*. New York: Pensuin Books, 2001.

Neillands, Robin. *The Bomber War: The Allied Air Offensive against Nazi Germany*. New York: Overlook Press, 2003.

Neyer, Rob, and Eddie Epstein. *Baseball Dynasties: The Greatest Teams of All Time*. New York: W. W. Norton, 2000.

Nowlin, Bill. *Ted Williams at War*. Burlington, Mass.: Rounder Books, 2007.

O'Connor, Leslie. *Official Baseball 1946*. New York: A. S. Barnes, 1946.

Peterson, Richard, ed. *The St. Louis Baseball Reader*. Columbia: University of Missouri Press, 2006.

Pietrusza, David. *Judge and Jury: The Life and Times of Judge Kenesaw Mountain Landis*. South Bend, Ind.: Diamond Communications, 1998.

Polner, Murray. *Branch Rickey: A Biography*. Rev. ed. Jefferson, N.C.: McFarland and Company, 2007.

Primm, James Neal. *Lion of the Valley: St. Louis, Missouri, 1764–1980*. 3rd ed. St. Louis: Missouri Historical Society Press, 1998.

Rains, Bob. *St. Louis Cardinals.* New York: St. Martin's Press, 1992.

Rossi, John P. *The National Game: Baseball and American Culture.* Chicago: Ivan R. Dee, 2000.

Savage, Charlie. *Takeover: The Return of the Imperial Presidency and the Subversion of American Democracy.* New York: Little, Brown and Co., 2007.

Scroop, Daniel. *Mr. Democrat: Jim Farley, the New Deal, and the Making of Modern American Politics.* Ann Arbor: University of Michigan Press, 2006.

Silber, Irwin. *Press Box Red: The Story of Lester Rodney, the Communist Who Helped Break the Color Line in American Sports.* Philadelphia: Temple University Press, 2003.

Slaughter, Enos, with Kevin Reid. *Country Hardball: The Autobiography of Enos "Country" Slaughter.* Greensboro, N.C.: Tudor Publishers, 1991.

Snow, Peter, and Dan Snow. *The World's Greatest Twentieth Century Battlefields.* London: BBC Books, 2007.

Snyder, John. *Cardinals Journal.* Cincinnati: Emmis Books, 2006.

Spink, J. G. Taylor. *Judge Landis and Twenty-Five Years of Baseball.* New York: Thomas Y. Crowell Company, 1947.

Story, Ronald. *Historical Atlas of World War Two.* New York: Oxford University Press, 2006.

Thomas, Joan M. *St. Louis' Big League Ballparks.* Charleston, S.C.: Arcadia, 2004.

Tieman, Robert L. *Cardinal Classics.* St. Louis: Baseball Historie, 1982.

Tygiel, Jules. *Past Time: Baseball as History.* New York: Oxford University Press, 2000.

Van der Vat, Dan. *The Pacific Campaign: World War II, The U.S.-Japanese Naval War 1941–1945.* New York: Simon and Schuster, 2992.

Voight, David Quinton. *American Baseball: From the Commission to Continental Expansion.* Vol. 2. University Park: Pennsylvania State University Press, 1988.

White, G. Edward. *Creating the National Game: Baseball Transforms Itself.* Princeton, N.J.: Princeton University Press, 1996.

Magazines

Baseball Collectors Digest
Baseball Digest
Baseball Magazine
Saturday Evening Post
National Pastime, The
Time Magazine

Newspapers

Brooklyn Eagle
New York Herald-Tribune
New York Times
St. Louis Globe-Democrat
St. Louis Post-Dispatch
St. Louis Star-Times
St. Petersburg Independent
St. Petersburg Times
Sporting News, The

Reference Works

Baseball Encyclopedia. 8th ed. New York: Macmillan Publishing Company, 1990.

Baseball Guide. 1942. St. Louis: C. C. Spink and Son, 1943.

Baseball Register. 1942. St. Louis: C. C. Spink and Son, 1943.

The Cardinals: The Complete Record of Redbird Baseball. New York: Collier Books, 1983.

Eisenbath, Mike. *The Cardinals Encyclopedia.* Philadelphia: Temple University, 1999.

Light, Jonathan Fraser. *The Cultural Encyclopedia of Baseball.* Jefferson, N.C.: McFarland and Company, 1997.

Missouri: The WPA Guide to the "Show Me" State. Reissue. St. Louis: Missouri Historical Society, 1998.

Neft, David S., Richard M. Cohen, and Michael L. Neft, eds. *The Sports Encyclopedia: Baseball 2007.* New York: St. Martin's Griffin, 2007.

Snyder, John. *Cardinals Journal: Year by Year and Day by Day with the St. Louis Cardinals since 1882.* Cincinnati: Emmis Books, 2006.

INDEX